A Linguistic Geography

CW00969814

More than forty years ago it was demonstrated that the African continent can be divided into four distinct language families. Research on African languages has accordingly been preoccupied with reconstructing and understanding similarities across these families. This has meant that an interest in other kinds of linguistic relationship, such as whether structural similarities and dissimilarities among African languages are the result of contact between these languages, has never been the subject of major research. The aim of this book is to show that such similarities across African languages are more common than is widely believed. It provides a broad perspective on Africa as a linguistic area, as well as an analysis of specific linguistic regions. In order to have a better understanding of African languages, their structures, and their history, more information on these contact-induced relationships is essential in order to understand Africa's linguistic geography, and reconstruct its history and prehistory.

BERND HEINE is Professor Emeritus of African Studies at the University of Köln, Germany.

DEREK NURSE is Henrietta Harvey Research Professor in the Linguistics Department at the Memorial University of Newfoundland, Canada.

Cambridge Approaches to Language Contact

General Editor
SALIKOKO S. MUFWENE
University of Chicago

Editorial Board
Robert Chaudenson, *Université d'Aix-en-Provence*
Braj Kachru, *University of Illinois at Urbana*
Raj Mesthrie, *University of Cape Town*
Lesley Milroy, *University of Michigan*
Shana Poplack, *University of Ottawa*
Michael Silverstein, *University of Chicago*

Cambridge Approaches to Language Contact is an interdisciplinary series bringing together work on language contact from a diverse range of research areas. The series focuses on key topics in the study of contact between languages or dialects, including the development of pidgins and creoles, language evolution and change, world Englishes, code-switching and code-mixing, bilingualism and second language acquisition, borrowing, interference, and convergence phenomena.

Published titles
Salikoko Mufwene, *The Ecology of Language Evolution*
Michael Clyne, *The Dynamics of Language Contact*
Bernd Heine and Tania Kuteva, *Language Contact and Grammatical Change*
Edgar W. Schneider, *Postcolonial English*
Virginia Yip and Stephen Matthews, *The Bilingual Child*
Bernd Heine and Derek Nurse (eds.), *A Linguistic Geography of Africa*

Further titles planned for the series
Guy Bailey and Patricia Cukor-Avila, *The Development of African-American English*
Maarten Mous, *Controlling Language*
Clancy Clements, *The Linguistic Legacy of Spanish and Portuguese*

A Linguistic Geography
of Africa

Edited by

Bernd Heine and Derek Nurse

CAMBRIDGE
UNIVERSITY PRESS

CAMBRIDGE UNIVERSITY PRESS
Cambridge, New York, Melbourne, Madrid, Cape Town, Singapore,
São Paulo, Delhi, Dubai, Tokyo, Mexico City

Cambridge University Press
The Edinburgh Building, Cambridge CB2 8RU, UK

Published in the United States of America by Cambridge University Press, New York

www.cambridge.org
Information on this title: www.cambridge.org/9780521182690

First published 2008
First paperback edition 2010

A catalogue record for this publication is available from the British Library

Library of Congress Cataloguing in Publication data

A linguistic geography of Africa / edited by Bernd Heine and Derek Nurse.
  p. cm. – (Cambridge approaches to language contact)
Includes bibliographical references and index.
ISBN-13: 978-0-521-87611-7
ISBN-10: 0-521-87611-7
1. African languages. 2. Languages in contact – Africa. 3. Linguistic geography.
1. Heine, Bernd, 1939– 11. Nurse, Derek. 111. Title. 1v. Series.
PL8005. L56 2007
496.09–dc22   2007013265

ISBN 978-0-521-87611-7 Hardback
ISBN 978-0-521-18269-0 Paperback

Contents

Maps

Figures

Tables

Contributors

PROFESSOR G. N. (NICK) CLEMENTS, Laboratoire de Phonétique et Phonologie (UMR 7018), CNRS / Sorbonne-Nouvelle, France

DR. JOACHIM CRASS, University of Mainz, Germany

PROFESSOR DENIS CREISSELS, Laboratoire Dynamique du Langage, MRASH, Lyon, France

PROFESSOR GERRIT J. DIMMENDAAL, Institut für Afrikanistik, University of Cologne, Germany

PROFESSOR ZYGMUNT FRAIJZYNGIER, Department of Linguistics, University of Colorado, USA

DR. TOM GÜLDEMANN, Max Planck Institute for Evolutionary Anthropology/Linguistics, Germany

PROFESSOR BERND HEINE, Institut für Afrikanistik, University of Cologne, Germany

PROFESSOR ROLAND KIEßLING, Asien-Afrika-Institut, Abteilung für Afrikanistik und Äthiopistik, University of Hamburg, Germany

DR. CHRISTA KÖNIG, Institut für Afrikanische Sprachwissenschaft, University of Frankfurt, University of Hamburg, Germany

DR. ZELEALEM LEYEW, Department of Linguistics, University of Addis Ababa, Ethiopia

DR. RONNY MEYER, University of Mainz, Germany

PROFESSOR MAARTEN MOUS, Department of Languages and Cultures of Africa, Leiden University, The Netherlands

PROFESSOR DEREK NURSE, Department of Linguistics, Memorial University of Newfoundland, Canada

DR. ANNIE RIALLAND, Laboratoire de Phonétique et Phonologie (UMR 7018), CNRS / Sorbonne-Nouvelle, France

Series editor's foreword

The series Cambridge Approaches to Language Contact (CALC) was set up to publish outstanding monographs on language contact, especially by authors who approach their specific subject matter from a diachronic or developmental perspective. Our goal is to integrate the ever-growing scholarship on language diversification (including the development of creoles, pidgins, and indigenized varieties of colonial European languages), bilingual language development, code-switching, and language endangerment. We hope to provide a select forum to scholars who contribute insightfully to understanding language evolution from an interdisciplinary perspective. We favor approaches that highlight the role of ecology and draw inspiration both from the authors' own fields of specialization and from related research areas in linguistics or other disciplines. Eclecticism is one of our mottoes, as we endeavor to comprehend the complexity of evolutionary processes associated with contact.

A Linguistic Geography of Africa diverges from the above tradition only in not being a monograph. We have made this exception because of the rich addition that the volume makes to the scholarly goals of CALC. Bernd Heine and Derek Nurse enrich the series with an outstanding collection of contributions that make evident how the linguistic history of a vast territory is naturally complicated by an intricate entanglement of genetic and areal ties. The backbone of the book consists of a few fundamental questions, including the following: why are the genetic and typological classifications of African languages not coextensive? Why are there so many typological features that cut across well-established genetic classifications of languages? How significant is the role of areal diffusion, therefore of language contact, in the structural affinities observable among so many languages?

From the perspective of language speciation, a number of other questions arise from the chapters of this book. For instance, what does this complex web of structural and genetic affinities suggest about patterns of population dispersal and subsequent inter-group communication over the millennia that have led to the present African linguascape? Can one do a genetic study of languages of any territory without sorting out among the following classic questions: among the features shared by a particular group of languages, which are the ones that have been inherited from a common ancestor? Which are those that are due to parallel, independent innovations after diversification from the proto-language? Which are those that are due to mutual influence during post-diversification contacts? How can one tell the difference? Are there any correlations between linguistic groupings and geographical characteristics of the relevant territories?

These questions, and many more, are addressed or brought up in complementary and often also overlapping ways by the contributors to *A Linguistic Geography of Africa*. The authors are all veteran field workers, typologists, and students of genetic classifications of African languages. Like the editors, many of them are also students of various forms of human contacts which produced not only creoles and pidgins but also varieties identified by some as "intertwined languages," those that display the most "global copying" or "grammatical replication." They are also aware of the danger of attributing too much to contact, as Derek Nurse had previously shown in his study, with other associates, of the evolution of Swahili. All the authors show that it would be too simplistic to stipulate, without qualifications, that Africa is a *Sprachbund* (also known as *convergence area*). Not even the Balkan-like situation of the Ethio-Eritrean area fits this sweeping characterization.

The bottom line is that one must combine techniques from both genetic and areal linguistics to account for the complex ways in which genetic and typological connections are literally intertwined in Africa and perhaps elsewhere too. Population movements, which lead to language contact, are an important dimension of the study of language evolution. The genetic classification of languages to reflect patterns of language diversification in a geographical space as vast as Africa is a much more complex topic than traditionally assumed. As the editors conclude, the contributors to this volume are just scraping the tip of the iceberg. There is much more to learn; and I hope *A Linguistic Geography of Africa* will be as seminal as other previous publications in this series, especially *Language Contact and Grammatical Change* by Bernd Heine and Tania Kuteva (2005). The books show the extent to which studies of language evolution and of language contact at the macro-level are interconnected. In the particular case of *A Linguistic Geography of Africa*, both the areal and genetic linguistics approaches help us make informed distinctions between convergence and diversification with common genetic inheritance, and/or, in some cases, articulate the relevant problems. The book also drives home the fact that language evolution is conditioned by a wide range of ecological factors, including those that pertain to geography, as these bear on population movements and all that ensue from them, economically and linguistically.

Salikoko S. Mufwene, *University of Chicago*

Acknowledgments

Many a student of African languages has pointed out that the way grammatical meanings and structures are expressed in a given language is strikingly similar to what is found in some neighboring language or languages, even though the languages concerned may be genetically unrelated or only remotely related. The main goal of this book is to show that such observations are far from coincidental – rather, that such similarities across African languages are more common than is widely believed and that they can be accounted for in terms of areal relationship. In editing this book, we have benefited greatly from discussions with and comments from many colleagues, in particular the following: Sasha Aikhenvald, Felix Ameka, Walter Bisang, Bernard Comrie, Norbert Cyffer, Östen Dahl, Bob Dixon, Paul Newman, Margaret Dunham, Ludwig Gerhardt, Lars Johanson, Tania Kuteva, Yaron Matras, Salikoko Mufwene, Robert Nicolai, Mechthild Reh, Suzanne Romaine, Marie-Claude Simeone-Senelle, Anne Storch, Thomas Stolz, Martine Vanhove, Erhard Voeltz, Rainer Vossen, as well as many others. Special thanks are also due to Monika Feinen and Will Oxford for their invaluable technical assistance, and to two anonymous referees for all the work they did on an earlier version of this volume.

The second-named editor would also like to thank the Henrietta Harvey Foundation for continued and generous support during the period of his work on this book. The first-named editor is deeply indebted to the Center for Advanced Study in the Behavioral Sciences, Stanford, and the Institute for Advanced Study, LaTrobe University, and in particular the Research Centre for Linguistic Typology in Melbourne and its directors Bob Dixon and Sasha Aikhenvald, who offered him academic hospitality to work on this book. We are grateful to these institutions for their generosity and understanding. Our gratitude also extends to our colleagues Lenore Grenoble and Lindsay Whaley, Dartmouth College, who offered the first-named editor academic hospitality and the means to work on this book when he was invited as a visiting professor in 2002. Finally, thanks are also due to the Netherlands Institute for Advanced Study (NIAS) and its rector Wim Blockmans for the outstanding hospitality that the first-named editor was able to enjoy in 2005/6 at the finalizing stage of the book.

Abbreviations

(In Bantu examples, numbers in glosses of nominal forms, or following '3:' in glosses of pronominal markers, indicate noun classes. Elsewhere, numbers indicate persons. For example, O3:2 means 'object marker, third person, class 2.')

A	agent, transitive subject function, aspect (Dimmendaal), verb class A, affirmative
AA	Afroasiatic
ABL	ablative
ABS	absolutive
ABS	absolute form of nouns
ACC	accusative, accusative system
AFF	affirmative, affix
AG	antigenitive
ALBU	Alagwa and Burunge
ANAPH	anaphora
ANN	annexion state
ANT	anterior
APPL	applicative
AP	antipassive
ASS	associative
ATR	advanced tongue root
AUX	auxiliary
B	verb class B
CAUS	causative, causative extension
CL	noun class marker
CMPL	complementizer
CND	conditional
CNV	converb
COM	comitative
COMP	comparative

COMPL	complement
CON	construct case
COP	copula, copulative
CSTR	construct state
D	dative object marker
DAT	dative, dative extension
DC	declarative sentence marker
DECAUS	decausative
DECL	declarative
DEF	definite
DEM	demonstrative
DET	determiner
DETR	detransitivization
DIM	diminutive
DIR	directional
DP	declarative particle
DS	dependent subject
DU	dual
E	evidential
E40	Mara Bantu languages
E50	Central Kenyan Bantu languages
EAB	East African Bantu
EE	end of event marker
ELA	Ethiopian Linguistic Area
ERG	ergative, ergative system
EXCL	exclusive
F	feminine
F10, F20, etc.	groups of the Bantu zone F
FAC	factive
FOC	focus
FF	far future
FP	far past
FPL	feminine plural
FSG	feminine singular
FUT	future
GEN	genitive
GO	go
HAB	habitual
IDEO	ideophone
IMP	imperative
INCL	inclusive
INDEF	indefinite

INDIR	indirect mood
INF	infinitive
INIT	initiator of reported speech
INST	instrumental
IO	indirect object
IPF	imperfective
IRR	irrealis
JUS	jussive
LINK	linker introducing a noun modifier
LOC	locative
LOCPRED	locative predicator
LOG	logophoric
M	masculine
MAL	malefactive
MNOM	marked nominative
MPL	masculine plural
MSG	masculine singular
N	neuter, noun
N.PRED	nominal predicate
NEG	negative
NF	near future
NFIN	non-finite
NOM	nominative
NOML	nominalizer
NP	near past, noun phrase
NS	Nilo-Saharan
NSM	non-interrogative sentence marker
NTS	non-topical subject
O	object, transitive object function, direct object marker
OBJOR	object orientation
OBL	oblique case
OPT	optative
PAST	past
PEC	Proto-Eastern Cushitic
PEE	possessee
PERF	perfect
PERS	persistive
PFV	perfective
PIRQ	Proto-Iraqwoid
PL	plural
PNM	predicate nominal phrase marker
POR	possessor

POS	positive (or affirmative)
POSS	possessive
POST	posterior
PRE	preposition
PRES	present
PROG	progressive
PSAM	Proto-Sam
PSN	Proto-Southern Nilotic
P(N,S)WR	Proto-(North, South) West Rift
PSV	passive
PURP	purpose
Q	question
QUOT	quotative
REL	relative
RSM	resumptive marker
S	subject, intransitive subject function
SC	subject concord
SEQ	sequential
SG	singular
SJN	subjunctive
SIM	similative
SPEC	specifier
SUB	subordination
SUBJ	syntactically marked case form
TA	tense–aspect
TAG	tag question
TAM	tense–aspect–modality
TMP	temporal
TR	transitive
V	verb
VEN	venitive (ventive)
VN	verbal noun
WR	West Rift
I	non-past verbal juncture
II	past verbal juncture
1, 2, 3	first, second, third person, or noun class 1, 2, 3, etc.
=	clitic boundary

1 Introduction

Bernd Heine and Derek Nurse

More than forty years ago, Joseph Greenberg (1963) demonstrated that the African continent can be divided into four distinct genetic phyla, or families as he called them, namely Niger-Congo (or Kongo-Kordofanian), Nilo-Saharan, Afroasiatic, and Khoisan. For subsequent generations of Africanists, this classification has served as a reference system to describe the relationship patterns among African languages. In this tradition, scholars doing comparative work on African languages were preoccupied to quite some extent with reconstructing and understanding similarities across languages with reference to genetic parameters. One effect this line of research had was that an interest in other kinds of linguistic relationship was never really pronounced. Especially the question of whether, or to what extent, structural similarities and dissimilarities among African languages are the result of areal, that is contact-induced relationship, has never attracted any major research activities beyond individual studies dealing with lexical borrowing and related subjects. Whether the African continent constitutes an areally defined unit, or whether it can be subclassified into linguistic areas (or sprachbunds, or convergence areas) remained issues that were the subject of casual observations or conjecture, or both, but not really of more detailed research.

Still, once more it was Greenberg who drew attention to the importance of areal relationship in Africa. Not only did he venture to point out major linguistic areas (1959), but he also was the first to come up with important findings on the areal distribution of phonological and morphosyntactic properties across Africa, and with hypotheses on the areal distribution of these properties (1983). The title of chapter 2 of this book echoes that of a paper by Joseph Greenberg (1959), and this choice is deliberate: with this book we wish to build on the foundations laid by Greenberg, demonstrating that in the course of the last decades some headway has been made in areal classification since his paper appeared nearly half a century ago.

A common thread to all the contributions of this volume is that genetic relationship is far from being a parameter for understanding many of the processes characterizing the history of and typological relationship among African languages, and the message implicit in these contributions is that for a better understanding of African languages, their structures, and their history, more detailed information on the areal relationship patterns is a *sine qua non* – not only for accounting for the relationship patterns among these languages, and for understanding Africa's linguistic geography, but also for reconstructing Africa's history and prehistory.

Work on linguistic areas or sprachbunds is not a new research line in Africa (see chapter 2 on the notion "linguistic area"). As early as 1976, an Ethiopian or, perhaps more appropriately, an Ethio-Eritrean area was proposed (Ferguson 1976), and this area is widely believed to constitute the only sprachbund-type unit to be found in Africa. However, doubts have been raised concerning the validity of this unit (Tosco 2000b). Tosco draws attention to the fact that there are a number of smaller, historically more immediately accessible areal groupings that can tell us more about the linguistic history of the macro-region concerned; chapter 7 will review this discussion and provide a summary and new findings on the nature of this sprachbund.

Otherwise, not much headway has been made in the search for linguistic areas within Africa. Some areas have been proposed, but the evidence to support the hypotheses concerned is in most cases not entirely satisfactory. An exception can been seen in Güldemann's (1998) attempt to define the Kalahari Basin as an areal unit. Based on the methodology developed by Nichols (1992), he argues that it is possible on quantitative grounds to set off the languages of this arid region of Botswana, Namibia, and South Africa from other African languages. The Kalahari Basin area includes a number of – though not all – Khoisan languages plus the Bantu languages Herero and Tswana.

As we will see in the following chapters, genetic relationship does not provide the only parameter for diachronic language classification in Africa; rather, there is reason to maintain that the African continent can equally well be classified in terms of areally defined groupings. Unlike the genetic stocks proposed by Greenberg (1963) these groupings are not really discrete and exhaustive, they exhibit overlapping structures and fuzzy boundaries. However, as we hope to demonstrate in this volume, the areal relationship patterns characterizing these groupings are immediately relevant for understanding structural properties of African languages.

Language contact

Areal relationship is the result of contact between languages, more precisely between the speakers of these languages. Language contact may have a wide range of implications for the languages involved, and it may affect virtually any component of language structure (see Thomason & Kaufman 1988). Grossly speaking, contact-induced influence manifests itself in the transfer of linguistic material from one language to another, where linguistic material can be of any of the following kinds:

(a) Form, that is, sounds or combinations of sounds
(b) Meanings (including grammatical meanings) or combinations of meanings
(c) Form-meaning units or combinations of form-meaning units
(d) Syntactic relations, that is, the order of meaningful elements
(e) Any combination of (a) through (d)

Language contact may involve simultaneously all kinds of transfer, that is, it may concern what Johanson (1992, 2002) calls global copying (*Global-kopieren*); but it may also involve only one kind of transfer, i.e. what Johanson calls selective copying (*Teilstrukturkopieren*). The data that are provided in this volume relate to both global and selective copying. But, as we will see in a number of chapters, there is one kind of transfer, namely (b), whose significance has been underrated in many previous studies of language contact: the transfer of meanings and combinations of meanings, occasionally discussed under the label "calquing," is the one that is most difficult to identify, but that is presumably as common as lexical borrowing or other kinds of (c). And perhaps even more importantly, (b) concerns not only the lexicon, but presumably more often the transfer of functional categories, that is, it qualifies as what is technically known as grammatical replication (Heine & Kuteva 2003, 2005, 2006).

While still ill-understood, grammatical replication appears to be a ubiquitous phenomenon in Africa. One of its main effects is that as a result of language contact, a language acquires a new use pattern or grammatical category, or a new way of structuring grammar. The following example may illustrate this effect. The Ilwana, a Bantu-speaking people living along the river Tana south of Garissa in eastern Kenya, have a history of over three centuries of contact with the Orma, who speak a dialect of the East Cushitic Oromo language. Bantu languages have a robust number distinction singular vs. plural, supported by the noun class system, where there is a singular marker regularly corresponding to a plural marker. Orma on the other hand has a prevailing pattern distinguishing three number categories: singulative vs. transnumeral (unmarked) vs. plural/collective. For example, ethnonyms tend to be used in the unmarked transnumeral form and a singular is formed by adding the singulative suffix. Ilwana speakers appear to have replicated this structure with ethnonyms, whereby the Bantu singular (noun class 1) prefix *mo-* was reinterpreted as a singulative prefix while the Bantu plural noun class 2 was replaced by noun class 10, which is unmarked for number – thereby giving rise to an unmarked plural resembling the transnumeral category of Orma (Nurse 2000b: 125; see also Nurse 1994). Thus, a Bantu structure illustrated in (1) was replaced in Ilwana by the structure shown in (2).

(1)   Swahili (Sabaki, Bantu)
        M-pokomo   Wa-pokomo (*plural*)   'Pokomo person'
(2)   Ilwana (Sabaki, Bantu; Nurse 2000b: 125)
        mo-bokomo   bokomo (*plural*)   'Pokomo person'

Change in typological profile

Cases such as the one just looked at will surface in a number of the following chapters: they concern the transfer of a structure from one language to another without involving any lexical or other form–meaning units. But we will also look at more dramatic cases of transfer, involving simultaneously a bundle of structural properties and leading to new typological profiles. With the term "new typological profile" we refer to cases where, as a result of grammatical replication, a language experiences a number of structural changes to the effect that that language is structurally clearly different from what it used to be prior to language contact (Heine & Kuteva 2006). Typically, these changes are in the direction of the model language, thus making the two languages structurally more equivalent and more readily inter-translatable – a process that in contact linguistics tends to be described as "convergence."

We may illustrate this process with the following example from the Kenyan language Luo. As we will see most clearly in chapter 6, East Africa is a region characterized by massive contact between languages belonging to different genetic stocks. Some of the linguistic effects of this contact concern Nilotic languages (belonging to the Nilo-Saharan family) that have been in contact with Bantu languages (belonging to the Niger-Congo family), especially Kalenjin (Southern Nilotic) and Luo (Western Nilotic) of south-central and southwestern Kenya. Nilotic languages may be called aspect-prominent, in that they commonly distinguish e.g. between a perfective and an imperfective aspect in verbs, mainly by way of tonal inflection. Bantu languages on the other hand are well known for their richness in tense distinctions, and the languages with which Kalenjin and Luo came into close contact are no exception to this rule. For example, the Bantu language Luhya (Luyia), which has been in contact with both Kalenjin and Luo, has among others the following tense categories expressed by verbal prefixes (Bukusu dialect of Luhya): Immediate Past, Near Past, Intermediate Past, Remote Past; Immediate Future, Inter-mediate Future, and Remote Future (Dimmendaal 1995a, 2001a, 2001b: 92; Kuteva 2000). While in Nilotic languages there are hardly any tense categories, the two languages for which there is an attested history of close contact with Bantu languages, viz. Kalenjin and Luo, have an array of tense distinctions comparable to that found among their Bantu neighbors. However, none of the tense markers in Kalenjin and Luo is etymologically related to corresponding

Table 1.1 *Past-tense markers in Luo (Dimmendaal 2001b: 101)*

Adverb of time	Verbal proclitic or prefix	Tense meaning
nénde	née, n-	'today in the past' (hodiernal)
nyóro	nyóo, ny-	'yesterday's past' (hesternal)
nyóca	nyóc(a), nyóc-	'the day before yesterday'
yandé	yand(é), yand-	'a few days ago'

tense markers in any of the Bantu languages concerned. Further, tense markers precede the verbal subject prefix in Kalenjin and Luo but follow the verbal subject prefix in the Bantu languages (Dimmendaal 2001: 93), and they have normally clearly affixal status in the Bantu languages but vary between clitic and affix status in Kalenjin and Luo.

Assuming that these two Nilotic languages replicated their tense categories from Bantu languages, the question arises as to what accounts for the structural difference between the two kinds of languages. Dimmendaal provides a cogent answer: the Nilotic languages received from their Bantu neighbors a range of tense concepts but neither the corresponding forms nor the morphosyntactic structures. Nilotic languages commonly use adverbs of time clause-initially (or clause-finally) to mark distinctions in time, and transfer had the effect that a set of such adverbs were grammaticalized to tense markers in clause-initial position; see table 1.1. Not surprisingly, therefore, these tense markers appear before the subject prefixes; in contrast to the model Bantu languages, which commonly have tense markers after the subject prefixes (Dimmendaal 2001b: 90–1). That this process happened independently in Luo from that to be observed in Kalenjin is suggested, for example, by the fact that the forms used in the two languages are not cognate (nor are they etymologically related to corresponding forms in the Bantu languages). There is one slight difference between the two Nilotic languages: while the grammaticalized tense markers have been adapted to the vowel harmony pattern of the verb stem in Kalenjin, they have not been affected by vowel harmony in Luo (Dimmendaal 2001b: 101).

To conclude, transfer appears to have had the effect that the Nilotic languages Kalenjin and Luo acquired a new functional domain (= tense) via the grammaticalization of adverbs of time.

The case just discussed is not an isolated instance of grammatical transfer from Bantu to Nilotic languages. Bantu languages are known for their rich paradigms of verbal derivational extensions marked by suffixes. There is nothing comparable in the Nilotic language Luo or its closest relatives, the Southern Lwoo languages of Uganda and the Sudan: verbal derivation is limited, mainly involving internal morphology in the verb root. Now, apparently on the model of neighboring Bantu languages, Luo speakers have

developed a set of what look like verbal suffixes, resembling structurally the
Bantu verbal suffixes, expressing functions typically encoded by the Bantu
derivational applied suffix *-id- ('for, to, with reference to, on behalf of'). Luo
speakers used the prepositions *ne* (or *nɪ*) benefactive, *e* locative, and *gɪ*
instrumental in order to develop verbal enclitics or suffixes; the following
example is confined to the benefactive preposition *ne*, where (3a) illustrates the
prepositional use and (3b), where *Juma* is topicalized, the use as a verbal suffix
(see also Dimmendaal 2001b: 101–2).

(3) Luo (Western Nilotic, Nilo-Saharan; Heine & Reh 1984: 51)

a.   jon   nego   diel   ne   juma
      John   is.killing goat   for   Juma
      'John is killing a goat for Juma'
b.   juma   jon   nego-   ne   diel
      Juma   John   is.killing- for   goat
      'John is killing a goat for *Juma*'

On the basis of such evidence one may argue that this Nilotic language is on the
verge of experiencing a gradual change of profile on the model of its Bantu
neighbors. To be sure, Luo is structurally still unambiguously a Nilotic language, but it is typologically no longer exactly as it was prior to language
contact with Bantu languages.

Areal distribution: word order

Areal diffusion, especially when it does not involve lexical borrowing or other
kinds of form–meaning units, is not easy to identify. Still, there are ways of
developing plausible hypotheses on how linguistic properties spread from one
language to another as a result of language contact. One of these ways concerns
the probability of linguistic change. For example, Thomason proposes the
following definition for contact-induced language change:

In my view, contact between languages (or dialects) is a source of linguistic change
whenever a change occurs that would have been unlikely, or at least less likely, to occur
outside a specific contact situation. This definition is broad enough to include both the
transfer of linguistic features from one language to another and innovations which,
though not direct interference features, nevertheless have their origin in a particular
contact situation. (Thomason 2003: 688)

Perhaps the most obvious procedure to seek for hypotheses on contact-induced
change concerns areal distribution among languages that are genetically
unrelated or only remotely related. This procedure has been employed in some
way or other by many students of contact-induced transfer (see especially
Aikhenvald 2002), and it is used in several of the chapters in this book.[1]

We may illustrate the procedure with the following example, relating to a number of cases discussed in this book. Africa is commonly divided into four distinct language families or phyla. Assuming that languages belonging to different phyla, that is, genetic stocks, do not share any genetic relationship, one can hypothesize that if there is a linguistic property that is found widely in Africa across language phyla, that property is likely to be due to areal diffusion, that is, to language contact. But it is possible to invoke alternative hypotheses. If one finds similarities in form, meaning, or structure between different languages then that can be due to a number of different causes: it may be due to universal principles of linguistic discourse and historical development, to shared genetic relationship, to parallel development or drift, to language contact, or simply to chance. Assuming that we can rule out genetic relationship, drift, and chance, this leaves us with the possibility that universal principles may be responsible for the widespread occurrence of the relevant property. In such a situation, areal distribution once more provides a convenient parameter for testing the hypothesis: if the relevant property is widespread in Africa but uncommon in other parts of the world then a hypothesis based on universal principles can essentially be ruled out.

As we will see in the following chapters, this procedure has been employed extensively to formulate hypotheses on areal relationship across African languages. But the procedure has also been used to propose areal discontinuities within Africa. The areal distribution of word order can be used as an example to illustrate this observation.

In some of the literature on contact linguistics it is claimed or implied that syntax belongs to the most stable parts of grammar, and that it is most resistant to change. As we will see in this book, such a view is in need of revision: syntactic structures are easily transferred from one language to another. With regard to the classic distinction between verb-initial (VSO), verb-medial (SVO), and verb-final languages (SOV), none of the African language families exhibits any consistent word-order behavior: all three word orders are found in the Afroasiatic and the Nilo-Saharan phyla, and the Niger-Congo and Khoisan phyla exhibit two of the these orders, namely SVO and SOV.[2]

But word order shows significant correlations with areal distribution. There is a large areal belt extending from Lake Chad to the west to the Horn of Africa to the east, where essentially only SOV languages are found (see chapter 9 concerning the complexity of this word-order type). This belt includes in the same way Nilo-Saharan languages such as Kanuri, Kunama, or Nobiin (Nile Nubian), furthermore all Omotic, Ethio-Semitic and, with one exception, also all Cushitic languages. In view of this areal contiguity and the genetic diversity involved, language contact offers the most plausible explanation to account for this typological similarity (Heine 1976). The areal-diffusion hypothesis receives further support from the fact that there is one Cushitic language that has basic SVO order. This language, Yaaku, is spoken in central Kenya and is surrounded by languages such as Maasai and Meru that have, respectively, VSO and SVO rather than SOV word order.

Another example of areal patterning concerns what Heine (1975, 1976) calls type B languages. These languages are characterized by head-final word order (*nomen rectum – nomen regens*) in genitive (i.e. attributive possessive) and noun–adposition constructions, but otherwise head-initial order prevails, that is, nominal qualifiers such as adjectives and numerals tend to follow the head noun. What distinguishes them from SOV (i.e. type D) languages mainly is the fact that adverbial phrases follow the main verb. Type B languages are crosslinguistically uncommon; it is only in Africa that they are found in significant numbers. While occasional cases are found in various parts of the continent and in all African language families except Afroasiatic, the largest number exists in West Africa: there is a compact area extending from Senegal in the west to Nigeria in the east where virtually only type B languages are found (Heine 1976: 41–2).

One might argue that this concentration of type B languages in West Africa is genetically induced since with one exception all languages belong to the Niger-Congo phylum. But there are arguments against such a hypothesis. First, the area cuts across genetic boundaries, in that all Kwa languages located within this geographical region are type B, while eastern Kwa languages are not. Second, type B languages do not correlate with the genetic relationship patterns within the Niger-Congo phylum, that is, they do not form a genetic unit within Niger-Congo. And third, there is only one Nilo-Saharan language spoken in this West African region, namely Songhai, and it is exactly this Nilo-Saharan language which is type B.

A third example demonstrating that word order in African languages patterns areally rather than genetically is provided by what Heine (1976: 60) calls the Rift Valley (not to be confused with the Tanzanian Rift Valley area discussed in chapter 6). VSO languages form a distinct minority among African languages. Ignoring the Berber languages of northwestern Africa, whose status as VSO languages is not entirely clear, and a few Chadic languages, all African VSO languages are concentrated in a small geographical belt within or close to the East African Rift Valley stretching from southern Ethiopia to central Tanzania. While these languages belong with one exception to the Nilo-Saharan phylum, they consist on the one hand of Eastern Nilotic, Southern Nilotic, and Surmic (Didinga-Murle) languages, and on the other hand of the Kuliak languages Ik, Nyang'i and So, whose genetic position within this family is largely unclear. But perhaps most importantly, the area also includes Hadza (Hadzapi), which some classify as a Khoisan language while others prefer to treat it as a genetic isolate. On account of this areal patterning, the most convincing explanation for this typological clustering again is one in terms of areal relationship.

These are but a few examples showing that it is possible to formulate hypotheses on areal groupings within Africa on the basis of word-order characteristics. Some of these characteristics are also relevant in order to locate Africa typologically vis-à-vis other parts of the world. For example, as has been shown by Dryer (forthcoming), negation markers placed at the end of the clause can be found in a vast area extending from the river Niger in the west to the river Nile in the east, and including a wide range of languages belonging to Niger-Congo, Afroasiatic, and Nilo-Saharan, that is, to three of the four African phyla[3] (see chapter 4, pp. 163–5). The fact that the distribution of this typological property patterns areally and at the same time cuts across genetic boundaries is strongly suggestive of areal relationship. But verb-final negation does not only stand out typologically within the areal landscape of Africa; rather, it is also of worldwide significance: there appear to be only few languages outside Africa that have it.

Micro-areas

Our focus in this book is on macro-situations, that is, on areal perspectives dealing with Africa as a whole or with significant regions of the continent. In doing so, we are aware that most of the data that are relevant for a better understanding of the mechanisms leading to areal diffusion in Africa have come not from macro-surveys but rather from micro-analyses of contact situations involving a limited number of different speech communities, in many cases only two, where one serves as the donor or model while the other acts as the receiver of linguistic transfers. We are not able to do justice to this rich research that has been carried out in Africa in the course of the last decades; suffice it to draw attention to a couple of studies resulting in fairly well-documented micro-situations of long-term and intense language contact. These studies have been volunteered by Nurse (2000b) on East African contact situations. One of them concerns the Daiso people of northeastern Tanzania, who originate from the central Kenyan highlands and appear to have reached their present territory early in the seventeenth century. By now, they have a history of nearly four centuries of contact with the Tanzanian Bantu languages Shamba(l)a, Bondei, Swahili, and Digo in the course of which their language has been influenced in a number of ways by these languages. The second study deals with the Ilwana, a Bantu-speaking people living along the river Tana south of Garissa in eastern Kenya. They have a history of over three centuries of contact with the Orma, who speak a dialect of the East Cushitic Oromo language (Nurse 2000b), and as a result of Orma influence have experienced a range of grammatical changes.

Intense language contact may result in situations of stable bilingualism, but it can as well lead to language shift, where one language gives way to another.

A number of studies carried out in Africa deal with contact-induced linguistic transfer in this kind of situation. Arguably the most substantial work dealing with such transfers is that by Sommer (1995) on Ngamiland in northern Botswana, where there is a detailed linguistic and sociolinguistic documentation of the process of transition from the minority language Yeyi (Siyeyi) to the national language Tswana (Setswana).

The present volume

All the wealth of information that has been amassed in such studies has been made use of in the chapters to follow, but unlike these studies, the goal of this book is to present a more general perspective of areal relationship in Africa. The contributions are mainly of three kinds. First, there are those that argue that there is reason to consider the African continent as an areal-typological unit that stands out against the rest of the world. This perspective is highlighted in chapters 2, 3, and 4. In the subsequent chapters 5 through 7, specific linguistic regions of Africa are analyzed and evidence is presented to define them as linguistic areas. The remaining chapters 8 and 9 each highlight one particular typological feature with a view to exploring their significance as parameters for areal classification.

That there are a number of properties that are widespread in Africa but uncommon elsewhere has been pointed out by a number of scholars. The authors of chapter 2 go on to look for quantitative information to test this hypothesis, using a catalogue of eleven phonetic, morphological, syntactic, and semantic properties. The conclusion Bernd Heine and Zelealem Leyew reach confirms what has been established in earlier research, namely, that it is not possible to define Africa as an area in terms of a set of properties that are generally found in Africa but nowhere else. Nevertheless, they argue on the basis of their quantitative evidence that it is possible to maintain that areal diffusion must have played some role in shaping Africa's linguistic landscape and to predict with a certain degree of probability whether or not a given language is spoken on the African continent.

Another finding that surfaces in chapter 2 is that the highest concentration of Africa-specific properties is found in the Sudanic belt of west-central Africa, a region that includes languages of three of the four African language phyla, while northeastern and northern Africa are typologically quite different from the rest of the continent, sharing with the languages of western, central, and southern Africa hardly more properties than they share with languages in other parts of the world.

The question of whether Africa can be defined as a distinct area vis-à-vis other language regions of the world is also the central issue of chapter 3. Surveying a range of phonological phenomena and comparing their distribution with that to be found outside Africa, Nick Clements and Annie Rialland are able to establish that there are in fact significant clusterings of phonological properties in sub-Saharan Africa. They go on to demonstrate that these clusterings concern most of all the Sudanic zone (i.e. roughly what is referred to in chapter 5 as the Macro-Sudan belt), that is, the sub-Saharan region roughly between the rivers Niger and Nile.

A major finding presented in chapter 3 concerns the areal subgrouping of Africa: the authors propose to classify the continent on the basis of typologically salient phonological parameters into six zones, which they call the North, Sudanic, East, Rift, Center, and South zones. These areal groupings cut across genetic boundaries, being suggestive of contact processes that characterize the prehistory of Africa.

While chapter 2 presents a crude template for identifying African languages and for distinguishing them from languages in other parts of the world, chapter 4 provides an extensive analysis of the main morphological and syntactic characteristics of the languages spoken in Africa, thereby building on the foundations laid in works such as Welmers (1974), Meeussen (1975), or Gregersen (1977). But in this chapter, Denis Creissels, Gerrit Dimmendaal, Zygmunt Frajzyngier, and Christa König go far beyond the scope of such works in building on substantive typological information on languages in other parts of the world. In this way, they are able to offer a truly contrastive perspective, demonstrating that there is a range of typological properties that are found extensively within Africa but are rare elsewhere in the world, and vice versa. Accordingly, the authors of this chapter present a balanced profile of African languages and contrast it with that of other linguistic regions of the world. In addition, this chapter also focuses on the internal typological complexity of the continent, suggesting areal groupings of various kinds, and enabling the reader to determine, for example, what structural characteristics to expect from a West African as opposed to an East African language.

The authors conclude chapter 4 with a list of nineteen morphosyntactic properties suggesting that African languages show a distinct areal behavior vis-à-vis other languages, exhibiting either an extraordinarily high or a clearly low rate of frequency of occurrence. This list also includes a number of perhaps surprising areal generalizations, such as the fact that no African language has been found so far where the verb obligatorily agrees with the object,[4] or that a number of African verb-final (SOV) languages exhibit a typologically unusual behavior in that they consistently place adverbial constituents after the verb (SOVX) (see also chapter 9 on this issue).

Ever since Westermann (1911) published his classic on the *Sudansprachen*, the large belt in the northern half of Africa south of the Sahara between the Niger and the Nile valleys has been the subject of hypotheses on the genetic relationship patterns in Africa. While there were scholars who claimed that the affinities found between the languages spoken in this belt cannot be defined in terms of genetic relationship, no convincing alternative has been presented so far. Based on structural evidence from a wide range of languages, Tom Güldemann is able to demonstrate in chapter 5 that an areal approach offers the most convincing means to account for these affinities. A number of the typological properties studied by him are considered by some to be characteristic of Africa as a whole (see chapter 2), but their clustering in the vast area between West and East Africa – cutting across genetic boundaries, including those of three of the four African language phyla – in fact suggests that the Macro-Sudan hypothesis is a robust one, even if the boundaries of this area are fuzzy.

This chapter discusses a fundamental problem surfacing in some way or other in most contributions to this volume, namely: what do we really know about the genetic relationship patterns in Africa? Güldemann's suggestion that a number of the taxonomic units proposed by Greenberg (1963) may turn out to be more appropriately analyzable in terms of areal, that is, contact-induced relationship rather than in terms of genetic affiliation provides a challenge for future comparative linguistics in Africa.

The region of the Tanzanian Rift Valley is genetically one of the most complex linguistic regions of the world: it includes languages of all four African language phyla and, if one classifies Hadza as a genetic isolate, the region hosts even five different genetic stocks. The region therefore provides an ideal laboratory for the study of language contact, as Roland Kießling, Maarten Mous, and Derek Nurse aptly demonstrate in chapter 6.

The authors use what Campbell et al. (1986) call a historicist approach, that is, their areal description is based on properties that are likely to require an explanation in terms of language contact rather than of general typological similarities. However, the analysis on which this chapter is based is of a different nature from that characterizing Campbell et al.'s (1986) description of Meso-America as a linguistic area: rather than being confined to searching for a catalogue of properties that neatly define the linguistic area, Kießling, Mous, and Nurse go on to reconstruct the historical processes that can be held responsible for the presence of these properties and, hence, for the rise of the Tanzanian Rift Valley as a linguistic area.

The only sprachbund-type area in Africa figuring in textbooks of contact linguistics, on the same level as the Balkans, Meso-America, South Asia, etc., is the Ethiopian linguistic area (also called the Ethio-Eritrean area). More recently, however, some students of African languages have shown that defining this area as a sprachbund is not unproblematic; we have drawn attention to this research above. In chapter 7, Joachim Crass and Ronny Meyer offer a comprehensive appraisal of previous research. Based on their own recent field research, they come to the conclusion that the areal hypothesis is sound, and they add new evidence to further substantiate this hypothesis.

If there are genuinely African typological properties then marked-nominative systems are one of them: languages having a grammaticalized case system where the nominative is the functionally marked category are world-wide extremely rare; they are essentially confined to the African continent and are mainly concentrated in eastern Africa. As Christa König demonstrates in chapter 8, there is reason to assume that this regional patterning is due to some extent to genetic factors, but language contact also must have played some role in the diffusion of such systems across genetic boundaries. What is perhaps noteworthy is the fact that the area covered by marked-nominative languages cuts across the Ethiopian highland area and the lowland region of the Nile valley.

The author defines a number of typological properties characterizing case marking in the Afroasiatic and Nilo-Saharan languages of this area, among them being one according to which there is a generalization to the effect that in marked-nominative languages case is distinguished only after the verb, that is, there are no case distinctions before the verb; for obvious reasons, verb-final languages, such as Cushitic and Omotic languages, are not covered by this generalization.

Gerrit Dimmendaal's survey of verb-final languages in Africa in the final chapter 9 is not strictly on areal linguistics, but it is a demonstration of how areal forces and genetic inheritance interact in shaping the syntax of African languages. To be sure, there are strong correlations between SOV (subject–object–verb) word order and phrasal modifier–head order; as the author con-vincingly shows, however, labels such as "SVO" and "SOV" are not very helpful for understanding the dynamics underlying the syntax and the dis-course-pragmatic structure of the languages concerned. His detailed analysis demonstrates that some of the generalizations proposed for SOV languages are in need of revision, considering the enormous diversity of morphosyntactic structures to be found in the so-called verb-final languages of Africa.

Among the many issues discussed in this chapter there is one that raises general problems for the typology of clause combining. It is widely assumed that the distinction between coordination and subordination is typologically neat; as Dimmendaal shows, however, the situation in Africa – but probably elsewhere as well – is more complex, and a more fine-grained typology of clause combining is required.

The impression one may get when reading the contributions to this volume is that work on the contact-induced patterns of linguistic relationship in Africa is still in its infancy, even though for more than a century, students of African languages have been drawing attention to the fact that neighboring but genetically unrelated or only remotely related languages exhibit a high degree of conceptual and structural intertranslatability. The present volume offers a multitude of examples confirming such observations and proposing significant areal relationship patterns; still, it can achieve hardly more than revealing the peak of the iceberg. It is hoped that the volume makes it clear that Africa's linguistic geography, and the social dynamics of language contact underlying it, is a research topic that deserves much more attention than it has received in the past.

2   Is Africa a linguistic area?

Bernd Heine and Zelealem Leyew

The question raised in the title of this chapter has been posed by a number of students of African languages (e.g. Greenberg 1983; Meeussen 1975; Gilman 1986), it has figured in the title of a seminal paper by Greenberg (1959), and it is raised in various parts of this work (see especially chapters 3 and 4). In the present chapter it is argued that it is possible, on the basis of a quantitative survey on African languages of all major genetic groupings and geographical regions, to define a catalogue of phonological, morphosyntactic, and semantic properties that can be of help in defining African languages vis-à-vis languages in other parts of the world.[1]

2.1   On linguistic areas

Areal linguistics is a much neglected field of comparative African linguistics. While there are a number of studies that have been devoted to contact between individual languages or language groups (e.g. Mutahi 1991; Nurse 1994; 2000b; Sommer 1995; Bechhaus-Gerst 1996; Dimmendaal 1995a; 2001b; Storch 2003), not much reliable information is available on areal relationship across larger groups of languages. The following are among the questions that we consider to be especially important in this field:

(1) Can Africa be defined as a linguistic area vis-a-vis the rest of the world?
(2) Are there any clearly definable linguistic macro-areas across genetic boundaries within Africa?
(3) Are there any linguistic micro-areas?

While the majority of chapters in this book deal with questions (2) and (3), our interest in this chapter is exclusively with question (1). A variety of different terms have been proposed to refer to sprachbunds, such as linguistic area, convergence area, diffusion area, *union linguistique*, *Sprachbund*, etc. (see Campbell et al. 1986: 530). Perhaps the most frequently discussed sprachbunds are the Balkans (for convenient summaries, see e.g. Joseph 1992; Feuillet 2001),[2] Meso-America (Campbell et al. 1986), Ethiopia (Ferguson 1976),[3] South Asia (Masica 1976; Emeneau 1980), the East Arnhem Land (Heath 1978), the Amerindian Pacific Northwest (Sherzer 1973; Beck 2000), the Vaupés basin of northwest Amazonia (Aikhenvald 1996; 2002), Standard Average European (Haspelmath 1998; 2001), and the Daly River area of Australia (Dixon 2002: 674–9). Furthermore, there are quite a number of less widely recognized sprachbunds, such as the Circum-Baltic (Nau 1996; Koptjevskaja-Tamm & Wälchli 2001), the Middle Volga region (Johanson 2000), or the Circum-Mediterranean area (Stolz 2002).

Substantial work has been done to define sprachbunds, with the result that there are now a few areas in all major parts of the world that can be described in terms of language contact. With regard to defining sprachbunds, two different stances can be distinguished. On the one hand it is argued that a definition of sprachbunds should highlight the fact that they are the result of language contact, that is, of historical processes; the following is representative of this view:[4]

A *linguistic* area is defined . . . as an area in which *several* linguistic traits are shared by languages of the area and furthermore, there is evidence (linguistic and non-linguistic) that contact between speakers of the languages contributed to the spread and/or retention of these traits and thereby to a certain degree of linguistic uniformity with the area. (Sherzer 1973: 760)

On the other hand, sprachbunds are defined exclusively in terms of linguistic parameters without reference to the historical forces that gave rise to them. Emeneau's classic definition[5] is a paradigm case of such definitions; a more recent version is the following (see also Aikhenvald 2002: 7–8):

A linguistic area can be recognized when a number of geographically contiguous languages share structural features which cannot be due to retention from a common proto-language and which give these languages a profile that makes them stand out among the surrounding languages. (Haspelmath 2001: 1492)

In the present chapter, we will be confined to the second kind of definition, and we will assume that there is a sprachbund whenever the following situation obtains:

(4) Characterization of linguistic areas

a.   There are a number of languages spoken in one and the same general area.
b.   The languages share a set of linguistic features whose presence can be explained with reference neither to genetic relationship, drift, universal constraints on language structure or language development, nor to chance.
c.   This set of features is not found in languages outside the area.
d.   On account of (b), the presence of these features must be the result of language contact.

This characterization is fairly general, it is not meant to be a definition; rather, it is used as a convenient discovery device for identifying possible instances of sprachbunds. Note that this characterization does not address crucial problems that have been raised in the relevant literature, for example, how many languages and how many features (or properties or traits) are minimally required, whether these features should be shared by all languages, whether individual features should not occur in languages outside the sprachbund, whether the languages should really be geographically contiguous, whether the languages should belong to different genetic groupings, to what extent isoglosses of features need to bundle, how factors such as the ones just mentioned influence the strength of a sprachbund hypothesis, or whether sprachbunds have any historical reality beyond the linguistic generalizations proposed by the researchers concerned.

2.2   Earlier work

Pre-Greenbergian comparative African linguistics suffered from the fact that no systematic distinction between different kinds of historical relationship was made, that is, it remained for the most part unclear whether the linguistic classifications proposed were intended to be genetically, areally or typologically defined or, more commonly, were an amalgamation of all three kinds of relationship. Accordingly, most of the works published prior to 1959 do not offer unambiguous evidence on areal patternings within Africa or between Africa and other parts of the world.

Greenberg's contribution to areal linguistics was of two kinds. First, he proposed a genetic classification of the languages of Africa (1963). A crucial problem associated with many cases of crosslinguistic comparison concerns the fact that it frequently remains unclear whether a given similarity found between languages is due to genetic or to areal relationship. Once it has been established where genetic boundaries are it is possible to propose viable hypotheses on areal diffusion and areal relationship. With his genetic classification therefore, Greenberg made it possible to draw a clear demarcation line between genetic relationship and other kinds of relationship.

Second, Greenberg also made the first substantial contribution to areal relationship in Africa. In an attempt to isolate areal patterns both within Africa and separating Africa from other regions of the world, he proposed a number of what he called "special" features of African languages. The properties listed by Greenberg (1959) include in particular a number of lexical polysemies, such as the use of the same term for 'meat' and 'wild animal,' the use of the same term for 'eat,' 'conquer,' 'capture a piece in a game,' and 'have sexual intercourse,' and the use of a noun for 'child' as a diminutive, or of 'child of tree' to denote 'fruit of tree.'

Another noteworthy contribution to areal relationship within Africa appeared in the same year, 1959: Larochette (1959) presented a catalogue of linguistic properties characteristic of Congolese Bantu (Kikongo, Luba, Mongo), an Ubangi language (Zande), and a Central Sudanic language (Mangbetu), but a number of the properties proposed can also be found in other regions and genetic groupings of Africa. Another range of properties characterizing many African languages was proposed by Gregersen (1977) and Welmers (1974). Building on the work of Greenberg (1959) and Larochette (1959), Meeussen (1975) presented an impressive list of what he called "Africanisms," that is, phonological, morphological, syntactic, and lexical properties widely found in African languages across genetic boundaries. Quite a number of the "Africanisms" proposed by Meeussen are in fact promising candidates for status as properties that are diagnostic of Africa as a linguistic area (see section 2.3 below).

Another seminal work on areal relationship was published by Greenberg in 1983. He defined areal properties "as those which are either exclusive to Africa, though not found everywhere within it, or those which are especially common in Africa although not confined to that continent" (Greenberg 1983: 3). As an example of the former he mentioned clicks; as instances of the latter he discussed in some detail the following four properties ("characteristics"; Greenberg 1983: 4): (i) coarticulated labial-velar (or labiovelar) stops, (ii) labial (or labiodental) flaps, (iii) the use of a verb meaning 'to surpass' to express comparison, and (iv) a single term meaning both 'meat' and 'animal.' He demonstrated that these four properties occur across genetic boundaries and, hence, are suggestive of being pan-African traits, especially since they are rarely found outside Africa.

Greenberg (1983) went on to reconstruct the history of these properties by studying their genetic distribution. He hypothesized that (i), (iii), and (iv) are ultimately of Niger-Kordofanian origin even though they are widely found in other African language phyla, in particular in Nilo-Saharan languages. For (ii), however, he did not find conclusive evidence for reconstruction, suggesting that it may not have had a single origin but rather that it arose in the area of the Central Sudanic languages of Nilo-Saharan and the Adamawa-Ubangi languages of Niger-Congo.

Search for areal properties across Africa is associated to some extent with creole linguistics (see e.g. Boretzky 1983). In an attempt to establish whether, or to what extent, the European-based pidgins and creoles on both sides of the Atlantic Ocean have been shaped by African languages, students of creoles pointed out a number of properties that are of wider distribution in Africa. Perhaps the most detailed study is that by Gilman (1986). Arguing that a large number of African-like structures in Atlantic and other pidgins and creoles are best explained by influence of areal properties widely distributed among the languages of Africa, Gilman proposed an impressive catalogue of pan-African areal properties (but see section 2.5).

2.3 "Africanisms"

In the works discussed in section 2.2 there are a number of properties that – following Meeussen (1975) – we will call Africanisms. With this term we are referring to properties that satisfy the following set of criteria:

(a) They are common in Africa but clearly less common elsewhere.
(b) They are found, at least to some extent, in all major geographical regions of Africa south of the Sahara.
(c) They are found in two or more of the four African language phyla.

A number of properties that are clearly more widespread in Africa than elsewhere are not considered here, for the following reasons. First, because they appear to be genetically determined. The presence of gender or noun class systems is a case in point. Most instances of such systems to be found in Africa are presumably genetically inherited. This can be assumed to apply on the one hand to the nature-based noun class systems found in Niger-Congo and Khoisan languages, and on the other hand to the sex-based gender systems of Afroasiatic and Central Khoisan languages.[6]

Perhaps surprisingly, we will also not consider the presence or absence of clicks a relevant property, although it appears to be the only property that is confined exlusively to Africa, and although it satisfies all of the criteria proposed above. The reason for doing so is the following: the main goal of this chapter is to find out whether African languages resemble one another more than they resemble other languages and what factors can be held responsible for such resemblances. To be sure, clicks occur in three of the four African language phyla, not only in all Khoisan languages, but also in South African Bantu (Niger-Congo) languages, and in the Cushitic (Afroasiatic) language Dahalo; still, their occurrence is geographically restricted to southern Africa and three East African languages.

Furthermore, the fact that Khoisan languages are among the phonologically most complex languages in the world, some of them distinguishing more than 110 distinct phonemes, is ignored here since it does not appear to be characteristic of Africa as a linguistic area, being restricted to a few North and South Khoisan languages.

In the following we will discuss a catalogue of properties that have been proposed to be characteristic of Africa as a linguistic area (especially Greenberg 1959; 1983; Larochette 1959; Meeussen 1975; Gilman 1986). Our selection is to some extent arbitrary in that we will ignore some properties that have been mentioned by other authors but where we are not entirely convinced that they are possible candidates for status as "Africanisms."

2.3.1   Grammar

A general phonological property that has been pointed out by a number of students of African languages is the preponderance of open syllables and an avoidance of consonant clusters and diphthongs (Meeussen 1975: 2; Gilman 1986: 41). Furthermore, tone as a distinctive unit is characteristic of the majority of African languages, in most cases both on the lexical and the grammatical levels (see section 2.4).

Ignoring click consonants, there are a number of consonant types that are widespread in Africa but uncommon elsewhere (see chapter 3 for detailed treatment). This applies among others to coarticulated labial-velar (or labio-velar) stops (Meeussen 1975: 2; Greenberg 1983: 4; Gilman 1986: 41). Labial-velars may be voiceless (*kp*) or voiced (*gb*). There are also corresponding nasals and/or fricatives, but they do not show the wide distribution of stops, and their occurrence is largely predictable on the basis of stops (Greenberg 1983: 4). The distribution of this property is clearly areally constrained: labial-velar stops occur in a broad geographical belt from the western Atlantic to the Nile–Congo divide, and they are also occasionally found outside this belt (see Welmers 1974: 47–8), e.g. in Katla and Giryama. Still, they are found in three of the four African phyla; only Khoisan languages have no labial-velar stops (see chapters 3 and 5). Also, in the Afroasiatic and Nilo-Saharan phyla, their occurrence is restricted essentially to one branch each, namely Chadic and Central Sudanic, respectively (Greenberg 1983: 7). Outside Africa, coarticulated labial-velar stops are found only sporadically, especially in northeastern Papua New Guinea in the Kâte-Ono group of the Indo-Pacific languages,[7] in some languages of Melanesia, and in the Austronesian language Iai (Greenberg 1983: 5; Maddieson 1984: 215–16); see section 3.2.4 for more details.

Perhaps even more characteristic are labial (or labiodental) flaps, where the teeth touch well below the outer eversion of the lip, which is flapped smartly outwards, downwards (see chapter 3). They have been found in all African phyla except Khoisan, e.g. in Chadic of Afroasiatic (Margi, Tera), Niger-Congo (Ngwe, Ngbaka, Ngbaka Mabo, Ndogo-Sere, some Shona dialects), and Nilo-Saharan (Kresh, Mangbetu) (Gregersen 1977: 31; Greenberg 1983: 4, 11). Still, their occurrence is confined to a relatively restricted number of languages, and even there they show restrictions in their use as phonemic units; not infrequently, these sounds are found only in special vocabulary such as ideophones. In their survey of 250 African and 345 non-African languages, Clements and Rialland did not find a single non-African language, but at least 70 African languages having such flaps (see chapter 3).

A third type of consonants that is widespread in Africa can be seen in implosives, which – following Clements and Rialland (chapter 3) – we define as non-obstruent stops. To be sure, these can be found in non-African languages, such as the Indonesian language Auye (Mike Cahill, p.c.), but such languages are rare. Furthermore, word-initial prenasalized consonants, for the most part voiced stops, are widely found in Africa (Meeussen 1975: 2; Gilman 1986: 41), although they occur most of all in Niger-Congo languages.

An outstanding property relating to the vowel system can be seen in the presence of cross-height vowel harmony based on distinctions of the tongue root position, commonly known as ATR (advanced tongue root) vowel harmony. It is widespread in Niger-Congo and Nilo-Saharan languages across the continent but appears to be rare outside Africa; see chapters 3 and 5 for discussion.

Morphological properties that have been mentioned include reduplication of nouns and adjectives, used to express a distributive function (e.g. Swahili *tano tano* 'five each, in fives'; Gilman 1986: 40). Within the verbal word, many African languages are characterized by a wide range of verbal derivational suffixes expressing functions such as reflexive, reciprocal, causative, passive, stative, andative (itive), and venitive (ventive), and these suffixes can be combined in sequence (Meeussen 1975: 2; Gilman 1986: 43). However, both these properties can also be observed widely in non-African languages.

A conspicuous feature of nominal morphology is the paucity of languages having case inflections, and ergative structures are fairly uncommon, but northeastern Africa is a noteworthy exception: there are a number of languages across genetic boundaries that have case inflections, and the only languages exhibiting an ergative organization, Shilluk, Päri, Anywa, and Jur-Luwo, are found there (chapter 8). Northeastern Africa is also typologically remarkable in that there are quite a number of languages having a marked-nominative system, where it is the accusative rather than the nominative case that is unmarked – note that marked-nominative languages are crosslinguistically exceptional; see chapter 8 for discussion. A perhaps unique property of case systems is the presence of case marked exclusively by tonal inflection, which so far has been found only in African marked-nominative languages but nowhere else in the world (König 2006).

With regard to word classes, African languages have been said to be characterized by a paucity of adjectives and, in a number of languages, adjectives are claimed to be absent altogether; what tends to be expressed in non-African languages by adjectives is likely to appear as verbs of state in Africa (cf. Gilman 1986: 40). On the other hand, there is a word class of ideophones that appears to be remarkably salient in many African languages (Meeussen 1975: 3). While languages in other parts of the world have ideophones as well, African languages have been found to have them in distinctly larger numbers. Furthermore, ideophones expressing color distinctions have so far only been found in Africa (Kilian-Hatz 2001; Voeltz & Kilian-Hatz 2001).

In their arrangement of words, African languages of all four phyla exhibit a number of general characteristics such as the following. While on a worldwide level languages having a verb-final syntax (SOV) appear to be the most numerous, in Africa there is a preponderance of languages having subject–verb–object (SVO) as their basic order: roughly 71 percent of all African languages exhibit this order (Heine 1976: 23; see also Gilman 1986: 37). Furthermore, the placement of nominal modifiers after the head noun appears to be more widespread in Africa than in most other parts of the world. Thus, in Heine's (1976: 23) sample of 300 African languages, demonstrative attributes are placed after the noun in 85 percent, adjectives in 88 percent, and numerals in 91 percent of all languages. Another characteristic in the arrangement of meaningful elements relates to verbal structure: in most African languages, pronominal subject clitics or affixes precede the tense markers (93 percent), which again precede the verb (83 percent), while adverbs follow the verb 93 percent (Heine 1976: 24).

An arrangement of basic word order that occurs in a number of languages across the continent but is fairly uncommon outside Africa concerns what nowadays tends to be referred to as SOVX order. In languages having this order, the direct object precedes the verb but the indirect object and adjuncts follow the verb. SOVX languages are likely to have postpositions and to place the genitival modifier before its head while other nominal modifiers follow the head noun (cf. the type B of Heine 1976).

Serial verb constructions have been claimed to be more common in Africa than elsewhere (Gilman 1986: 41). Recent studies suggest in fact that they are not confined to Niger-Congo but exist also in Khoisan languages (Kilian-Hatz 2003; König 2003); still, the majority of African languages do not qualify as serial verb languages, and such languages are not uncommon in some other parts of the world.

With reference to information structure, mention has been made of front-focusing of nouns by means of some kind of cleft construction, frequently used obligatorily in word questions, where *who went?* is expressed by *who is it who went?* (Gregersen 1977: 50–1; Gilman 1986: 39). In addition to noun phrase focusing there is also front-focusing by means of verb copying, where the verb appears first in the focus position and is repeated in the main clause (Gilman 1986: 39); the exact distribution of this phenomenon across Africa, however, is unknown. Note that focus marking by means of verbal inflections has so far only been found in African languages (see chapter 5).

In addition, there are construction types that are said to be found in a number of African languages but to be rare outside Africa. One of them is called anastasis by Meeussen (1975: 4); this consists of the swapping of subject and complement participants within the clause, for example, it is possible to express 'Worms enter the corpse' by saying 'The corpse enters worms.' It is unknown how widespread anastasis is in Africa, and it would seem that it is not all that uncommon in other parts of the world (Felix Ameka, p.c.).

Logophoric marking constitutes another construction type that has been claimed to be specifically African. Logophoric pronouns indicate coreference of a nominal in the non-direct quote to the speaker encoded in the accompanying quotative construction, as opposed to its non-coreference indicated by an unmarked pronominal device (Hagège 1974; Güldemann 2003a; see also Güldemann & von Roncador 2002). Thus, whereas (5a) illustrates a logophoric structure, (5b) is a plain, non-logophoric structure.

(5) Ewe (Kwa, Niger-Congo)

a. é   gblɔ   bé   ye-   dzó
   3SG   say   that   LOG-   leave
   'She$_i$ said that she$_i$ left'
b. é-   gblɔ   bé   é-   dzó
   3SG-   say   that   3SG-   leave
   'She$_i$ said that she$_j$ left'

Logophoric structures are with very few exceptions concentrated in a large belt extending from the southeastern corner of Ethiopia to the east up to the Niger River in the west and are found in three of the four language phyla (Güldemann 2003a; von Roncador 1992: 173); see chapter 5 for discussion.

Finally, there are a number of conceptualization strategies that might qualify as Africanisms. This applies in particular to what is called the goose-file model of spatial orientation (Heine 1997: 12–14), to be found in at least three of the four African language phyla, described by Meeussen in the following way:

Imagine a place from which a house can be seen, and further away a small hill. In such a situation the hill will be referred to in African terms as being 'in front of the house,' and the house as being 'behind the hill,' whereas in European languages the reverse expressions will be used. (Meeussen 1975: 3)

The following example from the Kuliak language So may illustrate the goose-file model, where an item to be located is conceptualized not as facing the speaker but rather as facing the same direction as the speaker.

(6) So (Kuliak, Nilo-Saharan)

nɛ́kɛ   yóG   sú-   o   sóG
be.at   people   behind- ABL   hill
'There are people in front of the hill'

There is another conceptualization strategy that has been proposed as an Africanism (Meeussen 1975), being one manifestation of what is usually called the inclusive or inclusory construction, which is used in reference to a plural that refers to a set of individuals and includes two explicit constituents. The form the construction typically takes in African languages is illustrated in (7).

(7) Swahili

sisi	na	wewe
we	and	you

'I and you'

It is unknown how widespread this construction type is; it is by no means restricted to Africa, being found in various other parts of the world (Blake 1987; Singer 1999; Moravcsik 2003: 479).

Another strategy to be found in all four language phyla, which is not restricted to Africa but is perhaps more widespread in Africa than elsewhere, is that in affirmative answers to negative questions the speaker wants to know if the propositional content of the question is correct or not, e.g. 'Didn't you sleep?' – 'Yes, I didn't' or 'No, I did' (Meeussen 1975: 4; Gregersen 1977: 44; Felix Ameka, p.c.).

2.3.2   Polysemy and grammaticalization

Perhaps the most conspicuous area where one might expect to find Africanisms can be seen in lexical and grammatical polysemies. The following are a few examples that have been pointed out by students of African languages.

Within the domain of nominal polysemy, a paradigm case can be seen in the fact that the same noun is used for 'meat' and 'animal' or, alternatively, that there are different but etymologically related nouns for 'meat' and 'animal' (Greenberg 1959, 1983: 4) – a case described by Lichtenberk (1991) more appropriately as heterosemy. Perhaps remarkably, if one of the two meanings is derived from the other then it goes from 'meat' to 'animal' rather than vice versa.[8] This is suggested at least by the fact that whenever the two are distinguished by means of some derivational, compounding or other mechanism then it is the item for 'meat' that is likely to be unmarked and 'animal' to be marked; cf. the examples in table 2.1 (for an example from the Bantu language Tonga, see Greenberg 1983: 16).

To be sure, such a polysemy can also be observed in other parts of the world, but it appears to be much more frequent in Africa than elsewhere (see section 2.4).

Another nominal polysemy that has been claimed to be pan-African is that of nouns denoting both 'hand' and 'arm', or nouns denoting both 'foot' and 'leg' (and 'wheel') (Gilman 1986: 43). Note, however, that these polysemies are also widespread outside Africa. Thus, in the worldwide survey by Witkowski and Brown (1985: 203), 50 out of 109 languages have a 'hand'/'arm' polysemy and 42 out of 109 languages a 'foot'/'leg' polysemy (see Heine 1997: 136).

Examples of polysemies involving verbs include verbs for 'eat,' which are said to also denote 'conquer,' 'capture a piece in a game,' and 'have sexual

Table 2.1 *Related Nouns for 'meat' and 'animal' in Hausa and !Xun*

Language	'meat'	'animal'
Hausa (Chadic, Afroasiatic)	nāmà	nāmàn dáɟì 'wild animal' ('meat of the bush')
!Xun (North Khoisan)	‖'hā	‖'hā-mà ('animal-DIM')

intercourse' (Greenberg 1959), verbs for 'die,' which tend to have many non-literal meanings in African languages such as 'be in a painful condition,' 'break down' (cf. Meeussen 1975: 4), verbs for 'lie (down)' also meaning 'sleep,' or verbs for 'hear' (to a lesser extent also 'see') also denoting other kinds of perception, such as 'smell,' 'feel,' 'taste,' 'understand' (Meeussen 1975: 4–5). Meeussen (1975: 4) furthermore notes that the use of words for 'good' also tend to express 'nice,' 'beautiful,' and 'fine' in African languages. The status of some of these polysemies as Africanisms, however, is far from clear. For example, meaning ranges expressed by verbs for 'die' in African languages may also be found in Australia or the Americas (Felix Ameka, p.c.), and much the same applies to polysemy involving 'hear' (see e.g. Evans & Wilkins 1998 for evidence on Australian languages).

Another area where Africa provides a wide range of common properties concerns grammaticalization processes, whereby the same conceptual schemas and constructions are employed to develop grammatical categories. Perhaps the most widely discussed example concerns comparative constructions based on what in Heine (1997) is called the Action Schema, taking either of the forms [X is big defeats/passes Y] or [X defeats/passes Y in size], i.e. the use of a verb meaning either 'defeat,' 'surpass,' or 'pass' to express comparison (Meeussen 1975: 4; Greenberg 1983: 4; Gilman 1986: 39). To be sure, this contact-induced grammaticalization occurs also in other parts of the world, for example in Sinitic languages, Thai, Vietnamese, Hmong and Khmer, where a verb for 'to cross' has given rise to a standard marker of comparison (Ansaldo 2004: 490ff.), but outside Africa it is extremely rare, while roughly 80 percent of the African languages have it (see table 2.1); we will return to this issue in section 2.4.

Furthermore, there is a grammaticalization process involving verbs for 'say' which are widely grammaticalized to quotatives, complementizers, purpose clause markers, etc. (Larochette 1959; Meeussen 1975: 3; Gilman 1986: 44; Güldemann 2001). However, this grammaticalization appears to be also fairly common outside Africa (see Ebert 1991; Heine & Kuteva 2002).

Body-part terms used metaphorically for deictic spatial distinctions are found throughout the world; for example, nouns for the body part 'back' are the conceptual source for spatial terms for 'behind' in most languages. But this general grammaticalization process appears to be more common in Africa than elsewhere, and there are some developments that are likely to happen in Africa but unlikely to happen elsewhere (Meeussen 1975: 3; Gilman 1986: 42). Such developments include, but are not confined to, the grammaticalization of body parts for 'stomach/belly' to spatial concepts for 'in(side),' or of 'buttocks/anus' to 'below' and/or 'behind' (Heine 1997: 37ff.). Furthermore, sex distinctions used for the grammaticalization of the spatial concepts 'right' (< 'male, strong hand') and 'left' (< 'female, weak hand') have been proposed as pan-African features (Gilman 1986: 42), but such metaphorical transfers are by no means confined to Africa.

Further grammaticalization processes widespread in Africa involve the use of nouns for 'man' and 'woman' as attributive or derivational markers for sex distinctions (cf. Gilman 1986: 42), whereby, for example, the noun for 'girl' is historically a 'woman child' and 'bitch' a 'woman dog.' Finally, the grammaticalization of nouns for 'body' to reflexive markers has also been proposed as characterizing common African conceptualization processes (Gilman 1986: 42; Heine 2000) but, once again, this is a process that is by no means restricted to Africa.

2.3.3   Conclusion

The properties that have been discussed in this section may have given an impression of the kind of structural characteristics to be expected in African languages. It would seem that they can be classified into the following categories:

(8) Properties that seem to be essentially restricted to Africa:

a.   clicks
b.   labial flaps
c.   several types of vowel harmony (described by Clements and Rialland in chapter 3)
d.   ideophones expressing color distinctions
e.   case inflections expressed exclusively by tone (so far only found in African languages, all of the marked-nominative type; see chapter 8)
f.   lack of obligatory agreement of transitive verbs with their object (see chapter 4)

(9) Properties that are distinctly more common in Africa than elsewhere. These are properties that are typologically remarkable, but many of them are either genetically or areally restricted in their occurrence:

a.   labial-velar stops
b.   implosives, which Clements and Rialland (this volume, chapter 3) define as non-obstruent stops

c. ATR-based vowel harmony
d. word-initial prenasalized stops
e. noun class systems
f. marked-nominative case systems
g. marking negation at the end of the clause
h. logophoric pronouns (which indicate coreference of a nominal in the non-direct quote to the speaker encoded in the accompanying quotative construction, as opposed to its non-coreference indicated by an unmarked pronominal device)
i. focus marking by means of verbal inflections
j. SOVX as a basic word order (where the direct object precedes while the indirect object and adjuncts follow the verb)

On the other hand, there are also linguistic features that occur in other parts of the world but are hard to find in Africa. Thus, so far only four African languages (Shilluk, Päri, Anywa, and Jur-Luwo) have been found to show an ergative organization. Furthermore, while noun class systems are more common in Africa than elsewhere in the world, languages with noun classifiers are comparatively rare, systems such as the genitival classifiers of the Ubangian language Dongo-ko and the numeral classifiers of the Cross River language Kana being exceptions. And finally, no clear cases of polysynthetic or noun-incorporating languages have so far been found in Africa.

Still, in spite of all the work that has been done on Africa as a linguistic area, there is no entirely convincing evidence to answer the question raised in the title of this chapter, for the following reasons. First, although there is some fairly comprehensive information on the areal distribution of some of the properties dealt with above (see e.g. Greenberg 1983; Heine 1976; see also chapters 3 and 5), we lack corresponding information on languages in other parts of the world in order to determine whether, or to what extent, we are really dealing with Africa-specific structures. Second, there is a genuine problem that any project aimed at defining Africa as a linguistic area is confronted with – one that has been described appropriately by Greenberg in the following way:

Ideally, if what is meant by an African areal characteristic is one which is found every-where in Africa but nowhere else, then clearly none exists . . . (Greenberg 1983: 3)

What this means is that it does not seem to be possible to define Africa as a linguistic area in the same way as, for example, Meso-America has been defined (Campbell et al. 1986), that is, in accordance with the characterization proposed in (4), more specifially in terms of a set of linguistic features that are not found outside that area (see (4b) and (4c)). In the remainder of this chapter we will argue, however, that there nevertheless is a way of approaching this general issue.

2.4   A survey

Being aware that it does not seem possible to find a set of properties that clearly separate Africa from the rest of the world in accordance with (4), we decided to use an alternative approach. Following Greenberg (1983), we selected a set of eleven properties or characteristics and we asked colleagues working on African languages to provide information on the presence vs. absence of these properties in the language or languages studied by them. In this way we received information on 99 African languages.[9] This sample is neither genetically nor areally entirely balanced but represents all major genetic groupings of Africa: of the 99 languages, 55 belong to the Niger-Congo, 23 to the Afroasiatic, 15 to the Nilo-Saharan, and 6 to the Khoisan phylum. It also includes all major regions with the exception of north-central Africa, which is clearly underrepresented.

Choice of properties was determined by the following considerations. We were aiming at finding phenomena that are likely to set Africa off from other parts of the world. Accordingly, we chose properties that previous authors had claimed to be widespread in Africa but less so elsewhere in the world, that is, a range of properties discussed in section 2.3. But a number of these properties turned out to be unsuitable for our survey, either because there is lack of appropriate information on them in many of the languages concerned or because we suspected that their distribution might be genetically motivated. In the end we were left with eleven properties that could be expected to be relevant for an areal analysis.

2.4.1   The data

Table 2.2 lists the eleven properties used in the survey as well as the overall results of the survey, namely the relative frequency of occurrence of these properties. What it suggests is that the properties are roughly of three kinds: first, there are some properties (3, 5, 6, 7, 8, and 10) that occur in at least two-thirds of the African languages of our survey; second, there are properties that are found in a minority of African languages (1, 2, 4, and 9); and finally, there is one property (11) that is found in roughly every second African language.

To test whether these properties are in fact characteristic of African languages, we asked experts of non-African languages and received information on an additional fifty languages. The results of the survey are summarized in table 2.3. What this table suggests is the following:

(a) Africa stands out against other regions of the world in having on average 6.8 of the eleven properties, while in other regions clearly lower figures are found.

Table 2.2 *Relative frequency of occurrence of eleven typological properties in African languages (sample: 99 languages. Parameters 3, 7, and 8 have two options, A and B; if one of the options applies this is taken as positive evidence that the relevant property is present)*

Property used as criteria	Number of languages having that property	Percentage of all languages
1 Labial-velar stops	39	39.4
2 Implosive stops	36	36.4
3 Lexical (A) and/or grammatical tones (B)	80	80.8
4 ATR-based vowel harmony	39	39.4
5 Verbal derivational suffixes (passive, causative, benefactive, etc.)	76	76.7
6 Nominal modifiers follow the noun	89	89.9
7 Semantic polysemy 'drink (A)/pull (B), smoke'	74	74.7
8 Semantic polysemy 'hear (A)/see (B), understand'	72	72.7
9 Semantic polysemy 'animal, meat'	40	40.4
10 Comparative constructions based on the schema [X is big defeats/ surpasses/ passes Y]	82	82.8
11 Noun 'child' used productively to express diminutive meaning	50	50.5

(b) Outside Africa, no language has been found to have as many as five properties, while African languages have between five and ten properties. There are a few exceptions, to be discussed below.

(c) While the African area can be set off from the rest of the world, it seems that there is also a worldwide north/south division: languages of the southern hemisphere have clearly more of the properties than languages of the northern hemisphere.

A slightly different picture emerges if one draws a line within Africa, separating sub-Saharan from northern Africa. With northern Africa we refer to Afroasiatic languages with the exception of the Chadic branch, that is, it includes Ethio-Semitic, Cushitic, Omotic, and Berber languages. Accordingly, sub-Saharan Africa includes Chadic as well as all languages of the other three language phyla. As table 2.4 suggests, this distinction is justified on account of the distribution of properties: whereas northern Africa does not behave much differently from other parts of the world, exhibiting similar figures as, for example, the languages of Australia and Oceania, it is sub-Saharan Africa that stands out typologically, with an average figure of 7.2 properties.

Table 2.3 *Distribution of eleven typological properties according to major world regions (sample: 99 African and 50 non-African languages)*

Region	Total of languages	Total of properties	Average number of properties per language
Europe	10	11	1.1
Asia	8	21	2.6
Australia/Oceania	12	37	3.0
The Americas	14	48	3.4
Africa	99	669	6.8
Pidgins and creoles[a]	6	14	2.3
All regions	*149*		

[a] Three of the six pidgin and creole languages are spoken in Africa and the rest in the Americas and in New Guinea.

2.4.2   Isopleth mapping

Isopleth mapping is a technique that has been employed in linguistic areas whose status is fairly uncontroversial, such as South Asia (Masica 1976), the Balkans (van der Auwera 1998), and Meso-America (van der Auwera 1998). Isopleth maps are designed on the basis of the relative number of features that languages of a linguistic area share: languages having the same number of properties, irrespective of which these properties are, are assigned to the same isopleth and, depending on how many properties are found in a given language, the relative position of that language within the linguistic area can be determined.[10]

What isopleth maps achieve is that they show the geographical distribution of the relative number of features making up a sprachbund. For example, on the basis of ten features characteristic of the Balkan languages, van der Auwera (1998: 261–3) finds that Bulgarian is the most central Balkanic language, being "included in all isoglosses," i.e. showing all ten Balkanic features (for a discussion of isopleth maps, see Heine & Kuteva 2006).

Applying isopleth mapping to Africa yields the following results: the most inclusive languages are Western Chadic, Gur (Voltaic), some Plateau and Guang languages, having nine to ten of the eleven properties considered. A secondary isopleth center is found in the Cameroon–Central Africa area, where up to nine properties are found. Clearly less central are languages further to the west and south, that is, Atlantic and Mande languages on the one hand, and Bantu languages on the other, where around six properties are found. Peripheral Africa consists of the Ethiopian highlands on the one hand, and northern (Berber) Africa, where less than five properties are found.

Table 2.4 *Distribution of eleven typological properties: sub-Saharan Africa vs. rest of the world (Sample: 99 African and 50 non-African languages. Northern Africa = Afroasiatic minus Chadic; sub-Saharan Africa = Africa minus northern Africa)*

Linguistically defined region	Total of languages	Total of properties	Average number of properties per language
World minus Africa	47	119	2.6
Northeastern Africa	13	46	3.7
World minus sub-Saharan Africa	60	165	2.8
Sub-Saharan Africa	86	635	7.2

Isopleth research in general and in Africa in particular is far from encouraging, for the following reasons. First, what it achieves is roughly what one would expect without drawing on a quantitative technique: languages spoken in the center of the area are likely to show the largest number of isopleths, and thus to be most central to the linguistic area concerned, and the farther languages are removed from the center, the fewer properties they tend to share, that is, the more peripheral they are to the area concerned. Second, the contribution that isopleth mapping can make to reconstructing linguistic history in particular and history in general is a modest one, since there is no coherent way of correlating isopleth structures with specific historical processes. Nevertheless, as we hope to demonstrate in the next section, the isopleth technique can be of use for specific issues relating to areal relationship.

2.4.3   Genetic vs. areal distribution

In order to test how our typology survey relates to individual language areas within Africa, we had a closer look at the situation in a particular region characterized by a high degree of genetic diversity, namely northern Nigeria. In the region between the Niger–Benue confluence and Lake Chad there is a multitude of languages belonging to three of the four language phyla of Africa: there are Chadic languages of the Afroasiatic family in the north, the Saharan languages Kanuri and Kanembu of Nilo-Saharan in the northeast, and Niger-Congo languages of the Atlantic, Benue-Congo, and Adamawa branches in the south. That there was massive language contact in this region across genetic boundaries is fairly uncontroversial (see e.g. Wolff & Gerhardt 1977); the question we wish to look into here is whether there is any significant correlation between the relative number of shared properties and the genetic affiliation of the languages concerned.

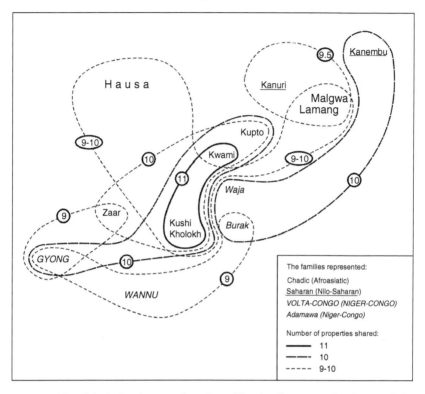

Map 2.1 A sketch map of northern Nigerian languages: isoglosses of the number of shared typological properties (encircled numbers = numbers of shared properties)

To this end we decided to ignore the procedure of isopleth mapping used in section 2.4.2, which is based on the absolute number of properties found in the languages concerned, and instead adopt a modified procedure relying on dyadic comparisons between all languages concerned. Comparison is based not only on whether two given languages share a certain property but also on whether they both lack some property, that is, typological similarity is not only determined in terms of presence but also in terms of shared absence of a property. Accordingly, if two languages were found to have labial-velar stops then this was interpreted as being just as typologially relevant as if they both lack labial-velar stops. Altogether fourteen languages were compared, of which eight are Chadic (= Afroasiatic), two Saharan (= Nilo-Saharan), two Adamawan, and two Volta-Congo (= both Niger-Congo); selection was determined primarily on the basis of the availability of survey data. The results of these dyadic comparisons are listed in table 2.5.

Table 2.5 *Number of typological properties shared by selected languages of northern Nigeria*

Language	Genetic grouping	1	2	3	4	5	6	7	8	9	10	11	12	13
1 Kanembu	Saharan													
2 Kanuri	Saharan	8.5												
3 Hausa	Chadic	7	8.5											
4 Kholokh	Chadic	7	7.5	9										
5 Kupto	Chadic	7	7.5	9	11									
6 Kushi	Chadic	6.5	7	9.5	10.5	10.5								
7 Kwami	Chadic	7	7.5	9.5	11	11	10.5							
8 Lamang	Chadic	8	9.5	9	8	8	7.5	8						
9 Malgwa	Chadic	7	9.5	10	9	9	8.5	9	10					
10 Zaar	Chadic	6	6.5	8	10	10	9.5	10	7	8				
11 Gyong	Plateau	7.5	8	8	9.5	9.5	9	9.5	6.5	7.5	9			
12 Burak[a]	Adamawa	9/10	6.5/10	5/10	7/10	7/10	6.5/10	7/10	5/10	5/10	7/10	8/10		
13 Waja	Adamawa	10.5	8.5	7.5	7.5	7.5	7	7.5	7.5	7.5	6.5	8.5	8.5/10	
14 Wannu	Jukunoid	8.5	7	5.5	7.5	7.5	7.5	7.5	5.5	5.5	8.5	8.5	9.5	8

[a] For Burak, only ten of the eleven properties were available.

The results of table 2.5 are presented in the form of an isopleth structure in map 2.1. Considered are only shared figures of nine or more properties on the basis of data presented in table 2.5. The overall picture that arises from this map yields one important finding: it suggests that the distribution of typological properties is not determined primarily by genetic relationship. While there are some genetic clusterings, combining e.g. the Chadic languages Kwami, Kushi, and Kholokh (11 properties), or the Niger-Congo languages Gyong, Wannu, and Burak (9 properties), more commonly the isopleth lines cut across genetic boundaries. This is suggested by the following observations:

(a) The Saharan language Kanuri shares more properties (9.5) with the Chadic languages Malgwa and Lamang than with the fellow Saharan language Kanembu.
(b) The Saharan language Kanembu shares more properties (10) with the Adamawan languages Waja and Burak than with the fellow Saharan language Kanuri.
(c) The Adamawan languages Burak and Waja share more properties with the Saharan language Kanembu than with their fellow Niger-Congo languages Gyong and Wannu.
(d) At the same time, Waja shares more properties with Kanembu (10.5) than with any other fellow Niger-Congo language.

While we do not wish to propose any generalizations beyond the data examined in this section, what these data suggest is that, on the basis of eleven properties used, areal clustering provides a parameter of language classification that is hardly less significant than genetic relationship.

2.5   Conclusions

The analysis of our survey data suggests that there is evidence to define Africa as a linguistic area: African languages exhibit significantly more of the eleven properties listed in table 2.2 than non-African languages do, and it is possible to predict with a high degree of probability that if there is some language that possesses more than five of these eleven properties then this must be an African language. The data also allow for a number of additional generalizations based on combinations of individual properties. For example, if there is a language that has any two of the properties 1 (labial-velar stops), 2 (implosive stops), and 4 (ATR-vowel harmony), then this must be an African language (see chapter 3 for more details).

Not all of the properties, however, are characteristic of Africa only; in fact, some are more common in other regions of the world. Property 5 (verbal derivational suffixes) appears to be more common in the Americas than in Africa, property 11 (noun 'child' used productively to express diminutive meaning) is as common in South America as it is in Africa, and property 6 (nominal modifiers follow the noun) is equally common in the Americas and Australia/Oceania. What is relevant to our discussion is not the distribution of individual properties but rather the combination of these properties, where the African continent clearly stands out against the rest of the world on the basis of the eleven properties examined.

What this means with reference to (4) is that our characterization of linguistic areas needs to be revised to take care of the quantitative generalizations proposed in section 2.4, by rephrasing (4c) in the following way: "This set of properties is not found at a comparable quantitative magnitude in languages outside the area."

The survey data presented are also of interest with reference to an issue concerning the genesis and explanation of creole languages. One of the main hypotheses advocated by students of these languages has it that the structure of creole languages, in particular of Atlantic and Indian Ocean creoles, can be explained at least in part with reference to substrate influence from African languages, more specifically from languages spoken along the West African coast (see e.g. Boretzky 1983; Holm 1988). In its strongest form this hypothesis maintains that creole languages such as Haitian Creole have the structure of African languages, especially of Fon (Fongbe), with a European superstrate grafted on (see especially Lefebvre 1998). While we are not able to assess this hypothesis here, our data do not lend any support to such a hypothesis: with the exception of the Portuguese-based creole Angolar (Maurer 1995), creole languages do not exhibit any noticeable typological affinity with African languages on the basis of our survey data (see table 2.3).

To offer a diachronic interpretation of the results presented would be beyond the scope of this chapter. An attempt in this direction has been made by Greenberg (1983), whose main goal was to identify sources for the spread of four areal properties in Africa (see section 2.2). In that paper he argued that labial-velar stops (our property 1) originated in Niger-Congo and then diffused into Chadic and Central Sudanic languages, and he suggested that comparatives based on the Action Schema (our property 10) are of Niger-Congo origin (1983: 15). In a similar fashion, he found evidence for a Niger-Congo origin for the 'meat'/'animal' polysemy (1983: 18; our property 11). On the basis of our data there is nothing that would contradict these reconstructions. But, as we will see in chapter 5, there is also an alternative perspective to this situation.

3   Africa as a phonological area

G. N. Clements and Annie Rialland

3.1   Phonological zones in Africa

Some 30 percent of the world's languages are spoken in Africa, by one current estimate (Gordon 2005). Given this linguistic richness, it is not surprising that African languages reveal robust patterns of phonology and phonetics that are much less frequent, or which barely occur, in other regions of the world. These differences are instructive for many reasons, not the least of which is the fact that they bring to light potentials for sound structure which, due to accidents of history and geography, have been more fully developed in Africa than in other continents. Just as importantly, a closer study of "variation space" across African languages shows that it is not homogeneous, as some combinations of properties tend to cluster together in genetically unrelated languages while other imaginable combinations are rare or unattested, even in single groups; crosslinguistic variation of this sort is of central interest to the study of linguistic universals and typology. A further important reason for studying phonological patterns in Africa is the light they shed upon earlier population movements and linguistic change through contact.

In preparing this chapter, we initially set out to examine characteristics that are more typical of the African continent as a whole than of other broad regions of the world (a goal initially set out by Greenberg 1959, 1983). However, this goal quickly turned out to be unrealistic. From a genetic-historical point of view, Africa contains several independent or very distantly related language groups, each of which show characteristics different from the others. Apart from contact areas where these languages meet, the features of any one region tend to coincide with inherited features of the languages spoken in it, often over thousands of years. From a geographical point of view, Africa is a vast expanse consisting of many regions differing in the conditions they offer for movement and exchange among peoples. For these reasons there is little reason to expect any great overall linguistic uniformity.

Our preliminary research quickly confirmed that there is no characteristically African phonological property that is common to the continent as a whole, nor even to the vast sub-Saharan region. Indeed, many of the characteristics for which Africa is best known to non-specialists, such as its clicks, its labial-velar

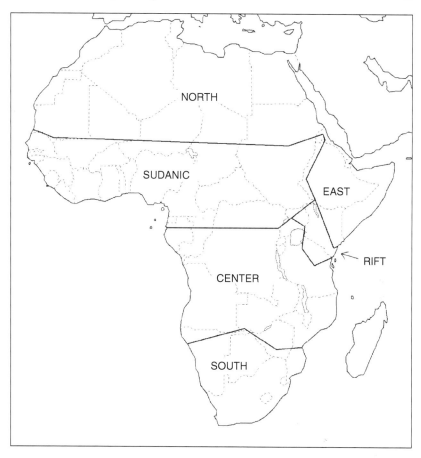

Map 3.1 Six phonological zones in Africa

consonants or its tongue-root-based (ATR) vowel harmony, are geographically restricted. In view of this fact, we found it more enlightening to focus our study on properties that are characteristic of smaller, more specific regions.

The central thesis of this chapter is that the African continent can be divided into six major zones, each of which is defined by a number of phonological properties that occur commonly within it but much less often outside it. These will be referred to by the neutral term "phonological zone" in order not to prejudge the question whether the shared features arise from common inheritance, diffusion, or other factors. These zones are shown in map 3.1.

Needless to say, it is impossible to draw rigid boundaries around assumed linguistic regions, and these boundaries should not be taken too literally. All such boundaries are porous, and shift as populations move and intermingle over time. In a few cases, boundaries correspond roughly to geographic or climatic frontiers – e.g. the Sudanic belt is bounded roughly by the Sahel to the north and the Congo basin to the south – but even these boundaries are not perfectly sharp, and it is usually best to recognize "transition zones" showing features of the zones on either side. Geographic features are not a sure guide in placing boundaries, and where doubt arises we have taken the linguistic evidence as decisive.

The largest zone we call the *North*, defined broadly to include the Mediterranean coastal region, the Sahara and the Sahel. This zone is fairly homogenous from a linguistic point of view, as its phonological properties coincide largely with those of the Arabic and Berber languages spoken within it. This is less true toward the south and east of the zone, where alongside local forms of Arabic and Berber (and Beja in the east) a number of non-Afroasiatic languages are spoken, including northern varieties of Fulfulde and Songay, the Saharan languages Tedaga, Dazaga, and Zaghawa, and the Nile Nubian languages Nobiin (or Mahas) and Kenuzi-Dongola.

A second zone, which we call the *East*, encompasses the Horn of Africa (Ethiopia, Eritrea, Djibouti, and Somalia). This zone is linguistically more diverse than the North. Though nearly all its languages are usually classed in the Afroasiatic phylum, they involve three independent stocks: Ethio-Semitic in the north, Cushitic in the east and south, and Omotic in the west. Linguistic features within Ethiopia tend to hug genetic boundaries to a certain extent (Tosco 2000b), though a few, such as the common presence of implosives in consonant inventories, cross boundaries as well. Due in large part to the common Afroasiatic heritage, many linguistic features of the East are shared with the North, though as we shall see it also has characteristic traits of its own.

The linguistically most dense of the six zones is one we call the *Sudanic belt*, or *Sudan* for short.[1] This region includes the vast savanna that extends across sub-Saharan Africa bounded by the Sahel to the north, the Atlantic Ocean to the west and southwest, Lake Albert to the southeast, and the Ethiopian–Eritrean highlands to the east, and corresponds roughly to the "core area" recognized by Greenberg (1959). This region is linguistically diverse, containing all non-Bantu (and some Bantu) languages of the Niger–Congo phylum, the Chadic subgroup of Afroasiatic, southern varieties of Arabic, and most Nilo-Saharan languages except for peripheral members in the north and southeast. Where these languages come into contact, we find evidence of phonological diffusion across genetic lines. (For further discussion of the (Macro-)Sudanic belt, with maps of several of its linguistic features, see Güldemann, chapter 5 of this volume.)

A fourth large zone, which we call the *Center*, comprises south-central and southeast Africa and includes most of the equatorial forest, the Great Lakes region, and the subequatorial savanna to the Kalahari Basin in the south and the Indian Ocean in the east. This geographically diverse zone is almost exclusively Bantu-speaking and is characterized by the linguistic features typical of Bantu languages. (For overviews of Bantu phonology see Hyman 2003 and Kisseberth & Odden 2003.)

A fifth zone, which we call the *South*, comprises the remainder of the continent to the south and includes semi-desert, savanna, and temperate coastal regions. While its phonological characteristics derive from those of the Khoisan and Bantu languages spoken within it, several of them are shared rather widely across genetic boundaries, and it is these that define this zone in phonological terms. This zone contains some of the richest consonant and vowel inventories of the world's languages, led perhaps by !Xóõ (Southern Khoisan) with some 160 distinct phonemes (Traill 1985). (For discussion of the Kalahari Basin area, see Güldemann 1998.)

A final zone, called the *Rift Valley* (or simply *Rift*), includes much of the eastern branch of the Great Rift Valley in northern Tanzania and western Kenya. In this region, languages of all four of Greenberg's super-families[2] (Afroasiatic, Nilo-Saharan, Niger-Congo, Khoisan) meet in a jigsaw-like pattern. In general, their phonological features do not appear to be widely shared among different groups, except as a result of independent genetic heritage. However, a number of apparently contact-induced features in an area southeast of Lake Victoria have been described by Kießling, Mous, and Nurse in chapter 6 of this volume.

Many micro-areas can be identified within these broad zones, some of which have received detailed study in other publications. Our purpose here, however, will not be to refine these zones but to examine their defining characteristics and interrelationships.

This chapter is organized around two "core" sections, the first dealing with segmental phonological properties and the second with prosodic properties. Each begins with a brief overview and then examines a number of selected features in more detail. In our selection of features we have given priority to those that are well documented in a large number of languages, that appear in genetically distant (but not necessarily totally unrelated) languages in a contiguous area, that are broadly represented across smaller genetic units within this area, and that appear with much less frequency in languages outside the area, and outside Africa. The chapter concludes with a review of proposed diagnostics of the major zones.

3.2   Segmental features

3.2.1   Preliminaries

As noted above, no "typically" African sound is found throughout the African continent. Properties that are widely shared across the continent as a whole

Table 3.1 *Number of languages having each of three consonant types in 150 African languages and 345 non-African ("non-Afr") languages. African languages are given by zone. The total number of languages in each set is indicated in parentheses*

Consonant type	Sudanic (100)	North (7)	East (12)	Center (13)	Rift (9)	South (9)	Non-Afr (345)	Ratio % Sudanic / % non-Afr
labial flaps	12	0	0	1	0	0	0	–
labial-velar stops	55	0	0	0	0	0	2	94.9
implosives	46	0	6	2	2	2	13	12.2

amount to little more than typologically unmarked features, such as the near-universal presence of voiceless stops, or a preference for open syllable structure. Once we restrict our attention to particular zones, however, certain relatively unusual features emerge.

In order to study the distribution of speech sounds across zones in quantitative terms, we constructed a database of 150 African phoneme systems representing all major linguistic groupings and geographic regions of the continent. This database is divided into six subsets corresponding to the six zones described above. It emphasizes languages of the Sudanic belt (N = 100) in keeping with their large numbers and genetic diversity, but also contains representative languages from the other zones (N = 50). All African languages in the database are listed in tables 3A and 3B of the appendix to this chapter. These languages are complemented by a further set of 345 non-African languages which provide a basis for comparison. The full database of 495 languages forms the basis for our quantitative generalizations, though our qualitative discussion is based upon an independent survey of the available literature and on our first-hand experience.[3]

3.2.2   Three Sudanic consonant types

A study of the database brings to light three consonant types that are especially representative of languages spoken in the Sudanic belt: labial flaps, labial-velar stops, and implosives. Table 3.1 shows their distribution in African and non-African languages. The last column shows the ratio of the percentage of occurrence of each sound in the Sudanic belt (% Sudanic) over the percentage of its occurrence outside Africa (% non-African).

The first two sounds are nearly unique to the Sudanic belt. Labial flaps occur in 12 of the 100 Sudanic languages in our sample and in only one language elsewhere in Africa.[4] Labial-velar stops occur in over half the Sudanic languages of the sample (55 percent) but in none of the other African languages and only

two non-African languages (0.6 percent).[5] As shown in the last column, these
sounds are over ninety times as frequent among Sudanic languages as among
non-African languages. Third on the list, but still much commoner in Sudanic
languages (46 percent) than in non-African languages (3.8 percent), are
implosive stops, which are about twelve times as frequent in the Sudanic belt as
outside Africa. Labial flaps and labial-velar stops will be discussed in the next
two sections, and implosives will be examined in section 3.2.7.

3.2.3   Labial flaps

Greenberg (1983) was first to point out the widespread occurrence of labial flaps
across a broad zone in north-central Africa. Due to their rarity and often marginal
status, these sounds have tended to be overlooked in the past, but have been
correctly described since the early twentieth century. In Shona S10,[6] the Bantuist
Clement M. Doke described the labiodental version of this sound as follows
(1931: 224): "It is a voiced sound in the production of which the lower lip is
brought behind the upper front teeth with tensity. The teeth touch well below the
outer eversion of the lip, which is flapped smartly outwards, downwards." (See
also his photographs, p. 298.) Bilabial versions of this sound have also been
described, but are not known to contrast with the labiodental variant. As far as
their phonology is concerned, these sounds usually constitute independent
phonemes and may occur in "crowded" phoneme systems containing many
competing labials. For example, in Higi, a Chadic language of northeast Nigeria,
the labial flap /ѷ/ occurs in a consonant system also containing five other voiced
labials / b ɓ m v w /, though its use is restricted to a few ideophones such as
ѷáѷáѷá 'signal of distress' (Mohrlang 1972). For more information, the reader is
referred to Olson and Hajek's thorough survey (2003).

  These sounds have been reported in at least seventy African languages, heavily
concentrated in the center of the Sudanic belt in an area encompassing northern
Cameroon, the Central African Republic (CAR), and adjoining parts of Nigeria,
Chad, Sudan, and the Democratic Republic of the Congo (DRC). (See the lan-
guage list in Olson & Hajek 2003 and map 3.6 in Güldemann, chapter 5 of this
volume). In this area, they occur in language families of three different phyla,
Chadic (Afroasiatic), Central Sudanic (Nilo-Saharan), and Adamawa-Ubangi
(Niger-Congo), as well as in a few neighboring northern Bantoid languages
(Niger-Congo). A separate concentration is found in the Nyanja (Bantu N30) and
Shona (Bantu S10) language groups spoken in Malawi, Zimbabwe, and adjacent
areas of Botswana and Mozambique. Outside Africa, labial flaps have been
reported only in one language, Sika, an Austronesian language of Indonesia.

  Labial flaps are not widely distributed across the Sudanic belt. In
spite of their concentrated distribution, common inheritance from a single
proto-language can be ruled out. Olson and Hajek (2003) suggest that they

Table 3.2 *Frequencies of four types of labial-velar stops in the African database (total languages with labial-velar stops = 55)*

	Number	Percent of total
gb	54	98.2
kp	54	98.2
Ngb	13	23.6
ŋm	7	12.7

might have arisen in Adamawa-Ubangi languages of Cameroon and spread from there into the eastern CAR and Sudan, from whence they would have been borrowed by Central Sudanic languages. How these sounds arose in the first place (i.e. via sound change, in ideophones, just once or several times independently) is still uncertain.

3.2.4   Labial-velar stops

Almost equally unique to Africa, and to the Sudanic belt in particular, are labial-velar stops. These are doubly articulated sounds produced with overlapping labial and velar closures (see Connell 1994 and Ladefoged & Maddieson 1996 for detailed phonetic descriptions). In spite of their complex articulation, they constitute single phonemes, as is shown by a number of diagnostics. For example, they cannot be split by epenthesis, they are copied as single units in reduplication, and they typically occur in syllable-initial position where consonant clusters are not otherwise allowed. In general, labiovelar sounds, including stops and the glide /w/, tend to pattern with labial rather than velar sounds in phonological systems (Ohala & Lorentz 1977). However, in homorganic nasal–stop sequences, it is the dorsal feature that typically spreads to the preceding nasal, yielding [ŋmgb] or [ŋgb].[7] A fuller discussion of their phonology can be found in Cahill (1999).

The commonest labial-velar stops are a voiced oral stop /gb/, a voiceless oral stop /kp/, a nasal stop /ŋm/, and a prenasalized stop /Ngb/ usually realized as [ŋmgb] or [ŋgb]. One or more of these sounds occur in 55 of the 150 African languages in our database (see table 3.2).

Other types of labial-velar sounds are very rare in our data, the most unusual being the labial-velar trills reported in the Bantu language Yaka C104 (Thomas 1991). As the numbers in table 3.2 suggest, /kp/ and /gb/ usually accompany each other in a system. This fact may seem unusual, given the crosslinguistic tendency for voiced stops to be less frequent than voiceless stops. In the Sudanic belt, however, this tendency does not hold; within our sample, only 4 percent of Sudanic languages lack voiced stops, and these are all Bantu

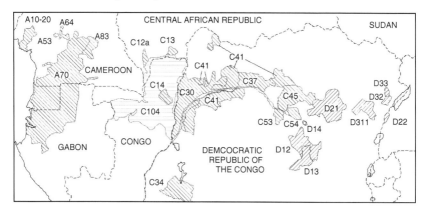

Map 3.2 Northern Bantu languages with labial-velar stops. Languages are identified by their Guthrie codes as revised and updated by Maho (2003); see text for language names

languages spoken in the transitional zone in the south. A regular pairing of /gb/ and /kp/ is therefore to be expected in this area.[8]

As far as their geographic distribution is concerned, labial-velar stops are found in over half the languages of the Sudanic belt in our sample, but are extremely infrequent in languages outside this area, whether in Africa or elsewhere. They occur across the entire Sudanic belt from the Atlantic Ocean in the west to Lake Albert and the Nubian Hills in the east. They are well represented in all major branches of Niger-Congo except Dogon, including, along the periphery of this zone, central and southern Atlantic languages (e.g. Biafada, Bidyogo, Temne, Kisi, and Gola), several Grassfields Bantu languages (e.g. Mundani, Aghem, Yamba, and Nweh), and a Kordofanian language (Kalak/Katla). In Nilo-Saharan they are typical of Central Sudanic languages, and also occur in Dendi Songay, spoken in Benin, and a few Nilotic languages (Kuku Bari of southern Sudan, Alur of the DRC). They are also found in a few Chadic languages (Bacama in north-eastern Nigeria, Daba, Mofu-Gudur, Kada/Gidar, and the Kotoko cluster in Cameroon). As an areal feature which cuts across genetic lines, they constitute a primary phonological diagnostic of the Sudanic belt. (See Greenberg 1983 for a fuller description of their geographical spread, and Güldemann, chapter 5 of this volume, for further discussion and a map of their distribution.)

Labial-velar stops are not common in Bantu languages. However, they occur in a fair number of northern Bantu languages of zones A, C, and D spoken in the equatorial forest and Congo Basin from the Atlantic in the west to Lake Albert in the east, as shown in map 3.2.

The zone A languages, spoken from southeastern Cameroon well into Gabon, include several members of the Lundu-Balong group A10 such as

Londo A11, Bafo A141, and Central Mbo A15C, several of the western Duala languages A21–3, Kpa/Bafia A53, Tuki A64, the Ewondo-Fang group A70, and Makaa A83. The zone C languages, spoken in the central Congo Basin, include several members of the Ngundi group C10 (notably Yaka/Aka C104, Pande C12a, Mbati C13, and Leke C14), many members of the Bangi-Ntumba group C30 spoken between the Ubangi and Congo Rivers, Ngombe C41 with 150,000 speakers, and further upstream along the Congo River, Beo/Ngelima C45, Topoke/Gesogo C53, and Lombo C54. Among zone D languages, labial-velar stops are found in the Mbole-Ena group D10 including Lengola D12, Mituku D13, and Enya D14, in Baali/Bali D21, and far to the east in several members of the Bira-Huku group D30 including Bila D311, Bira D32, Nyali D33, and Amba D22, the latter spoken in the northern foothills of the Ruwenzori mountains and adjacent areas of Uganda. Well to the south of the Congo River at the southern limit of the tropical forest, labial-velar stops occur in a few roots in Sakata C34. This list is very likely incomplete, as information for most languages in the area is sparse.[9] The Bantu languages in this broad zone are (or presumably have been in the not distant past) in contact with other Sudanic languages having labial-velar stops: southern Bantoid languages in the west, Adamawa-Ubangi languages in the center, and Central Sudanic languages in the east.

In the Rift zone of eastern Africa, labial-velar stops occur in several Bantu languages spoken on the southern Kenyan coast, including Giryama E72a, where they have arisen through internal change (e.g. Giryama E72a *kua > [kpa], *mua > [ŋma]).[10]

It is usually thought since Greenberg (1983) that labial-velar stops originated in Niger-Congo languages and diffused from there to neighboring Central Sudanic languages, constituting a block from whence they spread to Chadic languages in the north, Nilotic languages in the east and Bantu languages in the south. Labial-velar stops have also arisen through internal change from labia-lized stops (usually velar, but sometimes labial), but such evolution has happened predominantly in areas where labial-velars are already present in neighboring languages, constituting a regional norm (the Kenyan Bantu languages mentioned above are exceptional in this respect).

Although labial-velar stops are extremely rare on other continents, the African diaspora has carried them to northeastern South America where they occur in some West-African-based creole languages such as Nengee, spoken in French Guiana, and Ndyuka and Saramaccan, spoken in Surinam. They have arisen independently in a number of Papuan languages including Kâte, Amele, and Yeletnye, as well as at least two Eastern Malayo-Polynesian languages, Iai (see note 5) and Owa, spoken in the Solomon Islands. In sum, though not entirely unique to Africa, they are one of the most characteristically African, and specifically Sudanic, speech-sound types.

Table 3.3 *African languages in our sample with nasal vowels*

African languages with nasal vowels:	26.7%
Sudanic:	34.0%
elsewhere in Africa:	12.0%
Non-African languages with nasal vowels:	21.2%

3.2.5   Nasal vowels and nasal consonants

Another characteristically Sudanic feature is the presence of a series of phonemic nasal vowels. We first consider the distribution of nasal vowels in Africa, and then take up the question of languages lacking (contrastive) nasal consonants.

While nasal vowels are not uncommon in the world's languages, they are especially common in the Sudanic belt. Statistics are given in table 3.3.

In our sample, nasal vowels are 60 percent more frequent in the Sudanic belt than they are outside Africa, and about three times more frequent in the Sudanic belt than they are elsewhere in Africa. The only other area in which they are frequent is among Khoisan languages of southern Africa. This heavy skewing is reflected in map 3.3.

Outside the two principal areas just mentioned, distinctive nasal vowels are found in a small number of Bantu languages in the west Central zone, including Bembe H11 and Umbundu R11, shown on the map, some varieties of Teke B70, and Yeyi R41 in the South. Here, however, contextual vowel nasalization is much more widespread than phonemic nasalization. In spite of their scarcity, Dimmendaal (2001a) cites comparative evidence suggesting that contrastive nasal vowels may have been present in Proto-Bantu and have undergone historical loss in all languages but Umbundu.

To this geographic restriction corresponds a genetic distinction. Contrastive nasal vowels are common in Niger-Congo and Khoisan, but rare in Nilo-Saharan and Afroasiatic languages. Within Niger-Congo they are especially common in Mande, Kwa, Gur, and Adamawa-Ubangi languages, as well as much of non-Bantoid Benue-Congo in Nigeria. In Nilo-Saharan, nasal vowels are found in Songay, which straddles the border between the Sudanic and Northern zones, and in the Mbay variety of Sara (Central Sudanic), which borders on Adamawa-Ubangi. We have found no examples among Chadic languages. This genetic and geographical distribution suggests that nasal vowels have had at least two separate origins in Africa, one in a proto-core group of Niger-Congo languages (as proposed by Stewart 1995) and one in the Khoisan languages of southern Africa, including at least Proto-Khoe (Central Khoisan) as reconstructed by Vossen (1997a).

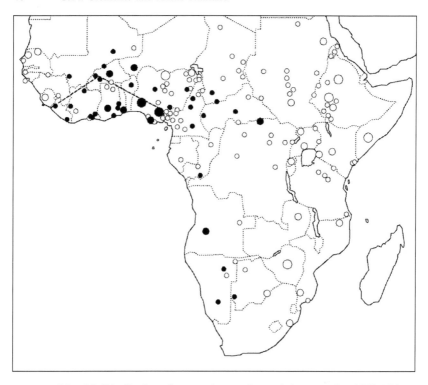

Map 3.3 Distribution of contrastive nasal vowels in a sample of 150 African languages. The area enclosed in dashes contains languages reported to lack distinctive nasal consonants

Outside Africa, too, nasal vowels are not distributed randomly but have strong areal limitations. Hajek (2005) shows that outside Africa they are primarily concentrated in equatorial South America, south-central Asia, and parts of North America. They thus tend to form clusters in certain areas and to be absent in others.

Looking more closely at the Sudanic belt, we find the typologically unusual phenomenon of languages lacking contrastive nasal consonants. Such languages have been widely reported in a continuous zone including Liberia in the west, Burkina Faso in the north and eastern Nigeria in the east. This area, enclosed in dashed lines in map 3.3, lies squarely within the nasal vowel zone. These languages, so far as they are known to us at present, are listed in table 3.4.[11]

Such languages typically have an oral vs. nasal contrast in vowels, and two sets of consonants. Members of set 1 are usually all obstruents and are realized as oral regardless of whether the following vowel is oral or nasal. Members of set 2 are usually non-obstruents, and are realized as oral sounds before oral

Table 3.4 *Languages reported to lack distinctive nasal consonants*

Liberia:	Kpelle (Mande); Grebo, Klao (Kru)
Burkina Faso:	Bwamu (Gur)
Côte d'Ivoire:	Dan, Guro-Yaoure, Wan-Mwan, Gban/Gagu, Tura (Mande); Senadi/Senufo (Gur); Nyabwa, Wè (Kru); Ebrié, Avikam, Abure (Kwa)
Ghana:	Abron, Akan, Ewe (Kwa)
Togo, Benin:	Gen, Fon (Kwa)
Nigeria:	Mbaise Igbo, Ikwere (Igboid)
CAR:	Yakoma (Ubangi)

Table 3.5 *Ikwere consonants*

Set 1: obstruents	p b t d c j k g k^w g^w f v s z
Set 2a: oral non-obstruents	ɓ 'ɓ l r y ɣ w h h^w
Set 2b: nasal non-obstruents	m 'm n r̃ ỹ ɣ̃ w̃ h̃ h̃^{w}

Note: ɓ and 'ɓ are voiced and preglottalized non-obstruent stops, respectively; see Clements & Osu (2002) for a phonetic study.

vowels and as nasal or nasalized sounds before nasal vowels. For example, the dental sonorant may be realized as [l] before oral vowels and as [n] before nasal vowels. In most cases, the corresponding oral/nasal pairs never contrast in any context, so that nasality is entirely non-distinctive in consonants.

The analytic line between languages which lack and do not lack contrastive nasal consonants is not sharp. A particularly clear case of a language that lacks them is Ikwere, an Igboid (Benue-Congo) language of Nigeria as described by Clements and Osu (2005). That nasality is distinctive in vowels is shown by pairs like *ódó* 'mortar' vs. *òdọ̀* 'yellow dye' (vowel nasality is indicated by subscript tildes). The full consonant system is shown in table 3.5. The key observations are that each oral consonant in set 2a has a nasal counterpart in set 2b and vice versa, and that the paired consonants are in complementary distribution before vowels, those of set 2a appearing only before oral vowels and those of set 2b only before nasal vowels. Examples are given in (1).

(1) before oral vowels (set 2a)   before nasal vowels (set 2b)
    áɓá   'paint'   ámà   'matchet'
    á'ɓá   'companionship'   à'mà   'path, road'
    ɔ-lú   'to marry'   ɔ-nú   'to hear'
    érú   'mushroom'   ẹ́rụ́   'work'
    à-yá   'to return'   áỹậ   'eye'

Since the paired consonants are in complementary distribution elsewhere as well, they can be derived from a single series of phonemes unspecified for nasality, e.g. [ḅ] and [m] from a phoneme /B/, [l] and [n] from a phoneme /L/, etc. A constraint *[+nasal,+obstruent] prohibits the assignment of nasality to obstruents, and the nasalized consonants are derived by an exceptionless rule spreading nasality from a nasal vowel to any segment that does not bear [+obstruent]. As in many other languages of this type, this rule is independently supported in Ikwere by regular patterns of alternation. For example, it accounts for alternations in the verbal suffix *rʊ̀* as illustrated in the words ɔ̀ *byà-rʊ̀* 's/he came ...' vs. ɔ̀ *wɔ̀-r̃ʊ̀* 's/he drank ...'

Such analyses explain an otherwise puzzling fact about the distribution of nasal consonants in languages of this type: prevocalic nasal consonants typically fail to appear before vowels that do not occur with distinctive nasalization. For example, if the oral vowels /e/ and /o/ have no distinctive nasal counterparts, nasal consonants typically do not appear before [e] and [o], nasalized or not. (Lexical exceptions may arise from reduplications, loanwords, frozen compounds, and the like.) Such gaps provide an independent diagnostic of the absence of distinctive nasality in consonants.

Not all systems are as straightforward as that of Ikwere, however. For example, most varieties of Gbe (the closely knit group of Kwa languages including Ewe, Gen, and Fon) are similar to Ikwere in relevant respects except that set 2a contains two obstruents, *b* and *ɖ*, matched with the set 2b sonorants *m* and *n*. Though the complementary distribution between sets 2a and 2b is still complete, the class of nasalizing sounds is no longer phonologically natural, as it contains both obstruents and sonorants. Stewart (1995) offers comparative evidence showing that the present-day obstruents *b* and *ɖ* are reflexes of Proto-Gbe-Potou-Tano (= tentative Proto-Kwa) implosive stops *ɓ* and *ɗ* which shifted to ordinary explosives in all Gbe languages. This shift explains the modern pattern. Nasal spreading applied in Pre-Gbe just as it does in Ikwere, affecting the full set of non-obstruents. Once the implosives shifted to explosives, however, the uniformity of the class of nasalizing segments was destroyed, leading to the "unnatural" rule of the present-day Gbe lects.

Other systems differ from those of Ikwere and Gbe in that there is a surface contrast between one member of the class of nasals, typically *m*, and its oral counterpart, such as *b* or *ɓ*. In the Nigerian language Gokana (Benue-Congo, Cross River), as discussed by Hyman (1982), we find a distribution of consonants into sets 1 and 2 as above. As in Gbe, set 2a contains obstruents as a result of evolutions from earlier sonorants (*w > v, *y > z). In Gokana, however, unlike Gbe, *b* appears before both oral and nasal vowels and contrasts with *m*, as is shown by minimal contrasts like *bá* 'arm, hand' vs. *bá̃* 'pot' vs. *má̃* 'breast.' In other relevant respects, the system resembles that of Gbe and Ikwere. In a later analysis of these facts, Hyman (1985) proposes to treat all set 1 consonants, including the *b* that fails to nasalize, as underlyingly specified for the feature [−nasal], which serves to protect them from nasalization. However, the feature [+obstruent] would equally well serve this purpose if we assume the general constraint *[+nasal,+obstruent] as in Ikwere. Surface *b* then comes from two underlying stops, one belonging to set 1 and the other to set 2. Set 1 /b/ is specified as [+obstruent], consistent with its realization, while the paired set 2a/2b stops [b]/[m] constitute a single phoneme /B/ unspecified for both obstruence and nasality. If /B/ occurs in a nasal context, it receives the features [+nasal] and [−obstruent], while if it occurs in an oral context it receives the features [−nasal] and [+obstruent] by default, merging with /b/. What crucially distinguishes Gokana from Gbe, then, is the presence of an underlying /b/ vs. /B/ contrast. (It is tempting to interpret the non-obstruent /B/ of Gokana as the reflex of an earlier non-obstruent stop such as ɓ, in parallel to Gbe, but we have no information on the historical source of this sound.)

The analysis of nasality is often intricate, and there are legitimate grounds for disagreement among linguists. Disagreement often has as much to do with one's theoretical framework as with the nature of the facts. It seems, nevertheless, that many West African nasal systems can be ranged along a continuum in regard to the plausibility of a "no-nasal" analysis, with fairly transparent systems like Ikwere occurring at one end, systems like Gbe in the middle, and more complex systems like those of Gokana, containing a basic /b/ vs. /B/ contrast but still lacking an underlying nasal phoneme /m/, at the other end. The position of a language on the continuum corresponds, in part, to the degree to which it has become "denaturalized" by subsequent historical evolution.

It is not clear to us whether nasal systems of this type have been inherited from a common source, whether they result from diffusion, or whether they have evolved independently in different languages. Within Africa, we know of no similar systems in other zones. Outside Africa, however, some South American languages have typologically similar systems, occasionally with the additional twist that voiceless obstruents are skipped in the spread of nasality, yielding discontinuous nasal spans such as . . . *ãtã* . . . (see Peng 2000 for examples and discussion). Systems of this type are rare in Africa, if they occur at all. Elsewhere in the world, languages without underlying nasal consonants are reported in North America (e.g. Hidatsa, Puget Sound Salish, and Quileute) and in certain languages with very small consonant inventories, such as Rotokas, a language of Papua New Guinea.

3.2.6   *Vowel systems and vowel harmony*

Africa has three types of vowel harmony systems which are apparently unknown elsewhere in the world, found in three non-overlapping areas. We discuss them in turn.

3.2.6.1   ATR vowel harmony   One of the best-known and most-discussed features of African phonology is the widespread use of the feature of tongue-root advancing (ATR = advanced tongue root) in creating systems of word-level vowel harmony. Such vowel harmony systems are found widely through the Sudanic belt and in adjacent areas to the east, ranging from the Atlantic language Diola-Fogny in the west to the Cushitic languages Somali, Boni, and Rendille in the east. (See map 5.3 in chapter 5, this volume.)

In its commonest variety, as first described for Akan by Stewart (1967), ATR harmony is found in languages with two series of high vowels and two series of mid vowels. The higher vowels in each series, usually including /i u e o/, are characterized by the feature [+ATR] and the lower vowels, usually including /ɪ ʊ ɛ ɔ/, by the feature [−ATR]. Within a word, all non-low vowels, including those of harmonizing prefixes and suffixes, agree in the feature [+ATR] or [−ATR]. In many such systems, the low vowel has no [+ATR] counterpart and remains neutral, combining with vowels of both series. In some languages, however, such as Kalenjin (Southern Nilotic), the low vowel has a [+ATR] counterpart, often /ɜ/ but in Kalenjin /ɑ/, as is illustrated by the following examples (Hall et al. 1974).[12]

(2) Cross-height ATR vowel harmony in Kalenjin
    [−ATR] roots *par, kɛr*   [+ATR] root *keːr*
a. kɪ-a-par-ɪn 'I killed you'   ki-ɑ-keːr-in 'I saw you'
b. ki-ɑ-ker-e 'I was shutting it'

In (2a), affix vowels agree with the [ATR] value of the root vowels, and are thus [−ATR] with the [−ATR] root *par* 'kill'; and [+ATR] with the [+ATR] root *keːr* 'see.' In (2b), the non-harmonizing suffix vowel /e/, which is invariantly [+ATR], requires all vowels, including the underlying [−ATR] vowel /ɛ/ of the root *kɛr* 'shut,' to take [+ATR] values. Such systems have been called "cross-height vowel harmony" since they operate *across* vowel heights; thus a [+ATR] vowel in mid vowels – such as the suffix vowel /e/ in the above examples – requires [+ATR] in high vowels and vice versa. In systems of this type, the value [+ATR] is usually dominant (i.e. phonologically active), though in some languages [−ATR] is active as well.

A reduced form of ATR harmony is found in languages with two series of high vowels but only one series of mid vowels. A typical vowel phoneme inventory in such languages would be /i u ɪ ʊ ɛ ɔ a/. In these languages too, [+ATR] is usually the dominant value, and as in Kalenjin, [−ATR] mid and high vowels shift to [+ATR] in the context of [+ATR] high vowels. Examples from Nande (Bantu DJ42) are shown in (3), from Mutaka (1995); we have replaced his vowel symbols to agree with those used elsewhere in this chapter.

Table 3.6 *Frequency of vowel systems in 150 African languages, classified by number of contrastive vowel heights*

Vowel heights	Sudanic (100)	North (7)	East (12)	Center (13)	Rift (9)	South (9)
2H–2M	22	1	2	0	3	1
2H–1M	6	0	0	2	0	0
1H–2M	46	0	1	2	2	0
1H–1M	25	5	9	9	4	8
1H–0M	1	1	0	0	0	0

(3) Reduced ATR harmony in Nande

    [−ATR] roots *yɪr, hʊm*   [+ATR] roots *yir, hum*

a. ɛrɪ-yɪr-a 'to have'   eri-yir-a 'to dislike'

b. ɛrí-hʊm-a 'to roar'   erí-hum-a 'to move'

c. erí-hum-is-i-a 'to make someone roar'

In (3a,b), prefixes have [−ATR] values before [−ATR] roots (left column) and [+ATR] values before [+ATR] roots (right column). In (3c), the non-harmonizing [+ATR] suffixes -*is* and -*i* require [+ATR] prefix and root vowels. This system differs from that of Kalenjin in that the [+ATR] mid vowels [e o] created by harmony are allophonic, not phonemic.

It is usually the case, outside Bantu, that if an African language has two sets of high vowels it has ATR harmony as well. We can therefore get a fairly good idea of the distribution of ATR vowel harmony in non-Bantu languages by examining the distribution of vowel systems with two series of high vowels.[13]

Table 3.6 shows the distribution of five types of vowel systems, classified by number of contrastive vowel heights, across the six zones. "2H" designates a language with two series of high vowels, "2M" one with two series of mid vowels, and so forth.

It will be immediately seen that 2H systems, as shown in the first two rows – that is, those which like Kalenjin typically have ATR harmony – are very largely concentrated in the Sudanic belt. Here they occur in 28 percent of the languages in our survey. This is typologically unusual, as outside Africa 2H systems occur in only 2 percent of our sample languages. 2H systems are very likely to have two series of mid vowels as well, as shown in the first row. This is even more unusual, as 2H–2M systems are 73 times more frequent in our Sudanic languages (22 languages, 22 percent) than they are in our non-African languages (1 language, 0.3 percent). 2M systems are also strongly favored even in languages with just one high vowel series, where they outnumber 1M systems by a ratio of 46 to 25 (rows three and four). Thus, Sudanic languages do not follow the common crosslinguistic preference for the five-vowel system /i u e o a/, preferring instead to double the number of mid vowels, high vowels, or both by the use of the feature [ATR].

In geographic terms, 2H systems (usually with ATR harmony) are found commonly across the Sudanic belt, but they are not ubiquitous. The strongest concentrations are in southeastern Mande, Kru, Kwa, Gur, Ijoid, many Benue-Congo languages (Edoid, Igboid, Cross River (Central Delta)), and then again, within Nilo-Saharan, in Central Sudanic (especially the Moru-Madi, Mangbetu and Lendu languages in southern Sudan, northeastern DRC, and northwestern Uganda) and the Nilotic languages. In Western Nilotic languages such as Shilluk, Nuer, and Dinka, ATR differences are often reinforced, supplemented or replaced by voice quality differences such as "breathy" vs. "creaky."

Within this broad zone there are areas where such systems are *less* common:

- most Atlantic languages
- eastern Kwa (notably the Gbe languages)
- Defoid (Yoruba, Itsekiri)
- most Idomoid (except Igede), Platoid, Jukunoid, northern Bantoid
- southern Grassfields Bantu and northwestern Bantu languages (zones A–D)
- Adamawa-Ubangi, except the Zande group (Azande has a system resembling that of Nande as described above except that vowel raising is non-neutralizing in high vowels as well as mid, Tucker & Hackett 1959).

2H systems become less frequent toward the north (northern Mande, Fulfulde, Songay, Dogon, Chadic), the northeast (where the rare 2H systems include the Kordofanian languages Jomang and Tima and several East Sudanic languages including Tama, Tabi, Nyimang, and Temein), and the far east, where rare 2H systems include Hamer (Omotic) and strikingly, Somali (Cushitic) with thoroughgoing ATR harmony. Bantu 2H systems will be discussed below.

This scattered pattern has given rise to a still-unresolved debate whether 2H vowel systems with ATR vowel harmony are derived from a 2H-2M proto-system /i u ɪ ʊ e o ɛ ɔ ɜ a/ in Niger-Congo, with losses in separate areas due to the merger of one or more of the marked vowels /ɪ ʊ ɜ/ with their less-marked neighbors (Williamson 1983–4), or from a simpler 2H–1M or 1H–2M system with a fourth height series arising by diffusion or internal change. In some cases, good arguments for the latter view can be made. Thus, Przezdziecki (2005) presents persuasive evidence that an innovative series of [−ATR] high vowels evolved in Akure Yoruba out of a more standard 1H–2M variety of Yoruba lacking ATR harmony as a result of phonetically motivated internal change. Dimmendaal (2001a) reviews a number of cases in which ATR harmony appears to have evolved by diffusion. An example is the Chadic language Tangale, whose ATR harmony system is anomalous within Chadic languages but can be plausibly explained by long-term contact with neighboring Benue-Congo languages.

Outside Africa, 2H vowel inventories (and vowel harmony systems based upon them) are rare, except when accompanied by length differences as in English. Vowel harmony systems resembling African ATR systems have been described in Nez Perce (Penutian, North America), Khalkha Mongolian (Altaic), and several languages of northeast Asia including Chukot/Chukchi (Chukotko-Kamchatkan) and the Manchu-Tungus languages (Altaic). However, these systems usually have reverse polarity in which tongue-root retraction acts as the dominant value, and might be better viewed as RTR (retracted tongue root) systems.

3.2.6.2   Bantu vowel harmony   ATR harmony is absent in the great majority of Bantu languages, where instead we find a quite different type of vowel harmony, which again appears to be unique to Africa. This type has three common variants according to the vowel system in question, as shown in (4) below.

(4) *Vowel system*   *Vowel harmony*
a. i u ɪ ʊ ɛ ɔ a   ɪ   is replaced by ɛ   after stem vowels ɛ   ɔ
                         ʊ   is replaced by ɔ   after stem vowel   ɔ
b. i u e o ɛ ɔ a   e   is replaced by ɛ   after stem vowels ɛ   ɔ
                         o   is replaced by ɔ   after some vowels ɛ   ɔ
c. i u ɛ ɔ a   i   is replaced by ɛ   after stem vowels ɛ   ɔ
                         u   is replaced by ɔ   after stem vowel   ɔ

Harmony applies within the stem (root plus suffixes), usually triggering suffix alternations. Kikuyu E51 illustrates a type B system (Armstrong 1967); here, harmony controls both root vowel sequences and the -ɛr ~ er alternants of the applicative suffix:

(5) *after root vowels /ɛ ɔ/*   *after root vowels /i u e o a/*
    ko-mɛɲɛr-ɛr-a 'to take care of'   ɣokiɲ-er-a 'to catch up with'
    kw-ɛrɔ́r-ɛr-a 'to look on at'   ko-rut-er-a 'to work for'
                                                 ɣw-ekér-er-a 'to pour out for'
                                                 ko-hetók-er-a 'to pass by'
                                                 ko-ɣamb-er-a 'to bark at'

Whether the operative feature in such systems is [ATR] or a feature of relative vowel height remains a matter of debate (see Maddieson 2003a for phonetic evidence that both types of systems may be present among Bantu languages). Type C systems are commonly found across the center of the Bantu-speaking area, type B in the northwest, and type A in the east, though there is a good deal of intermingling. Of course, not all Bantu languages have

vowel harmony. See Hyman (1999) for a comprehensive overview of Bantu
vowel harmony systems and maps showing their distribution.

A few northern Bantu languages have been described as having some features of cross-height ATR harmony as found in non-Bantu languages. Where
evidence is available, it appears that these systems have evolved as a result of
internal innovation and/or diffusion from neighboring languages, rather than
from inheritance from a common ancestor. They are found in two clusters:

1. One is located in a region in northeastern DRC including several mostly
   adjacent languages of zone D30. In Bila D311, as described by Kutsch
   Lojenga (2003), ATR harmony applies in verbs but not in nouns, where
   instead we find a more conventional B-type harmony. Grégoire (2003)
   suggests that these systems might have originated from long-term contact
   with neighboring Central Sudanic languages.
2. The other is located in a region in southwest Cameroon including mostly
   adjacent languages of zones A40–60 such as Nen A44, Numaand A46,
   Kaalong/Mbong A52d, and Gunu Yambasa A62a. Some dialects of Nen
   have two phonetically identical vowels /o/, one of which patterns as a
   [+ATR] vowel and the other as a [−ATR] vowel; in other dialects, the
   corresponding vowels are phonetically distinct (Mous 2003b). Stewart
   (2000–1) argues that the [+ATR] mid vowels are an innovation, resulting
   from earlier [−ATR] mid vowels through assimilation to the [+ATR]
   high vowels /i u/.

In the case of Nen, it might be argued that [+ATR] was already present in
the system as a distinctive feature, if we assume, following Stewart, that all
varieties of Nen had two series of high vowels, [+ATR] and [−ATR], at the
point when mid vowel raising took place. It should be noted, however, that two
series of high vowels is not a necessary precondition for mid vowel raising. In
Zulu S42, whose phonemic vowels are /i u ɛ ɔ a/, the mid vowels /ɛ ɔ/ shift to
[e o] before the redundantly [+ATR] high vowels /i u/. Raising of this type is
found elsewhere in Africa, as in the five-vowel system of Kaado Songay
(Nicolaï & Zima 1997).

3.2.6.3   Raising harmony in the Sotho-Tswana languages   A yet different
type of vowel harmony, again apparently unique among the world's languages,
is found in the Sotho-Tswana group of Bantu languages (S30) in the South
zone. Atypically among Bantu languages, Southern and Northern Sotho and
Tswana have nine distinctive vowels, /i u ɪ ʊ e o ɛ ɔ a/, of which the upper mid
vowels /e o/ are recent innovations. These languages have regressive vowel
harmony according to which /ɛ/ and /ɔ/ are raised to /e/ and /o/ if the next
syllable contains a higher vowel. This raising is not conditioned by the feature

[+ATR], as the [−ATR] vowels /ɪ/ and /ʊ/ are included among the triggers. In addition, /ɪ ʊ/ have raised allophones before a high vowel /i u/, creating an auditorily distinct third high vowel series. For further discussion and examples see Krüger and Snyman (1986), Khabanyane (1991), Gowlett (2003), and references therein.

This chapter cannot review the great variety of ways in which ATR vowel harmony can be implemented in Africa nor the several further types of vowel harmony to be found in African languages. Studies giving some idea of the diversity of African vowel harmony systems include Clements (1991), Archangeli and Pulleyblank (1994), Kabore and Tchagbalé (1998), and Williamson (2004).

3.2.7   Implosives and other non-obstruent stops

Another characteristic African sound is the implosive. As we saw in table 3.1, implosive stops, especially ɓ and ɗ, are frequent in languages of the Sudanic belt, where they are about twelve times commoner than elsewhere in the world. Implosives occur even more frequently, it appears, in Cushitic and Omotic languages of the East zone, and are also found in Bantu languages of the South. We give special attention to these sounds due to their broad distribution and their typological and genetic importance.

According to the typical textbook definition, implosives are produced with an ingressive glottalic airstream. In this view, the lowering of the closed glottis during the stop closure rarifies the air behind the closure, causing a rapid inflow of air into the mouth when the closure is released. Following this definition, field linguists have tended to use the terms "implosive" and "glottalized stop" interchangeably, and many phonologists use a feature of glottal construction to distinguish implosives from other sounds.

However, more recent research, much of it by Peter Ladefoged (see Ladefoged 1968; Ladefoged et al. 1976; Ladefoged & Maddieson 1996), has shown this definition to be incomplete, if not misleading. It is now known that

- "implosives" may be non-glottalized, that is, produced with no glottal closure or significant laryngealization (e.g. Lindau 1984);
- "implosives" may involve no negative oral air pressure or ingressive airstream (e.g. Lex 2001);
- larynx lowering is not unique to "implosives" but often accompanies the ordinary voiced stops of languages such as English and French (e.g. Ewan & Krones 1974);
- ingressive airflow can be produced with no larynx lowering (Clements & Osu 2002);

- normally (modally) voiced "implosives" do not correlate with glottalized sounds in phoneme inventories, while ejectives and laryngealized sounds do (Clements 2003).

These observations suggest that implosives cannot be neatly distinguished from non-implosive sounds in terms of an alleged glottalic airstream mechanism.

In view of these difficulties, Clements and Osu (2002) have proposed to define implosives and related sounds as *non-obstruent stops*. Non-obstruents are, in phonetic theory, sounds that are produced with no buildup of air pressure behind the constriction in the oral cavity (Stevens 1983). As there is no buildup of air pressure, there is no explosion at release. The full class of non-obstruent stops therefore includes not only prototypical implosives, produced with negative air pressure behind the primary closure, but also unimploded sounds, involving neither negative nor positive air pressure and lacking an explosive burst. This more general definition of implosives, which does not require glottal closure or larynx lowering, is consistent with the various observations above, and accommodates less typical types of non-explosive sounds along with the "classical" implosives of the textbooks.

A direct advantage of this definition is that it explains why implosives, unlike explosive stops, are typically voiced; this is because voicing is the normal realization of non-obstruent sounds in general (Creissels 1994). It also explains why implosives, unlike other voiced stops, do not trigger voicing assimilation (for Oromo, see Lloret 1995); this is because such assimilation typically takes place between obstruents only. Another observation is that implosives frequently pattern with sonorants; for example, implosive ɓ often alternates with *m* in nasalization contexts, as we have seen in Ikwere (section 3.2.5), if we allow that the non-explosive stop (ḅ) of this language is a type of implosive under the more general definition proposed above. Similarly, implosive ɗ often alternates with *l* or *r* (see e.g. Kaye 1981). Facts such as these have sometimes led linguists to view implosives as liquids or as sonorant stops. However, non-explosive stops lack several properties associated with true sonorants, such as the ability to form syllable nuclei. For this reason Clements and Osu conclude, with Stewart (1989), that implosives are both non-obstruent and non-sonorant sounds.

If implosives are not inherently glottalized, we should expect to find contrasts between plain and glottalized implosives, just as we do between plain and glottalized explosives. This is just what we do find. Contrasts between two types of implosives, variously described in the literature as "plain vs. voiceless" or "plain vs. preglottalized," have been examined phonetically in Owere Igbo by Ladefoged et al. (1976), in the closely related Ikwere language by Clements and Osu (2002), in Ngiti by Kutsch Lojenga (1994), and in the closely related Lendu language by Demolin (1995).[14] These studies have shown that the voiceless member of the contrast is usually produced with full glottalization (that is, a complete glottal stop) somewhere during the occlusion, usually toward the beginning. While there is some variation in the way such sounds are realized, from a phonological point of view it appears sufficient to recognize two categories of non-explosive stops, plain (modally voiced) and laryngealized/glottalized (produced with glottal creak or glottal closure). In languages lacking a contrast between these two types, implosives may have little if any laryngealization as in most Bantu languages, strong glottalization as in Hausa (Lindau 1984; Lindsey et al. 1992), or more rarely, complete glottal closure as in Bwamu (Manessy 1960).

The term "non-obstruent stop" may therefore replace the older term "lenis stop." The latter term has been used in the Africanist literature to refer to various unrelated sounds: (i) non-explosive stops which are not necessarily implosive (e.g. Stewart 1989); (ii) extra-short sounds which contrast with sounds of normal length (e.g. Elugbe 1980); and (iii) sounds of normal length which contrast with extra-long sounds (see Faraclas 1989 and references therein). These three senses are quite different, but have often been used interchangeably, leading to some confusion. For example, the extra-long "fortis" consonants of some Plateau and Cross River languages of Nigeria, which contrast with "lenis" sounds in sense (iii), have arisen from a relatively recent fusion of consonant clusters (e.g. Hoffman 1963) and have nothing to do with "lenis" stops in senses (i) and (ii).

Let us now consider the geographic distribution of implosives in this larger sense. The occurrence of voiced and laryngealized implosives in our sample is shown in map 3.4.

This map shows that implosives occur primarily in a broad band across the center of Africa, taking in most of the Sudanic belt, and extending eastward into the East and Rift zones as well. Implosives are not common in the Grassfields Bantu languages of southwestern Cameroon, but reappear in northern Bantu languages where their geographical distribution parallels that of labial-velars (Grégoire 2003). Implosives occur again in southern Africa (Guthrie's Zone S), appearing in the Shona group S10, the Nguni group S40, and Copi S61.

There is an important isogloss dividing the broad west-to-east implosive area into two smaller regions. According to Greenberg (1970), if a language has only one implosive, it is almost always the labial ɓ. This is true of all but one of our Sudanic languages (Berta, see just below) and all of our Bantu languages. However, it is not true in Ethiopia, Somalia, and Kenya, where a lone implosive is always ɗ; examples include the Omotic languages Kullo and Wolaytta, the Cushitic languages Oromo, Somali, Sidamo, and Rendille, and Berta, a Nilo-Saharan language spoken in the Sudan–Ethiopian border area. The presence of "only-ɗ" languages appears to be a unique feature of eastern Africa.

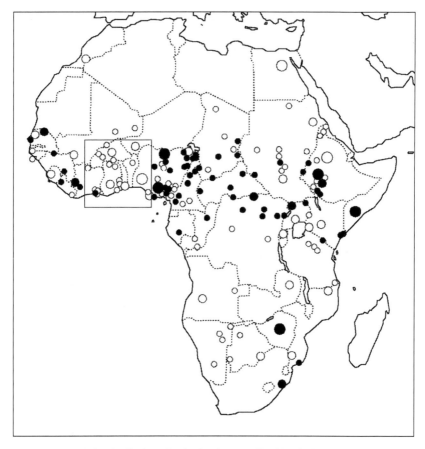

Map 3.4 Distribution of voiced or laryngealized implosives in a sample of 150 African languages. Black circles show languages with implosives. The square at left highlights an area in which implosives are mostly absent. (Small circles = languages with less than 1m speakers; medium-sized circles = languages with 1–10 m speakers; large circles = languages with over 10 m speakers)

The box in map 3.4 highlights a large area in which implosives are statistically rare. This area extends from the Bandama River in central Côte d'Ivoire to the Niger River in central Nigeria, continuing inland to the Sahara. Within this area, except for Fulfulde, implosives are lacking in most languages including Songay, Dogon, Senoufo, Mòoré, Kabiyé, Baatonum, Akan, Guang, Gbe, Yoruba, most Edoid languages, and Izon. In contrast, implosives are well represented on both of its flanks; indeed, the sole Edoid and Ijoid languages with implosives (Delta Edoid, Kalabari, Defaka, etc.) are those that are spoken on the east bank of the Niger. The major language families represented in this zone of exclusion are Songay, Gur, and Kwa. (i) According to data in Nicolaï and Zima (1997), implosives are absent in representative varieties of Songay. (ii) According to Manessy (1979), implosives are absent in the core section of Gur (Central Gur), though implosive, glottalized or "lenis" /b d/ occur in some western Gur languages (Naden 1989), including Bwamu as mentioned above. (iii) According to Stewart (1993), implosives are absent in all Kwa languages except Ega and Avikam, isolates lying outside this zone to the west, and the Potou Lagoon languages Ebrié and Mbatto, spoken just 100 km east of the Bandama River. Here, then, we are dealing with "a wave of proscription over a wide area," to use Stewart's apt phrase.

Such phenomena can sometimes be explained by sound shifts. In this case there is comparative evidence that earlier implosives shifted to non-implosive sounds, e.g. $ɓ > b/v, ɗ > d/ɖ/l$ in Central Gur (Manessy 1979) and the two largest Kwa units, Tano (including Anyi-Baule, Akan, and the Guang group) and Gbe (including Ewe, Gen, and Fon) (Stewart 1995). These appear to be parallel developments, perhaps influenced by contact.

As one might expect from their broad distribution, implosives are found in several different genetic units. Among Niger-Congo languages of the Sudanic belt, the western implosive area includes Atlantic, Kru, and southeastern Mande languages and the eastern area includes eastern Ijoid (Kalabari, Defaka), southern Edoid (Isoko, Delta Edoid), southern Igboid (Igbo, Ikwere), Cross River (Central Delta, a few Upper Cross languages), Adamawa-Ubangi, and northern Bantu languages. In Nilo-Saharan, implosives are prevalent in Central Sudanic and occur in several East Sudanic groups (Surmic, Tama, Daju) as well as Gumuz, Koman, and Kado. Within Afroasiatic, all Chadic languages have $ɓ$ and $ɗ$, according to Schuh (2003); these sounds are usually glottalized to some extent, and for this reason they are usually classified as glottalized or laryngealized stops in descriptions of Chadic languages. Glottalized implosives $ɗ$ and $ɠ$ also occur in varieties of Arabic spoken in southwestern Chad, where they have replaced emphatics (Hagège 1973).

In the East and Rift zones, implosives are again distributed through several genetic units. In Afroasiatic, they occur distinctively in Omotic languages (e.g. Hamer and Kullo) and in Cushitic languages as far south as Dahalo on the central Kenyan coast. In Eastern Sudanic (Nilo-Saharan), they occur in the Kuliak languages of Uganda and in several Nilotic languages (e.g. Bari, Alur, Päkoot, and Maasai). In eastern Bantu languages, they occur in the Swahili group G40 and continue southward into southern Kenya and Tanzania, occurring in at least E70 (e.g. Pokomo E71 and Giryama E72a), some members of G30 (e.g. Sagala G39), and G50 (Nurse & Hinnebusch 1993: 570–6).

This wide distribution does not suggest a pattern of diffusion from a single source, at least in recent times. Indeed implosives have been reconstructed for Chadic (Newman 1977), for core sections of Niger-Congo (Stewart 2002) and

Nilo-Saharan (Bender 1997), and for a number of smaller units such as Central Gur (Manessy 1979), possibly Mande (Grégoire 1988), Edoid (Elugbe 1989b: 297), and Proto-Sabaki, comprising Bantu E71–3 and G40 (Nurse & Hinnebusch 1993: 61). In Bantu languages, implosives are usually reflexes of Proto-Bantu *b and *d, sometimes thought to have been implosives themselves. Of course, the fact that so many proto-units have implosives raises the question of whether diffusion might have been at work in the distant past.

Not all implosives are inherited directly from proto-languages. Bilabial implosives, for example, often evolve from earlier labial-velars. In Isoko (Edoid) and southern Igboid languages (Owere Igbo and Ikwere), voiced and voiceless labial-velars are in various stages of transition to velarized bilabial implosives; this pattern of evolution accounts for at least some of the "only-ɓ" languages in the Sudanic belt. In Surmic languages of western Ethiopia (East Sudanic), implosives ɓ, ɗ, ɠ have developed out of voiced geminate consonants (Yigezu 2001).

Outside Africa, as noted above, implosives are unusual sounds, occurring notably in Mon-Khmer languages (e.g. Vietnamese and Khmer/Cambodian), Tibeto-Burman (Karen languages), and a small number of languages of North and South America.

Thus implosives are a characteristic feature of broad areas of Africa. They are of typological interest not only in themselves, but in the fact that they occur commonly alongside voiced and voiceless stops, creating a nearly unique exception to the usual rule that triple stop systems have only one voiced series (Hopper 1973).

3.2.8   Ejectives, aspirated stops, and clicks

Here we review stop consonant types that are especially characteristic of the South zone: ejectives, aspirated stops, and clicks. These consonants are much more frequent in the South zone than they are outside Africa. In our sample, ejectives are over four times more common in the South than outside Africa, and aspirated stops are over twice as common (table 3.7). Clicks are immensurably more common as they occur in all the South zone languages of the sample (Bantu and Khoisan alike) and none of the non-African languages.

We consider the distribution of these sounds in turn.

Ejective stops are a major feature of eastern Africa, covering nearly half the continent. In the South, ejectives are ubiquitous in Khoisan languages and very common in Bantu languages (a partial list will be given in table 3.8 below). But they are found elsewhere as well. In the East zone, these sounds occur widely in Ethiopian Semitic, Cushitic, and Omotic languages. In the Rift they are represented in a number of genetically diverse languages including Ik (Kuliak, Uganda), Dahalo (Cushitic, Kenya), Sandawe and Hadza (Khoisan, Tanzania), and the coastal Bantu languages Upper Pokomo E71, Ilwana E701, and

Table 3.7 *Frequency of three characteristic consonant types of the South zone*

Consonant type:	South (9)	Sudanic (100)	North (7)	East (12)	Center (13)	Rift (9)	Non-Afr (345)	Ratio % South / % non-Afr
ejective stops	6	4	0	9	1	3	52	4.4
aspirated stops	7	3	0	1	2	2	105	2.6
clicks	9	0	0	1	0	2	0	–

Giryama E72a. In the Sudanic belt they are very rare outside Hausa, occurring mostly near the Sudan/Ethiopian border (e.g. Berta, Gumuz, Koman, and the Surmic languages Me'en and Koegu). In Bantu, however, they are usually only weakly ejective and sometimes vary with plain voiceless stops; for example, Jessen (2002) notes variation between ejective and non-ejective realizations in Xhosa S41, and Dickens (1987) finds that the ejectives described in earlier studies of Qhalaxarzi/Kgalagadi S31d are now mostly realized as simple voiceless stops. Ejectives are nearly absent in the Center.

Map 3.5 shows the distribution of emphatic consonants and ejectives in our sample languages.

As a comparison of maps 3.4 and 3.5 shows, ejective consonants occur largely in areas where implosives do not. Indeed, it was earlier thought that implosive and ejective consonants never contrast. However, they contrast in just the two areas where their distribution overlaps. The first is eastern Africa, where a four-way contrast among voiceless stops, voiced stops, ejectives, and implosives is found in Koma (Nilo-Saharan) and Kullo (Omotic) in Ethiopia, Oromo (Cushitic) in Ethiopia and Kenya, Dahalo (Cushitic) in Kenya, and Ik (Kuliak) in Uganda. The second area is southern Africa, where implosives and ejectives contrast in the Nguni group of Bantu languages including Xhosa S41, Swati S43, and, at least historically,[15] Zulu S42.

The geographic distribution of ejectives is due in part to common inheritance. Glottalized sounds, including ejectives, are reconstructed for Proto-Afroasiatic (Wedekind 1994; Hayward 2000a) and Proto-Khoe (Vossen 1997a). In other languages, however, where ejectives are not reconstructed, contact or independent innovation may have been at work.

Contrastive *aspirated* stops are rare in most of Africa. The major exception is the South, where contrastive aspirated stops occur in nearly all Khoisan and Bantu languages. They also occur in Swahili coastal dialects from Mozambique to southern Somalia, and in some adjacent languages along the coast and inland. Elsewhere they occur notably in Owere Igbo (Igboid, Nigeria), Kohomuno (Cross River, Nigeria), several northern Bantu languages such as Beembe/Bembe (H11, Republic of the Congo), and Sandawe and Hadza in

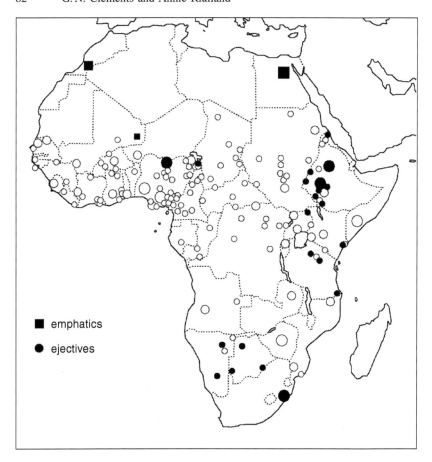

Map 3.5 Distribution of emphatic and ejective consonants in a sample of 150 African languages. Black squares show languages with emphatic consonants, and black circles show languages with ejectives. Symbol size varies with number of speakers as in Map 4

Tanzania. Aspirated stops are reconstructed for Proto-Khoe, but not for Bantu, where they have typically evolved from prenasalized stops (e.g. $nt > t^h$) or from unaspirated stops before high vowels (e.g. $ti > t^hi$).

A third characteristic feature of the South zone, and the most notorious, is the widespread presence of *clicks*. Among the world's languages, clicks are found in just five groups of languages, all spoken in Africa:

• all Khoisan languages of southern Africa
• two Khoisan isolates, Hadza and Sandawe, spoken in Tanzania

- Dahalo, a Cushitic language of Kenya
- several southwestern Bantu languages (the Kwangari cluster K33, Yeyi R41), spoken in northwest Botswana and northeast Namibia
- many southeastern Bantu languages, including at least two Sotho-Tswana languages (Southern Sotho S33, Qhalaxarzi/Kgalagadi S31d), the Nguni group S40, the Tsonga group S50, and also Copi S61, spoken in Mozambique

Elsewhere in the world, clicks as regular speech sounds have been reported only in Damin, a ceremonial form of the Lardil language (Hale & Nash 1997).

Clicks originated in Khoisan languages and subsequently spread into Bantu languages through contact. Yeyi has borrowed most extensively, with four basic click places of articulation (dental, alveolar, lateral, and palatal) crossclassified by up to nine accompaniments ("effluxes"), including a unique prenasalized glottal accompaniment that apparently does not occur even in Khoisan languages. Zulu and Xhosa have three places of articulation (dental, alveolar, and lateral) which combine with six or seven accompaniments. Most other Bantu click languages are less well endowed. For further discussion of the history and spread of clicks in Bantu languages, see Herbert (1990) and Vossen (1997b).

It is a common, but misleading practice in introductory textbooks to discuss clicks out of the context of the larger consonant systems in which they are embedded. This makes them appear much more unique than they actually are. Apart from their phonetic complexity, clicks are stop consonants much like any others and contrast along many of the same feature dimensions, including aspiration and ejection. This can be seen by an examination of table 3.8, which shows parallel non-click and click consonant types in a number of Khoisan and Bantu languages.

As Table 3.8 shows, the click accompaniments of aspiration and glottalization strictly parallel the distinctive features of aspiration and glottalization found in non-click consonants. If a language has one of these click accompaniments, it always has the corresponding feature in non-clicks, at least in the languages shown here. A treatment of these "effluxes" as a feature unique to clicks would fail to explain this generalization.[16]

Table 3.8 shows a fourth consonant type that belongs to the syndrome of southern African characteristics. The southern Bantu stops represented by the symbol D^h are usually described as murmured, weakly voiced, or completely voiceless sounds, followed in some languages by some amount of breathy voice. In Zulu they are voiced only in nasal clusters, mb, nd, $ŋg$. These characteristics resemble the description of the "slack voice" phonation type described by Ladefoged and Maddieson (1996). Since they often function as phonological tone depressors, they might perhaps be assigned the feature [+slack vocal cords], as we have suggested in the table (see also Jessen & Roux 2002). These sounds contrast with plain voiceless stops in Copi, and with plain voiced stops in

Table 3.8 *Some varieties of non-click and click consonants in Khoisan and southern Bantu languages.* + = *occurs contrastively at least one place of articulation in each language,* ( ) = *rare or marginal.* T = *plain voiceless stops,* T' = *ejective stops,* T^h = aspirated voiceless stops, D = plain voiced stops, D^h = slack voiced stops, # = simple oral clicks, #' = post-glottalized clicks, $\#^h$ = aspirated clicks. (Data from Güldemann 2001b and other sources)

KHOISAN	T	T'	T^h	#	#'	$\#^h$
Sandawe	+	+	+	+	+	+
Hadza	+	+	+	+	+	+
!Xũ (!Kung)	+	+	+	+	+	+
Jul'hoan	+	+	+	+	+	+
Gǀui	+	+	+	+	+	+
Kxoe	+	+	+	+	+	+
Nama	+	−	+	+	+	+
!Xóõ	+	+	+	+	+	+
ǂKhomani	+	+	+	+	+	?
ǂHõã	+	+	+	+	+	+
BANTU	$T/D/D^h$	T'	T^h	#	#'	$\#^h$
Zulu	$T{\sim}D^h$	+	+	+	−	+
Xhosa	D^h	+	+	+	+	+
Swati	D^h	+	+	+	−	+
Ndebele	D^h	+	+	+	−	+
Tswana	D	+	+	(+)	−	−
Southern Sotho	D	+	+	−	−	+
Qhalaxarzi	D	+	+	+	−	−
Tsonga	D^h	−	+	+	−	−
Copi	D^h	−	+	+	−	+
Shona (Ndau)	D	+	+	−	−	−

Tsonga and Zulu.[17] However, we know of no southern Bantu language that has a three-way contrast between plain voiced, slack voiced, and plain voiceless stops.

In sum, ejectives, aspirates, and clicks form part of a syndrome of characteristically southern African sounds. All have been reconstructed for Proto-Khoe, while their presence in Bantu, at least in the case of clicks, is due to diffusion. Even when these sounds have not been acquired through direct lexical borrowing – Southern Sotho, for example, evolved its glottalized and aspirated series from prenasalized stops (e.g. *mp > p^h, *mb > p') – the fact that the features [spread glottis] and [constricted glottis] are prominent in the contact situation sets up conditions favorable to their acquisition and generalization.

3.2.9   Languages without P-sounds

It has been noted since Houis (1974) that many African languages lack
P-sounds (voiceless labial stops) in their core phoneme inventories. In these
languages, P-sounds either fail to occur, or occur only in loanwords or proper
names, or are reserved for the expressive vocabulary (ideophones, interjec-
tions, etc.).

An example of a language that lacks a P-sound completely is Kikuyu (Bantu
E51). According to Benson (1964), /p/ occurs in three ideophones (*pa* 'sound
made by a door, box, gourd, etc. when struck,' *pɛ* 'description of breaking or
splintering,' *pii* 'description of bullet passing close'). Even in these words, *p* is
only likely to be used by those acquainted with Swahili and English, other
speakers using *b* instead. In loanwords, /p/ is replaced by /mb/ or /b/: *mbaoni*
'pound (sterling),' *bɔɔthita* 'post (office),' *mbaka* 'cat' (< Swahili *paka*). The
absence of /p/ in Kikuyu is due to the shift of earlier **p* to *h* (Guthrie 1967–71:
vol. 2).[18]

A language in which P-sounds occur only in loanwords is Tigrinya, a
Semitic language of Ethiopia and Eritrea. According to Woldu (1985), /p/ does
not exist in the phonology of Tigrinya, though schooled Tigrinya speakers have
little difficulty in pronouncing and perceiving it. It is mostly used for Italian
loanwords (*pane, polizia, posta,* etc.). The absence of /p/ in Tigrinya and
other Ethio-Semitic languages is due to the shift of an earlier **p* to *f* (Hetzron
1987: 657).

A language in which P-sounds occur only in loanwords and ideophones is
Tem, a Central Gur language of northern Togo. According to Tchagbale
(1977), /p/ is found in loanwords from English and Akan, in word-initial
position in ideophones, and nowhere else. Even in loanwords it is often
replaced by the native phonemes /f/ or /kp/. Comparison with other Central Gur
languages such as Winye, Phwi (Phwo), and Sisaala-Tumuli, which have /p/,
suggests that its absence in Tem may be due to a recent, local shift of **p* to *f*.

Statistics from our database are shown in table 3.9. A language is counted as
lacking a P-sound if it has at least one voiceless non-labial stop but lacks a
voiceless labial stop, or has such a stop only marginally, or only in ejectives,
geminates, *mp* clusters, etc.

These figures confirm that P-lessness is an African feature. However, its distribution is unequal. In the North and East zones, the absence of P-sounds is about
eight times as frequent as it is in other parts of the world. This feature is virtually
ubiquitous in Semitic and Berber languages in the North, and is present in
neighboring Nilo-Saharan languages, including the Songay and Nile Nubian
groups. It also occurs in roughly one out of two languages in the East, including
all major groups (Semitic, Cushitic, and Omotic).

Table 3.9 *African and non-African languages lacking P-sounds*

African languages lacking P-sounds:	21.3%
North and East:	63.2%
Sudanic:	16.0%
Other zones:	12.9%
Non-African languages lacking P-sounds:	8.1%

P-lessness spills over into adjacent areas of the Sudanic belt, where we find it for example in Hausa (northern Nigeria) and several northern Nilo-Saharan languages including Maba and Tama (central Chad), Nyimang (Sudan), and Kunama and Nera (Eritrea). Elsewhere in the Sudanic belt, P-sounds are generally more common. However, there is an important region in the Sudanic belt in which P-sounds are widely absent. This region extends from the Bandama to the Niger rivers – the same area, it will be recalled, in which implosives are also generally absent (see map 3.4). P-less languages here include Guro, Gban, Alladian, and Anyi-Baule (Côte d'Ivoire), most varieties of Gbe (Ghana to Benin), Yoruba (Benin and Nigeria), and an Edoid enclave (Ehuẹun and Ukue) in the Yoruba-speaking area. Among these P-less languages, labial stops tend to be represented by /b kp gb/. A second region, or perhaps a continuation of the first, extends from southeastern Nigeria through Cameroon into Gabon, and is represented by Lower Cross languages such as Efik, by Noni (Beboid), by several Grassfields Bantu languages including Aghem and Ngiemboon, and by some northwestern Bantu languages (the Ewondo-Fang group A70, Makaa A83). A third region, adjoining the first on its northwest flank, comprises most northern Mande languages including the Mandekan group (Grégoire 1988). We do find languages with p in these areas, but in many cases it is a fairly recent innovation. Akan, for example, lost its p when it shifted to f but got it back again when kp shifted to p (Stewart 2002). Gen (a variety of Gbe) acquired its p through rephonemicization by Akan- and Ga-speaking immigrants (Bole-Richard 1983a). Overall, as table 3.9 shows, P-less languages are about twice as frequent in the Sudanic belt as they are outside Africa.

In the Center, the facts are a bit harder to put together due to the large number of languages and the frequent absence of reliable descriptions. However, Guthrie's data (1967–71) suggest that the loss of Proto-Bantu *p was widespread in the Bantu-speaking area, taking place across a broad and largely contiguous region in the center, west, and northeast.[19] (Complicating the pattern, however, is the fact that some languages that lost *p later reintroduced it though borrowing or internal change.)

Turning to Khoisan, a phoneme *p is reconstructed for Proto-Khoe by Vossen (1997a) and is widely retained in daughter languages. However, P-sounds are less common in southern Khoisan languages, where in !Xóõ, for example, the voiceless labial stops /p pʰ/ occur only in a few borrowings (Traill 1985).

In sum, P-lessness occurs widely across Africa from north to south, with special concentrations in the North and East, in much of the Sudanic belt, and in broad areas of the Bantu-speaking Center and East. In most cases, as in Semitic and Bantu languages, it arises from the historical shift of an earlier *p to a fricative (h, f or Φ). Outside Africa, P-less languages are much less common, but examples can be found in the eastern Malayo-Polynesian languages of Indonesia, the Solomon Islands and the Philippines, in several languages of Australia and Papua New Guinea, and in several language families of the Americas.

What might explain the special concentration of this phenomenon in Africa? None of the usual explanations – chance, external factors, shared inheritance, parallel development, language contact – seems fully adequate on its own:

- chance can be eliminated, since the occurrence of P-lessness within Africa is vastly more frequent than in most other parts of the world;
- it is unclear what external factors might explain the phenomenon;[20]
- shared inheritance from a proto-language might account for Berber, Arabic, Ethio-Semitic, Cushitic, perhaps Omotic, and some western and central Nilo-Saharan languages, but even so, why so many proto-languages in the area should share this feature remains unexplained;[21]
- parallel development due to universal phonetic principles cannot explain why p should be so much more unstable in Africa than elsewhere.

A final hypothesis, language contact, explains much of the residue left after other factors are duly considered. To a very large extent, we find that if a given language lacks P-sounds, its neighbors tend to do so, even when they are not closely related.

3.2.10   Features of the eastern Sudanic belt

We conclude this section with a brief review of features of the northeastern sector of the Sudanic belt, as originally noted by Schadeberg (1987). In general, this region – which includes most of central Chad and Sudan, as well as the western lowlands of Ethiopia and Eritrea – tends to lack the characteristic Sudanic features described earlier, including labial flaps, labial-velar stops, ATR vowel harmony, and nasal vowels. Furthermore, while nearly all Sudanic languages have a contrast between voiced and voiceless explosive stops, this contrast seems to be more fragile in the east; indeed, most Kordofanian languages lack a voicing contrast altogether, as do Southern Nilotic languages spoken farther south.

Table 3.10 *Some languages of the eastern Sudan displaying minimal contrasts between dental and alveolar or retroflex consonants*

Niger-Congo, Kordofanian:	most Kordofan, e.g. Moro, Jomang, Katcha, Tima
Nilo-Saharan, Central Sudanic:	Kresh, Lugbara, Madi, Mangbetu
Nilo-Saharan, East Sudanic:	Temein, Nyimang, Tabi (fricatives only), Hill Nubian, Western Nilotic (Dinka, Nuer, Shilluk, Luo)
Nilo-Saharan, other:	Maba, Kadugli, Berta (fricatives only)
Cushitic:	Beja

There is one positive feature that distingishes the eastern Sudan from the rest of the Sudanic belt. This is the characteristic presence of two series of coronal stops (or less commonly, fricatives), one usually described as dental and the other as alveolar or retroflex. The latter sounds are distinct from implosives and sometimes contrast with them, as in Kresh, Mangbetu, and the Moru-Madi group (all Central Sudanic); in these languages, stops of the more retracted series are realized as retroflex affricates, as in Kresh and Lugbara, or as post-trilled *tr dr (ndr)*, as in Mangbetu and most Moru-Madi languages. In some languages, such as Shilluk (Gilley 1992), the sounds of the two series are subject to a harmony constraint according to which only one series can appear in any root.

This contrast, relatively uncommon elsewhere in the world's languages, is found in several distantly related and unrelated languages, including those shown in table 3.10.

Elsewhere in Africa this contrast is much less common. Scattered examples include Temne (Atlantic), Kabiyè (Gur), Ewe-Gen (Kwa), Isoko (Edoid), coastal varieties of Swahili (Bantu), and Dahalo (Cushitic). In some cases, such as Ewe, the retroflex *ɖ* evolved from an earlier implosive *ɗ*.

On the basis of these characteristics, the eastern Sudan might merit consideration as a zone of its own (Schadeberg 1987). However, two characteristic Sudanic features are found to its east, implosives and multiple tone heights (for the latter, see section 3.3.2 below), raising the question whether the Sudanic belt as defined here might not have been linguistically more homogeneous in the past.

3.3   Prosodic features

We now consider prosodic features of African languages. We begin with an overview and then examine two selected features more closely: number of tone levels, and yes/no question intonation.

3.3.1   Overview

Most African languages (about 80 percent in the sample discussed by Heine &
Leyew, this volume) are tone languages, in which tone serves a lexical and/or
grammatical function. A smaller number, including Somali and many Bantu
languages, are tonal accent languages, in which a distinctive or demarcative
accent is expressed by a toneme of high pitch. An even smaller number
(including Wolof) are neither tone languages nor tonal accent languages.
Predictable stress-accent occurs across most varieties of Arabic, and penultimate stress-accent is found in a number of non-tonal eastern Bantu languages
starting with coastal Swahili and leading across southern Tanzania into Malawi
(Derek Nurse, p.c.).

African tone languages, especially in the Sudanic and Central zones, differ
from typical East Asian tone languages in several fundamental ways. A first
difference concerns the nature of contour (rising, falling) tones. While contour
tones in East Asian languages are often unitary, that is, non-decomposable into
smaller sequences, contour tones in African languages can almost always be
analyzed into sequences of level tones. For example, a rising tone in an African
language with two level tonemes, H (high) and L (low), will typically exhibit
phonological behavior showing that it consists of a L tone followed by a H
tone. Almost any careful account of a West African or Bantu tone system will
give ample evidence for such an analysis. This fundamental distinction may
arise in part from the different historical origins of tone in the two cases. The
ancestor of Niger-Congo languages is thought to have been a tone language
with two basic levels, H and L, though there still exists no widely agreed-upon
reconstruction. In East Asian languages, lexically distinctive tone arose
through the influence of consonants (see e.g. Haudricourt 1954 for Vietnamese, and Karlgren 1960, Pulleyblank 1991, and Baxter 1992 for Chinese).
Since these languages are typically monosyllabic, they offer little potential for
the often pervasive patterns of tonal alternation found in many African languages which often provide the main evidence for tonal decomposition.

A second fundamental difference concerns the nature of tone *register*. By
register we mean the subdivision of the overall pitch range within which a
given tone or tone sequence is realized. A high tone produced in a low register
will be lower in pitch – often distinctively so – than a high tone produced in a
higher register. The fundamental difference between African and East Asian
tone languages is that register functions typically in a *syntagmatic* manner
in Africa and in a *paradigmatic* manner in Asia. That is, in African tone
languages, register most often takes the form of downstep, a significant
lowering of the register in which subsequent tones are produced, while in an
East Asian language such as Chinese, register takes the form of a choice between two lexically distinctive registers, upper and lower. In African languages,

downstep may hold across spans containing many words, while in Chinese the domain of register (and most else in the phonology) is the word. A further difference is that register is recursive in African languages, which typically allow a potentially unbounded number of downsteps within a single span. All these differences, too, stem ultimately from the different origin of tone on the two continents.

Another characteristic feature of African tone languages, rare or marginal in Asian languages, is the common occurrence of *floating tones* – tones which occur in the tone sequence but have no direct segmental realization. Floating tones originate in various ways, for example:

- through loss of a tone-bearing vowel, whose tone remains afloat
- through spreading of an H tone onto an adjacent syllable, dislodging its L tone
- through the mapping of a "tone melody" onto a word with fewer tone-bearing units than tones, leaving a final L tone without support

It is usually (though not always) the case that if an African language has floating tones, it also has distinctive downstep. This is mainly because some of the best synchronic evidence for floating tones comes from their function as downstep triggers. Other diagnostics of floating tones include (i) the failure of some word-final low tones to undergo final lowering, which can often be explained by positing a final floating H tone, and (ii) tonal alternations in which a floating tone "docks" onto an available vowel, creating a contour tone. For more detailed discussion of the nature of tone in African languages, see Clements and Goldsmith (1984), Creissels (1994), Odden (1995), Rialland (1998), Hyman and Kisseberth (1998), and Yip (2002), among others.

While African tonology has attracted considerable attention from linguists, genuine crosslinguistic databases are few. Databases have occasionally been collected for specific purposes, but there still exists no database for tonal inventories comparable, for example, to the UPSID database for phoneme inventories. We will therefore limit our discussion to two features of African languages for which enough data has been collected that some generalizations can be drawn: (i) the number of discrete tones (tone levels) in a given system, and (ii) non-segmental markers for yes/no questions (general questions). We will show that each of these features has an interesting areal distribution.

3.3.2   Number of tone levels

One might say, for typological convenience, that the number of distinctive tone levels in African languages varies from zero to five. Non-tonal languages have no tone at all (thus "zero tone levels"). A language making use of a contrast between H tone and its absence, i.e. one in which H tone functions as a privative feature as in typical tonal accent systems, can be counted as a one-level language. Such languages have sometimes been described as tonal, and sometimes as accentual. It is hard to place a sharp boundary between tonal accent languages and tone languages, and there exist transitional systems which behave as tonal in some respects and accentual in others. Many systems which seem largely accentual have derived historically from tone systems, especially in the Bantu domain, where Proto-Bantu is usually reconstructed with an H vs. L contrast.

Somewhat more straightforward are systems with two or more tone levels, though even here too, problems arise. A number of languages make use of non-distinctive tone levels which are just as well-defined phonetically as their distinctive tone levels. A well-known case is the Gbe language cluster, including Ewe and Fon, whose three discrete surface tone levels – H, M, and L – can be reduced to a basic H vs. non-H contrast in underlying representation. Another example is the interesting system of Mupun (Chadic, Nigeria), which has three lexically contrastive levels but four surface levels as the result of a process by which verb tones are "stepped up" by one degree with respect to noun tones; thus, a verbal M tone is realized at the same level as a nominal H tone, while a verbal H tone is realized on an extra-H level (Frajzyngier 1993).

At the other end of the spectrum we find languages with as many as five tone levels, which appears to be the maximum if we exclude register effects such as downstepped tones and extra-L sentence-final tones. For example, five distinctive tone levels are attested in the Santa variety of Dan (a southern Mande language spoken in the Côte d'Ivoire), as illustrated by the following nouns (Bearth & Zemp 1967):

(6) gba^1 'caterpillar'
    gba^2 'shelter'
    gba^3 'fine'
    gba^4 'roof'
    gba^5 'antelope'

(1 = highest tone, 5 = lowest tone). It seems that five represents the maximum number of contrastive tone levels, not only in Africa but in Asia and the Americas as well (Maddieson 1977; Yip 2002).

If we consider the geographic distribution of languages according to the number of tone levels they possess, we find a number of clear areal tendencies. As a broad generalization, non-tonal languages (those with "zero tone levels") are located primarily from the west, north, and east perimeter of the continent, to the Sahel in the south. In the west, we find non-tonal languages in the Atlantic family (Wolof, Seereer, Diola, etc.), including Fulfulde, spoken as far east as Cameroon; the Atlantic family is the only member of Niger-Congo whose members are mostly non-tonal. In the north and north-east, most Semitic languages have non-distinctive stress. In the east, as mentioned above, most forms of Swahili as spoken along the coast from Kenya to Mozambique have stress-accent systems.

The great majority of the remaining African languages are either tonal accent languages (especially Cushitic and many Bantu languages) or fully tonal. Consider the Niger-Congo language families spoken in the Sudanic belt. All except Atlantic are preponderantly tonal. Most appear to include no non-tonal languages at all (Williamson 1989). Within Afroasiatic, all Chadic languages are tonal; since Proto-Afroasiatic was probably not tonal, the most likely source of tone in Chadic is early and continued contact with non-Afroasiatic tone languages (Schuh 2003). The origin of the predominantly tonal or tonal accent systems of Omotic languages in the western Ethiopian highlands is more of a problem; if this group is a member of Afroasiatic, as is widely assumed, it is unclear where their tone systems might have come from. Most Nilo-Saharan languages are tonal and exhibit features similar to those of Niger-Congo languages, except that grammatically distinctive tones are sometimes commoner than lexically distinctive tones. Finally, Khoisan languages are tone languages. In sum, the widespread distribution of tone across sub-Saharan Africa owes both to shared genetic inheritance and diffusion.

It is instructive to consider the geographic distribution of tone languages according to the number of tone levels they possess. Just as toneless languages have an areal distribution, so do "tonally loaded" languages, that is, those with three to five tone levels. It was first observed by Wedekind (1985) that most such languages are located within a vast belt extending from Liberia in the west to the Ethiopian highlands in the east. This is roughly similar to our Sudanic belt, together with southwest Ethiopia. A second such area lies in the Khoisan-speaking region in adjacent areas of Botswana and Namibia. These two areas are enclosed in rectangles in map 3.6, which shows 76 languages with three or more contrastive tone levels. (The complete list of languages is given in the appendix, table 3C.)

As map 3.6 shows, languages with four tone levels (shown with black circles) or five tone levels (shown with black squares) are found in several pockets within these two large areas. These are located in: (i) southern Côte d'Ivoire (Kru, southeastern Mande, and Kwa languages); (ii) northern Togo and Benin (Gur languages); (iii) the eastern Nigeria–western Cameroon border area (Bantoid and Adamawa-Ubangi languages); (iv) the southwestern CAR–northwestern DRC border area (Bantu and Adamawa-Ubangi languages); (v) northeastern DRC and northwestern Uganda (Central Sudanic languages); (vi) southwestern Ethiopia (Omotic languages); and (vii) Botswana (Khoisan languages). The rare languages with five contrastive tone levels are spoken

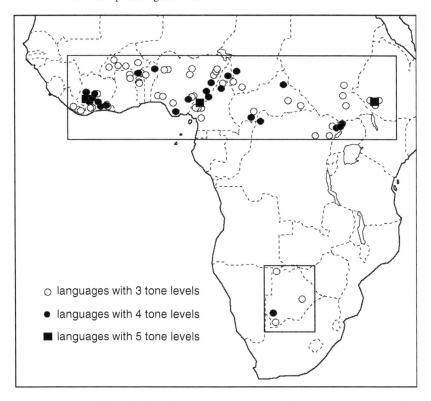

Map 3.6 Distribution of 76 African languages with three or more distinctive tone levels. The two major concentrations are enclosed in rectangles. Languages with three, four, and five tone levels are indicated by white circles, black circles, and black squares, respectively

inside these zones: Santa Dan (Mande, Côte d'Ivoire), Bench Gimira (Omotic, southwest Ethiopia), and perhaps Mbembe (Cross River, Cameroon).

Three of the areas with four or five tone levels are genetically heterogenous. In the Ivorian zone, such systems are found in three families in contact: Kru, southeastern Mande, and Kwa. In the Nigerian–Cameroon zone, such systems are found in several distantly related families within Niger-Congo: Adamawa-Ubangi (Tupuri, Yendang), Idomoid (Igede), Cross River (Kana), Jukunoid (Mbembe), and Northern Bantoid (Mambila, Ndoola). The CAR–DRC border zone contains such systems in two Niger-Congo language families, Adamawa-Ubangi (Munzombo) and Bantu (Mbati C13).

Where do such "tonally loaded" systems come from? Wedekind (1985) has argued that the five distinctive tone levels of Bench Gimira are related to its strong tendency toward monosyllabism, created by the historical loss of vowels, consonants, and even syllables, which one can reconstruct by comparison with closely related languages. Such an account is relevant for other languages as well. The link between segmental attrition and the appearance of an extra tone level can be illustrated by a comparison of examples from Moba, a four-level Gur language as spoken in northern Togo, with cognate forms from the closely related three-level language Gulmancema, spoken in Burkina Faso (Rialland 2001).

(7)   Gulmancema   Moba

   a. ò kándì [ka̋ndì]   ù ka̋nt   's/he stepped over ... '
   b. ò kándí [ka̋ndí]   ù kánt   's/he steps over ... '
   c. (kī) bígā   bík̚   'the child'
   d. (kú) fàagū   fàòg̚   'the leaf'

Example (7a) shows how a distinctive extra-H tone came into being in Moba following the loss of a final vowel, retained in Gulmancema. The redundantly extra-high realization of a H tone before a L tone which we see in the Gulmancema form was phonologized as a new phonemic tone level in Moba following the loss of its final vowel. Examples (7b) and (7c) show that H tones before H and M tones in Gulmancema did not shift to extra-H in Moba, and examples (7c) and (7d) shows that final M tones became floating L tones in Moba. Synchronically, the extra-H tone in Moba (7a) contrasts with H tone both finally (7b) and before floating L tones (7c). The tonal evolution in Moba is linked to several factors: the loss of the final vowel of bisyllabic verbs (7a,b), the loss of the final vowel of noun class suffixes (7c), and the incorporation of a final vowel into the preceding syllable (7d). All of these changes result in monosyllabic forms.

Southeastern Mande languages are also preponderantly monosyllabic. Typical roots are of the form CV, CLV, or CVV. Northern Mande languages (Bambara, Soninke, etc.) have many bisyllabic roots as well. The explanation for this difference is that in southeastern Mande languages, word-internal intervocalic consonants have fallen out. In Dan, initial syllables dropped out in just those dialects that have four or five tone levels (see the examples given earlier in (6)). Interestingly, however, the attrition of tone-bearing elements through loss of consonants and vowels is not the only mechanism at work in these languages; the formation of new tones also seems to have arisen from the phonologization of consonantal influences on tones (Vydrine 2004). Such processes are comparable to those that gave rise to tones in Asian languages.

While systems with multiple tone levels usually arise from internal factors, the fact that such systems cluster together suggests areal diffusion, if not of multiple tonal levels directly, then of the phonological factors (loss of syllables, etc.) that underlie them.

3.3.3   "Lax" question markers: an areal feature?

A second characteristically African prosodic feature involves a special type of marker used for yes/no questions. It is often taken for granted that the use of rising or high-pitched intonation to signal yes/no questions is universal, or nearly so. High-pitched question intonation markers have been viewed as the grammaticalization of a natural tendency shared by all humans. For example, Ohala writes (1984: 2):

> [This] pattern is too widespread to be explained by borrowing, descent from a common linguistic source, or chance. It follows that there is something common to all human speakers, at all stages in history, which creates this phenomenon.

However, a review of yes/no question markers in African languages shows that alternative types of question markers exist as well.

While a few databases on question intonation exist, they are dated (Hermann 1942; Ultan 1969; Bolinger 1978). The first two are known primarily through citations in Bolinger (1978), and we do not know which African languages were included. Given this inadequacy, we have begun to compile a database of yes/no question markers which includes seventy-five languages at present. This database does not aim at genetic or geographical balance, and languages spoken in the Sudanic belt are greatly overrepresented (see the appendix, table 3D for a complete list of languages; Rialland (forthcoming) provides a detailed list of sources and references). An important further problem is that sources vary in quality, and most do not include actual phonetic data, such as pitch (f0) contours. In spite of these limitations, a trend has emerged from this study: while many of the question markers found in Africa are commonly used elsewhere in the world, one type appears to be unique, or near-unique, to this continent: this consists of markers that do not involve high pitch or pitch raising. No less than thirty-four languages in our sample – almost half – are reported to have question markers of this type.

The following discussion briefly reviews the occurrence of the more familiar types of question markers (section 3.3.3.1), and then takes a closer look at question markers that do not involve high pitch or raising (section 3.3.3.2).

3.3.3.1   Type 1 question markers, involving H pitch or raising
A common type of "raising" question marker takes the form of a sentence-final rise. This marker is very common crosslinguistically, especially in non-tone languages. For an English- or French-speaking person, it is the prototypical question intonation. In our database, however, it is far from being the majority type. Where it appears, it is widely dispersed among language families; we find it in Atlantic (Fulfulde), Mande (Mende), Kru (Klao), Gur (Kulango), Benue-Congo (Edoid languages such as Isoko and Yekhee), Songay (Zarma), Chadic

(Hausa), and a number of Bantu languages including Chewa N40, Saghala E74b, and Ganda E15. Question markers consisting of a HL tone melody are reported in four languages in our database: Farefare (Gur), Dahalo (Cushitic), Jita (Bantu EJ25), and Swahili (Bantu G41–3).

Another family of "rising" patterns involves operations on register. These patterns include reduction or suppression of downdrift, raising of a H tone or H tone series (usually final), and suppression of final lowering. We consider them in turn.

Reduction or suppression of downdrift occurs in our database in non-tone languages (e.g. Wolof), in tonal accent languages (e.g. Rundi), in languages with two tone levels (e.g. Hausa), and in one language with three levels (Nama). This type of question marker has a wide geographical distribution, ranging from Atlantic languages in the west to Nilotic languages in the east and Bantu and Khoisan languages in the south. In such diverse languages as Wolof, Efik, the Bantu languages Rundi DJ62 and Jita EJ25, and the Chadic language Miya it marks yes/no questions by itself. It is often associated with other markers as well, such as rising intonation, as in Fulfulde, Mende, and Chewa N40, a segmental marker such as -à, as in Hausa and Turkana, or a reduction of penultimate lengthening, as in some southern Bantu languages (see further discussion in section 3.3.3.3). Reduction of downdrift in questions is far from unique to African languages, and is found in many other languages of the world (Bolinger 1978).

Raising of a H tone or H tone series is much less common. In our sample, it is reported in several Chadic languages, including Hausa, Tera, Angas, and Sayanci (Leben 1989) and in Bantu languages such as Ganda E15 (Lindsey 1985) and Dzamba C322 (Bokamba 1976). In Nama, a yes/no question marker has the effect of raising the second syllable in an initial H–H sequence to H–XH (extra-high) in subjectless sentences (Haacke 1999).

Suppression of final lowering is reported in just three languages of our sample: Ga, a Kwa language, Mongo-Nkundu or Lomongo, a Bantu language (C61), and Arbore, a Cushitic language. However, we suspect that it may be more common than descriptions suggest.

We might include among this first group of question markers the so-called polar tone, usually realized as a H tone after a L tone and as a L tone after a H tone. It is reported in two Bantu languages in our sample, Holoholo D20 and Nyanga D24. In three-level systems, a M tone may serve a similar function, as in the Mande language Samo.

3.3.3.2   Type 2 question markers, not involving H pitch or raising   A second type of question marker does not involve H pitch or raising. This type takes several forms, which we describe in turn.

A first marker of this type consists of a *final L tone* or *falling intonation*. Our database shows that this marker is well represented in the western sector of the

Sudanic belt. The near-totality of Gur languages in our sample are reported to have it: Ncam, Akaselem, Kusaal, Nateni, Moyobe, Mòoré, Dagaare, Gulmancema, Kasem, Kabiyé, Tem, Nawdem, and Lobiri. It has also been reported in Mande (Baule and Guro), Kru (Bassa and Grebo), Kwa (Adioukrou, Akan, Gun, and Fon), Idoid (Nembe and Degema), and Edoid (Isoko). Farther east it is reported in one of our Adamawa-Ubangi languages (Munzombo) and in Bagiro, a Nilo-Saharan language. These languages include two-level languages (Mòoré, Dagaare, Kabiye, Tem, Baule, and Gun) as well as three- and four-level languages (Munzombo, Ncam, Akaselem, Gulmancema, and Kasem).

We have found no Bantu, Afroasiatic, or Khoisan language that has this marker without having register expansion or H tone raising as well. However, due to the limitations of our database we cannot exclude the possibility that such systems may exist in these families too, or that they might even prove to be quite common.

Let us consider *final lengthening* next. In our database only two languages, Nupe (Benue-Congo) and Wobé (Kru), use final lengthening as their only question marker. In a very few contexts, Tikar (Bantoid) also uses this marker alone. In other languages, final lengthening is usually associated with other question markers, especially falling intonation as in Mòoré, breathy termination as in Moba, or both as in Ncam (all of which are Gur languages). Lengthening may add a mora, and thus a tone-bearing unit, to the last syllable, but there may be even greater durational effects. Falling intonation greatly lengthens the final vowel, and the breathy termination marker draws it out even more. Thus while lengthening can be self-sufficient, it is more often used in conjunction with other markers.

Breathy termination, characterized by a lengthening of the final vowel, is produced by a progressive opening of the glottis. It may contrast with the brusque termination produced by a sudden glottal closure (glottal stop) characterizing statements. Breathy termination occurs in Moba, where together with final lengthening it constitutes the only marker of yes/no questions (Rialland 1984). Breathy termination is also found in other Gur languages such as Mòoré, Ncam, Akaselem, and Gulmancema. However, in these languages it is associated with falling intonation (Mòoré, Ncam, Akaselem, and Gulmancema) or occurs in alternation with rising intonation (Gulmancema, which has both rising and falling question intonation patterns). We have not found breathy termination markers in other language families, but it would be surprising if it were restricted just to Gur, and we suspect that it may have been overlooked in descriptions of other languages.

We have included *open vowels*, especially [a], among type 2 question markers, due to the fact that it is always related to an L tone or falling intonation in our data. The adjunction of a final open vowel is found in Vata and Tikar, where it harmonizes in place of articulation with the last vowel of

the root. Thus in Tikar we find [ɛ] after a root ending in any of the front vowels [i e ɛ], and [a] after a root ending in a back vowel [u o a] (Stanley 1991). The geographic distribution of this question marker is particularly vast. We find it in Kru (Neyo, Odie, and Seme/Siamou), Kwa (the Gbe languages Ewe, Fon, Gun, etc.), Chadic (Pero, Sayanci, and Angas), and sporadically in other groups: Gur (Ncam and Akaselem), Edoid (Engenni), Adamawa-Ubangi (Banda-Linda), non-Bantu Bantoid (Tikar and Ejagham), and even Nilotic (Turkana). No Bantu language in our database is reported to have it, though some, such as Shi DJ53 and Southern Sotho S33, have CV markers ending in [a].

Interestingly, the open vowel question marker appears in combination or alternation not only with falling intonation (or final L tone) but also, on occasion, with the breathy termination marker. Such variant realizations can be observed within a single language and between dialects of closely related languages. For example, in Ncam (Gur), these markers vary according to the following pattern (Cox 1988, 41; L tone marks falling intonation):

(8) a.   *-a* appears after a consonant-final root:

ù cò ˈ m̄   'S/he walks'   ù cò ˈ mā ꞌꞌ   'Did s/he walk?'

   b.   a final long vowel has extra length, with no change in quality:

ań sū Ꞌ   'It's rotten'   ań sū ꞋꞋꞋ   'Is it rotten?'
ù pɔ̄ ꞋꞋ   'S/he is well'   ù pɔ̄ ꞋꞋꞋ   'Is s/he well?'

   c.   *-a* replaces a short final *i*, which is most often epenthetic:

ù ŋáŋkì   'S/he repaired'   ù ŋáŋkà ˈˈ   'Did s/he repair?'

   d.   *-a* is added after other short vowels, where it undergoes a variety of assimilations

   e.   falling intonation, final lengthening and breathy termination are regularly present

In (8a), the M tone borne by the final *m* in the statement shifts to the lengthened vowel *-a* in the question. The *-a* marker is absent in other languages of the Gurma group, such as Moba and Gulmancema, as discussed earlier. Outside the Gurma group, Mòoré uses a pattern of question marking similar to that of Ncam (vowel lengthening, breathy termination, falling intonation), but without the *-a* marker.

In Kru languages, one also finds a number of variant patterns involving open vowels, vowel lengthening, and L tones. For example, one finds languages

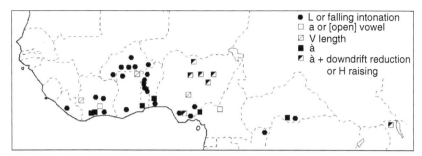

Map 3.7 Distribution of "lax" question prosody markers, which occur in 41 of a sample of 75 African languages for which relevant information was found

with final -à (Neyo, Godié, and Seme/Siamou), languages with a [+open] vowel (Vata), languages with only vowel lengthening (Wobé), and languages with a final lengthened vowel and L tone (Bassa and Grebo). We have so far found no mention of the breathy termination marker in Kru languages (see Marchese 1983; Vogler 1987). In the Gbe languages (Kwa) spoken from Ghana to Benin, the -à marker is particularly frequent. Though it is usually the sole marker of yes/no questions, L tone may be used alone in the Porto-Novo dialect of Gun (Fréchet 1989).

In the Adamawa-Ubangi group, Banda-Linda has final -à while Munzombo uses a simple L tone on a lengthened vowel. In Edoid languages, there is similar variation between L-toned -à or -è in expressions of doubt (Engenni) and L tone alone (Isoko and Degema). Of our two Bantoid languages, Tikar has an open vowel and Ejagham has L-toned -à.

In Chadic, Hausa employs an optional L tone in addition to its usual vowel lengthening and breathy termination, while Sayanci and Angas have final L-toned -aà.

The cluster of properties just reviewed – open vowels, L tones, sentence-final falling intonation, and lengthening, often in combination – constitutes a syndrome of what might be called *lax* features, centering around a relaxation of the vocal cords inducing pitch lowering and the presence of low vowels, bearing intrinsically low phonetic pitch. One might be tempted to speak of a "lax prosody" opposed to a "tense prosody," the latter involving rising intonation, tense vocal cords, and/or a raised larynx. This feature provides another diagnostic of the Sudanic belt, with a particular concentration in the western sector.

Map 3.7 shows the geographical distribution of lax question prosodies, broken down into their main forms (L tone/falling intonation, vowel lengthening, [open] vowel, -à) as well as a hybrid form (-à associated with a downdrift reduction or final H raising). The map only shows the Sudanic belt, as this feature, even in its hybrid form, was not found elsewhere.

We speculate that this cluster of features might have originated in a single historical source form such as a L-toned -*a*, perhaps accompanied by breathy termination, which might have been transmitted from one or more source languages to neighboring languages through contact. One or another of these features is found throughout most of the Sudanic belt, but appears most commonly in Niger-Congo languages (Atlantic, Mande, Kru, Gur, Kwa, Benue-Congo, and Adamawa-Ubangi), which seem to be its most likely historical source. Though "lax" markers occur outside Niger-Congo, they usually assume a hybrid form combining L-toned -*à(a)* with downdrift reduction or final H raising, as is found for example in Chadic languages such as Hausa, Angas, Sayanci, and Pero, and further to the east in Turkana (Nilotic). Apart from these cases, it is not represented in our small sample of non-Chadic Afroasiatic languages and Nilo-Saharan languages, nor have we found it in our sample of Bantu languages.

3.3.3.3   Cancellation of penultimate lengthening   A further mark of yes/no questions consists of the suppression or absence of penultimate lengthening in languages that employ such lengthening in statements. The H register is also expanded, raising H tones to extra-high, and downdrift is reduced. This cluster of features is restricted to the southern Bantu languages Zulu S42 and Southern Sotho S33 in our data. Compare, for instance, the following Zulu forms (Taljaard & Bosch 1988):

(9) a.   ukhali:le   'S/he cried'   (statement)
     b.   ukhalile?   'Did s/he cry?'   (question)

3.3.3.4   Conclusion: a "lax" question marker in African languages   To summarize, question intonation in African languages is much more diverse than one might have expected. Most strikingly, many question markers involve no high pitch or pitch raising, such as are often thought to be universal. Our database, incomplete though it is, has brought this diversity to light, and has shown the Sudanic belt to constitute a prosodic area, characterized not only by multiple tone heights but by the widespread use of a typologically unusual feature of "lax" question intonation.

3.4   Summary and discussion

Table 3.11 summarizes some of the main phonological features of African languages, as they occur across zones.

Table 3.11 *Phonological characteristics of African languages, by zone.*
(xxx = very common or ubiquitous, xx = common, x = infrequent, − = very
rare or absent, (x) = Omotic and/or Cushitic, /x/ = Bantu, [x] = Khoisan)

	North	East	Sudanic	Center	South	Rift
absence of P-sounds	xxx	xx	x	xx	−	x
emphatic consonants	xx	−	−	−	−	−
non-tonal prosody	xxx	x	−	−	−	−
labial flaps	−	−	x	x	−	−
labial-velar stops	−	−	xx	−	−	−
implosives	−	(xx)	xx	x	/x/	x
nasal vowels	−	−	xx	−	[xxx]	−
two series of high vowels	−	(x)	xxx	xx	x	xx
3+ tone levels	−	(x)	xx	−	[x]	−
"lax" question markers	−	−	xx	?	−	?
ejective stops	−	xx	−	−	xxx	x
aspirated stops	−	−	−	−	xxx	/x/, [xxx]
clicks	−	−	−	−	xx	[xxx]
slack voiced stops	−	−	−	−	/xx/	−

How well does this table support a division of the African continent into phonological zones? We again emphasize, as we did at the outset, that no zone is airtight. Because of this, neighboring zones, as the table shows, often show features of both. For example, implosives and 2H vowel systems with ATR vowel harmony occur well beyond the eastern limit of the Sudanic belt in the East and Rift zones. Moreover, phonological isoglosses rarely coincide. A typical example is labial-velar stops: while these sounds have diffused widely into the Congo Basin, labial flaps, nasal vowels and 2H–2M vowel systems have not.

While the patterns are therefore complex, there appears to be some justification for the main thesis of this chapter, which is that Africa is best viewed as a set of zones rather than a single linguistic area. Three of the proposed zones, at least, are sharply distinguished by independent, marked phonological features that occur across major genetic lines and which show substantial overlap. Let us review them briefly.

The North, as we see from an examination of the first three features in table 3.11, is set apart by the absence of P-sounds, the presence of an emphatic series of consonants, and the prevalence of non-tonal prosodic systems. These features span a major genetic boundary, that between Arabic and Berber. These two units share many other characteristic features, including a series of "guttural" consonants, contrastive consonant gemination, and small vowel inventories doubled by contrastive vowel length, the latter also found in most Nilo-Saharan languages in the region.

The Sudanic belt is well defined by the next group of features: labial flaps, labial-velar stops, implosives, nasal vowels, 2H vowel systems, multiple tone levels and "lax" question prosodies, among others. None of these features are as common in other zones. Nor, as we have seen, are they equally distributed within it; however, their overlap defines the Sudanic belt quite well, with the exception of the extreme northwest (northern Atlantic languages) and the northeast (the eastern Sudan, as discussed in section 3.2.10).

A third zone, the South, is sharply delineated by the remaining features in table 3.11: ejective and aspirated stops, clicks, and slack voiced stops. To these features we could add their characteristic series of lateral affricates and fricatives. All these features are widely shared by Khoisan and Bantu languages in the region.

Less well demarcated is the East zone, whose languages share many features with those of the North due to their common Afroasiatic heritage. Nevertheless, the two non-Semitic families in this zone, Omotic and Cushitic, display several features different from those of the North, notably the widespread presence of tone or tonal accent systems, and the common occurrence of implosives and ejectives (sometimes in the same language). We have seen that only in this zone does ɗ occur as the unique implosive. Ejectives also occur in Ethio-Semitic languages (see Crass 2002 for a fuller account).

The Center is well defined by the inherited features of the Bantu languages spoken within it, and does not as a whole display the characteristic features of the Sudanic languages spoken to the north nor the Khoisan and Bantu languages spoken to the south. We have seen that it is well characterized by a unique system of vowel harmony.

As far as the more diverse Rift zone is concerned, this survey has not succeeded in identifying large-scale diffusion of phonological features across major genetic boundaries, the hallmark of a genuine phonological area. This fact might well call the independence of this zone into question. It remains to be seen, however, whether further study will reveal cases of such diffusion, at least in micro-areas.

Appendix

The African phoneme database used for this study is composed of most of the African languages contained in the UPSID database (Maddieson & Precoda 1989) together with others that we have added, mainly in the Sudanic belt, in order to improve the geographical coverage. It is divided into six parts, according to zone. It contains 88 Niger-Congo languages, 30 Nilo-Saharan languages, 27 Afroasiatic languages, and 5 Khoisan languages, for a total of 150 languages spoken indigenously on the African continent. We have corrected and updated information on certain UPSID languages based on more

Table 3A *Composition of the Sudanic database, by genetic groups*

NIGER-CONGO (66)	
Dogon:	Dogon
Atlantic:	Wolof, Pulaar, Diola, Konyagi, Ndut, Temne, Bidyogo, Kisi
Mande:	Kpelle, Bambara, Bobo-Fing, Dan, Bisa
Kru:	Aizi, Klao, Bete
Gur:	Dagbani, Mòoré, Bwamu, Tampulma, Senadi, Bariba
Kwa:	Alladian, Adioukrou, Attié, Akan, Gã, Lelemi, Siya, Ewe-Gen
Ijoid:	Ijo (Izon)
West Benue-Congo:	Yoruba, Isoko, Igbo, Gwari, Igede
East Benue-Congo:	
non-Bantoid:	Amo, Birom, Tarok, Kpan, Efik, Ogbia, Kohumono
Bantoid, non-Bantu:	Mambila, Ejaghem, Noni, Aghem, Fe'fe'
Bantu:	Kpa/Bafia, Ewondo, Makaa, Basaa, Yaka/Aka, Egbuta, Bila
Adamawa:	Doayo, Mumuye, Mbum, Lua
Ubangi:	Gbeya, Azande, Mba (Mba-Ne), Sango
Kordofanian:	Moro, Jomang
NILO-SAHARAN (23)	
Central Sudanic:	Yulu, Sar, Furu/Bagiro, Kresh, Lugbara, Ngiti, Mangbetu
Eastern Sudanic:	Nera, Nyimang, Tama, Mursi, Tabi, Temein, Daju, Dinka
Other:	Zarma, Central Kanuri, Maba, Fur, Berta, Kunama, Koma, Kadugli
AFROASIATIC, CHADIC (11)	
West:	Hausa, Kanakuru, Angas, Ngizim
Biu-Mandara:	Tera, Margi, Kotoko, Higi
East:	Kera, Dangaléat
Masa:	Lamé

Table 3B *Composition of the North, East, Rift, Center, and South databases*

NORTH (7)	
Afroasiatic, Berber:	Shilha, Tamasheq
Afroasiatic, Semitic:	Egyptian Arabic
Afroasiatic, Cushitic:	Beja
Nilo-Saharan:	Tedaga, Nobiin, Koyraboro Senni Songay
EAST (12)	
Afroasiatic, Semitic:	Amharic, Tigre, Chaha
Afroasiatic, Cushitic:	Awiya/Awngi, Oromo, Somali, Dahalo
Afroasiatic, Omotic:	Dizi, Hamer, Kefa/Kafa, Kullo
Niger-Congo, Bantu:	Swahili

Table 3B (*Cont.*)

RIFT (9)	
Afroasiatic, Cushitic:	Iraqw
Nilo-Saharan, Nilotic:	Luo, Maasai, Sebei
Nilo-Saharan, Kuliak:	Ik
Niger-Congo, Bantu:	Kikuyu, Ganda
Khoisan:	Hadza, Sandawe
CENTER (13)	
Niger-Congo, Bantu:	Tsogo, Teke, Beembe, Mongo-Nkundu, Lega, Rwanda, Bemba, Mwera, Makhuwa, Luvale, Umbundu, Herero, Zezuru Shona
SOUTH (9)	
Central Khoisan (Khoe):	Nama
Northern Khoisan:	!Xũ (!Kung)
Southern Khoisan:	!Xóõ
Niger-Congo, Bantu:	Gciriku/Diriku, Tsonga, Yeyi, Copi, Tswana, Zulu

Table 3C *Composition of the tone level database*

NIGER-CONGO (55)	
Mande:	Samo (3), Guro (3), Santa Dan (5), Tura (4), Bobo-Fing (3)
Kru:	Wobé (4), Bété (4), Vata (4), Godié (3), Neyo (3), Dewoin/ De (3), Nyabwa (4), Krahn (3)
Gur:	Togolese Moba (4), Bariba (4), Ncam (3), Akaselem (3), Nateni (3), Gulmancema (3), Kasem (3), Nuni (3), Biali (3)
Kwa:	Attié (4), Abbé (3), Alladian (3)
West Benue-Congo:	Nupe (3), Igede (4), Kana (4), Gwari/Gbari (3), Yoruba (3), Yala (3), Igala (3)
East Benue-Congo:	
non-Bantoid:	Mbembe (5?), Jukun (3), Birom (3), Kpan (3)
Bantoid, non-Bantu:	Tikar (3), Mambila (4), Ndoola (4), Bafut (3), Babanki (3)
Bantu:	Ewondo A70 (3), Mbati C13 (4?), Nyali D23 (3), Bira D21 (3), Bila D311 (3)
Adamawa-Ubangi:	Banda-Linda (3), Ngbaka (3), Zande (3), Sango (3), Tupuri (4), Yendang (4), Munzombo (4), Doayo (4), Mumuye (3)
NILO-SAHARAN (8)	
Central Sudanic:	Moru-Madi (4), Lugbara (4), Mangbetu (4), Bedionde (3), Yulu (4)
Nilotic:	Dinka (3), Shilluk (3), Nuer (3)
AFROASIATIC (9)	
Chadic:	Tera (3), Ga'anda (3), Angas (3), Kera (3), Lame (3)
Omotic:	Dizi (3), Sheko (3), Yem (3), Bench Gimira (5)
KHOISAN (4)	Nama (3), Kxoe (3), Tsoa (3), !Xóõ (4)

Table 3D *Composition of the question intonation database*

NIGER-CONGO (60)	
Atlantic:	Wolof, Fulfulde
Mande:	Mende, Baule, Samo, Guro
Kru:	Godié, Neyo, Bassa, Klao, Wobé, Vata
Gur:	Togolese Moba, Mòoré, Ncam, Akaselem, Kusaal, Nateni, Moyobe, Farefare, Dagaaré, Gulmancema, Kasem, Kabiye, Tem, Nawdem, Lobiri
Kwa:	Adioukrou, Akan, Ga, Ewe, Gun, Fon
Adamawa/Ubangi	Banda-Linda, Munzombo
Ijoid:	Ijo (Izon), Nembe
West Benue-Congo:	Isoko, Igbo, Yekhee, Degema, Engenni, Nupe
East Benue-Congo	
non-Bantoid:	Efik
Bantoid, non-Bantu:	Tikar, Ejagham
Bantu:	Bafut, Bajele, Mongo-Nkundu, Holoholo, Dzamba, Nyanga, Rundi, Shi, Saghala, Jita, Chewa, Southern Sotho, Zulu, Swahili
NILO-SAHARAN (6)	
Songay:	Zarma
Central Sudanic:	Bagiro, Ngiti
Nilotic:	Dholuo, Turkana, Nandi
AFROASIATIC (8)	
Chadic:	Hausa, Angas, Sayanci, Pero, Miya, Tera
Cushitic:	Dahalo, Arbore
KHOISAN (1)	Nama

recent or more accurate information. Non-African phoneme systems have been drawn from the unmodified UPSID database.

Table 3A shows the genetic composition of the Sudanic database. A few units, notably Gur, Kainji-Platoid, Cross River, Adamawa, Ubangi, and Chadic, are underrepresented in proportion to their numbers, but as these units are centrally located in the Sudanic belt this should not lead to a severe underestimation of shared Sudanic properties.

Table 3B gives the composition of the North, East, Rift, Center, and South databases.

Table 3C gives the composition of the tone level database, consisting of 76 languages with three or more contrastive tone levels. The number of contrastive levels in each language is shown in parentheses.

Table 3D gives the composition of the yes/no question intonation database, containing 75 languages for which relevant information was found.

4   Africa as a morphosyntactic area

Denis Creissels, Gerrit J. Dimmendaal, Zygmunt Frajzyngier, and Christa König

4.1   Introduction

The aim of the present chapter is to review a list of morphosyntactic features, involving categories and their syntactic functions, which are likely to provide a typological characterization of languages in general. The properties in question are investigated from the following two points of view:

(i)   Does the proportion of African languages possessing a given feature (or being devoid of it) seem to be roughly similar to the proportion observed at world level, or to be significantly different?

(ii) Are the features whose frequency or rarity characterizes Africa as a whole evenly distributed, or are there geographical clusterings, i.e. areas with a particular concentration of languages possessing or lacking the features in question, and if so, to what degree do such clusterings coincide with or diverge from genetic groupings?

We do not proceed by systematically testing the features we consider on the basis of a language sample pre-established on the basis of statistical methods that would ensure its representativity. Apart from a few reference works whose quality can be taken for granted, this chapter mainly relies on the authors' first-hand knowledge of African data. This undoubtedly limits the bearing of our conclusions (or rather suggestions), but the set of African languages documented in a sufficient way to be systematically used in such a study is so limited that it is simply impossible to extract from it a sample representative of the diversity of African languages.

4.2   Core grammatical relations

4.2.1   The recognition of subjects and objects

The relevance of a syntactic function "subject" grouping together the only argument of semantically monovalent verbs (hereafter S) and the more agent-like argument of semantically bivalent verbs (hereafter A) is obvious only for languages in which, regardless of the precise semantic nature of the verb, both have the same coding characteristics (in terms of case marking, indexation, and/or constituent order). In other languages, the possibility of recognizing a syntactic function "subject" is less obvious, since it cannot be justified on the basis of immediately visible coding properties, but only on the basis of behavioral properties in mechanisms such as reflexivization, relativization, questioning, focalization, or clause chaining; in some languages, it may happen that (some of) these mechanisms function in a way that does not justify grouping together S and A, which in turn may raise doubts about the relevance of the notion of subject for the description of such languages.

From this point of view, African languages can be characterized as languages in which the notions of subject and object are not problematic, and most often, the clearest manifestation of these notions can be found in systems of pronominal affixes of a type particularly widespread among Bantu languages (see section 4.2.3), in which the same set of pronominal affixes is used to represent S and A, and another set is used to represent the patient of prototypical action verbs, and more generally the less agent-like argument of semantically bivalent verbs.

Outside Africa, some language groups (e.g. Caucasian languages) show a marked tendency towards a closer correspondence between semantic and syntactic roles, whereby verbs tend to divide into classes characterized by different constructions according to the type of event they represent and the types of semantic roles they assign to their arguments, and the assimilation of the construction of semantically bivalent verbs to that of prototypical transitive verbs is systematically limited by semantic conditions. The available documentation on African languages suggests a strong predominance of the opposite tendency: to the best of our knowledge, syntactic descriptions of African languages do not mention the existence of systematic semantic limitations to the assimilation of the construction of semantically bivalent verbs to the prototypical transitive construction, and variations in the morphosyntactic treatment of the single argument of semantically monovalent verbs are exceptional in African languages.

4.2.2 Subject/object case marking typology

In this section, case marking is taken in a wide sense, including not only morphological case, but also the use of adpositions to code the distinction between subjects and objects.

In the majority of African languages, both subjects and objects are unmarked for case, i.e. they do not exhibit any marking (affix, adposition, or prosodic contour) distinguishing noun phrases in subject or object function from noun phrases quoted in isolation, or used in an extra-syntactic function of pure designation. However, the situation is not exactly the same in all phyla and in all geographical areas of Africa.

In Khoisan, as a rule, there is no case marking of the distinction between subject and object. However, in some languages, the status of certain morphemes as marking the discourse roles topic/focus or the syntactic roles subject/object is not entirely clear.

Case-marked subjects or objects are exceptional in Niger-Congo languages; in the few Niger-Congo languages in which a case distinction between subjects and objects may be recognized, it results from recent historical developments: either the reanalysis of a verb 'take' in a serial verb construction as a preposition introducing objects, in some Kwa languages (Lord 1993), or the reanalysis of a distinction between a definite and an indefinite form of nouns as a case distinction, in some western Bantu languages – see Blanchon (1999), Schadeberg (1999). The western Bantu languages that have "tone cases" constitute an compact geographical area from Gabon to Angola. The following example is from Ngangela (Maniacky 2002):

(1) a. nouns in quotation, or in extra-syntactic function of pure designation:
    kánike 'child', kaθúúmbi 'hen'
   b. kanike   námonó   kaθúúmbi
      12:child:SUBJ   TAM:see   12:hen:ABS
      'The child has seen the hen'

Case distinctions between subjects and objects are less rare in the other two phyla (Afroasiatic and Nilo-Saharan). Within Afroasiatic, the majority of Chadic languages have no case system, but some Central Chadic languages use prepositions to code objects, and many Berber, Omotic, Cushitic and Ethio-Semitic languages distinguish between subject and object by way of morphological case on nouns. Thus, in the Omotic language Maale, case suffixes (whose form depends on gender and definiteness) as well as tonal inflection are used to distinguish these two core functions (Amha 2001: 56–8). Compare:

(2) a. na-att-á   bayi   yenk'-á-ne
       child-PL-SUBJ   cattle:ABS   herd-IPF-POS:DECL
       'Children herd cattle'
    b. ʔ́ózó   na-att-ó   naʃk-á-ne
       3MSG:SUBJ   child-PL-ABS   like-IPF-POS:DECL
       'He likes children'

Within Nilo-Saharan, case marking is common in a range of language groups stretching from Nigeria in the west to Ethiopia and Eritrea in the east, more specifically in primary branches such as Saharan, Maban, For, various

Eastern Sudanic groups, e.g. the Tama group, Nara, Nubian, Surmic, and Nilotic. Within this phylum, case-marking systems appear to be absent in a number of Eastern Sudanic groups in the Nuba Mountains and west of this area (Temein and Keiga Jirru, the Daju group) and in Central Sudanic.[1] Since these groups are spoken in areas where Niger-Congo languages are found (which typically lack case marking), areal contact may have played a role in the disappearance of case.

An inventory of African languages having case contrasts between subjects and objects can be found in König (2004a, 2004b, and this volume).

In African languages that have case-marking systems distinguishing subjects from objects, this distinction is often marked by tonal differences. This is the case not only in all western Bantu languages that have a case distinction (see above), but also, for example, in the Cushitic language Somali, or in the Nilotic languages Dinka and Maasai. As shown by Amha (2001) for Maale, and by Andersen (1988) for the Nilotic language Päri, case marking through tonal inflection may be used in tandem with suffixation. In Päri, the two strategies appear to be entirely phonologically conditioned (Andersen 1988: 294–5). With nouns ending in a consonant in the absolutive, the ergative is formed by doubling the final consonant if the latter is a sonorant, and by adding a low-toned suffix -i or -I (depending on vowel harmony). With vowel-final nouns, the final vowel is replaced by the same suffix if the final root vowel is high, and by -e or ε (depending on vowel harmony) with non-high vowels. If both vowel replacement and tone addition apply vacuously, the ergative form is phonologically indistinguishable from the absolutive form:

(3)   Absolutive   Ergative
        tóŋ   tóŋŋ-ì   'spear'
        léɛp   léɛp-ì   'tongue'
        kìd-í   kíd-î   'stone'
        wìɲ-ɔ́   wìɲ-ɛ̂   'bird'
        jóob-ì   jòob-ì   'buffalo'
        pàl-ɛ̀   pàl-ɛ̀   'knives'

The drift towards loss of segmental layers and the maintenance of tonal marking is part of a more general areal tendency to use tone as an exponent of some inflectional or derivational process in African languages (similar observations can be made, for example, regarding the expression of TAM distinctions, or of definiteness distinctions see section 4.2).

Among the languages that have a case distinction between core syntactic roles with the same case form for S (intransitive subject) and A (transitive subject), and a different case form for O, the most common type worldwide is that in which the case form for S and A (nominative) coincides with the form

of nouns used for quotation or in the extra-syntactic function of pure designation, whereas the form for O, traditionally called Accusative, is a form
occurring only in certain syntactic conditions. By contrast, the type of case
marking in which the quotation or designation form of nouns is used for O, a
case form distinct from the quotation or designation form of nouns being used
for both S and A, is very rare at world level. But African languages show a
very different ratio of these two variants of the accusative type of case
marking (König 2004a, 2004b). The first variant, which very strongly predominates at world level, is not particularly common on the African continent; in particular, it seems to never occur in case-marking systems
involving tonal distinctions. By contrast, so-called "marked-nominative"
systems (i.e. systems in which the quotation or designation form of nouns is
used for O, and a case form distinct from the quotation or designation form is
used for both S and A)[2] are very common among African languages that have
case. Such systems are found in three different areas of the African continent.
The case systems found in Berber languages and western Bantu languages
(see the Ngangela example (1) above) all belong to the "marked-nominative"
type, and this type is also relatively common among the northeast African
languages that have distinct case forms for subjects and objects: most case
systems found in Nilotic, Surmic, Omotic, and Cushitic languages belong to
the "marked-nominative" type; for a detailed inventory, see König (2004a,
2004b, and this volume).

A fairly common type at world level is the ergative type of case marking, in
which S and O share the same case form (absolutive), and A takes a special
case form (ergative). In general, ergativity is not a common phenomenon
among African languages; most manifestations of ergativity observed in
African languages can be characterized as "ubiquitous" or "pervasive" ergativity, i.e. manifestations of ergativity that tend to occur even in the most robust
accusative languages. In particular, the ergative type of case marking is
exceptional on the African continent. It has been recognized only in some
Western Nilotic languages, i.e. in a language family in which case systems of
the "marked-nominative" type are predominant. According to Andersen
(1988), in basic sentences in Päri, S and O precede the verb and are in a form
that coincides with the quotation or designation form, whereas A follows the
verb and shows a different form, identifiable as ergative case:

(4) a. dháagɔ̀   áŋɛ̀ɛthɔ̀
       woman:ABS   TAM:laugh
       'The woman laughed'

    b. dháagɔ̀   áyàaɲ   ùbúrr-ì
       woman:ABS   TAM:insult   Ubur-ERG
       'Ubur insulted the woman'

A similar system has been reported for the closely related Western Nilotic languages Anywa (Reh 1996), Jur-Luwo (Buth 1981), and Shilluk (Miller & Gilley 2001). With respect to the situation commonly found in non-African languages that have a case marking of core syntactic roles of the ergative type, the most striking characteristic of these Western Nilotic languages is a strong correlation between word order and case marking. This is a general property of Nilotic and Surmic case-marking systems: in Nilotic and Surmic languages with case marking of the "marked-nominative" type, it is common that only postverbal subjects are inflected for case; the same applies to the Western Nilotic languages having a case-marking system of the ergative type, with the additional constraint that in ergative systems, intransitive subjects (but not transitive subjects) are restricted to occur in preverbal position.

In the languages of the world, definiteness and case marking often correlate, and some northeast African languages that have case-marked core constituents confirm this tendency: the use of an accusative marker correlates with the definiteness distinction in Semitic languages like Amharic or Tigre,[3] as well as some Cushitic and Omotic languages. In the Omotic language Haro, subjects as well as objects are inflected for case only when they are definite (Woldemariam 2004).

4.2.3   Subject/object indexation typology

4.2.3.1   Types of pronominal markers In this section, the term "pronominal marker" is applied to bound morphemes possessing the following characteristics:

- A pronominal marker refers to an entity that is represented elsewhere in the same clause by a noun phrase, or could be represented by a noun phrase in a clause identical in all other respects.
- A pronominal marker is attached to a word in a certain syntactic relation with the noun phrase that represents or could represent the entity to which it refers.[4] Most commonly, pronominal markers attach to verbs and represent arguments of the verb they are attached to, but this is not the only possible situation: so-called "possessive affixes" are pronominal markers attached to nouns (see section 4.4.6), and pronominal markers may also attach to adpositions (see section 4.5).
- A pronominal marker shows variations reflecting, either semantic characteristics of the entity it refers to, or grammatical features of a noun phrase referring to the same entity.

Pronominal markers typically show variations expressing distinctions that parallel those expressed by free pronouns, in particular distinctions in person and number.[5]

Generally speaking, three subtypes of pronominal markers can be distinguished on the basis of their conditions of cooccurrence with the corresponding noun phrases. Diachronically, these three subtypes represent successive stages in an evolution whose starting point is the cliticization of free pronouns (Creissels 2005).

Stage I pronominal markers are in complementary distribution with the corresponding noun phrase within the limits of the clause, and the choice between the pronominal marker and the corresponding noun phrase depends on the discourse structure of the clause.

Stage II pronominal markers are obligatory, even if a noun phrase or a free pronoun referring to the same entity is present in subject or object function, whereas the corresponding noun phrases or free pronouns are not obligatory constituents of the clause.

Stage III pronominal markers share with stage II pronominal markers the property of obligatoriness, but they differ from them by not being able to represent by themselves the entity they refer to.[6]

Most African languages have subject markers attached to verbs, and a number of them have also object markers. When juxtaposed to each other, such combinations of pronominal subject-object marking frequently fuse and result in syncretism, as in the Nilotic language Maasai, where a verbal prefix *kɪ* occurs when the subject refers to either a second or third person (singular or plural) and the object refers to either a first or second person singular. In some languages with so-called double object constructions, verb forms may include two object markers, and sometimes (e.g. in Rwanda and some other Bantu languages) up to six, where the applicative is involved, as in the Rwanda verb form *y-aa-bi-ha-yi-mu-mu-h-er-e-ye* 'He gave it (food) to it (dog) there from her for him (chief)' (Robert Botne, p.c.).

The Cushitic language Oromo (Griefenow-Mewis & Bitima 1994) is similar to Latin in that it has stage II subject markers suffixed to verbs, but uses exclusively free pronouns to pronominalize objects. This situation seems to be relatively common among Cushitic and Omotic languages, but rather uncommon in the other African language families.

Maale (Amha 2001) is a clear case of an African language in which pronominal markers attached to verbs have only a very marginal status: in Maale, the verb is inflected for person and number in the imperative and in the optative only; and apart from that, the pronominal morphemes of Maale are all very clearly free pronouns. But such cases are not frequent among African languages. In particular, the pronominal morphemes of many Mande or Songhay languages may at first sight give the impression of uniformly behaving as free pronouns, but precise descriptions always make apparent the existence of allomorphic variations that affect at least certain pronominal morphemes in certain contexts, and that can be accounted for neither as case distinctions nor as the result of postlexical phonological processes operating at ordinary word junctions – see for example Heath (1999) for Gao Songhay.

Many descriptions of African languages do not identify pronominal markers appropriately, treating them as independent words. The reason is that stage I pronominal markers, i.e. pronominal markers minimally different from free pronouns, are particularly frequent in African languages. But once pronominal markers are recognized correctly, it appears that an overwhelming majority of African languages do have pronominal markers, and that the vast majority of them have both subject markers and object markers.

4.2.3.2   Obligatory vs. discourse dependent subject/object markers   Subject or object markers functioning as pure agreement morphemes (i.e. subject or object markers whose variations refer to an argument encoded as a noun phrase in subject or object function but that cannot by themselves represent the argument they refer to) are not common in the languages of the world. Not surprisingly, examples of pronominal markers of this type are very difficult to find in African languages.

Among African languages, one commonly encounters both languages with discourse dependent subject markers and languages with obligatory subject markers. Stage I subject markers are particularly common in some language families (e.g. Kwa) and stage II subject markers in others (e.g. Bantu), but it is difficult to say which of these two types predominates at the level of the African continent.

By contrast, discourse-dependent object markers are very common in African languages, but third-person object markers necessarily present in transitive constructions, even in the presence of the corresponding noun phrase, do not seem to be attested (though such object markers may be obligatory for first or second person). The following example from Tswana illustrates a situation in which even first- or second-person object markers attached to the verb forms always represent topics and are therefore in complementary distribution with noun phrases or free pronouns, the choice between an object marker and a free pronoun in the canonical position of objects being pragmatically significant.

(5) a. kì-χ ̀u-bídítsè
      S1SG-O2SG-call:TAM
      'I *called* you' (how is it possible that you didn't hear me?)

   b. kì-bídítsè   wèná
      S1SG-call:TAM   2SG
      'I called *you*' (and nobody else!)

Many languages (for example, the Bantu language Swahili) have object markers that can be classified as stage I in the sense that they are not always present in transitive constructions, but that depart from the typical behavior of stage I object markers in the sense that at least in certain conditions, they must be present even if the corresponding noun phrase or free pronoun is also present. Swahili also illustrates a situation in which definiteness is not overtly marked at noun phrase level, but triggers the presence of an object marker that constitutes the only clue to the definiteness of common nouns in object function.

(6) a. ni-me-ku-ona
       S1SG-ANT-O.2SG-see
       'I have seen you'

    b. *ni-me-ona   wewe
       S1SG-ANT-see   2SG

    c. u-me-leta   chakula
       S2SG-ANT-bring   7:food
       'Have you brought (some) food?'

    d. u-me-leta   chakula
       S2SG-ANT-O3:7-bring   7:food
       'Have you brought the food?' (which I told you to bring)

A situation parallel to Swahili exists in a number of Chadic languages, e.g. Gidar. If the object is determined, i.e. marked for previous mention or marked by a deictic determiner, it must be coded on the verb. But the coding on the verb may also be the sole marker of the definiteness of the object. The nominal object in such cases need not have a determiner of its own. In Chadic languages the verbs of movement can also code the definiteness of their locative complement, which may point to a tendency to assimilate locative complements to the syntactic role of direct object.

In Mupun (West Chadic) the coding of a pronominal object following the verb is constrained by tense in the following way: in the past tense, the third-person inanimate object pronoun cannot be used even if its antecedent has been mentioned in the preceding discourse; in the future tense, again, the third-person inanimate object pronoun cannot be omitted (Frajzyngier 1993).

4.2.3.3   Weak pronouns representing core arguments but attached to a word other than the verb   Subject/object markers attached to the verb are particularly common, but other types of attachment are possible for weak pronouns (or bound pronouns) representing core arguments of the verb.

Another relatively common type of attachment, in the languages of the world, is that in which subject/object pronouns behave as second-position clitics. This type is found in some Khoisan languages (e.g. Nama), but does not seem to occur elsewhere in Africa.

In Mande languages, the order of the constituents of the clause is S (v) O V X, where (v) indicates the possible presence of a grammatical word (or clitic), often called "predicative marker," which expresses TAM and polarity distinctions.[7] In some languages, depending on the TAM and polarity value of the clause, the predicative marker may be absent, but in others, the predicative marker is an obligatory element of the clause. In Mande languages, the verb itself is never inflected for subject, but in some of the Mande languages in which the predicative marker is an obligatory element of the clause (e.g. Dan), its variations express person–number distinctions that refer to the subject of the clause.

In Cushitic languages in which verbal predication similarly implies the presence of a grammatical word (often called "selector"; see chapter 6) morphologically distinct from the verb but expressing semantic distinctions typically expressed through verb morphology, both the selector and the verb may be inflected for subject, and object markers may be attached to the selector (Mous 2006).

In Somali, verbs are inflected for subject, but in independent clauses, subject markers also occur attached to "mood classifiers" and focus markers, and in subordination, subject markers attach to the complementizer *ín* 'that' and to noun phrases modified by relative clauses.

In the East Chadic languages Lele (Frajzyngier 2001) and East Dangla (Shay 1999), subject pronouns cliticize on complementizers.

In the Omotic language Zayse (Hayward 1990), the sentences having focused constituents are characterized by the attachment of the clitic copula to the head of the focused phrase, and if the focused constituent is not the subject, a clitic subject pronoun obligatorily follows the copula functioning as a focus marker.

Another interesting case in point is Ewe. With ordinary transitive verbs, the object pronouns of Ewe are necessarily attached to the verb, but in the construction of verbs like 'give,' the noun phrase representing the thing given precedes the noun phrase representing the recipient, and the recipient can be represented by an object pronoun attached to the last word of the noun phrase representing the thing given, as in the following example (Felix Ameka, p.c.):

(7) a. é-ná   tsi-i
       S3SG-give   water-O3SG
       '(S)he gave him/her water'

   b. é-fíá   dɔ-ɛ
       S3SG-show   work-O3SG
       '(S)he taught him/her a profession'

   c. é-fíá   teΦé   áɖé-e
       S3SG-show   place good   INDEF-O3SG
       '(S)he showed him/her a nice place'

4.2.3.4   Distinctions in the shape of subject and object markers   Subject and object markers sharing the same semantic features may have identical phonological forms. However, in a number of African languages, even among those that have no case distinction between subjects and objects, subject markers differ from the corresponding object markers, at least in some persons. For example, in Tswana (as in many other Bantu languages), subject markers and object markers have distinct segmental forms in the first person singular, in the second person singular, and in noun class 1; in the first and second person plural, and in the classes other than class 1, they have the same segmental form, but their tonal properties are always very different.

In African languages, differences in the phonological shape of pronominal markers sharing the same semantic features almost always have a straight-forward explanation in terms of the traditionally recognized syntactic functions subject and object.

Anywa and other Western Nilotic languages with ergative properties appear to be an exception to this general rule. As shown by Reh (1996), Anywa has two sets of pronominal markers attached to verbs, but there is no one-to-one correspondence between these two sets and the syntactic functions subject and object, and Reh analyzes the correspondence as a case of split ergativity: in certain constructions, indexation follows an ergative pattern, with prefixes used to represent A, and suffixes used to represent S or O, whereas in other constructions, the same suffixes are used to represent S or A, resulting in an accusative pattern. The same holds for Päri. Some Kordofanian languages have fused S and O verbal prefixes, e.g., Orig *Musa adi-fagna* (Musa 3SG.1. SG-beat) 'Musa beat me' (Schadeberg & Elias 1979).

The active pattern (in which intransitive verbs divide into two classes, the intransitive subject markers being identical with the subject markers of transitive verbs in one class, and with the object markers in the other) and the direct/inverse pattern (in which a given combination of persons in transitive verb morphology is encoded without taking into account the respective roles of the arguments referred to) are also very rare in Africa; it has however been proposed to recognize an indexation system of the direct/inverse type in Maasai (Payne et al. 1994), and indexation systems showing features that can be analyzed as pointing to an active pattern have been signaled in the Saharan languages Berti and Beria, in the Mande language Loma, and in some Berber languages (König 2004a).

4.2.4   Special treatment of indefinite or non-referential objects

Several African languages treat indefinite or non-referential objects differently from definite or referential ones. The distinction may concern case marking (in Haro, only definite objects take the accusative suffix; see Woldemariam 2004) or indexation (in Swahili, definite objects trigger the presence of an object marker attached to the verb). Alternatively, the verb stem may be modified, as in the Nilotic language Bari (Spagnolo 1933). In the following example, if the object is left out in sentence (a), the sentence means 'I cooked it'; if the object is left out in sentence (b), the meaning is 'I was cooking / I cooked'; as Spagnolo (1933: 138) has put it, "the thought is on the verb" in such clauses, which means that the complement simply specifies the kind of cooking involved:

(8) a. nan   a   dɛr   sukuri
       1SG   PERF   cook   chicken
       'I cooked the chicken'
    b. nan   a   dɛr-ja   sukuri
       1SG   PERF   cook-DETR   chicken
       'I cooked a chicken'

This use of a detransitivizing derivation (antipassive) in order to avoid indefinite (or non-specific) objects is common in languages that have a coding of core syntactic roles of the ergative type; according to Miller and Gilley (2001: 42–3), this function of the antipassive is attested with some verbs in Shilluk.

By contrast, systematic incorporation of non-referential objects is not common in African languages. However, some African languages have productive incorporation or incorporation-like mechanisms, in particular with indefinite, non-referential or generic nouns. Sasse has described interesting degrees of incorporation in three Eastern Cushitic languages, Dullay, Dhaasanac (Dasanetch), and Boni. In all three Cushitic languages the mechanism of noun incorporation is to "serve the tendency towards a clear distinction of discourse prominence" (Sasse 1984b: 255).

4.2.5   *The status of the "indirect object" (or "dative")*

In the preceding sections, the properties of subjects and objects have been discussed with reference to prototypical transitive verbs, i.e. verbs that have two arguments to which they assign the roles of agent and patient. In this section, we examine the grammatical organization of the valency of verbs with an argument frame similar to that of *give*.

We first draw a distinction between primary and secondary verbs of giving. Primary verbs of giving are verbs that can enter an argument frame of the type *giver – given – recipient* (whatever the morphosyntactic coding of this frame may be) without necessitating a morphological marking, or the addition of another verb in a serial construction.

Many African languages have a very limited set of primary verbs of giving, which implies a wide use of applicative affixes, or of applicative periphrases, in

order to use basically bivalent verbs with an argument frame similar to that of
give. For example, in many African languages, the equivalent of *write* is
strictly bivalent, and the only way to encode a possible recipient (*write
something to somebody*) is to use the applicative form of this verb, as in
Tswana (9), or to use an applicative periphrasis in which a strictly bivalent verb
meaning *write* forms a so-called serial construction with another verb whose
basic meaning is *give*, as in Baule (10).

(9) a. kì-kwálá   lòkwálɔ̀
    S1SG-write:TAM   11:letter
    'I'm writing a letter'

   b. kì-kwálɛ́lá   màlómɛ́   lùwálɔ̀
    S1SG-write:APPL:TAM 1:uncle:1SG 11:letter
    'I'm writing a letter to my uncle'

(10) a. kòfí   klèlì   flúwá
     Kofi   write:PERF letter
     'Kofi wrote a letter'

   b. kòfíá   klèlì   flúwá   mànnìn   kuàjó
     Kofi   write:PERF letter   give:PERF Kuajo
     'Kofi wrote a letter to Kuajo'

In languages that use applicative derivation to incorporate a recipient or a
beneficiary into the argument frame of verbs that do not include such a participant in their basic argument frame, secondary verbs of giving are derived
verbs whose construction is identical to that of a non-derived verb meaning
'give.' For example, in Tswana, *kwálélá*, applicative form of *kwálá* 'write,' has
the same construction as the non-derived verb *fá* 'give.'

Serializing languages tend to code events involving three participants by
means of combinations of two verbs (see section 4.3.6). However, in African
languages commonly considered as typical serializing languages, it is generally possible to identify a verb meaning 'give' in a construction that involves
no other verb, and in which the argument fully assimilated to the patient of
typical transitive verbs is the recipient. This verb 'give' commonly functions
also as the second term of serial constructions in which it takes a unique
complement representing a recipient or a beneficiary, and the serial construction in which a verb 'give' combines with a verb 'take' is synonymous
with the ditransitive construction of 'give'; this is consistent with the existence
of serial constructions in which the patient of typical transitive verbs is introduced by a verb whose meaning in single-verb constructions is 'take' (Lord
1993). This is illustrated by the following example from the Kwa language
Kposo (Eklo 1987):

(11) a. kúmá   á-ká   kɔ̄kʊ́   ìtùkpá
         Kuma   S3SG:TAM-give   Koku   goat
         'Kuma gave Koku a goat'

    b. kúmá   á-jɔ̄   ìtùkpá   ká   kɔ̄kʊ́
         Kuma   S3SG:TAM-take   goat   give   Koku
         'Kuma gave Koku a goat'

    c. kúmá   á-ɰè   ɛ̀gà   ká   kɔ̄kʊ́
         Kuma   S3SG:TAM-lend   money   give   Koku
         'Kuma lent money to Koku'

The distinction between primary and secondary verbs of giving proves to be useful for analyzing the situation of languages in which the existence of such a distinction is not at first sight obvious. For example, in the Chadic language Hausa, the verb *baà* 'give' (12) very clearly has a construction in which the recipient is treated exactly the same as the patient of typical transitive verbs:

(12) a. yaa   baà   audù   àbinci
         S3MSG:TAM   give   Audu   food
         'He gave food to Audu'

    b. yaa   baa-nì   àbinci
         S3MSG:TAM   give-O1SG   food
         'He gave me food'

By contrast, the other verbs of giving (or verbs of transfer in constructions involving a recipient) as in (13), have a construction currently analyzed as one in which the recipient is the complement of a preposition *wa/mV-* (where *V* represents an underspecified vowel):[8]

(13) a. yaa   kaawoo   wa   audù   àbinci
         S3MSG:TAM   bring   to   Audu   food
         'He brought food to Audu'

    b. yaa   kaawoo   mi-nì   àbinci
         S3MSG:TAM   bring   to-1SG   food
         'He brought food to Audu'

It has been said above that in most African languages there is no difficulty in recognizing the traditional notions of subject and object. By contrast, African languages (at least among those belonging to certain families) provide considerable evidence against the hypothesis of the universality of a third core grammatical relation, called "indirect object" or "dative", typically encoding the recipient of transfer verbs.

The traditional notions of "indirect object" or "dative" apply without difficulty to languages in which nouns have case variations, and the thing given is typically represented by a noun in the same case as the patient of prototypical two-argument verbs, whereas the noun representing the recipient stands in a more or less specialized dative case. This situation can be observed in Omotic languages like Maale:[9]

(14) ʔiini   ʃooc'-atsi-m   goys'-o   ɗaww-é-ne
     3MSG:SUBJ guest-M:ABS-DAT   road-ABS   show-PERF-POS:DECL
     'He showed the road to the guest'

Similarly, specialized dative prepositions are found in some Chadic languages, including Gidar (Central Chadic) and Lele (East Chadic) (Frajzyngier 2001).

Alternatively, the noun phrase representing the thing given can be represented by the same object markers as the patient of prototypical two-argument verbs, whereas special dative markers are used to encode the recipient, as in the Berber language Kabyle (Naït-Zerrad 2001):

(15) a. yefka   weqcic   aksum   i   wemcic
        give:S3MSG   boy:ANN   meat   to   cat:ANN
        'The boy gave the meat to the cat'

     b. yefka-t   weqcic   i   wemcic
        give:S3MSG-O3MSG   boy:ANN   to   cat:ANN
        'The boy gave it (the meat) to the cat'

     c. yefka-yas   weqcic   aksum
        give:S3MSG-D3MSG   boy:ANN   meat
        'The boy gave the meat to it (the cat)'

     d. yefka-yas-t   weqcic
        give:S3MSG-D3MSG-O3MSG boy:ANN
        'The boy gave it (the meat) to it (the cat)'

Such situations are particularly common among European languages, but there are other possible ways of organizing the construction of such verbs. A second possibility is to treat the recipient in a way that does not distinguish it clearly from the oblique arguments of, for example, motion verbs. A third possibility (marginally attested in English: *present somebody with something*) is to fully assimilate the recipient to the grammatical role object (i.e. to treat it in exactly the same way as the patient of prototypical transitive verbs), and to treat the thing given as an oblique, as in the following example from the Benue-Congo language Yoruba:

(16) a. òjó   fún   iyá   ní   owó
        Ojo   give   mother   PRE   money
        'Ojo gave mother money'

b. òjó   fún-un   ní   owó
Ojo   give-O3SG   PRE   money
'Ojo gave her money'

So-called "double object constructions" represent a fourth possibility, in which both the thing given and the recipient are represented by noun phrases that show at least some object-like characteristics, and no obvious indication of an oblique status, as in the following example from Tswana:

(17) a. kì-fílé   bàná   lùkwálɔ̀
S1SG-give:TAM   2:child   11:lamp
'I've given the lamp to the children'
b. kì-lú-bà-fílè
S1SG-O3:11-O3:2-give:TAM
'I've given it to them (the lamp)'

The analysis of "double object constructions" shows that the two objects always differ in the extent to which they possess the properties that characterize prototypical objects of transitive verbs. In some languages (e.g. Tswana) the difference is minimal, in other languages (e.g. Swahili) one of the two objects has very few objectal properties, but what is crucial is that the noun phrase representing the recipient is always more object-like than that representing the thing given, and can therefore conveniently be called "primary object".

This suggests the following typology (Creissels forthcoming):

Type I: the argument that fully assimilates to the patient of prototypical transitive verbs is the thing given, with a possible subdivision between type Ia (the recipient is treated as an oblique) and type Ib (there exists a third core grammatical relation –"dative object"– typically used to encode the recipient);

Type II: the argument that fully assimilates to the patient of prototypical transitive verbs is the recipient, with a subdivision between type IIa (the thing given is treated as an oblique) and type IIb (the noun phrase representing the thing given shows no obvious indication of an oblique status, and has at least some object-like properties – "double object construction").

Among European languages, type I is dominant, and the subtype Ib (in which the recipient typically has properties that distinguish it both from the direct object and from obliques) is not uncommon, which explains the tendency of many grammarians to postulate the universality of the "indirect object." By contrast, type I is not particularly common in Africa as a whole, and clear cases of the subtype Ib are particularly uncommon in some families.

Among Niger-Congo languages, type Ia (in which the thing given is fully assimilated to the patient of prototypical transitive verbs, and the recipient clearly has an oblique status) is not rare (it is particularly common in Mande languages), but we know of no Niger-Congo language whose case marking or indexation system would justify the introduction of a grammatical relation "indirect object" or "dative" similar to that traditionally recognized in descriptions of European languages. In most language families included in the Niger-Congo phylum, especially among Bantu and Atlantic languages, type IIb ("double object constructions") is predominant.

The situation is different in other phyla, particularly among Afroasiatic languages. Double object constructions exist for example in Somali (Saeed 1987: 8), but among Afroasiatic languages, constructions of type I (including the variant Ib, in which the recognition of a syntactic role "dative" is fully justified) are also very common.

In Hausa (see (13) above), the dative is introduced by a special preposition and precedes the direct object (if there is one), and a separate set of dative pronouns can be recognized. More generally, Chadic languages have a grammatical role "dative" both distinct from direct object and obliques, with variations in the way individual Chadic languages distinguish it from other grammatical roles (use of specialized adpositions, distinct sets of dative pronouns, or other devices).

Berber languages have indexation systems including special dative markers (see (15)).

Omotic languages tend to use a separate case distinction for the argument expressing a recipient, benefactive or malefactive. A specialized dative case exists also in some Cushitic languages (e.g. Oromo).

Several non-Niger-Congo languages have an interesting type of mixed construction belonging to type I as regards case marking, but to type II as regards indexation: object markers identical to those representing the patient of prototypical transitive verbs, when attached to verbs with an argument frame similar to that of 'give,' exclusively refer to the recipient, but the noun phrase representing the recipient receives a distinct dative (or dative-allative) case marking. This situation is found in the Saharan language Kanuri, in the Ethio-Semitic language Amharic, and in the Chadic language East Dangla (Shay 1999). In such systems, there is no problem in recognizing a syntactic role "dative," since case marking ensures the distinction between dative and direct object, and indexation ensures the distinction between dative and obliques.

4.3   The verb

4.3.1   Presence vs. absence of a verbal inflection, and the use of grammatical words expressing the same types of distinctions as verbal inflection

In most languages, at world level as well as at the level of the African continent, the verb has an inflection considerably more complex than that of any other category. The verb may have a rich inflection system even in languages in which nominal inflection proper does not exist, in the sense that all of the grammatical morphemes operating at noun-phrase level have the status of phrasal affixes (or "clitics," in more traditional terminology) rather than that of affixes of the head noun. This situation is common for example among Kwa languages.

Languages really devoid of verbal inflection are very rare in Africa, but the available documentation on African languages may be misleading, since in many descriptions of West African languages, as already mentioned in connection with subject markers, verb prefixes are wrongly identified as free morphemes, with the result that languages with an entirely prefixal verb inflection (which is a fairly common situation among West African languages) are wrongly presented as languages devoid of verbal inflection.

An interesting case is that of languages in which the word constituted by the lexical verb and its inflectional affixes cannot be used alone (or only in very restricted conditions) and must be accompanied by a grammatical word expressing semantic distinctions that most languages tend to encode through verb morphology (TAM and polarity distinctions, argument indexation). Such languages are characterized by a complementarity (or sometimes redundancy) between the distinctions expressed at the level of this grammatical word ("predicative marker," or "selector") and those expressed at the level of the lexical verb. In the borderline case, illustrated by Zarma, all grammaticalized TAM distinctions appear at the level of the "predicative marker," and the lexical verb has no inflection proper.

In Africa, this type of organization of verbal predication is found mainly in two groups of languages:

- In West Africa, it is common among languages that have a constituent order SOVX (such languages are found in a geographically compact area including the languages of the Kru, Kwa, Gur, and Mande branches of Niger-Congo, and Songhay);
- In northeast Africa, it is common in some branches of Cushitic (see chapter 7).

The following example is from the Songhay language Zarma (Oumarou Yaro 1993):

(18) a. muusaa   *na*   feejoo   *wii*
        Moussa   PERF:POS   sheep:DEF   kill
        'Moussa killed the sheep'

    b. muusaa   *mana*   feejoo   *wii*
        Moussa   PF:NEG   sheep:DEF   kill
        'Moussa did not kill the sheep'

c. muusaa   *ga*   feejoo   *wii*
   Moussa   IPF:POS   sheep:DEF   kill
   'Moussa will kill the sheep'

d. muusaa   *si*   feejoo   *wii*
   Moussa   IPF:NEG   sheep:DEF   kill
   'Moussa will not kill the sheep'

4.3.2   Types of distinctions expressed through verbal inflection or variations of a grammatical word that obligatorily accompanies the verb

The meanings most commonly encoded through verbal inflection are argument indexation, TAM distinctions, and negation.[10]

Argument indexation has already been dealt with in section 4.2. Verb inflection systems in which argument indexation is expressed through variations of the verbal word, but TAM distinctions are expressed exclusively through auxiliaries or adverbs, are very rare; however, such systems are attested in Sara languages (Central Sudanic).

The systems of TAM distinctions expressed through verbal inflection vary in such a way that it does not seem possible to define an African type of TAM system, or even types that would characterize languages spoken in particular areas or belonging to particular families.

The TAM markers do not necessarily constitute one domain. In particular, in Chadic languages, modality markers may be coded differently from tense and aspectual markers. The deontic modality is often coded on the verb, while the tense and aspectual markers may be coded on the verb or before and/or after the verb. In some Chadic languages they are morphologically fused with subject pronouns (e.g. Hausa). In other languages, they may occur in clause-initial position (before subject pronouns), and in some languages, they may occur before and after the verb (e.g. in the Central Chadic language Mina).

Systems of verbal inflection expressing negation are particularly common in Africa. Very often, negation markers and TAM markers fuse together strongly, and the TAM distinctions expressed by negative verb forms may be different from those expressed by positive verb forms.

Among semantic distinctions less commonly expressed through verbal inflection, a remarkable feature of African languages is the relatively high proportion of systems of verbal inflection that directly express distinctions relating to various types of focus phenomena, or interfere with other focus-marking devices. Such systems seem to be very rare outside Africa. They are found in a number of languages belonging to various branches of the Niger-Congo phylum (Atlantic, Benue-Congo, etc.), and in Cushitic. For example, the Atlantic language Wolof uses distinct verbal inflections to express focalization of the verb, of the subject, or of a term of the construction of the verb other than the subject.

(19) a. gis na   yaayam
     see TAM:S3SG   mother:3SG
     'He saw his mother'
   b. moo   gis   yaayam
     FOC:S3SG   see   mother:3SG
     '*He* saw his mother'
   c. yaayam   la   gis
     mother:3SG   FOC:S3SG   see
     'He saw *his mother*'
   b. dafa   gis   yaayam
     FOC:S3SG   see   mother:3SG
     'He *saw* his mother'

Somali also has a prominent focus-marking system, as shown, for example, by Tosco (2003). Main declarative (positive) sentences in Somali receive focus marking by way of one of the two focus markers, *baa* and *ayaa*, which immediately follow noun phrases. When a noun phrase is not focalized in such a sentence, a "mood classifier" *waa* is used. *Waa* is basically a positive declarative mood classifier, and its verbal-focus effect is ascribed to the absence of nominal focus marking in sentences in which it occurs; see also Creissels (1996) on Tswana.

The exact extent of this phenomenon is however difficult to evaluate. This is not only a question of documentation. It seems common that the same morphological devices are used to focalize the choice of a particular verbal lexeme and to put emphasis on the assertive value of declarative sentences. Moreover, focalization may interfere with operations on valency or with tense/aspect in a way that sometimes makes it difficult to identify the precise nature of morphemes involved in the expression of such distinctions. In particular, Güldemann (2003b) presents evidence for a relation between verb focus and progressive aspect in Bantu, and the possibility of a relation between verb focus and antipassive should perhaps be considered.[11]

4.3.3 Auxiliary verbs and compound verb forms

Complex verb forms of the type commonly encountered in European languages (i.e. those consisting of an auxiliary verb and a dependent or nominalized form of another verb) are quite common in African languages too, and comparative data very often suggest that TAM markers that synchronically have the status of inflectional morphemes originate in ancient auxiliary verbs (future markers originating in an auxiliarized form of a verb 'come' or 'go' are particularly common in African languages). Auxiliary verbs are also a plausible source of grammatical words obligatorily accompanying the verb and expressing meanings commonly encoded through verb morphology.

A very general characteristic of Niger-Congo and Nilo-Saharan languages is that they tend to have auxiliary verbs expressing meanings commonly taken up by adverbial expressions in European languages, i.e. auxiliary verbs with meanings such as 'to do first,' 'to do again,' 'to do often,' 'to have previously done,' 'to have done the day before,' 'not to have done yet,' etc., as illustrated by the following examples from Tswana.

(20) a. kʊ́nʊ́pɔ̀   é   í-tsʰílà   ʊ́-qʰáʊ́χ-ílè
        9:button   9:DEM   S3:9-live   S3:9-tear-ANT
        'This button is always torn'

    b. rì-àtìsà   χʊ̀-jà   kérèké-ŋ̀
        S1P-increase   INF-go   9:church-LOC
        'We often go to church'

    c. ʊ̀-rát-ílé   χʊ̀-tʰùbà   pìtsá jàmí
        S2SG-like-ANT   INF-break   9:pot 9:my
        'You nearly broke my pot'

    d. púlá   í-léts-ì   í-nà
        9:rain   S3:9-spend the night-ANT   S3:9-fall (rain)
        'It rained last night'

    e. tsʰímʊ̀   é   í-(tɬáà-)tsʊ́χ-á   í-lìŋwá
        9:field   9:DEM   S3:9-(FUT-)rise   S3:9-plough:PSV
        'This field will be ploughed tomorrow'

    f. tsʰímʊ́   é   í-dík-ílè   í-lìŋwá
        9:field   9:DEM   S3:9-surround-ANT   S3:9-plough:PSV
        'This field was cultivated last year'

Similarly, there are a number of verbs in various Chadic languages whose function is to code the manner and the temporal characteristics of an event, such as 'spend the day doing,' 'keep on doing,' 'start doing,' 'cease, stop doing,' 'finish doing,' 'do a lot.'

A typical feature of languages in northeastern and north-central Africa is the use of compound verb formations that consist of an invariable non-verbal component determining the lexical meaning of the compound, and of an inflected form of a verb with the independent lexical meaning 'say' or 'do' functioning in such compounds as a mere bearer of inflectional marking (cf. Dimmendaal, this volume chapter 9, for further details). A similar use of a verb with the meaning 'say,' restricted however to combinations with ideophones, is sporadically found in Niger-Congo languages, as in the following example from Tswana; see Creissels (2003a) for more details.

(21) a. ú-nè   à-tsájá   ḿ-mídí   à-ú-rí   χ̀ùrù̀ fá   fàts^hí
         S3:1-AUX   S3:1:   3:maize   S3:1:SEQ-   IDEO PRE   on the
                      SEQ-take   O3:3-say   ground
        'He then took the maize and poured it out on the ground'

     b. nóts^hí   já-mù-rì   pó   mó   tsèbé-ɳ̀
         9:bee   S3:9:SEQ-   IDEO   PRE   ear-LOC
                     O3:1-say
        'The bee stung him on the ear"

4.3.4 Dependent verb forms

African languages commonly have dependent verb forms morphologically distinct from those that fulfill the predicate function in independent clauses. Many of these forms have uses broadly similar to those of the non-finite verb forms encountered in European languages (infinitives, participles, gerundives).

In addition to that, Niger-Congo languages often have special "consecutive" or "sequential" verb forms that characterize non-initial clauses in sequences of clauses reflecting a chronological presentation of events, and such dependent verb forms are also attested in Nilo-Saharan languages. The following example is from Tswana:

(22) lìpòdísí   lí-ts^hwérí   máχòdù   lá-à-tséɲá
     5:policeman   S3:5-catch:ANT   6:thief   S3:5:SEQ-O3:6-put

     dìhákàbóí   lá-à-ísá   tùróŋkóɳ̀
     10:handcuff   S3:5:SEQ-O3:6-go:CAUS   9:jail:LOC
     'The policeman caught the thieves, put them in handcuffs, and took them to the jail'

A common clause-chaining strategy of Afroasiatic languages in Ethiopia as well as of Nilo-Saharan languages to the west of this region (with an extension into Chad) is the use of so-called converbs in non-final clauses. These verb forms usually have a reduced system of inflectional morphology. Thus, in Maale, converbs lack the inflectional features that characterize independent verb forms (Amha 2001):

(23) ʔìzì   mís'-ó   tik'-áʔʔo makiin-aa c'aan-é-ne
     3MSG:SUBJ   tree-ABS   cut-CNV   car-LOC   load-PERF-POS:DECL
     'Having cut the wood he loaded it on a car'

Dependent verb forms such as the converb in this Maale example are "non-finite" in the sense that they lack some inflectional features characterizing the independent verb forms of the same language, but dependent verb forms with an inflection showing the same distinctions as that of independent verb forms arc attested. This is the case with the sequential form in the Tswana example above, and Tswana has another set of strictly dependent but morphologically finite verb forms, used in temporal subordinate clauses.[12]

Many Chadic languages have two tense/aspect systems, where there may exist two perfective, two imperfective, and two progressive/habitual aspects, as well as two future tenses. One system codes pragmatically independent clauses, i.e. clauses that can be interpreted on their own, and the other codes pragmatically dependent clauses, i.e. clauses that must be interpreted in connection with another clause. Pragmatically independent clauses are morphologicaly marked because they occur less frequently than pragmatically dependent clauses. Pragmatically independent clauses typically involve affirmative clauses, yes/no questions, matrix clauses in complex sentences, and comments on topicalized constituents. Pragmatically dependent clauses may involve specific questions (wh-questions), comments on focused elements, temporal sequential clauses, and relative clauses, i.e. comments on the head of the relative clause. Some negative clauses may also be coded as pragmatically dependent.

The use of bare verbs in contexts in which most languages tend to use morphologically marked dependent verb forms is typically found in languages commonly identified as "serializing" languages (see section 4.3.6), but also in Wolof and in many Bantu languages.

4.3.5   Transitivity and morphological coding of operations on verb valency

Verbs used in transitive constructions may be strictly transitive, if their use in intransitive constructions is restricted to elliptical constructions, but they may also have non-elliptical intransitive uses, with two possibilities: the subject of an ambitransitive verb used in an intransitive construction may receive the same semantic role as the subject of the same verb in a transitive construction (as in English eat: We ate fish vs. We ate slowly), or it may receive a role identical or similar to that of the object of the transitive construction (as in English break: He broke the plate vs. The plate broke). Both types of ambitransitivity are widely attested in African languages, and some language families may have marked preferences for one type or the other, but none can be said to be predominant for Africa as a whole. For example, the Mande language Bambara represents the extreme case of a language in which virtually every transitive verb has the behavior illustrated above by break, whereas the type of ambitransitivity illustrated by eat is almost non-existent in this language; by contrast, in Tswana, the type of ambitransitivity illustrated by *break* is almost non-existent, but transitive verbs generally accept intransitive uses of the type illustrated by *eat*.

Many Niger-Congo languages have rich systems of verb affixes encoding operations on verb valency, i.e. operations that modify the correspondence between semantic roles and grammatical relations. A particularly rich system is found in Wolof: Nouguier (2002) identifies ten verbal suffixes productively used in Wolof to code operations on valency, some of them being used to code two or more different types of operations. A typical Niger-Congo system of morphologically marked valency changes includes passive, reciprocal, decausative,[13] causative, and applicative derivations. In addition to that, reflexive object markers commonly tend to acquire a variety of uses that cannot be reduced to the notion of coreference, which may justify reanalyzing them as middle-voice markers.

The typologically salient feature of Niger-Congo systems are:

- the existence of distinct reciprocal and decausative forms (cross-linguistically, reciprocal and decausative meanings are commonly expressed by middle-voice forms that by themselves have a more general and abstract meaning);
- a particularly wide use of applicatives and, in particular, of obligatory applicatives:[14] in typical Niger-Congo systems, several semantic types of complements that crosslinguistically tend to be treated as obliques can occur only as (direct) objects of applicative verb forms, and the semantic interpretation of an applicative construction entirely depends on the lexical meaning of the verb and of the noun involved in the construction, since by itself, the applicative marker gives no clue to the semantic role of the object it licenses, as in the following example from Tswana:

(24) a. kì-bíd-ítsé   bàná / kì-bíd-ítsé   ŋákà
        S1SG-call-ANT   2:child S1SG-call-ANT   9:doctor
        'I have called the children' / 'I have called the doctor'

    b. kì-bíl-éd-ítsé   bàná   dìdʒɔ́
        S1SG-call-APPL-ANT   2:child   8/10:meal
        'I have called the children to eat'

    c. kì-bíl-éd-ítsé   bàná   ŋákà
        S1SG-call-APPL-ANT   2:child   9:doctor
        'I have called the doctor for the children'

In the other phyla, morphological coding of changes in the valency of the verb is also quite common. In particular, applicatives are widespread all over Africa (applicatives are found for example in Ik, Amharic, etc.). Their identification is most of the time straightforward, but in some cases their status from the point of view of a general typology of valency-changing devices is problematic, because they depart more or less from the prototype. For example, in Ik, the term licensed by the applicative derivation is treated as an oblique rather than a direct object; similarly, in North Khoisan languages, the presence of valency-external noun phrases may trigger a morphological marking on the verb, as in typical Niger-Congo obligatory applicatives, but this morphological marking may be triggered by the presence of terms that do not show the characteristics of objects (Güldemann & Vossen 2000). In Tswana, applicative derivation may change the semantic role of locative complements of motion verbs without changing the construction from a formal point of view (see section 4.15), or even simply put into focus a locative complement (Creissels 2002), etc. In many languages, the distinction between applicative and causative derivation is not clearcut: some languages, e.g. Wolof (Nouguier 2002), are described as using the same derivatives to code valency operations of the causative and of the applicative type, and in some others, derived forms of the verb currently identified as applicatives may have causative-like uses, e.g. in Kanuri (Hutchinson 1981), and vice versa, e.g. in Tswana (Creissels 2002).

In some Chadic languages, verbal morphology codes distinctions of "point of view" and/or "goal orientation." The representation of an event from the point of view of the subject invites the listener to consider what effects the event has on the subject, without indicating any specific effects. The subject in such a representation is in the scope of the event, which implies that no other argument (including the object) is there. The representation of an event from the point of view of the object means that it is the object that is in the scope of the result of the event. In some Chadic languages (e.g. Hausa), the point of view of the subject is the default point of view for the majority of transitive verbs, and putting the object in the scope of the result of an event involves the use of special morphological markers. Goal orientation in Hausa can be illustrated by the distinction between the verb 'to fall' (unmarked form) and 'to fall onto something' marked by the goal-oriented marker -a added to the verb. It appears that in Gidar, the category of goal orientation is in contrast with the point of view of the subject: the distinction between 'eat' and 'eat something' is marked by the suffix -a. In the following example from Gidar, the omission of the marker -a in sentence (b) codes the event from the point of view of the subject, and the addition of -a in sentence (d) codes object orientation; specific object coding on the verb, as in sentence (e), implies that the object is known, determined by deictics, or present in the speech environment:

(25) a. kə̀-vr-á-n-k   dʼə̀fá
      S2PL-hit-OBJOR-PL-PERF   man
      'You hit somebody'

b. kə̀-vrə́-n-kà
   S2PL-hit-PL-PERF
   'You hit'

c. à-kkə̀ɗ-kà
   S3M-polish-PERF
   'He polished'

d. à-kkə̀ɗ-á-n-kà
   S3M-polish-OBJOR-PL-PERF
   'They polished something'

e. à-kkə̀ɗ-ə́-kà
   S3M-polish-O3M-PERF
   'He polished it (M)'

It is likely that in some languages morphemes that are not currently analyzed as valency operators attached to the verb should perhaps be reanalyzed.
For example, Somali grammars mention the existence of four "prepositions"
that "differ from English prepositions in not being next to the noun they
govern but placed before the verb, regardless of the position of their noun"
(Saeed 1987), which suggests the possibility of reanalyzing these
"prepositions" as obligatory applicative markers. In Amharic, prepositions
have been incorporated into the verb, and thus can be analyzed as having
given rise to applicative suffixes (Amberber 2000). However, the analysis of
incorporated prepositions as applicatives may not be justified, at least in
some languages; moreover, this possibility of analysis largely depends on the
precise way the definition of "applicative" is formulated, so that we prefer to
leave this question open.

In this connection, antipassive is rarely mentioned in description of African
languages, but this question should perhaps be reconsidered too. Not surprisingly, reanalysis of some Western Nilotic languages as having an ergative
coding of core syntactic roles implies the recognition of an antipassive derivation that was not identified as such in previous analyses. Derived forms of
transitive verbs used to avoid the mention of the object of transitive verbs (or of
one of the two objects of ditransitive verbs) are attested even in languages that
show no trace of ergativity in the way they code core syntactic roles, as in the
following example from Wolof (Nouguier 2002).

(26) a. Xaj   bii   du   màtt-e
        dog   DEM   NEG.S3SG   bite-AP
        'This dog does not bite'

     b. Alal   du   jox-e   màqaama
        wealth   NEG.S3SG   give-AP   prestige
        'Wealth does not give prestige'

A possible connection between antipassive and mechanisms currently presented in terms of aspect or verb focus deserves consideration too (see note 11).

4.3.6   Serial verbs

The term *serializing languages* is often loosely used to refer to languages having constructions in which two or more verbal lexemes combine without any overt indication of a dependency between them: none of the verbs is morphologically marked as dependent, and there is no conjunction between them. In such constructions, each verb may show full verbal inflection, but it may also happen that only the first one shows verb inflection, the following ones taking the form of a bare lexeme. In addition to that, languages currently identified as serializing often use combinations of two or more verbal lexemes to encode events that crosslinguistically tend to be encoded by single lexemes.

However, these two features are logically independent, and in the absence of any overt indication of dependency relations in a sequence of verbs is not by itself an indication of the syntactic nature of the sequence. Nothing ensures that the constructions termed "serial verbs" in descriptive grammars are syntactically comparable, even in a single language, which makes the notion of serial verb difficult to use in a typological perspective.[15]

Syntactically, many constructions currently identified as "serial constructions" in descriptive grammars are combinations of clauses that differ from more usual types only superficially (for example, by the fact that a dependent verb takes the form of a bare lexeme instead of showing non-finite morphology). But a notion of serial verb construction including such situations is not very useful, and it is desirable to restrict the definition of "serial constructions" in such a way that it excludes from this notion constructions analyzable as sequences of clauses.

In this narrow sense, "serial constructions" are constructions that involve two or more verbs, but that, taken as a whole, have the behavior of a single predicate, and not that of a construction involving distinct predicates in some dependency relation.[16] Here again, some of these complex predicates do not seem to be very different from the more usual type *auxiliary + main verb*, apart from the fact that the auxiliated verb does not show non-finite morphology. But in some other cases, each verb constituting the complex predicate can combine with its own complement, which calls for another kind of analysis.

Functionally, an interesting case is that of verb sequences in which one of the verbs that constitute the complex predicate can be analyzed as giving the specific lexical meaning of the whole sequence (and assigning specific semantic roles to all NPs present in the construction), the others acting as valency operators that make explicit the general type of semantic role assigned to their complement (e.g. 'take' → instrument or patient, 'give' → recipient or beneficiary). For example, in Yoruba, the mention of a beneficiary in the construction of *rà* 'buy' necessitates the use of an applicative periphrasis in which the beneficiary is constructed as the complement of *fún* 'give':

(27) a. òjó   rà   ìwé   fún   ìyá
        Ojo   buy   book   give   mother
        'Ojo bought a book for mother'

     b. òjó   rà-á   fún-un
        Ojo   buy-O3SG   give-O3SG
        'Ojo bought it for her'

In Africa, this particular type of complex predicate is very common in a restricted area including Kwa languages (e.g. Ewe) and Western Benue-Congo languages (e.g. Yoruba). It has been recognized also in the North Khoisan language !Xun.

Some Chadic languages have a very robust system of serial verb constructions, e.g. Mupun, West Chadic (Frajzyngier 1993), and some languages have verbal extensions, many of which are the result of the reduction of serial verb constructions (e.g. Gidar, Central Chadic). Serial verb constructions involving the expression of spatial relations code the parameters of point of view, manner, and directionality, including the ventive and andative categories. There is no evidence that these constructions arose from the combination of clauses. There is, however, evidence that they arose using a particular verb because it already coded the needed semantic characteristic. Example (25) illustrates the coding of directionality, path, and manner of the event by means a serial verb construction in Mupun.

(28) a. wa   mu   siam   n-tulu
        return   1PL   descend   PRE-home
        'We went down home'

     b. mo   taa   ɗee   n-panksin
        3PL   fall   stay   PRE-Pankshin
        'They stopped over in P'

     c. a   naa   mbi   nə   dəm   kam   nə   lee
        2M   see   thing DEF   go   show   ANAPH   make

        tkə   n-wu   pan   ɗee   ɗi   a   gurum
        OPT   PRE-3M   do a little   become   ANAPH   COP   person
        'You see, the thing shows, it has caused him to become a little wiser
        (lit. he became a man)'

4.3.7   Verbal number

Prototypically, number marking is an inflectional property of nouns (Corbett 2000). However, in many African languages, number does not manifest itself in nominal morphology only, but also in the existence of plural (or "pluractional") verbs expressing frequentative or iterative actions, or actions involving a plurality of participants.

In Chadic languages, verbal number codes plurality of the object, plurality of the subject of intransitive verbs, and plurality of the event. It specifically does not code the plurality of the agent of transitive verbs. In some languages (e.g. Pero, West Chadic) there exists only verbal number, to the total exclusion of nominal number (number distinction does exist, however, in pronouns). See, for example, Frajzyngier (1977) and Newman (1990) for a detailed account of this phenomenon in the Chadic branch of Afroasiatic.

Pluractional marking is an areal feature attested not only in Chadic, but also in a variety of Niger-Congo and Nilo-Saharan languages, including languages where number marking is not a prominent inflectional feature of noun phrases. Compare the Central Sudanic language Ngiti (Kutsch Lojenga 1994: 283–90), where such derived verbs are expressed by way of a stem-initial vowel ʉ or u:

(29) a. ma   mí   ìndrì   nádha
      1SG   SC.AUX   goat   RSM.pull:NOMZ
      'I am pulling one goat, or a group of goats simultaneously'
      (collective plural)

  b. ma   mí   ìndrì   nʉ́dhà
      1SG   SC.AUX   goat   RSM.pull:PL:NOMZ
      'I am pulling several goats one by one (distributive plural), or
      one goat several times'

Very far from the area where verbal plural has been noted as particularly widespread, the North Khoisan language !Xun has roughly fourteen verbs, frequently used, with a suppletive plural form; in !Xun, verbal plural encodes actions involving a plurality of subjects in intransitive clauses, and a plurality of objects in transitive clauses, but not frequentative or iterative actions. Also far from the area where it was first noted, pluractionality occurs in the Bantu languages of Mozambique (Derek Nurse, p.c.).

4.3.8   Evidentiality

A common property of languages in South America as well as South Asia is the morphological coding of the source through which particular information was derived, i.e. whether one knows something because one witnessed it oneself or, instead, whether the information was derived from hearsay.

More recently, it has been shown that similar distinctions occur in African languages as well. Thus, in the Western Nilotic languages, different past tense markers are used when describing a particular event depending on the kind of evidence the speaker has for his proposition (Miller & Gilley forthcoming) on Shilluk, Storch (forthcoming) on Luwo. Compare the following examples from Shilluk (Miller & Gilley 2001: 51–2):

(30) a. ḓyàŋ   á-ˈkwāì   yī   cūl
        cow   PST:E-steal:TR   ERG   Col
        'Col stole the cow (and I saw him do it)'

  b. ḓyàŋ   ú-kwālɔ̂   yī   cūl
        cow   PAST:NonE-steal:TR   ERG   Col
        'Col stole the cow (I didn't see the action, but I've been assured
        that he did it)'

Evidentiality marking as a category of information source may be more widespread in African languages, but its study constitutes a poorly known domain so far.

4.4   The noun and the noun phrase

4.4.1   Nominal classification

Classifier systems of the type encountered in languages of East Asia or of the Pacific are extremely rare in Africa. Pasch (1985) describes a system of genitival classifiers in the Ubangian language Dongo-ko, and Ikoro (1994) describes a system of numeral classifiers in the Cross River language Kana, but these are quite exceptional cases.

By contrast, one commonly finds in Africa noun classification systems in which nouns are divided into several subsets on the basis of their agreement properties with modifiers, verbs, and pronouns. Two types of gender systems are common among African languages:

(a) Systems with two genders mainly based on the sex distinction (masculine vs. feminine) are common in all branches of Afroasiatic;[17] in Nilo-Saharan, they occur in a number of Daju languages, in Nilotic,[18] as well as in Kadu, a group of languages spoken in the Nuba mountains which may belong to Nilo-Saharan, or which, alternatively, constitute a genetic isolate; in Khoisan, such systems are found in Khoe languages and in the isolated languages Sandawe, Kwadi, and Hadza. A third gender similar to the Indo-European neuter has been reported to exist in Eastern Nilotic languages and in Khoe languages.

(b) Another type of gender system, in which the sex distinction plays no role, is encountered in all major branches of the Niger-Congo phylum, with the sole exception of Mande, and in non-Khoe Khoisan languages. In addition to the irrelevance of the masculine vs. feminine distinction, Niger-Congo gender systems, usually referred to as "noun class systems," share the following characteristics:

- The number of genders is relatively high; gender systems with something like twenty genders are not exceptional among Bantu or Atlantic languages.
- The semantic distinction most transparently taken into account in the allocation of nouns to genders is always the *human vs. non-human* or *animate vs. inanimate* distinction.
- Nouns generally include obligatory affixes that indicate to which class they belong.
- Gender and number interfere in a particularly intricate way: it is imposssible to isolate plural markers distinct from gender markers; nouns that belong to the same concord class in the singular often belong to different concord classes in the plural, and conversely; alternate plural forms (with sometimes more or less subtle shades of meaning) corresponding to the same singular form are not uncommon.
- The distinction between inflection and derivation tends to blur, since on the one hand gender cannot be dissociated from number, which is a typically inflectional notion, but on the other hand allocation of nouns to genders largely relies on typically derivational notions or distinctions, such as augmentative, diminutive, concrete vs. abstract, tree vs. fruit, etc., and in deverbative nouns, gender markers straightforwardly express distinctions usually conveyed by distinct derivational morphemes (deverbative nouns in the "human" gender denote agents, etc.).[19]

This particular type of noun classification is mainly bound to a particular phylum rather than to a particular area – and within the area occupied by Niger-Congo languages, its most typical representatives are found among Atlantic languages and Bantu languages, i.e. in two areas very distant from each other.

It has however been said above that noun classification systems of a similar type are found in North and South Khoisan. They share with Niger-Congo systems the existence of important discrepancies between the classification of nouns in the singular and in the plural, resulting in a number of genders higher than the number of classes (for example, in !Xõõ, five classes result in nine different singular–plural groupings). They differ from Niger-Congo systems in that the number of classes in Khoisan never exceeds five. Another difference is that, in Khoisan, class membership generally does not manifest itself in noun morphology, but only in agreement. Among Khoisan languages that have noun class systems, there are variations in the range of syntactic relations governed by agreement (in North Khoisan, there is no agreement on the verb), but similar variations exist in Niger-Congo too.

According to Güldemann (forthcoming, a), !Xõõ has a distinction between intra-sentential and inter-sentential agreement, with five classes distinguished at clause level, but a distinction between animate and inanimate only in inter-sential agreement. The tendency to reorganize inter-sentential agreement on the basis of a binary distinction *human vs. non-human* or *animate vs. inanimate* is very common in Niger-Congo languages too. Even in languages having a noun class system of the Niger-Congo type in its most typical form (e.g. Tswana), the concord rules involving coordinated NPs and long-distance anaphora may neutralize class distinctions, and take into account the distinction *human vs. non-human* or *animate vs. inanimate* only. A radical reorganization of the noun class system along these lines is well attested among Gur languages, as well as in the Cameroonian language Kako, certain Bantu languages in the northeastern DRC, and Pidgin Swahili, as spoken in Nairobi. These languages have in common a reduction of the noun class system to two or three classes, keeping only the distinctions ±human or ±animate.

A few Niger-Congo languages (e.g. Ijo, the Ubangian language Zande, the Mande language Jo) are reported to have a *masculine vs. feminine* distinction, but it concerns only "pronominal" gender and does not manifest itself at the level of the relation between the noun and its modifiers. These languages do not correspond to any grouping definable in genetic or geographic terms: they are sporadically found in several branches of Niger-Congo, in areas very distant from one another.

4.4.2   Referentiality and definiteness

Languages with and without definite articles are encountered in virtually all language families and in all parts of the African continent. This distribution shows that the grammaticalization process "demonstrative → definite article" is very frequent in the evolution of languages,[20] but also that definite articles are relatively unstable: processes leading to their loss or to a change in their status are also frequent. There is a very general tendency for definite articles proper to expand their use to include both definite determination and non-definite referential uses, giving rise to what Greenberg (1978) calls stage II of the definite article. Articles at this stage of their evolution are particularly common in Africa, and the relatively high proportion of African languages with drastically eroded "stage-II articles" is remarkable: in a number of African languages, "stage-II articles" manifest themselves only through a change in tone at the beginning or at the end of the word they are attached to, which results from the erosion of former prefixes or suffixes.

Arabic illustrates the somewhat exceptional case of a language with a definite article affixed to nouns and with agreement in definiteness between the noun and its adjectival modifiers, as in *al-baytu l-kabi·ru* 'the big house,' literally 'the-house the-big.'

On definiteness and referentiality, see also sections 4.2.3.2 and 4.2.4.

4.4.3 Number

In the languages of the world, plural marking restricted to a narrow range of nouns is not uncommon (Corbett 2000), but most African languages have bound morphemes encoding plurality without particular restrictions on the semantic nature of nouns, e.g. on whether noun phrases occupy a relatively high position in the animacy hierarchy.

However, the total lack of plural markers is illustrated by the Western Benue-Congo language Igbo. In this language, the two nouns meaning 'child' and 'person' have suppletive plural forms, but with nouns that are not compounds having 'person' or 'child' as their first formant, plurality can be expressed only by adding numerals or quantifiers such as 'several,' 'a few,' 'many,' etc. Such a situation is found also in some languages of the Chadic family (Gwandara, Pero), but on the whole, it is rather exceptional in Africa.

The same can be said of systems of plural markers restricted to a narrow range of nouns (mainly human and animate), but such a situation is found in Ngiti (Kutsch Lojenga 1994), and in some languages of the Chadic family, e.g. in Masa (see Frajzyngier 1977, 1997).

A common number-marking system attested in a wide range of Nilo-Saharan languages involves a three-way distinction between (i) nouns inflected for number in the plural, (ii) those inflected for number in the singular, and (iii) those taking a number marker both in the singular and the plural (Dimmendaal 2000), as in the Maban language Aiki (Runga), described by Nougayrol (1989):

(31)   Singular   Plural
       àyó-k   àyó   'leaf'
       kɔ̀lɔ́   kɔ̀lɔ̀-t   'snake'
       dɔ̀dí   dɔ́dú   'leg'

Similarly, in the Maa dialect Samburu there is no coherent correspondence between a morphologically unmarked form referring to singular and a derived form corresponding to plural. Instead, each noun gets a prototypical interpretation. With certain nouns the morphologically unmarked form stands for singular, with others for plural. The morphologically unmarked form *l-akír* has the meaning 'stars.' The singulative has to be derived from this morphologically unmarked form by a suffix *-a*: *l-akír-á* 'star'; similarly, *l-pápít* 'hair' and *l-pápít-á* 'hair, a single one.' Furthermore, one and the same suffix indicates with some nouns a singular and with others a plural interpretation, compare *n-kópir-ó* 'feather' and *soit-ó* 'stones.' In 'stones'-*o* functions as a plural marker, in 'feather' as a singulative.

Collective entities such as 'leaf,' 'hair,' or 'tooth,' or words referring to items naturally occurring in pairs, such as 'shoe,' 'eye,' or 'wing,' tend to be morphologically unmarked in the plural in these Nilo-Saharan languages; the corresponding singular expresses an individuated item from a collective or from a pair. This type of singulative marking is also found in Cushitic and Semitic languages.

As regards the use of plural markers not restricted to a small subset of nouns, two opposite tendencies emerge among African languages, which are not bound to any particular genetic or geographical grouping, but rather seem to correlate both with the morphological nature of plural markers and with the presence vs. absence of a gender system:

(a) Languages devoid of a gender system frequently have a single plural marker with the morphological status of a phrasal affix, and such plural markers tend to be used on a "pragmatic" basis, i.e. to be employed only when plurality is both communicatively relevant and not implied by the context, at least in the case of nouns that do not refer to persons. In Corbett's (2000) terms, such languages have a *general/singular vs. plural* rather than *singular vs. plural* distinction.

(b) Languages that have gender generally have a morphologically complex plural marking, characterized by a fusion of gender and number markers, and variations in gender and number manifest themselves through morphemes affixed to the head noun and to (some of) its modifiers, in an agreement relationship. In these languages, plural marking tends to function on a 'semantic' basis, which means that plural markers tend to be present in every noun phrase referring to a plurality of individuals, irrespective of their communicative relevance (in Corbett's terms, such languages tend to have a true *singular vs. plural* opposition).

Extreme cases of morphologically complex number (singular, plural, and collective) marking are encountered in an area including the Eastern Sudanic branch of Nilo-Saharan and all branches of the Afroasiatic phylum.

Among the possible types of number systems presented in Corbett (2000), only the most common ones are well represented among African languages; among the less common types, the following ones are however attested:

(a) A three-way number set-up including dual (singular/dual/plural) for both nouns and pronouns exists only in the Central Khoisan phylum; in the western dialects of the North Khoisan language !Xun there is a trial in addition. In the other language families of Africa, dual is extremely rare, and always restricted to pronouns. Several languages of the Sara-Bongo-Bagirmi subgroup of Central Sudanic and some Chadic languages have a distinct dual form in the first person only.

(b) The Cushitic language Bayso has a general number morphologically distinct from both singular and plural, and the same three-way distinction is found in the Fouta Jalon dialect of Fula, but only for a part of the noun inventory (Corbett 2000).

(c) Bayso also has a paucal, used for reference to a small number of individuals, from two to about six (Corbett 2000). A similar system is attested in the neighboring Omotic language Haro (Woldemariam 2004: 56–62), probably as a result of contact with Bayso.

(d) "Greater plural" is relatively common among Atlantic and Bantu languages, i.e. among the Niger-Congo languages that have the Niger-Congo noun classification system in its most typical form; in these languages, singular and plural are distinguished by class affixes, and some noun stems at least can combine with two distinct class affixes to express a distinction between ordinary plural and "greater plural", as in Southern Sotho *pere* 'horse,' *lipere* 'horses,' *mapere* 'a great many horses.'

4.4.4   Morphological coding of the syntactic role of noun phrases

Variations in the role of a noun phrase as a constituent of a larger construction may bring into play two types of bound morphemes commonly called case affixes:

(a) phrasal affixes, i.e. bound morphemes attached to the first or to the last word of the noun phrase irrespective of the precise nature of this word;[21]

(b) bound morphemes affixed to the head noun and to (some of) its modifiers, in an agreement relationship.

Case systems of type (b) (i.e. systems in which nouns are inflected for case and modifiers agree in case with the noun they modify) have not been reported for any African language to our knowledge.

With case suffixes of type (a), if the noun phrase is head final, case inflections normally appear on the head noun, but can be transferred to a modifier, either because the head noun is absent (i.e. in elliptical phrases), or because the modifier is emphasized and, accordingly, occurs in a non-basic position. Such a system is found in Omotic languages like Maale (Amha 2001). A slightly different system is found in Nilo-Saharan languages like Tama, a language in which possessives and demonstratives precede the noun they modify, whereas other modifiers, such as adjectives, follow the head noun. When these latter occur, the case marker appears on the modifier, as in the following examples, where the accusative marker -$V\eta$ attaches to either the noun or the adjective (Dimmendaal, unpublished data):

(32) a. tòòjíȋ̃ŋ   nùùttùŋó
    children:ACC   S1SG:see:PERF
    'I have seen/saw the children'

b. tòòjù   ìllíìŋ   nùùttùŋó
    children   small:ACC   S1SG:see:PERF
    'I have seen/saw the small children'

Therefore, morphemes analyzable as case affixes in descriptions of African languages are of a type not always easy to distinguish from adpositions, and in current practice, the distinction is not always made in a consistent way. For example, Bambara "postpositions" and Kanuri "case suffixes" exhibit no significant difference in their behavior: both are bound morphemes attached to the last word of a noun phrase, and both exhibit a moderate degree of phonological interaction with their host.

Functionally, a distinction may be drawn between case affixes encoding core syntactic roles (subject/object) and case affixes encoding the semantic role of noun phrases in oblique syntactic role. The first type has been dealt with in section 4.2.2. No significant generalization seems to be possible about the second type: in African languages, as in languages spoken in other parts of the world, case affixes of this type code semantic roles such as instrument, comitative, location, source, or direction; from a syntactic point of view, these roles tend to involve optional extensions of predications, and are commonly coded by adpositions rather than by case affixes. Note however that languages making a wide use of obligatory applicatives (which is rather common among Niger-Congo languages) systematically code some of these roles, not as oblique syntactic roles, but as direct objects of applicative verb forms; not surprisingly, such languages typically lack case affixes and/or adpositions coding the roles in question. Note also that in many African languages, locative affixes or adpositions do not code the distinction between location, source and direction; see section 4.15.

4.4.5   Linkers and construct forms

Postnominal noun modifiers may require the use of a linker immediately to their left, or trigger the use of a special "construct form" or "construct state" of the head noun.

The following example illustrates a system of linkers in Tswana. Internal evidence and comparison with other Bantu languages show that these linkers are former demonstratives that, in the context *noun ... modifier*, have lost their deictic value and have acquired a purely syntactic function. It is characteristic of linkers that they are maintained in elliptical constructions in which the head noun is omitted:

(33) a. dìpúdì   tsé   díntsʰù   tsé   dìqʰúlú   tsé
         8/10:goat   8/10:LINK   8/10:black   8/10:LINK   8/10:big   8/10:LINK

         kí-dì-rékílè-ŋ́
         S1SG-O3:8/10-buy-ANT-REL
         'the big black goats that I bought'

b. <u>tsé</u>   dîntsʰʊ̀   <u>tsé</u>   dìqʰʊ́lʊ́   <u>tsé</u>
   <u>8/10:LINK</u>   8/10:black   <u>8/10:LINK</u>   8/10:big   <u>8/10:LINK</u>

   kí-dì-rékílè-ŋ́
   S1SG-O3:8/10-buy-ANT-REL
   'the big black ones that I bought'

"Multifunction" linkers of the type illustrated by this Tswana example are not common. By contrast, linkers used specifically to introduce postnominal relatives are common throughout Africa; see section 4.14.3.

In the languages that have a construct form of nouns, the construct form may appear in combination with a particular type of modifier only (typically, in combination with genitival modifiers only), or with various types of modifiers. Note that, in genitival constructions, the use of a construct form of the head noun must be carefully distinguished from the obligatory use of possessive affixes attached to the head noun, which is crosslinguistically a much commoner way of marking the genitival relation; see section 4.4.6.

The notion of construct form, traditional in Semitic linguistics, is rarely explicitly mentioned in descriptive grammars of non-Semitic languages, but in fact, morphological variations of nouns governed by the presence of (particular types of) modifiers are found in many African languages that do not belong to the Semitic family, for example Wolof, Tswana, Hausa, or the Cushitic language Iraqw.[22] The following example is from Wolof.

(34) a. fas   wu   ñuul
        horse   CL:LINK   be:black
        'black horse'

     b. suma   nijaay
        1SG   uncle
        'my uncle'

     c. suma   fas-u   nijaay   wu   ñuul
        1SG   horse-CSTR   uncle   CL:LINK   be:black
        'my uncle's black horse'

According to Andersen (2002), construct forms are common in Western Nilotic languages (Dinka, Shilluk, DhoLuo, Päri, and Anywa). In other families, in particular in those included in the Niger-Congo phylum, they seem to be rather sporadic. Note however that in Tswana, the distinction between the absolute form and the construct form of nouns is purely tonal, and it may well be that a similar distinction has been missed in descriptions of other languages.

4.4.6   *The genitival modifier*

It has been mentioned in section 4.4.5 that the genitival construction may involve a special "construct form" of the head noun. The genitival construction may also involve a genitive marker attached to the genitival modifier, or so-called "possessive affixes."

As regards the use of genitive markers, case-marked genitives are relatively common in Africa, even in languages devoid of case contrast between subject and object. By contrast, genitival constructions involving obligatory possessive affixes even in the presence of a noun phrase in genitive function are not very common, but they are found in different language families and in different parts of the African continent, and the same can be said of genitival constructions involving a construct form of the head noun; see section 4.5.

Crosslinguistically, gender–number agreement of the genitival modifier is not very common, but it occurs in the most typical Niger-Congo noun class systems (particularly in Bantu languages).

A number of African languages have more than one possible way of combining a noun with a genitival modifier, most commonly with a distinction in meaning so that the variant with more morphological material (genitive markers or possessive affixes) is used with "non-intimate" (or "alienable") types of relations, and that with less morphological material with "intimate" (or "inalienable") types of relations. As a rule, the inalienable form involves mere juxtaposition. This type of distinction is particularly common in some language groups (e.g. Mande languages), but it is not really bound to particular families or areas.

For example, a distinction between alienable and inalienable possession exists in many Chadic languages. In Lele, when the possessor is nominal, if the possessum is alienable, the order is *possessor possessum-pronoun*, a pronoun coding gender and number of the possessor being suffixed to the possessum (Frajzyngier 2001):

(35) a. kíwé   dìngàw-rò
        leopard   ferocity-3FSG
        'the ferocity of the leopard'

    b. gùmnó   dìngàwr-ìy
        buffalo   ferocity-3MSG
        'the buffalo's ferocity'

When the possessor is nominal, if the possessum is alienable, the order is *possessum–possessor kè-pronoun*:

(36) a. kúlbá   cànìgé   kè-y
        cow   Canige   GEN-3MSG
        'cow of Canige'

b. gìrà   cànigé   kè-y
   dog   Canige   GEN-3MSG
   'dog of Canige'

c. gúrbálò   karma   kè-gè
   cloth   children   GEN-3PL
   'children's clothes'

d. kolo   yé-y   kò-rò
   word   mother-3MSG   GEN-3FSG
   'news of his mother'

4.4.7   The adjectival modifier

We will return with this item in section 4.6.

4.4.8   Noun phrase coordination

In most African languages, the same morpheme serves as a comitative adpo-sition (*with*) and as a noun phrase coordinator with an additive meaning (*and*). The sample of languages used in Stassen's typological study of noun phrase coordination (Stassen 2000) includes a number of African languages, and provides interesting insights on their status in a typology of coordination.

4.5   Adpositions

Most African languages have relatively few monomorphemic words acting exclusively as adpositions, and make a wide use of adposition-like words or expressions that clearly have a nominal or verbal origin. This pattern is widespread, for example, in the Nilo-Saharan phylum, where adpositions derived from nouns frequently serve to specify the search domain for an object ('on top of,' 'underneath'), whereas non-derived adpositions tend to introduce other types of adjuncts, for example phrases introducing semantic roles such as instrument, beneficiary, or recipient.

A feature common to languages that have obligatory applicatives and to languages that have the type of complex predicates presented in section 4.3.6 is that, in comparison with other languages, they make only a very limited use of adpositions, since adpositions typically encode the semantic role of obliques, and both mechanisms result in giving the status of direct objects to various semantic types of complements that in other languages tend to be treated as obliques.[23]

Adpositions derived from nouns (usually referring to body parts) may take pronominal markers identical to the possessive affixes attached to nouns in order to express 'next to / on top of / behind / ... him/her.' Similarly, adpositions derived from verbs may take pronominal affixes reflecting a former mechanism of object indexation on the verb. For example, in Gidar (Central Chadic), the dedicated dative and associative prepositions code the gender and number of the complement noun, which may indicate the verbal origin of both prepositions. An adposition inflected for gender has been signaled in the South Khoisan language !Xõõ, and the Kuliak language Ik has case-inflected adpositions (König 2002). However, on the whole, inflected adpositions seem less widely attested in Africa than in some Eurasian or American language families.

Some languages, e.g. in the Kwa branch of Niger-Congo (see Ameka 2003 on Ewe), have both prepositions and postpositions, each originating from different sources.

4.6   The adjective

The languages of the world greatly differ in the way they treat adjectival concepts (i.e. concepts that tend to be expressed through adjectival lexemes in languages in which the existence and the delimitation of a category "adjective" are not controversial). In principle, one can imagine languages having a class of adjectives whose behavior would be equally distinct from that of verbs and from that of nouns, and some languages (e.g. Japanese, Bambara) stand fairly close to this ideal type, but in most languages, the grammatical behavior of lexemes expressing typically adjectival concepts is more or less similar, and sometimes identical, either to that of nouns, or to that of verbs. See Creissels (2003b) for a general introduction to the question of adjectives in African languages.

In some languages (e.g. Mupun, West Chadic), even if adjectives behave like verbs in predicative constructions, they behave differently from verbs in attributive constructions, and therefore do constitute a separate lexical category (Frajzyngier 1993). A similar situation is found, for example, in Songhay (Creissels 2003b).

Languages do not necessarily treat typically adjectival concepts in a uniform way: some languages (e.g. Baule) use both noun-like adjectives and verb-like adjectives to encode even the most typical adjectival concepts.

Contrary to what is observed in other areas, both languages with a predominance of noun-like adjectives and languages with a predominance of verb-like adjectives are common all over Africa. A number of African languages have a category that consists of a very small number of non-derived adjectives (sometimes less than ten), and that cannot be expanded by derivation from other categories. For example, Igbo is famous for having a class of adjectives consisting of eight members, semantically four pairs of antonyms. In Africa, this situation does not seem to be restricted to particular language families or areas.

In many African languages, true adjectival modifiers (i.e. adjectival modifiers distinct from relativized verbs) have very limited possibilities of expansion: they can combine with single words (adverbs or ideophones) expressing intensity, but cannot be used as the head of adjective phrases similar to those encountered in European languages, in which adjectives take full phrases ("maximal projections") as their complement (as in *a man [proud [of his son]]*, or *a man [ready [to fight]]*). Turkana is however an exception: in this language, adjectives can be expanded with a prepositional phrase (Dimmendaal 1983b: 334–5); this phenomenon may be more widespread, but the literature on this topic is rather scanty.

4.7   Adverbs and ideophones

Among the various types of words traditionally called adverbs, languages often have a productive class of "manner adverbs" mainly derived from adjectives, or adjectives that can be used as verb modifiers to express the same kind of meaning. But in many African languages, the possibility of deriving manner adverbs from other categories, or to use adjectives as verb modifiers, is very limited. There are however exceptions to this generalization. In particular, some Chadic languages have a large class of modifiers that can serve as both adjectives and adverbs, and a common feature of many Chadic languages is the derivation of adverbs through the reduplication of verbs, nouns, and even numerals (e.g. in Mina, Gidar, Central Chadic).

In languages that have only limited possibilities of deriving manner adverbs from adjectives or to use adjectives as manner adverbs, the meaning commonly conveyed by manner adverbs in other languages may be expressed either by nouns in oblique function, or by cognate object constructions (e.g. the equivalent of *He walked slowly* may be something like *He walked with slowness* or *He walked a slow walk*). But there is also considerable overlap between the role fulfilled by manner adverbs in European languages and that fulfilled in African languages by ideophones.

In descriptions of African languages, ideophones are often recognized as a category of words that does not correspond to any of the categories traditionally recognized in descriptions of European languages. But it may well be that this is a matter of descriptive tradition, rather than a characteristic feature of African languages. Ideophones are generally described as having not only phonological properties that set them apart from other categories (which is commonly viewed as the manifestation of a semantic feature of expressivity), but also distributional characteristics that justify analyzing them as constituting a distinct syntactic category.

There are however important crosslinguistic variations in the distribution of ideophones:

(a) It may happen that the occurrence of ideophones is conditioned by individual verbs or adjectives, each ideophone combining only with a particular verb or adjective (or with a very limited set of verbs/adjectives).

(b) It may happen that all the ideophones combine with a verb meaning 'be,' 'do,' or 'say.' In such combinations, the verb in question loses the meaning and the subcategorization properties it has when it functions by itself as the predicative center of a clause, and the meaning as well as the subcategorization properties of the combination *be/do/say* + *ideophone* are entirely determined by the ideophone.

(c) It may happen that ideophones occur in verbless clauses in which they determine the semantic roles assigned to the noun phrases with which they combine.

The use of 'say' as a light verb introducing ideophones is particularly widespread in Nilo-Saharan and Afroasiatic languages ranging from Ethiopia to Lake Chad, but the same phenomenon is sporadically attested in other areas, e.g. in Wolof, or in Tswana (Creissels 2001; 2003a; 2003b).

For a recent survey, see the studies in Voeltz and Kilian-Hatz (2001).

4.8   Word-order typology

Among the logically possible clause-constituent orders, the most commonly used in the languages of the world with the status of basic constituent order are those in which the subject precedes both the verb and the object, i.e. SOV and SVO. Constituent orders with the verb in first position (VSO and VOS) are less commonly used as basic constituent order, and languages having a basic constituent order with the object in first position are very rare.

The family in Africa with the most important variations in constituent order seems to be Kordofanian. Some Kordofanian languages are recorded with SVO, some with SOV, at least one with VSO, and at least one (Lafofa) with OSV in a series of tense–aspect forms (Thilo C. Schadeberg, p.c.). This is an area that deserves more investigation.

African languages confirm the strong predominance of subject-initial orders (SOV and SVO), and the proportion of verb-initial African languages is roughly comparable to that observed at world level. But in some respects, clause-constituent order is a domain in which the diversity observed at the level of the African continent differs from that observed at world level.

The proportion of African languages with a particularly rigid clause-constituent order is relatively high. Sandawe, a poorly documented language spoken in Tanzania, has been reported to have a relatively flexible clause-constituent order (see Dalgish 1979), but such cases are exceptional in Africa, and none of the well-documented African languages exhibits a "free" clause-constituent order (i.e. a constituent order pragmatically rather than syntactically determined) of the type encountered in Russian, Hungarian, or in some Australian languages.

Syntactically conditioned variations in constituent order are not rare among African languages. Most of the time, they are trigered by the TAM value of the verb or by negation. For example, a few Central Chadic languages (e.g. Hona, Ga'anda) have a different word order in the perfective (verb-initial, VSO) and in the imperfective (SVO), and several Kwa languages have a variation between SVO and SOV with a similar conditioning. For variations in the constituent order triggered by negation, see section 4.12.

The proportion of subject-initial languages (SOV or SVO) taken as a whole is roughly comparable to that observed at world level, but the proportion of languages with a basic SVO order is considerably higher (and the proportion of those with a basic SOV order considerably lower) among the languages of Africa than at world level, at least from a strictly numerical point of view (genetically balanced samples show a higher proportion of verb-final languages).

Heine (1976) argues that a strict dichotomy between an SVO and an SOV type cannot be held in African linguistics, and that a satisfying account of the patterns of word-order variation observed in the African languages requires recognizing four main types, in the definition of which the position occupied by the genitive modifier and by noun phrases in oblique function is more important than that of the object.

Heine's type A corresponds to what is often considered as the "consistent" SVO type. Languages of this type have a basic SVOX clause-constituent order, prepositions and, within the noun phrase, all of the modifiers (including the genitival modifier) follow the head noun. In Africa, this type is found in all phyla, but it is particularly predominant in Niger-Congo. In particular, virtually all Atlantic and Benue-Congo languages belong to it.

A minor type, viewed as a subtype of type A, differs from type A proper in the position of the adjectival modifier: in this subtype, the adjectival modifier precedes the head noun (but all other kinds of modifiers follow it, as in type A proper). This subtype is found in a geographically defineable area including mostly Adamawa-Ubangian languages, but also some Benue-Congo and Chadic languages (in particular Hausa).

Type B is defined by the following characteristics: languages of this type have postpositions; within the noun phrase, the genitival modifier precedes the head noun, but all other kinds of modifiers follow it; at clause level, type B languages may have an SVOX order, or an SOVX order, or both. In other words, this type groups together SVO languages that differ from the "consistent" SVO type in putting the genitival modifier before the noun it modifies, and SOV languages that differ from the "consistent" SOV type by putting the obliques after the verb. The reason for grouping together these two sets of languages and for considering as irrelevant the position of the object is that

(a) in all languages that have both constituent orders SVOX and SOVX in complementary distribution, the genitival modifier precedes the noun it modifies, which makes it possible to explain the emergence of an alternative SOVX order in languages that originally have a rigid SVOX order;[24]

(b) languages with SOVX as the only possible clause constituent order share many more properties with SVO languages than with "true" SOV languages (i.e. consistently verb-final languages): in consistent SOV languages, heads systematically follow their modifiers, whereas in type B languages, most constructions conform to the *head + modifier* order: attributive adjectives follow the noun, auxiliaries precede the main verb, complementizers precede the complement clause, etc.

Type B is widespread in Africa, but relatively uncommon outside the continent. It is mainly located in West Africa, in a geographically compact area including the languages of the Kru, Kwa, Gur, and Mande branches of Niger-Congo and Songhay, but it occurs also sporadically in others parts of the African continent. Mande languages, with their rigid SOVX clause-constituent order, can be viewed as its most typical representatives.

Heine's Type C corresponds to the type known in the literature as VSO. It differs from type A in the position of the subject only. It shares with it the use of prepositions and the position of the noun modifiers (including the genitival modifier) after the noun they modify. Apart from Ancient Egyptian and a few Chadic languages, uncontroversial examples of this type are largely confined to the Eastern Sudanic group of Nilo-Saharan. It has been reported to exist also in the Berber and Semitic branches of Afroasiatic, but this question is somewhat controversial. The point is that there may often be hesitations in identifying the basic constituent order of individual languages as SVO or VSO, due to the fact that languages that have a basic VSO constituent order always have at least SVO as a possible alternative.[25] Reh (1983) describes an exceptional case of a verb-initial language with postpositions.

Type D is mainly found in East Africa, and is particularly uncommon among Niger-Congo languages (Ijo is the only Niger-Congo language belonging to this type). This language type is further discussed elsewhere in this volume (chapter 9).

Note that this typology was elaborated prior to the reanalysis of some Western Nilotic languages as having a coding of syntactic roles of the ergative type (see section 4.2.2 above), and therefore does not take into account recent analyses according to which these languages have a basic OVA order in transitive clauses, and SV in intransitive clauses.

The patterns of word-order variation presented above call also for the following remarks:

(a) In a number of African languages with an SVOX or SOVX clause-constituent order, the genitival modifier is the only type of modifier that precedes the noun, whereas at world level, the tendency of the genitival modifier towards preceding the noun is not particularly strong in comparison with other types of modifiers such as numerals or demonstratives.

(b) In some other languages with an SVOX or SOVX clause-constituent order, the adjectival modifier is the only type of modifier that precedes the noun, which contradicts the fact that in the languages of the world, the adjectival modifier is among the types of modifiers that exhibit a marked tendency towards following the noun they modify.

As regards adpositions, by and large, African data confirm that languages in which the genitival modifier precedes the noun generally tend to have postpositions, whereas those in which the genitival modifier follows the noun tend to have prepositions. The obvious explanation for this correlation is that, historically, the reanalysis of *genitive + noun* constructions is universally an important source of *noun phrase + adposition* constructions. However, the reanalysis of *object + verb* constructions is another widely attested source, and this may explain the development of both postpositions and prepositions, for example, in Kwa languages in which the genitive precedes the noun it modifies, but the object follows the verb; see in particular Heine, Claudi, and Hünnemeyer (1991) and Ameka (2003) for Ewe.

4.9   Non-verbal predications and copulas

Non-verbal predications are commonly encountered in clauses expressing identification, existence, location, or attribution of qualities, but are often restricted to clauses expressing a TAM value identical to that expressed in verbal predication by the verb tenses commonly labeled indicative present. Uncontroversial examples of non-verbal predications are those involving mere juxtaposition of non-verbal words or constituents devoid of any predicative marking (noun phrases, adposition phrases, adverbs), as in the following example from Kanuri:

(37) a. bíntu   féro
     Bintu   girl
     'Bintu is a girl'

   b. músa   káno-lan
     Musa   Kano-LOC
     'Musa is in Kano'

   c. nyí   kúra
     2SG   big
     'You are big'

This type exists also, for example, in the equational clauses of some Chadic languages, but on the whole, it is not particularly frequent in Africa.

Copulas with clearly verbal properties are also attested – for example, in Baule (Kwa), in the Khoisan language !Xun, and in the Kuliak language Ik – but this is not a very common situation either.

By contrast, in clauses expressing identification, existence, location, or attribution of qualities, constructions involving predicative words with very few verbal properties, or even entirely devoid of morphological properties that would identify them as verb forms, are particularly common all over Africa. Certain descriptive traditions tend to analyze such predicative words as irregular verbs, but labels such as "non-verbal predicative" or "non-verbal copula" are also current in descriptions of African languages. For example, *bé* 'be located at' is analyzed as a non-verbal predicative in most recent descriptions of Bambara; this analysis accounts for its limited combinability with TAM morphemes, but its syntactic distribution is clearly that of a verb, and it combines with a past marker; consequently, one may prefer to view it as an irregular verb. Historically, there is in many cases comparative evidence that such predicatives originate in decategorialized verbs, but this is not their only possible source (in particular, they may originate also in demonstratives).

Frajzyngier, Krech, and Mirzayan (2002) propose a correlation between the occurrence of the copula in equational clauses and the form of the modifying construction involving two nouns.

Some African languages also have what may be analyzed as a predicative inflection of nouns. For example, in many Bantu languages, a prefix identical to the verbal prefix expressing agreement with the subject in positive tenses of the indicative is attached to nouns in predicate function. However, in Bantu languages, the predicative inflection of nouns is always limited to person–number(–gender), and possibly negation. A similar phenomenon occurs in the Nilotic language Luo, where it may have originated as part of a more general typological shift towards a Bantu-type of language with noun classes and tense marking on verbs (Dimmendaal 2000). Compare the parallel inflection of verbs and predicative nouns in Luo – data from Tucker (1994):

(38) a. án　　　ráwɛra
　　　1SG　　boy
　　　'I am the boy (e.g. they were looking for)'

　　b. a-ráwɛra
　　　S1SG-boy
　　　'I am a boy'

　　c. a-ŋéyo　　　　dhó-lúô
　　　S1SG-speak　　mouth-Luo
　　　'I speak/know Luo'

Historically, predicative morphemes attached to nouns may originate in former copulas, since cliticization of copulas is a very common phenomenon crosslinguistically. No African language has been reported to have a situation identical to that attested by some Amerindian languages in which the predicative inflection of nouns expresses all TAM distinctions occurring in verbal inflection, although some languages, e.g. the Jukun language Hone (Storch forthcoming), come remarkably close to such a system.

4.10   Possessive predications

Languages generally have clauses that present the possession of a certain (type of) entity as a property attributed to a possessor, and that do not specify (or specify only minimally) the precise nature of the relation between possessor and possessum.

All types of possessive predication identified in the literature are attested among African languages. For example, languages with a transitive verb similar to English *have* are not rare in Africa, and possessive predications more or less similar to existential predications are not rare either. But the comitative type (i.e. possessive clauses whose literal meaning is 'possessor is with possessum') seems to be more frequent in Africa than in other parts of the world (Creissels 1979).

4.11   Sentence types

4.11.1   *Declarative sentences*

Crosslinguistically, declarative sentences tend to be formally unmarked, and African languages generally conform to this tendency. However, in Maale, there are no unmarked independent sentences, and all sentence types, including declarative, are overtly marked by special verb suffixes (Amha 2001). An overt marking of declarative sentences has been observed also in some Gur languages (e.g. Bele; see Burns 1986) and in Khoc (Central Khoisan). In the western dialect of !Xun (North Khoisan), declarative sentences take an obligatory topic marker *má* (except for some specific clause types).

Particles combining assertion marking and focus marking are also found in some languages (see section 4.13). Verbal inflections expressing verb focus are commonly used also to emphasize the assertive value of declarative sentences, and sometimes morphological devices that have been described as expressing verb focus (e.g. for the Cushitic language Rendille) should perhaps be reanalyzed as default marking of declarative sentences in the absence of any focalization (Oomen 1978).

4.11.2   Imperative sentences

Special imperative verb forms are universally common, and tend to mark the distinction between singular and plural adressee. African languages do not contradict these generalizations. Typologically, the construction of imperative sentences in most African languages does not seem to call for particular remarks. Note, however, that in the Kuliak language Ik the object of imperative sentences does not appear in the accusative case (which as a rule is the default case for O in this language), but in the morphologically unmarked form called oblique case by König (2002):

(39)   bi-á   ɗa-ée   saɓ-ée   loŋót[a]
       you-NOM   go-IMP.2SG   kill-IMP.2SG   enemies.OBL
       'You go and kill enemies'

4.11.3   Interrogative sentences

4.11.3.1   Yes/no questions   No African language marking yes/no questions exclusively by a special constituent order has been identified to our knowledge. However, this is not very surprising, since the use of a special constituent order in yes/no questions is common among European languages but rare at world level.

In African languages, verbal systems including special interrogative forms are not common, and apart from intonation, yes/no questions most commonly involve only the addition of a question marker at the beginning or the end of the sentence. Clause-final interrogative particles are particularly common. In !Xun (North Khoisan), yes/no question markers have a fixed position between subject and verb, which is a rather uncommon pattern.

4.11.3.2   Constituent questions (or "wh-questions")   Three types of strategies are available in the construction of constituent questions:

(a) the interrogative word may occupy the same position as the corresponding constituent in an assertive sentence (Bambara);
(b) the interrogative word may be treated in the same way as a focalized constituent in an assertive sentence (Ik, !Xun);
(c) the interrogative word may undergo a special treatment that cannot be analyzed as a particular case of a more general focalizing strategy available for constituents of assertive sentences.

(a) and (b) are very common among African languages, and many languages use both more or less freely. By contrast, (c), very common in Europe, is relatively rare in Africa. It is, however, attested in Chadic: in some Chadic languages, interrogative words are moved to clause-final position, and in some languages they are moved to clause-initial position, but even in languages in which interrogative words are in clause-initial position, this cannot be analyzed as a particular case of a more general focalizing strategy.

In many languages (particularly, but not exclusively, in the Chadic family), so-called "question words" are not the sole markers of questions: they code an unspecified participant (a human, a thing, a place, etc.), hence the need for an additional strategy to code specific interrogative clauses. One of these strategies in Chadic is a clause-final interrogative marker, which in many languages differs from the clause-final interrogative marker for yes/no questions. Another strategy is the use of tense–aspect systems coding pragmatically dependent clauses.

In many Chadic languages there exist morphological and syntactic means to distinguish between participants that are completely unknown and participants that belong to a known set. The first group corresponds to English *who* and *what*, and the second to English *which one*. In Lele, the questions involving the two different types of human participants are coded by morphological means. The distinction between the two types of non-human participants is coded by syntactic means. Fronting of the specific non-human interrogative marks it as belonging to a known group; keeping it *in situ* marks it as belonging to an unknown group (Frajzyngier 2001).

Very often, different strategies are used depending on whether the questioned constituent is in subject function or in another function, and constraints on the discursive or referential status of the subject may provide an explanation. For example, in Tswana, interrogative words can substitute for constituents in functions other than subject without changing anything else in the construction of the clause, but they can never merely substitute for constituents in subject function, and the sentence must be reformulated (by means of a passive construction, or an impersonal construction, or a cleft construction) in order that the interrogative word does not figure in subject function.

It is also true for many Chadic languages that there are different strategies for asking questions about the subject and questions about other terms. These differences are a result of the fact that the question words code only the features human, non-human, place, time, etc. Therefore, the grammatical role must be marked by other means if the question word does not remain in situ. A posssible strategy is the use of two different sets of subject pronouns where set indicates that the question word represents the subject, and the other indicates that the question word represents the object (e.g. Gidar, Central Chadic).

4.12   Negation

4.12.1   Predicate negation (i.e. negation affecting the sentence as a whole)

As already mentioned above (see section 4.3.2), negative marking internal to the verbal word is particularly frequent among African languages, but the following two strategies are also relatively common all over Africa:

(a) the use of special negative auxiliaries;
(b) the use of negative particles in clause-final position (combined or not with a modification of the verbal word).

According to Dryer (forthcoming), clause-final negation is rare outside Africa. Clause-final negation is particularly widespread in Central Africa, in an area roughly between the rivers Niger and Nile. In particular, negation in Chadic is always coded by a clause-final marker; in some languages, there is also a negative marker occurring before the verb, or after the verb and before the object, and in some others, the verb of negative clauses must have the tense–aspect inflection characteristic of dependent clauses; see section 4.3.4.

Ngiti (Kutsch Lojenga 1994: 242–5) has negative particles that can occur in clause-initial position, which is a less usual pattern than clause-final negation – see below for a possible explanation of clause-initial negation, at least in some languages.

Changes in the constituent order triggered by negation are widely attested in Africa. In Niger-Congo, changes in the constituent order triggered by negation are particularly common in Kru languages, as illustrated by the following example from the Kru language Dida (Guéhoun 1993), in which negation involves a negative marker that cliticizes on the subject noun phrase, and clause-final position of the verb:

(40) a. dàāgɔ̄   lìpì   flàásū
       Dago   speak:PERF   French
       'Dago spoke French'

   b. dáāgɔ̄-ɔ́   flàásʊ   lìpì
       Dago-NEG   French   speak:PERF
       'Dago did not speak French'

In the case of Kru languages, and in some others, this seems to be the consequence of the transformation of a former negative auxiliary into an uninflected negative marker attached to the preceding word, the particular position of the verb in negative clauses still reflecting the order of the original construction in which a nominalized or non-finite form of the verb was formerly the complement of a negative auxiliary.

Other languages have an alternation between VSO for positive sentences and SVO for negative sentences: the East Nilotic language Teso (Heine & Reh 1984), the Surmic language Tennet (Randal 1998: 248; Payne 1997); the following example is from Tennet:

(41) a. k-á-cín-ɪ   anná   lokúli   íyókó   nɛ́kɔ̀
        S1SG-IPERF-see-S1SG   1SG   Lokuli   now   DEM
        'I see Lokuli now'

   b. ɪrɔ́ŋ   anná   k-a-cín-ɪ   lokúli
      NEG   1SG   S1SG-IPERF-see-S1SG   Lokuli

      íyókó   nɛ́kɔ̀
      now   DEM
      'I do not see Lokuli now'

   c. k-í-cín-ɪ   anná   lokúli   balwáz
      S1SG-PERF-see-S1SG   1SG   Lokuli   yesterday
      'I saw Lokuli yesterday'

   d. ŋanní   anná   k-í-cín   lokúli   balwáz
      NEG   1SG   S1SG:SJN-see   Lokuli   yesterday
      'I did not see Lokuli yesterday'

Here again, the initial position of the negative particles seems to reflect the position of a former negative auxiliary, and the use of the subjunctive when the verb combines with the negative particle *ŋanní* strongly supports this hypothesis. More generally, grammaticalization theory would predict that sentence-initial negative markers are likely to occur in VSO languages, and this is what we actually observe (e.g. Maasai, Ik, So).

Clause-final negation marking combined with a shift of the verb to the end of the clause is found in a range of languages from southwestern Ethiopia to Cameroon, although not in a geographically contiguous area. The Surmic language Me'en constitutes an example of such a system (Dimmendaal 1998c:68):

(42) a. ɛdɛ   or   kobuʔo
        3PL   see   chickens
        'They see the chickens'

   b. ɛdɛ   kobuʔo   or-oŋ
      3PL   chickens   see-NEG
      'They don't see the chickens'

Inherently negative copulas or existential verbs (i.e. copulas or existential verbs whose lexical meaning includes negation, and that consequently express negation in constructions devoid of any morphosyntactic negative marking) are very common throughout Africa. Their usual English equivalent is 'not to be,' but they are better glossed as 'be different from,' 'be absent.' For example, Chadic languages, in which the use of clause-final negative particles is general, have negative existential verbs that do not trigger the presence of negative markers in clause-final position.

Focalized negation is as a rule expressed through negative cleft-like constructions (*It is not X that* ...).

4.12.2   *Existential quantification negation*

The linguistic expression of this logical type of negation commonly involves a negative pronoun or adverb replacing the corresponding constituent of a positive sentence, or the addition of a negative determiner to a noun, and this substitution or addition of a negative word may combine or not with the morphosyntactic modifications that by themselves express predicate negation (*There is no person X such that I saw X → I didn't see anybody*, but *There is no X such that X came → Nobody came*).

In African languages, the second strategy (in which negative pronouns, adverbs, or determiners occur in sentences devoid of any other negative marking) is not common.

Some languages (e.g. Tswana) show an interesting correlation between the restrictions concerning the accessibility of negative and interrogative pronouns to the subject function: in Tswana, both negative and interrogative pronouns are excluded from the subject function, and passive or impersonal reformulations must be used in order to avoid the presence of a negative pronoun in subject function.

4.13   Focus

Some languages (e.g. English) primarily use intonation (higher pitch) to emphasize one word or phrase over the others and signal it as the focus of the sentence, without changing anything in its construction. Few African languages can use intonation alone to focalize a word or phrase; focus most commonly involves morphosyntactic alterations in Africa. The importance of lexical and grammatical tone in most African languages may provide an explanation for this tendency to avoid a purely intonational strategy of focus marking.

Several types of morphosyntactic devices can be used to mark the focus of a sentence, and it is common for a language to use more than one of them.

Cleft-type constructions are extremely common in African languages, but they rarely constitute the only possible way of marking focus. Since the main clause in cleft constructions is treated as a relative clause, it is not surprising that many languages have cleft constructions, or cleft-type constructions presumably derived from former cleft constructions, with subordination markings characteristic of relative clauses (Rendille, Somali, Tswana).

A striking characteristic of African languages taken as a whole is the frequent use of changes in the verb form, or of special auxiliaries, to express focus (see section 4.3.2).

Focus particles that place emphasis on the noun phrase they immmediately precede or follow are also very common in African languages. The introduction of a focus particle may leave the constituent order unchanged (e.g. in Bambara, Arbore), but much more commonly focus particles combine with a change in the constituent order (e.g. in Ik).[26]

In most Chadic languages, focus on any element is coded through some extraposition (clause-initial, clause-final, or for objects, position before the verb) and the use of the dependent tense–aspect systems in the comment clause. In other words, focus on the extraposed element is coded in the comment clause. In Chadic languages, extraposition alone, without the use of the dependent tense–aspectual systems, indicates topicalization.

The contribution of constituent order to the expression of focus is particularly obvious in languages in which focalized constituents move to a position left empty in the basic constituent order (e.g. in Turkana and other verb-initial languages of northeast Africa in which emphasized subjects or objects move to the preverbal position (Dimmendaal 1983b), but it may also happen that a position occupied by a constituent in the basic constituent order has properties that require analyzing it as functioning (at least to some extent) as a focus position.

For example, Tswana has a basic (and fairly rigid) constituent order SVOX, but at least the following two mechanisms suggest that the position immediately to the right of the verb is basically a focus position:

(a) interrogative pronouns and adverbs tend to immediately follow the verb, even if the constituent of the affirmative sentence they replace is obligatorily separated from the verb by another constituent;
(b) there is an impersonal construction, whose function is to detopicalize the subject of intransitive verbs, in which the NP corresponding to the subject of the basic construction occurs in postverbal position.

The use of the position immediately following the verb as an "unmarked focus position" has been signaled in other Bantu languages, but this phenomenon does not seem to be a general property of SVO languages.

Outside Africa, the mirror image of this situation is attested by a number of strict verb-final languages (e.g. Turkish), and is found also in languages with a syntactically flexible constituent order (e.g. Basque, Hungarian), in which the position immediately to the left of the verb is a focus position. According to Amha (2001), the same phenomenon occurs in Maale and other Ethiopian languages (e.g. Amharic).

The question of verb focalization calls for two remarks. First, as already mentioned, in languages that use special verb forms for verb focalization, these forms are commonly used not only to emphasize the choice of the verbal lexeme, but also to express emphatic assertion, in particular in sentences uttered with the intention to provide some explanation; they may also have aspectual implications. Second, crosslinguistically, cleft-type constructions, or constructions in which a focalized constituent marked by a focus particle moves to the left edge of the sentence, tend to be restricted to non-verbal terms of the clause (noun phrases, adposition phrases, adverbs), but some languages use them to focalize also verbs, without however moving the verb from its canonical position: many Kwa and Western Benue-Congo languages focalize verbs by means of cleft constructions, or other constructions used to focalize nouns, in which the focus position is occupied by a word identical to the verbal lexeme or derived from it, syntactically analyzable as a nominalized form of the verb fulfilling the role of a cognate object, as in the following example from Yoruba:

(43) a. mo   fún   òjó   ní   owó
          S1SG   give   Òjó   PRE   money
          'I gave some money to Ojo'

    b.   òjó   ni   mo   fún   ní   owó
          Ojo   FOC   S1SG   give   PRE   money
          'I gave some money to *Ojo*'

    c.   nwón   pa   òjó
          S3PL   kill   Òjó
          'They   killed   Ojo'

    d.   pípa   ni   nwón   pa   òjó
          kill:NOML   FOC   S3PL   kill   Òjó
          'They *killed* Ojo' (lit. 'It is *killing* (that) they killed Ojo')

For a relatively recent survey, see Bearth (1999).

4.14   Complex constructions

4.14.1   *Clause coordination*

The only clear generalization about coordinating words used to link clauses is that, in most African languages, the morpheme used as the equivalent of English *and* in noun phrase coordination (which generally also serves as the comitative adposition 'with' (see section 4.4.8) cannot be used for clause coordination. Exceptions to this generalization are only sporadic, and never extend to entire families or areas.

4.14.2   Sequential (or consecutive) constructions

The following types of clause sequences iconically reflecting a chronological presentation of events may be recognized:

(a) the sequence may be constructed as a mere juxtaposition of clauses in which every clause has the same form (in particular, regarding verb inflection) as an independent sentence;

(b) the sequence may be constructed as a sequence of clauses that are linked by conjunctions, but otherwise have the same form (in particular, regarding verb inflection) as independent sentences;

(c) only the first clause of the sequence shows the formal characteristics of an independent clause, and non-initial clauses are characterized either by a reduction or lack of verbal inflection, or by the use of special dependent verb forms ("consecutive," or "sequential");

(d) only the last clause of the sequence shows the formal characteristics of an independent clause, and non-final clauses use some dependent verb form ("gerundive," or "converb").

(a), (b), and (c) are all common in Africa; (c) seems to be particularly common, at least in Niger-Congo. It is also found in many Chadic languages, where sequential clauses are coded by the dependent tense–aspectual system. (d) is geographically more restricted, and its occurrence seems to be restricted to verb-final languages: it is found in Kanuri, in Central Khoisan languages, and is common in the SOV languages of East Africa.

4.14.3   Relativization

Most African languages have postnominal relatives, i.e. embedded relatives treated as noun modifiers that follow the noun they modify. This is not surprising, given the general tendency of African languages towards postponing the modifiers to the noun and the well-known fact that, in comparison with other types of modifiers, relative clauses are particularly prone to follow the noun they modify.

Prenominal relatives are found in Amharic, Afar, Maale, and other verb-final Afroasiatic languages of northeast Africa. Prenominal relatives are also found in Ngiti (Kutsch Lojenga 1994), a Central Sudanic language with a constituent order alternating between SVO and SAuxOV, depending on tense–aspect distinctions. By contrast, verb-final Nilo-Saharan languages spoken to the west of the verb-final Afroasiatic languages use a postnominal relative clause strategy, as shown by the following example from Tama (Dimmendaal; unpublished data):

(44) a. ɛ̀rɛ̀bíyɛ́-r-!gí   núúnú-ŋó
      car-SPEC-INST   S1SG:come-PERF
      'I came by car'

   b. ɛ̀rɛ̀bíyɛ́   núúnú-ŋó-r   tùŋg-òŋó
      car   S1SG:come-PERF-REL   steal:PAST-PERF
      'The car with which I came was stolen'

Bambara illustrates another type of relativization strategy in which the relative clause is not embedded in the main clause (some authors exclude this type from relative clauses proper). In this construction, relativization entirely relies on the presence of a relative marker within the relative clause, the location of the relative marker signaling the relativized position. When the relative clause precedes the main clause (which is the most common construction), this gives a construction whose literal transposition in English would be something like *The dog-REL bit the child, I saw that one* for 'I saw the dog that bit the child,' and *The dog bit the child-REL, I saw that one* for 'I saw the child that the dog bit.' This is the only available relativization strategy in most Northern Mande languages; it has also been reported to occur in some Gur languages.

The relativization strategy in which a relative clause embedded in the main clause includes the noun whose referent is determined by the property expressed by the relative clause ("head-internal" relatives embedded in the main clause) is not common crosslinguistically, and we know of no sure attestation of it among African languages.

It has often been pointed out that in prenominal relatives the verb tends to be in a non-finite form ("participial relatives"), whereas verb forms identical to those used in independent clauses are predominant in postnominal relatives. However, a number of African languages have postnominal relatives in which the verb has forms different from those used in independent declarative clauses, which contradicts this generalization. In particular, in Chadic languages distinguishing dependent and independent tense–aspect systems, the verb in relative clauses has the dependent tense–aspect system.

As shown by Andersen (1991: 290), the basic position of subjects in Dinka is postverbal, where they are marked for case. Preverbal noun phrases are topics, whose underlying grammatical relation can be that of subject, object, adverbial, or possessor. This latter constituent order is also found in relative clauses, as in the following example:

(45) mòɲ   cì í   jɔ̂ɔŋ-dè̖   mè̖th   câam
      man:AG   PERF:NTS   dog-3SG   child   eat:NFIN
      'the man whose dog has bitten the child'

As regards the treatment of the relativized role, Amharic has prenominal relatives that systematically include resumptive pronouns, which constitute a counterexample to the well-known generalization that the resumptive pronoun strategy is very rarely used in prenominal relatives; in postnominal relatives, African languages conform to a general tendency to use the gapping strategy if the relativized role stands relatively high in the accessibility hierarchy, the resumptive pronoun strategy being preferred if the relativized role stands relatively low in this hierarchy.

Postnominal relatives are commonly (but not always) introduced by relativizers, and are often followed by determiners in languages that place determiners at the right edge of noun phrases (which is a particularly common phenomenon in West African languages). The following example from Kanuri illustrates postnominal relatives immediately juxtaposed to their antecedent, but followed by a definite marker. Note that the use of a resumptive pronoun in the relativization of the dative, but not of the direct object, conforms to the generalization mentioned above.

(46) a. kâm   [kasúwu-lan   rúmma]-dɔ́
        person   market-LOC   see.TAM.S2SG-DEF
        'the person you saw at the market'
        cf. shí-ga kasúwu-lan rúmma 'you saw him/her at the market'

     b. kâm   [shí-ro   goro   yíkɔ́na]-dɔ́
        person   3SG-DAT   cola   give.TAM.S1SG-DEF
        'the person to whom I gave cola'
        cf. shí-ro goro yíkɔ́na 'I gave him/her cola'

Relativizers analyzable as pure subordination morphemes (which very often are also used as complementizers, such as English *that*) are common in African languages. True relative pronouns are very rare, if this notion is restricted to words that stand at the edge of the relative clause but show variations in their form and syntactic properties (e.g. combinability with adpositions), strongly supporting the hypothesis that they are pronouns fulfilling the relativized role but occupying a non-canonical position. But a third type of relativizer is very common in Africa; relativizers of this type can conveniently be called *relative linkers*. They are often confused with relative pronouns, because they show variations in gender and number governed by the antecedent of the relative clause, and can represent it; but nothing in their morphosyntactic properties can be viewed as evidence that they are constituents of the relativized clause in a non-canonical position, and very often (e.g. in Tswana, or in Arabic) they systematically co-occur with resumptive pronouns. The following example is from Arabic:

(47) a. ar-raʒulu   llaði: daraba   muħammadan
        DEF-man   LINK:MSG   hit.PERF:S3MSG Muhammad:ACC
        'the man who hit Muhammad'

b. ar-raʒulu   llaði: qatalu:-hu
   DEF-man   LINK:MSG   kill.PERF:S3MPL-O3MSG
   'the man they killed' (lit. 'the man that one they killed him')

c. al-bintu   llati: ðahabtu   maʕa-ha: ʔila:
   DEF-girl   LINK:FSG   go.PERF:S1SG   with-3FSG   to

   s-su:qi
   DEF-market:GEN
   'the girl with whom I went to the market' (lit. 'the girl that one
   I went with her to the market')

Diachronically, there is often evidence that such relativizers originate from demonstratives in a sequence *noun + demonstrative + relativized clause* in which the demonstrative has become obligatory and has changed into a mere linker. In Tswana, the same linkers are obligatory with adjectival modifiers too (see section 4.4.5).

4.14.4   Complementation

In a number of African languages, the clausal complement of verbs of saying, perceiving, and thinking, and of verbs expressing desire, intention, command, etc., is introduced by a complementizer that is quite transparently a grammaticalized form of a verb 'to say' (or of a non-verbal predicator used in quotative constructions), but this is a common typological feature in other parts of the world too.

There are languages with several types of complementizers. In Lele there is a *de dicto* complementizer *na*, coding complements of verbs of saying and coding indirect perception after verbs of perception, and a *de re* complementizer *go*, coding direct perception after verbs of perception (Frajzyngier 2001).

In many Chadic languages, and also in Nigerian Arabic, the coding of the subject of the embedded clause as object of the matrix clause has the function of coding direct perception verbs, and realis wish with volitional verbs. This phenomenon also occurs in English (Frajzyngier 1996; Frajzyngier & Shay 2003).

Among the SOV languages of Africa, clausal complements preceding the verb (i.e. occupying the same position as nominal complements fulfilling a similar function) are found for example in Kanuri, Amharic, Somali, and in most Central Khoisan languages (although frequently in a reduced form), but clausal complements may follow the verb even in languages that otherwise behave like strict SOV languages, as illustrated by the following example from Ijo:

(48) a. erí   kɛnɪ   dúʊ   gbaamɪ
        he   one   tale   told
        'He told a tale'

b. erǐ   gba   ámεέε   erǐ   boŋgimi
   he   said   that   he   will.come
   'He said that he would come'

More generally, discrepancies between the position of nominal and clausal complements of the same verbs are not uncommon. In some VS languages of the Chadic family (e.g. Hdi), the clausal complement of verbs of saying precedes the matrix clause, but the nominal complement of verbs of saying follows the matrix clause, whereas the clausal complement of verbs of perception follows the matrix clause (Frajzyngier & Shay 2002).

However, this is not always the case: an interesting particularity of Somali is to fully assimilate complement clauses in subject or object function to NPs: no complementizer is present, and the last word of the complement clause (i.e. the verb) is case-marked exactly in the same way as the last word of an NP fulfilling the same function.

4.14.5   Switch-reference in complex constructions and logophoricity

Comrie (1983) cites Gokana (an Ogoni language spoken in Nigeria) as an exceptional case of an African language in which the morphology of dependent verb forms marks the presence or absence of coreferentiality between the subject of the dependent verb and the subject of the main clause. However, Amha (2001) indicates that switch-reference marking on dependent verb forms is widely attested in Omotic and in Cushitic languages. Mina (Central Chadic) has a third-person pronoun whose function is to code contrastive focus on the third person; another function of this pronoun is to code switch-reference, more precisely, coding that the subject of the clause is different from the immediately preceding subject.

Another type of reference tracking, namely, "logophoricity," is much more common in African languages, in an area ranging from Senegal in the west to Ethiopia in the east, and cutting across genetic boundaries. Logophoricity and switch-reference are functionally similar, but logophoricity involves special third-person pronouns occurring in dependent clauses only and expressing coreferentiality with the subject of the main clause.

In the Chadic language Mupun, there are two sets of logophoric pronouns. As illustrated by the following example, one set has the subject of the verb of saying as its antecedent (sentences a and b with subject pronouns, and sentences c and d with object pronouns), and the other set has the addressee of the verb of saying as its antecedent (sentences e-f). This is perhaps the richest logophoric system attested (Frajzyngier 1993).

(49) a. wu/wa/mo   sat   nə   wu/wa/mo   ta   ɗee   n-jos
        he/she/they say   CMPL   he/she/they   stop   stay   PRE-Jos
        'He₁/she₁/they₁ said that he₂/she₂/they₂ stopped over in Jos'

   b. wu/wa/mo   sat   nə   ta   ɗɪ/ɗe/ɗu   ɗee   n-jos
      he/she/they say   CMPL   stop   he/she/they stay   PRE-Jos
      'He₁/she₁/they₁ said that he₁/she₁/they₁ stopped over in Jos'

   c. wu/wa   sat   nə   n-nas   wur/war
      he/she   say   CMPL   1SG-beat   him/her
      He₁/she₁ said that I beat him₂/her₂'

   d. wu/wa   sat   nə   n-nas   ɗin/ɗe
      he/she   say   CMPL   1SG-beat   him/her
      'He₁/she₁ said that I beat him₁/her₁'

   e. n-sat   n-wur   nə   wur   ji
      1SG-say   PRE-3SG   CMPL   3SG   come
      'I told him₁ that he₂ should come'

   f. n-sat   n-wur   nə   gwar   ji
      1SG-say   PRE-3SG   CMPL   3SG   come
      'I told him₁ that he₁ should come'

See Güldemann and von Roncador (2002) for a recent survey.

A system of anti-logophoricity marking has been reported by Kouadio (1996: 384–9) for the Kwa language Attie, and by Andersen (1999) for the Western Nilotic language Mabaan. In these languages, in indirect speech, third-person pronominal forms identical to those used in independent clauses indicate coreferentiality with the subject of the main clause, whereas other third-person referents are represented by special pronouns ("fourth-person forms"), as illustrated by the following example from Mabaan:

(50) a. ʔɛ́kɛ̀   gɔ́kɛ̀   ʔágē   ʔɛ́kɛ̀ kâɲɟ́ɛ́
        3SG   say:AP:3   INIT.3SG   swim:FUT:INDIR:3SG
        'He₁ says that he₁ will swim'

   b. ʔɛ́kɛ̀   gɔ́kɛ̀   ʔágē   ʔêktá kâɲɟ́ɛ́
      3SG   say:AP:3   INIT.4SG   swim:FUT:INDIR:4
      'He₁ says that he₂ will swim'

4.15   The grammatical coding of spatial relations

Most languages use locative case markers or adpositions to encode basic spatial relations (*in/on/at* N), but in many Niger-Congo languages, among those that have the noun class system characteristic of this phylum in its most typical form, this function is fulfilled by noun class markers: class affixes inherently associated with the noun 'place' may also be added to the inherent prefix of other nouns; nouns combined with locative class markers fulfill the function of locative argument or adjunct without necessitating the addition of any case marker or adposition, but, at least in the languages that have this mechanism in its most typical form, the locative morpheme clearly remains a noun class marker, since non-locative nouns combined with it lose their inherent concordial properties and behave in concord rules like the noun 'place.' This is consonant with the fact that in many Bantu languages, locative constructions may function as syntactic subjects or objects of verbal predications involving motion verbs, postural verbs, or verbs of existence and availability. This strategy as well as other strategies whereby locative constructions are treated as core, rather than peripheral, constituents, are further discussed in Dimmendaal (2003).

Another remarkable feature of the grammatical coding of spatial relations in Niger-Congo languages is that, as a rule, the locative adpositions or affixes do not code the distinction between *location at/movement towards/movement from*, which implies the existence of two distinct classes of motion verbs assigning the role of goal or source to a locative complement. In addition to that, the set of motion verbs that can assign the role of source or direction to their complement is often very limited, hence the frequent use of verb sequences in order to code the starting point and the direction of a motion (for example, 'run from A to B' is often rendered literally as *leave A run reach B*), even in languages that otherwise show no marked tendency towards serialization.

Similarly, in some Chadic languages, directionality away from a source or towards a goal is coded through serial verb constructions, where each verb codes just one parameter, such as 'go,' 'leave,' 'arrive,' 'pass'; in some other languages, the verbs that once were part of a serial verb construction have become extensions to the main verb.

In languages that have an applicative derivation, a possible use of the applicative (observed in particular in Bantu languages) is to derive verbs assigning the role of goal to a locative complement from verbs that, in their non-derived form, either don't have any locative argument, or have a locative argument to which they assign the role of source, as in the following example from Tswana:

(51) a. kì-tɬàà-húdúχ-à   kó   kàɲɛ́
       S1SG-FUT-move-FUT   PRE   Kanye
       'I am going to move from Kanye'
   b. kì-tɬàà-húdúχ-ɛ́là   kó   χàbʊ́róní
       S1SG-FUT-move-APPL-FUT   PRE   Gaborone
       'I am going to move to Gaborone'

c. kì-tɬàà-húdúχ-à   kó   kàɲɛ́   kì-húdúχ-él-ì   kò
   S1SG-FUT-move-FUT   PRE   Kanye   S1SG-move-   PRE
                                            APPL-SEQ

χàbʊ́rónì
Gaborone
'I am going to move from Kanye to Gaborone'

The chadic language Mina has a "locative predicator" used with locative predications when the predicate is inherently non-locative. A locative preposition is used only when the complement is inherently non-locative. If both the predicate and the complement are inherently locative, neither the predicator nor the preposition is used. In the following example, the locative predicator *á* must be used in sentence (a) because the main verb 'called' is not inherently locative; in sentence (b), *tsú* 'went' is inherently locative, and the locative predication does not require the locative predicator:

(52) a. nd-á   yà   ngùl   ngə̀n   á   bìŋ
        go-GO   call   husband   3SG   LOCPRED   room
        'And [she] called her husband into the room'

     b. séy   mə̀   ngùl   tìy   á   tìy-ù   wàl
        so   REL   husband   see   3SG   see-3SG   wife
        tsú   zə̀   dámù
        went   EE   bush
        'So the husband saw that the wife went into the bush'

The tendency to code the distinction *location at / movement towards / movement from* exclusively on verbs is typical of languages spoken in a large area including the whole of Niger-Congo languages, but not of African languages in general. In particular, if more or less grammaticalized uses of a verb 'leave' are not taken into account, ablative case affixes or adpositions seem to be totally absent from Niger-Congo languages; by contrast, ablative case affixes or adpositions are common in several branches of Afroasiatic and Nilo-Saharan.[27]

As regards the grammatical coding of spatial relations, another very common phenomenon in African languages (not restricted to particular families or areas) is that place names in locative argument or adjunct function need not combine with the locative case affixes or adpositions that are obligatory for common nouns fulfilling the same function. The case of the Chadic language Mina has been mentioned above. In the Chadic language Hdi, the locative preposition has a different tone when occurring with a toponym than when occurring with an inherently non-locative noun (Frajzyngier & Shay 2002).

Directional morphemes (deictic or non-deictic) attached to the verb are not very common in African languages in general, but they are common in Nilo-Saharan languages (in particular venitive and andative) and are sporadically attested elsewhere (for example, Wolof has venitive and andative verb forms).

An interesting particularity concerning the grammatical coding of spatial relations in the Omotic as well as the Cushitic branch of Afroasiatic, is that locative complements of verbs of motion are frequently treated on a par with complements of prototypical transitive verbs such as 'eat' or 'beat,' i.e. as direct objects. Thus in Maale (a language with a case contrast of the "marked-nominative" type), the complement of the verb 'go' (accordingly best translated as 'reach (somewhere)') takes absolute case:

(53) a. ʔízí   hell-é-ne
       3MSG:SUBJ   reach-PERF-POS:DECL
       'He arrived'

    b. ʔíázíá   gurd-ó   hell-é-ne
       3MSG:SUBJ   village-ABS   reach-PERF-POS:DECL
       'He arrived in the village/He reached the village'

This phenomenon is sporadically found in other languages too, for example in the Southern Bantu language Tswana.[28]

4.16   Conclusion

As already observed in the introduction, our conclusions are limited by the fact that they are not backed by appropriate quantitative data, for example, in the form of a survey that would ensure a fine-grained picture of the linguistic diversity of the African continent. Moreover, in order to establish in an uncontroversial way to what extent Africa can be considered as a morpho-syntactic area really different from the rest of the world, similar data would be needed for the other parts of the world too.

As the preceding sections have shown, Africa's internal coherence cannot be established on the basis of features common to all African languages: the only morphosyntactic features found in all African languages are presumably universals, or quasi-universals (see chapter 2). It is however possible to list a set of features that certainly would deserve thorough investigation in further studies of the morphosyntactic diversity of African languages compared to the diversity observed in other parts of the world. What we propose below is a tentative list of morphosyntactic features that seem to concern a proportion of African languages significantly different (higher or lower) from that observed at world level.

Note however that, as mentioned in the relevant sections, most of these features are not evenly distributed on the African continent. In some cases, their distribution may cast doubt on their relevance from the point of view of areal typology, and suggests that the genetic factor may have been crucial, and that contact may have played only a limited role in their diffusion. In particular, several features listed below (for example, the relative rarity of case-marked subjects and objects, or the frequency of double object constructions), do not really characterize Africa as a whole, but rather an area including mostly Niger-Congo languages, plus possibly languages belonging to groups in relatively close contact with Niger-Congo languages (i.e. Songhay, Chadic, and Central Sudanic).

With all these caveats, leaving aside features that concern the majority of African languages but seem to be equally well attested in most other parts of the world, or features that concern a minority of African languages but seem to be equally rare in most other parts of the world, we would like to propose the following as the features most likely to be relevant, at the present state of documentation, for a characterization of the African continent as a morpho-syntactic area:

(a) The ergative type of core syntactic role coding is exceptional among African languages (section 4.2).

(b) Case-marked subjects or objects are less common among African languages than at world level (section 4.2.2).

(c) The so-called "marked-nominative" type of case contrast between subjects and objects is exceptional in other parts of the world but very common among African languages that have a case contrast between subjects and objects (section 4.2.2; see also chapter 8).

(d) Obligatory agreement of transitive verbs with their object does not seem to be attested among African languages (section 4.2.3.2).

(e) Second-position clitics are relatively common in the languages of the world, but exceptional among African languages (section 4.2.3.3).

(f) In a relatively high proportion of African languages, the construction of verbs with an argument frame of the type *giver – given – recipient* tends to assimilate the recipient (rather than the thing given) to the patient of prototypical transitive verbs, and double object constructions are particularly frequent (section 4.2.5).

(g) Focus strategies implying morphosyntactic alterations, and in particular focus marking by means of verbal inflection, are particularly common in Africa (sections 4.3.2 and 4.13).

(h) The use of special verb forms in sequential constructions is particularly widespread among African languages (sections 4.3.4 and 4.14.2).

(i) Applicatives are particularly common in Africa, and a relatively high proportion of African languages make a wide use of obligatory applicatives and of various types of non-canonical applicatives (section 4.3.5).

(j) Classifier systems are exceptional among African languages (section 4.4.1).

(k) Relatively few African languages are devoid of morphological plural, or have a morphological plural restricted to a subset of nouns occupying a high position in the animacy hierarchy (section 4.4.3).

(l) African languages that do not use the same morpheme as a noun phrase coordinator and as a comitative adposition are relatively rare (section 4.4.8).

(m) The proportion of languages with a syntactically flexible constituent order is much lower among African languages than at world level (section 4.8).

(n) The constituent order SOVX, relatively rare at world level, is relatively frequent among African languages (section 4.8).

(o) Clause-final negative particles occur among African languages much more frequently than in other parts of the world (section 4.12.1).

(p) Changes in the constituent order triggered by negation are particularly common among African languages (section 4.12.1).

(q) True relative pronouns are particularly rare in African languages (most words currently identified as relative pronouns are relative linkers), and the use of dependent verb forms in postnominal relatives, relatively rare in the languages of the world, is common among African languages (section 4.14.3).

(r) Logophoricity is particularly widespread among African languages (section 4.14.5).

(s) Systems of coding of spatial relations in which the distinction *location at / movement toward / movement from* manifests itself exclusively on verbs are more frequent in Africa than in most other parts of the world (section 4.15).

5 The Macro-Sudan belt: towards identifying a linguistic area in northern sub-Saharan Africa

Tom Güldemann

5.1 Introduction

It has been recognized for a long time that languages across a broad sub-Saharan belt from the western end of the continent to the escarpment of the Ethiopian Plateau in the east display certain linguistic affinities. At the same time, it has been difficult to identify precisely the nature and range of these affinities and to provide a plausible explanation for them.

I propose in Güldemann (2003a) that the distribution of logophoric marking in Africa follows an areal pattern in that it is regularly found in languages of the sub-Saharan belt referred to above, but is virtually absent from the rest of the continent. This finding is the starting point for a more systematic investigation of the following questions:

(a) Does this geographical region share other linguistic traits?
(b) If so, do these define some sort of linguistic area?
(c) If so, how has this area come into being?

I present in section 5.2 several linguistic features which appear to share a roughly similar distribution across the African continent, as well as additional candidate features which may support the evidence provided in this chapter. Section 5.3 briefly surveys previous approaches to the general observation of linguistic commonalities across the sub-Saharan belt, among which there is the proposal that most of the languages involved belong to a *genealogical* lineage comprising Greenberg's super-groups Niger-Kordofanian and Nilo-Saharan. On the basis of the data given here, section 5.4 argues against such an explanation and, in so doing, tries to make a case for an *areal* language group which I propose to call the "Macro-Sudan belt." Section 5.5 discusses a few preliminary points on the possible historical emergence of this linguistic area in the center of Africa. The final section 5.6 addresses the potential relevance of the hypothesis for areal-typological research in Africa as a whole.

To begin with, I will characterize the area at issue in more detail and outline the language groups involved. As remarked already, the area is a broad belt south of the Sahara and can be fairly well defined in purely geographical terms: it is, so to speak, sandwiched between the Atlantic Ocean and the Congo Basin in the south and the Sahara and Sahel in the north, and spans the continent from the Atlantic Ocean in the west to the escarpment of the Ethiopian Plateau in the east.

To a considerable extent, there are also linguistic correlates of the above external boundaries. That is, the area excludes regions which are more homogeneous in linguistic-genealogical terms, namely the Saharan spread zone in the north covered today by Berber, Saharan, and Arabic; the spread zone in the south colonized by Narrow Bantu; and finally the Ethiopian Plateau in the east dominated by Cushitic and Ethio-Semitic (see chapter 7; see Nichols 1992 for the general concept of a "spread zone").

Regarding the internal profile of the area, one needs to distinguish between different types of languages and language groups constituting it. That is, not all linguistic lineages concerned are involved to the same degree in certain distribution patterns of linguistic features.

The core of the area is formed by the following language families: Mande, Kru, Gur, Kwa, Benue-Congo (excluding Narrow Bantu), Adamawa-Ubangi, Bongo-Bagirmi,[1] and Moru-Mangbetu. The two easternmost families of Niger-Congo, Benue-Congo and Adamawa-Ubangi, as well as the two Central Sudanic families, Bongo-Bagirmi and Moru-Mangbetu, will be shown to hold a particularly prominent position in the core group and form again a compact geographical block.

Some lineages, which in geographical terms are all peripheral but still adjacent to the core, display an ambiguous behavior regarding linguistic commonalities with this area. These lineages are Atlantic, Dogon, Songhay, Chadic, Ijoid, Narrow Bantu, and Nilotic.

The above remarks suggest that genealogical language groups to be considered in this chapter are usually low-level units, called here "families," ignoring the four super-groups proposed by Greenberg (1963). Reasons for taking such smaller genealogical units as the reference of continental sampling will be postponed until section 5.4.2. Suffice it to say here that my approach has the advantage that a greater variety of languages will have to be included and no relevant genealogical group for which data are available is unduly omitted.

Clearly, if this breakdown were to be transferred into a genealogical classification this would be a far more splitting one. The present schema, which does not refer to groups like Khoisan, Nilo-Saharan, and Niger-Kordofanian,[2] should, however, not be viewed as an alternative classification proposal; to develop such a classification would be an endeavor in its own right. Low-level sampling is warranted by the particular topic of this chapter, which must consider the possibility that certain types of linguistic commonalities, when involving genealogical entities that are not yet based on solid evidence, may well have an explanation other than common inheritance, *inter alia*, one in terms of areal contact.

5.2   The linguistic features

The following section will discuss the linguistic features which are thought to
be relevant for establishing the linguistic area at issue. The methodology has
been to survey the presence/absence of a certain candidate feature in language
families across the entire African continent – this mostly in two steps: first,
relevant sources on a given feature have been consulted in order to assemble a
basic list of languages and families possessing it; when necessary, lineages not
mentioned there have been checked in a second phase as to the presence or
absence of the feature. The information here is based on group surveys;[3] my
own knowledge, particularly of the various Khoisan groups; and last but not
least personal communication from family specialists.[4] Sometimes, descriptions of individual languages have been consulted too.

A closer look at the languages and language groups surveyed will reveal that
several African lineages which would have to be considered according to the
family level chosen for this investigation are not included, generally or for
individual features. This is due to the lack of appropriate, reliable data. Such
omissions concern in particular Kordofanian and a number of poorly documented groups commonly subsumed under Nilo-Saharan. In geographical
terms, these languages cluster in three areas in the eastern domain of the
relevant part of Africa (indicated in the accompanying maps by means
of dotted areas), called here from east to west (a) "Ethiopian escarpment,"
(b) "Nuba Mountains," and (c) "Southwest Sudan border belt." These are
"fragmentation" zones in the sense that they display a considerable amount of
genealogical diversity.[5]

In ascertaining the distribution of a feature within a family, I make a basic
distinction between three degrees of frequency, namely (a) absent, (b) present,
and (c) frequent. The empirical limitations of the available data affect what is
behind these three classificatory values. The value "frequent" is the most
straightforward in the sense that it is intended exclusively to mean a fairly
homogeneous distribution and frequent presence of the feature across the relevant
group. When assigning to a family the value "present," this does not always
imply a frequency evaluation, because the available data may be insufficient;
usually it means that the feature is an occasional or even rather isolated phenomenon in the family, but it could also be more frequent. Finally, the value
"absent" stands in principle for the feature's absence in a family; but sometimes
this is merely inferred from the fact that I did not come across a relevant language.

Given the great number of African languages as well as their overall poor
state of description, it is clear that the data achieved in the analytical procedure
described above cannot be claimed to be complete. Hence, the distributional
patterns arising here are to a certain extent preliminary; at the same time, they
seem to be robust enough to be discussed from a wider African perspective.

Each feature survey is summarized in a table where the affected families (mostly followed by a letter code) and/or languages are listed. The above three-way split is represented by simply recording the values "present" and "frequent." Hence, lineages which do not appear in these tables are assumed to lack the property entirely. Where the value "frequent" is identified for a family, this is marked by a grey cell in the table column "Language or group" instead of giving the numerous possible attestations for such groups. In all other cases, the individual languages which possess the respective feature, according to reported data, appear in the relevant column.

A survey is also accompanied by a map showing the rough distribution of major language families in the wider area (smaller enclaves of a family are indicated by a line connecting them with the respective letter code). The families which have a given feature frequently are marked as a whole by dark grey. While this may represent an oversimplification of a potentially more heterogeneous picture in the family, I did not find any other solution that would not have inhibited the map's usability. The special pattern within Benue-Congo, namely that a feature is present except in most of Narrow Bantu, is reflected by the fading out of the grey shading. Where the occurrence of a feature is restricted to a more moderate number of languages, I indicate this both in the map and the legend by a numbered dot, also in dark grey. Hence, the continental distribution of a feature will be graphically discernible from the contrast of light vs. dark grey.

5.2.1   Logophoricity

Güldemann (2003a) is an investigation of the distribution of so-called "logophoric" markers in Africa. They are defined there as grammatical devices that indicate in non-direct reported discourse the *coreference* of a quote-internal nominal to its source, the speaker, who is mostly encoded in the construction accompanying/signaling the presence of the quote. Logophoric markers are mostly pronouns which contrast with other unmarked pronouns indicating non-coreference, as in (1) from Kera (Chadic).

(1) a. wə   míntí   tó   kóoré   vs.
       3M.Sx   QUOT   3M.S.LOGx   go.away
    b. wə   míntí   wə   kóoré
       3M.Sx   QUOT   3M.Sy   go.away
    'Er sagte, daß er weggehe' [he said he would go] (Ebert 1979: 260)

An essential criterion for diagnosing the presence of grammaticalized logophoricicty in a language is that the marking device is regular or even obligatory in this context; it does not mean that it is only used in this function, in other words, that it is a dedicated marker. On this basis, the distribution of

Table 5.1 *Logophoricity across African lineages*

Family		Stock	Language or group (branch)	Area
Bongo-Bagirmi	A	Central Sudanic	▓▓▓▓▓▓	
Moru-Mangbetu	B	Central Sudanic	▓▓▓▓▓▓	
Adamawa-Ubangi	C	N. Niger-Congo	▓▓▓▓▓▓	
Benue-Congo	D	N. Niger-Congo	except most of Narrow Bantu	
Kwa	E	N. Niger-Congo	▓▓▓▓▓▓	
Gur	F	N. Niger-Congo	▓▓▓▓▓▓	
Dogon	G	–	▓▓▓▓▓▓	Niger bend
Songhay	H	–	Koyra Chiini, Koyraboro Senni	Niger bend
Omotic	O	Afroasiatic	Gimira, Male, Wolaitta, Kafi-noono	Southwest Ethiopia
Nilotic	Q	Eastern Sudanic	Acholi, Lango (West)	North Uganda
Kado		–	Krongo	Nuba Mountains
Chadic	T	Afroasiatic	Mwaghavul, Angas, Tangale, Pero (West); Kera, Lele (East)	North Nigeria; Southeast Chad
Mande	W	–	Bisa, Boko-Busa (East)	Ghana, Burkina Faso, Benin, Nigeria

logophoricity across African languages and lineages has been determined as far as possible. The results are given in table 5.1.

That logophoricity occurs only in a few languages or just one sub-branch of a family holds, according to the available data, for Nilotic, Omotic, Chadic, and Mande. The other pattern of logophoricity distribution, according to which the feature is evenly distributed in the group, seems to apply to Songhay (Jeffrey Heath, p.c.) and Dogon (Culy & Kodio 1995), but the information does not yet allow a conclusive assessment. Two far larger groups can be identified with more confidence as lineages rich in logophoric languages: Central Sudanic (both member families affected) and Narrow Niger-Congo (all member families but Kru being affected). An important observation, to come up also in later sections, is that a considerable portion of Benue-Congo – a member of Narrow Niger-Congo – does not show the feature, namely the great majority of Narrow Bantu languages outside west-central Africa. These differ in this respect from the many non-Bantu Bantoid languages, their closest relatives, and even some Bantu languages in west-central Africa displaying logophoricity.

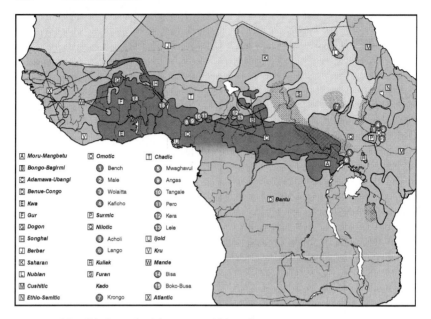

Map 5.1 Logophoricity across African lineages

The geographical pattern in map 5.1 shows that African languages with a logophoric system are concentrated in a fairly compact, broad belt stretching from northern Uganda in the east up to the Niger River in the west. Only Krongo in the Nuba Mountains and a few Omotic languages in Ethiopia are not directly integrated in this area, but are still close to it. It must be stressed that this area is not defined by any complete coverage by the feature at issue, but rather by its fairly consistent non-occurrence outside it.

In some lineages, member languages only possess logophoric marking when they are located in or close to the area, but lack it when they are farther away. This holds for Narrow Bantu, Chadic, Nilotic, and Mande; this can be discerned from the relevant languages listed in map 5.1 vis-à-vis the general position of their respective family. For Chadic, Frajzyngier (1985) has argued that logophoricity cannot be reconstructed to the proto-language and is better accounted for by contact-induced interference from non-Chadic languages. The same interpretation is likely for Mande and Nilotic.

5.2.2   Labial-velar consonants

Another feature relevant for the discussion is the presence of labial-velar consonants. Maddieson's (1984: 215–16) data on a world sample of 317 languages showed that these sounds are virtually restricted to Africa; outside this continent,

Table 5.2 *Labial-velar consonants across African lineages*

Family		Stock	Language or group (branch)	Area
Bongo-Bagirmi	A	Central Sudanic	░░░░░░░░░	
Moru-Mangbetu	B	Central Sudanic	░░░░░░░░░	
Adamawa-Ubangi	C	N. Niger-Congo	░░░░░░░░░	
Benue-Congo	D	N. Niger-Congo	except most of Narrow Bantu	
Kwa	E	N. Niger-Congo	░░░░░░░░░	
Gur	F	N. Niger-Congo	░░░░░░░░░	
Nilotic	Q	Eastern Sudanic	Kuku (West), Alur (East)	South Sudan, North Uganda
Chadic	T	Afroasiatic	Afade, Bacama (Central)	Northeast Nigeria, North Cameroon
Ijoid	U	–		
Kru	V	N. Niger-Congo		
Mande	W	–	░░░░░░░░░	
Atlantic	X	–	except North	

this survey yielded only Iai from Austronesian as having voiced /gb/. Maddieson (2005) presents a similar picture except that there are a few more cases of labial-velars in the Pacific, namely in the eastern end of New Guinea, including one language possessing a particularly elaborate system of such consonants.

Of great importance for this chapter is the distribution of labial-velars *within* Africa, because it resembles that of logophoricity. All African languages in Maddieson's sample with such consonants are spoken in or near the logophoricity area and establish a language set with a genealogical profile similar to that in table 5.1. His languages with labial-velars come from the following families: Moru-Mangbetu, Bongo-Bagirmi, Adamawa-Ubangi, Benue-Congo, Kwa, Gur, Atlantic, Mande, Chadic, and Ijoid. Kru and Nilotic can be added to this list, because they also have languages with these sounds, the former many, the latter only a few. The survey is summarized in table 5.2.

In some languages, labial-velar consonants occur as a feature which is untypical for the family; they are found in the geographical periphery of the area, namely in the extreme south (Bantu), east (Nilotic) and north (Chadic).

Most of Narrow Bantu lacks labial-velar consonants, while its closest relatives within and adjacent to the area frequently have them. According to Clements and Rialland (this volume chapter 3), most Bantu languages with labial-velars are spoken north of a line that stretches from northern Gabon in the west, along the northern sector of the Congo River to half-way between Lake Albert and Lake Edward.[6]

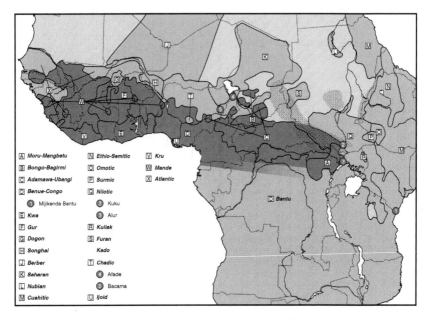

Map 5.2 Labiovelar consonants across African lineages

The feature in Nilotic and Chadic is in all probability an innovation due to contact with languages belonging to the core area. For Kuku and Alur from Nilotic, linguistic interference from Moru-Mangbetu is explicitly stated by Dimmendaal (1995b: 100–1, 103) to be responsible for the sound change. This is parallel to the peripheral status of Nilotic with respect to logophoricity. Since labial-velars are unusual in Chadic too, the contact explanation can also be applied to the few Chadic languages concerned; at least Bacama is still today the neighbor of Adamawa-Ubangi languages.

5.2.3   ATR vowel harmony

The well-known vowel-harmony type based on advanced tongue root (ATR) is another property of African languages with a distribution similar to the previous ones; see Clements and Rialland (this volume, chapter 3) for a characterization of this feature and more discussion. A survey of this feature, emerging from a summary of Hall et al. (1974), Blench (1995: 89–91), Dimmendaal (2001a: 368–73), and Casali (2003), singles out the following families: Moru-Mangbetu, Bongo-Bagirmi, Adamawa-Ubangi, Benue-Congo, Kwa, Gur, Kru, Atlantic, Dogon, Mande, Ijoid, Chadic, Cushitic, Omotic, Surmic, Nilotic, Nubian, and Kado. Hall et al. (1974) and Casali (2003) also list languages from Saharan, Maban, Furan, and Koman in the northeast (classified as Nilo-Saharan) as possibly having this vowel-harmony type, while

Table 5.3 *ATR vowel harmony across African lineages*

Family		Stock	Language or group (branch)	Area
Bongo-Bagirmi	A	Central Sudanic	▓▓▓▓▓▓	
Moru-Mangbetu	B	Central Sudanic	▓▓▓▓▓▓	
Adamawa-Ubangi	C	N. Niger-Congo	▓▓▓▓▓▓	
Benue-Congo	D	N. Niger-Congo	except most of Narrow Bantu	
Kwa	E	N. Niger-Congo	▓▓▓▓▓▓	
Gur	F	N. Niger-Congo	▓▓▓▓▓▓	
Nubian	L	Eastern Sudanic	Hill Nubian	Nuba Mountains
Cushitic	M	Afroasiatic	Somali (East)	Horn of Africa
Omotic	O	Afroasiatic	Hamer (South)	Southwest Ethiopia
Surmic	P	Eastern Sudanic	▓▓▓▓▓▓	
Nilotic	Q	Nubian	▓▓▓▓▓▓	
Kuliak	R	–	Ik, So	North Uganda
Kado		–	Krongo	Nuba Mountains
Chadic	T	Afroasiatic	Tangale (West)	Northeast Nigeria
Ijoid	U	–	▓▓▓▓▓▓	
Kru	V	N. Niger-Congo	▓▓▓▓▓▓	
Mande	W	–	except West	Côte d'Ivoire, Ghana, Burkina Faso
Atlantic	X	–	except most of South	

Blench (1995: 90) explicitly excludes them; all sources lack a more detailed discussion so that these cases remain open and are not listed in table 5.3.

In some families such as Chadic in the north and Nubian, Cushitic, and Omotic in the east, the property is exceptional. Hall et al. (1974) and especially Dimmendaal (2001a: 368–73) state that languages of some of these latter groups as well as individual subgroups within Narrow Niger-Congo (are likely to) have acquired the vowel-harmony type through contact with languages where the feature is well entrenched. Such a contact-induced interference has been treated more extensively for the Tangale group of Chadic by Kleine-willinghöfer (1990) and Jungraithmayr (1992/3); see also Drolc (2004) for vowel-harmony phenomena in Ndut (Cangin, Atlantic) induced by contact with Wolof, another Atlantic language from the Senegambian subgroup.

5.2.4   Word order S-(AUX)-O-V-X

At least since Heine (1976) it has become established that Africa hosts, besides languages with more or less consistent word-orders of the types S-V-O, S-O-V, and V-S-O, a considerable number of languages which have a kind of

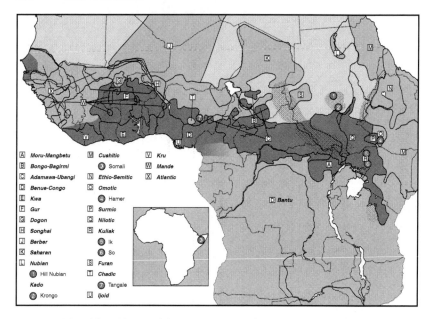

Map 5.3 ATR vowel harmony across African lineages

inconsistent word order (his type B). It is characterized in particular by the combination of S-V-O in the clause and by GEN-N in the noun phrase. This "mixed" type B is often associated with a second word-order pattern on the clause level, namely S-AUX-O-V-X (X = participant other than S and O). The possible alternation between the two orders is exemplified by (2) from Akan (Kwa).

(2) a. ɔ̀-fὲm-m̀   àbòfrá   nó   sìká
         3SG-lend-PAST   child   DEF   money
         'She lent the child money'
     b. ɔ̀-dὲ   sìká   fὲm-m̀   àbòfrá   nó
         3SG-AUX   money   lend-PAST   child   DEF
         'She lent [the] money to the child' (Manfredi 1997: 109)

The clause structure S-AUX-O-V-X, in which the object and another non-subject participant are separated from each other by the main verb, is in fact in some languages the only option (i.e. there is no S-V-O alternative); this holds particularly for the Mande family, as shown in example (3) from Koranko.

(3) ù   sí   wò   lá-bùì   yí   rɔ̀
     1SG   PROSPECTIVE   that.one   CAUS-fall   water   in
     'I'm going to throw her into the water' (Kastenholz 1987: 117)

It is thus an empirically salient and robust word-order type in Africa, which contrasts with the fact that it is crosslinguistically very rare (see Gensler 1994, 1997; Gensler & Güldemann 2003). Nevertheless, a continental survey of the feature turns out to be problematic, because it remains to be determined what the exact criteria are to view a language-specific structure as an instance of it. Several properties of S-AUX-O-V-X can be focused on: (a) the syntagmatic split within the predicate since the object intervenes between auxiliary and main verb; (b) the syntagmatic split between non-subject participants separated from each other by the main verb; and (c) the paradigmatic split within a language between S-AUX-O-V-X and S-V-O. The rationale for the following survey is not to view the involvement of an auxiliary as a necessary criterion and to consider languages which have either S-AUX-O-V-X or S-O-V-X as a major or the only word-order type.

The data are based on Gensler and Güldemann's (2003) survey, supplemented by information that was made available in connection with the workshop "Distributed predicative syntax" held at WOCAL 4, including Elders (2003) and Childs (2004). According to this material, S-(AUX)-O-V-X does not occur throughout the continent, but is restricted to languages of the following families: Songhay, Mande, Atlantic, Kru, Gur, Kwa, Benue-Congo, parts of Adamawa-Ubangi, and Moru-Mangbetu; it is also a possible structure in Ju (= Northern Khoisan) and the southern branch of Cushitic.

Heine and Claudi (2001: 43) claim that S-(AUX)-O-V-X "is neither a matter of common origin (= genetic relationship) nor of language contact (= areal relationship)." Instead, they exclusively entertain a grammaticalization explanation whose basic precondition is that a language combines S-V-O order in the clause with GEN-N order in the noun phrase (see the above article and Claudi 1993 for more details). This would suggest that the co-occurrence of these two word-order features is the ultimate common denominator of languages with S-(AUX)-O-V-X. However, this is not the case, *inter alia* because there are quite a few Benue-Congo and Adamawa-Ubangi languages with the pattern, but which have N-GEN. Therefore, the proposed functional explanation is unlikely to be an exhaustive account for the emergence and the geographical distribution of S-(AUX)-O-V-X in Africa (see also Gensler 1997 for some discussion).

In fact, there is no *a priori* reason why the marked word order should be a unitary phenomenon and thus have a single explanation for all its attested cases. Accordingly, a geographically isolated occurrence, as in Ju of southern Africa and South Cushitic of eastern Africa, does not rule out that the feature can be explained to a considerable extent in terms of genealogical and areal factors.

With respect to genealogical patterns, Gensler (1994, 1997) makes a case for reconstructing S-(AUX)-O-V-X to Proto-Niger-Congo (in Greenberg's Niger-Kordofanian sense), besides unmarked S-V-O. This becomes even more

Table 5.4 *Word order S-(AUX)-O-V-X across African lineages*

Family		Stock	Language or group (branch)	Area
Moru-Mangbetu	B	Central Sudanic		
Adamawa-Ubangi	C	N. Niger-Congo	Bolgo, Bua, Tunia, Niellim, Ndai, Samba Leko, Doyayo, Dii (A.); Mba, Dongo (U.)	South Chad, North Cameroon; Northeast DRC
Benue-Congo	D	N. Niger-Congo	except most of Narrow Bantu[a]	
Kwa	E	N. Niger-Congo		
Gur	F	N. Niger-Congo		
Songhay	H	–	except Koyra Chiini + Djenné Chiini	
Cushitic	M	Afroasiatic	Burunge, Iraqw (South)	North Tanzania
Kru	V	N. Niger-Congo		
Mande	W	–		
Atlantic	X	–		
Ju	Y	–		Namibia, Botswana

[a] The feature can be reconstructed for Proto-Bantu, presumably spoken in or very close to the relevant area. However, most of modern Narrow Bantu is not concerned; the clause order S-(AUX)-O-V-X, apparently restricted to just pronominal objects, has been petrified in the Savannah group as a morphotactic pattern in verbs, S-INFLECTION-O-VERB.STEM. The restriction to pronoun objects is generally salient in languages with S-(AUX)-O-V-X (cf. Childs 2004 for Atlantic) and it is indeed found in languages of other Benue-Congo branches and even Northwest Bantu, where it has not been grammaticalized as a word-level phenomenon (cf. Ikoro (1996: 206–13) for the Cross River language Kana, or Redden (1979: 126, 166f) for Ewondo).

attractive as soon as such uncertain members as Mande, Dogon, Ijoid, and Kordofanian are excluded from this stock, because there the feature has a very different status, as in Mande, or does not occur (Gensler & Güldemann 2003).

Regarding areal factors, the feature clearly clusters in northern sub-Saharan Africa. Moreover, Gensler and Güldemann (2003) and Güldemann (forthcoming c) observe that there is a geographical cline within this area regarding the functional load of the word-order pattern. Language families such as Moru-Mangbetu, Adamawa-Ubangi, Benue-Congo, and Kwa in the east, as well as Atlantic in the west mostly have S-(AUX)-O-V-X as a grammatically

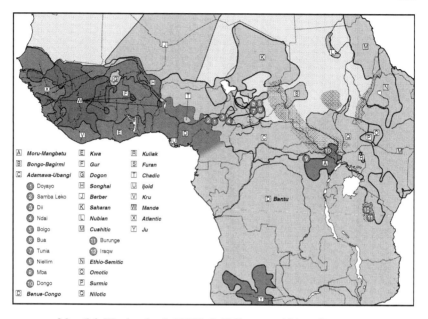

Map 5.4 Word order S-(AUX)-O-V-X across African lineages

conditioned phenomenon. That is, the preverbal position of objects is restricted to subclasses of objects (e.g. extrafocal participants, pronouns) or to special clause types (e.g. negation, progressive, certain modals); here, a common denominator of these contexts is arguably the object's status as extrafocal, non-asserted information (see Güldemann forthcoming c regarding Benue-Congo languages), possibly with the additional factor of its phonetic lightness (cf. the preference for pronouns). In the west, by contrast, especially in Mande, Songhay, Kru, and the Senufo branch of Gur, the structure is far more salient and is not (or is less) motivated by the above functional factors. Therefore, the increased salience in the westernmost Narrow Niger-Congo languages of the Gur and Kru families vis-à-vis their relatives in the east and, *pace* Childs (2004), possibly also the frequency of the pattern in the Atlantic language Kisi in the west can be interpreted as the result of contact with languages where O-V order does not have a salient V-O counterpart, as is the case in Mande and most of Songhai (with strong S-AUX-O-V-X) as well as Dogon (a true verb-final language).

5.2.5   Word order V-O-NEG

Another candidate for an areal isogloss whose geographical distribution is partly similar to that of previous features has been identified by Dryer (forthcoming). After showing that globally V-O languages display a preference

Table 5.5 *Word order V-O-NEG across African lineages*

Family		Stock	Language or group (branch)	Area
Bongo-Bagirmi	A	Central Sudanic	▓▓▓▓▓▓	
Moru-Mangbetu[b]	B	Central Sudanic	▓▓▓▓▓▓	
Adamawa-Ubangi	C	N. Niger-Congo	▓▓▓▓▓▓	
Benue-Congo	D	N. Niger-Congo	except most of Narrow Bantu	
Kwa	E	N. Niger-Congo	Ega	Côte d'Ivoire
Gur	F	N. Niger-Congo	Moré[a]	Burkina Faso
Gumuz		–	Gumuz	Ethiopian escarpment
Kado		–	Krongo[a]	Nuba Mountains
Daju		Eastern Sudanic	Shatt	Nuba Mountains
East Jebel		Eastern Sudanic	Gaam	Ethiopian escarpment
Chadic	T	Afroasiatic	▓▓▓▓▓▓	
Atlantic	X	–	Kisi[b]	Guinea-Conakry

Notes: [a] languages with double negation
    [b] languages with alternative S-AUX-O-V

for placing the negative marker before the verb, he identifies Central Africa as an area that goes against this general trend, because it hosts many V-O languages that have the negative word after the verb phrase or even at the very end of the clause. There are also V-O-NEG languages outside this area, for example, the South Atlantic language Kisi as shown in (4).

(4) wàŋndó   hὲnáŋ   pò   kóŋ   lé
     person   love   man   that   NEG
     'No one loves that man' (Childs 1995: 260)

Table 5.5 summarizes the data of Dryer's survey; I have also included his languages where (a) V-O-NEG occurs in one of two major clause orders, i.e. S-V-O (the other pattern being S-AUX-O-V, see section 5.2.4) and where (b) it is associated with a second negative before the verb.

The feature is particularly salient in Bongo-Bagirmi, Moru-Mangbetu, Chadic, Benue-Congo, and Adamawa-Ubangi, so that Dryer (forthcoming) concludes regarding the geographical pattern that "the area where VO&VNeg languages are common is one centered around the Central African Republic, extending north into the southern half of Chad, extending west to cover much of Cameroon and the eastern half of Nigeria, extending south into the Democratic Republic of the Congo, and extending east into Sudan." He also notes that there are some languages of the relevant type "outside this

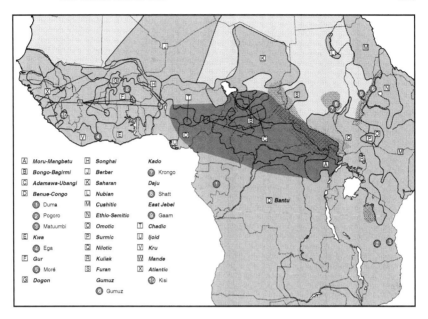

Map 5.5 Word order V-O-NEG across African lineages

immediate area which may represent historically unrelated instances of this order." This includes various languages from Narrow Bantu further south (e.g. in Tanzania, Angola, Democratic Republic of Congo), where the feature is a more recent innovation arising from the functionally motivated process of negation reinforcement.[7]

5.2.6   Labial flap consonants

Olson and Hajek (2003) give a survey of another typologically quirky sound property, labial flap phonemes. They are found so far in only three locations in the world: on the island of Flores (Indonesia) in the Austronesian language Sika, in southeastern Africa in a few Bantu languages, and in one larger area in Central Africa where quite a few languages of different genealogical affiliation are concerned, as shown in table 5.6. The families affected most are Bongo-Bagirmi, Moru-Mangbetu, and Adamawa-Ubangi.

The Central African area with labial flaps is defined by Olson and Hajek (2003: 159) "as the savannah of north central Africa and its immediate surroundings ... bounded to the north by the Sahara, to the south by the tropical rain forest, to the west by the Adamawa plateau, and to the east by the Upper Nile."

Table 5.6 *Labial flaps across African lineages*

Family		Stock	Language or group (branch)	Area
Bongo-Bagirmi	A	Central Sudanic	▓▓▓▓▓▓▓▓▓▓▓▓▓▓	
Moru-Mangbetu	B	Central Sudanic	▓▓▓▓▓▓▓▓▓▓▓▓▓▓	
Adamawa-Ubangi	C	N. Niger-Congo	▓▓▓▓▓▓▓▓▓▓▓▓▓▓	
Benue-Congo	D	N. Niger-Congo	Nungu (Platoid), Kwanja, Samba Daka, Tep (North Bantoid); Shona cluster, Nyanja Narrow Bantu)	East Nigeria, North Cameroon; Zimbabwe, Malawi
Chadic	T	Afroasiatic	Ron, Yiwom (West); Bana, Daba, Gude, Kamwe, Margi, Mofu-Gudur, Tera (Centr.); Gabri, Kera, Mukulu, Migaama (East); Pevé (Masa)	East Nigeria, North Cameroon, Southeast Chad

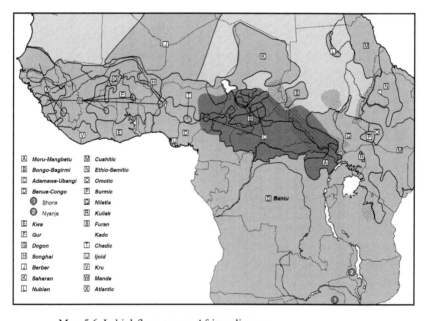

Map 5.6 Labial flaps across African lineages

5.2.7   Summary

I will now give a synopsis of the geographical and genealogical distribution of the six features presented in the previous sections. In order to make the distributional correlations between them more transparent, table 5.7 surveys them across a wider range of genealogical lineages of the entire African continent. Recall that such a survey cannot be complete, because it must disregard certain groups which are relevant for the present sampling level, viz. the "family," but on which the data are insufficient.

It can be seen that the middle of the table displays a cluster of language families with many grey cells, symbolizing the presence of a feature. This also reflects clustering in real geographical terms, because the language families are intentionally ordered in the table, to the effect that those within the area are put together, while those at the periphery or outside it are grouped around the former. This is indicated in the leftmost column in the order of increasing peripheral status: grey cell + bold script > grey cell > nothing.

The greatest cohesion exists in an area formed basically by four geographically adjacent language groups, the two easternmost Narrow Niger-Congo families Benue-Congo (minus Narrow Bantu) and Adamawa-Ubangi and the two Central Sudanic families Bongo-Bagirmi and Moru-Mangbetu. These are affected by virtually all features surveyed above, and mostly in a regular fashion; there is only one isogloss in which two of the families do not participate at all or very incompletely: S-(AUX)-O-V-X is not found in Bongo-Bagirmi and great parts of Adamawa-Ubangi. Also, more western Benue-Congo languages are excluded from V-O-NEG and labial flaps. The compact zone of these four families will be called here for convenience the areal "hotbed."

There is another grouping called here the "core," which comprises families that regularly possess at least three properties with intermediate or high frequency (marked by bold script and a grey cell in the left column of table 5.7). This core is formed by the following families (number of features in parentheses): Atlantic (3), Mande (3), Kru (3), Gur (4), Kwa (4), Benue-Congo (5), Adamawa-Ubangi (6), Bongo-Bagirmi (5), and Moru-Mangbetu (6).

Several lineages can be grouped together with the core in the sense that they are peripheral, but still adjacent to it and display the relevant feature set to an even lesser extent (marked by just a grey cell in the left column of table 5.7): Dogon, Songhay, and Ijoid. The number of moderately or frequently present features in them is one or two.

Finally, three lineages, Chadic, Nilotic, and Narrow Bantu, do not really belong to the area, as the features are mostly untypical for them; but they occur recurrently in member languages which border on the area and which thus could be viewed as participating in it. The numbers of properties concerned range on the group level from three in Nilotic, over five in Chadic, to

Table 5.7 *Distribution of linguistic features across African lineages*

Family	Stock	Logophoricity	Labio-velars	ATR harmony	S-(AUX)-O-V-X	V-O-NEG	Labial flaps
Berber	Afroasiatic						
Saharan							
Maban							
Furan							
Kordofanian							
Nubian	Eastern Sudanic						
Kunama (isolate)							
Nera (isolate)							
Semitic	Afroasiatic						
Cushitic	Afroasiatic						
Omotic	Afroasiatic						
Kado							
Chadic	Afroasiatic						
Dogon							
Songhay							
Atlantic							
Mande							
Kru	N. Niger-Congo						
Gur	N. Niger-Congo						
Kwa	N. Niger-Congo						
Benue-Congo	N. Niger-Congo						
Adamawa-Ubangi	N. Niger-Congo						
Moru-Mangbetu	Central Sudanic						
Bongo-Bagirmi	Central Sudanic						
Ijoid							
Bantu (Benue-Congo)	N. Niger-Congo						
Nilotic	Eastern Sudanic						
Surmic	Eastern Sudanic						
Kuliak							
Hadza (isolate)							
Sandawe (isolate)							
Khoe-Kwadi							
Ju							
Tuu							

Notes:
Family column: grey cell = families of the wider area; bold = families of the core area
Feature columns: dark grey = frequent, intermediate grey = present, light grey = rare, blank cell = absent or unknown

the maximum of six in Narrow Bantu. As mentioned above, Chadic and Nilotic repeatedly show a pattern whereby a feature in individual languages or sub-groups is fairly clearly due to contact with languages belonging to the core area.

In an abstract sense, the area as a whole can thus be conceived of as consisting of three concentric circles, where the sharing of features is particularly prominent in the innermost one, the "hotbed," is still strong in the intermediate one, the "core," but peters out in the outermost one, the "macro-area" as a whole.

Other candidate features for the macro-area and its subparts should be researched in the future in the light of the present hypothesis. Thus, Hajek's

(2005) worldwide survey of vowel nasalization reveals that this trait is unevenly distributed not only over the globe but also within Africa. Here, it patterns similarly to the area at issue, with two qualifications: it does not extend as far east as the previously mentioned features and it has a second, geographically separate hotbed in southern Africa not recognized in Hajek's survey, i.e. the languages subsumed under Khoisan; see Dimmendaal (2001a: 374–6) and Clements and Rialland (this volume, chapter 3) for more discussion. Moreover, Clements and Rialland's (this volume, chapter 3) African surveys of prosodic systems with three and more tone levels and of what they call "lax" question markers reveal as well clear parallels with the broader geographical pattern described here.

There is also more empirical support for the areal "hotbed." For example, a broader survey across the languages of Central Africa by Thomas (1972: 112) yields corroborating evidence regarding commonalities in sound structure in that seven phonological features (or absences) are identified as being virtually universal in this area; in addition to labial-velars and labial flaps discussed above, they are the presence of a voice–voiceless distinction and the absence of friction, of aspiration, of a uvular articulation place, and of consonant coarticulations (labialization, palatalization, velarization, pharyngealization). While the five additional traits are not very diagnostic due to their typological frequency, they still attest to a considerable degree of homogeneity of the area in terms of general sound patterns.

Finally, it is worth investigating features which define yet smaller zones within the area. For example, a typologically significant feature which seems to be relevant for a subzone in the Central African "hotbed" is the existence of pronoun systems of the so-called "minimal-augmented" type. Its important property is a fourth person category that combines the features "speaker" and "hearer" in one simplex form.[8] The pronoun system of Gula Sara (Bongo-Bagirmi, Central Sudanic) in (5) can serve as an example.

(5)   PERSON   MINIMAL   AUGMENTED
      1st + 2nd   zé   zégēgē
      1st   má   zígī
      2nd   í   ség
      3rd   nén, nēn   ɖéḡ   (after Nougayrol 1999: 106)

The African families where languages with a minimal-augmented system have been found so far are Benue-Congo, Adamawa-Ubangi, Bongo-Bagirmi, Chadic, Mande, Nilotic, and Kordofanian (the information is based on Greenberg 1988: 2 and Cysouw 2003: 140, p.c., but also includes a few more languages not mentioned there).[9] Since no lineage on the family level has been found to display the feature regularly, table 5.8 and map 5.7 only involve individual languages.

Table 5.8 *Minimal-augmented pronoun systems across African lineages*

Family		Stock	Language or group (branch)	Area
Kordofanian		–	Heiban, Moro (Heiban)	Nuba Mountains
Bongo-Bagirmi	A	Central Sudanic	Mbay (Sara-Bagirmi); Gula, Furu (Kara)	South Chad; Central African Republic, North DRC
Adamawa-Ubangi	C	N. Niger-Congo	Dii (A.), Belanda Viri (U.)	Cameroon, South Sudan
Benue-Congo	D	N. Niger-Congo	Ghomala, Ngiemboon, Mankon, Limbum, Vengo, Akoose, Makaa (Non-B. Bantoid)	Southwest Cameroon
Nilotic	Q	Eastern Sudanic	Nuer (West)	South Sudan
Chadic	T	Afroasiatic	Fyer, Ron, Sha, Kulere (West); Marghi, Lamang, Xedi, Gude, Buduma, Lagwan (Central); Lele (East)	North-central Nigeria; Lake Chad area; South Chad
Mande	W	–	Dan, Yaouré (East); Toma (West)	Côte d'Ivoire; Guinea

The distribution of this feature is fairly dispersed and does not qualify as an isogloss of some larger linguistic area. Nevertheless, two points are remarkable. Its general geographical and genealogical profile is comparable to that of the previous features in that it is synchronically restricted to the sub-Saharan belt at issue and straddles a similar set of families. More importantly, there is a clear concentration of the feature in an area that stretches from Lake Chad in a south-southwestern direction, which is arguably mediated by areal contact. In involving Chadic, Bongo-Bagirmi, Benue-Congo, and possibly Adamawa-Ubangi, it is reminiscent of the genealogical profile of the areal "hotbed." In contrast to most other features, in this case the possibility that some early language state of Chadic displayed this property is not excluded (cf. Newman 1990: 133, (a)).

5.3   Previous approaches

Looking back to the history of African linguistics, it should be recognized that the macro-area under consideration has various types of conceptual predecessors. These will be discussed briefly in the following section.

5.3.1   *Westermann's* Sudansprachen

The first study which dealt more extensively with linguistic similarities across the wider area at issue was Westermann (1911), proposing a language group

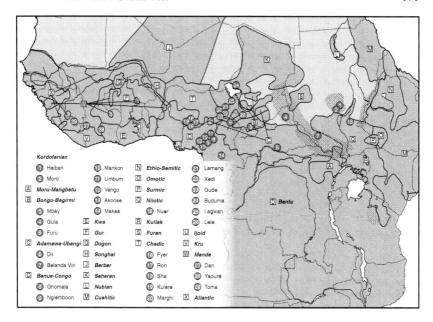

Map 5.7 Minimal-augmented pronoun systems across African lineages

Sudansprachen.[10] This concept, as expressed in this and later studies (1927, 1935, 1940), differs in several important respects from the linguistic entity proposed here.

First of all, Westermann stated explicitly that his Sudan language group is a unit defined in genealogical terms, while I interpret the commonalities identified above to reflect a linguistic *area* across different genealogical units. Also, a look at the sample languages of Westermann (1911) and the accompanying map reveals that his Sudan group is more inclusive in geographical terms. For example, his sample includes Ewe, Twi, Gã, Yoruba, Efik, and Dinka, which are inside or close to the area under consideration, but also Kunama (isolate) and Nobiin (Nubian), which are geographically quite remote.[11] Finally, it becomes evident from Westermann's writing that his motivations for including certain languages in the Sudan group and excluding others from it are often not of a purely linguistic nature. In accordance with the general approach to African linguistic classification at the time, he was also guided by criteria referring to cultural and biological characteristics of the respective speech communities. Accordingly, the Sudan languages as a genealogically defined unit have not played a major role in the later history of African linguistics (see, however, section 5.3.3 below).[12]

Despite these differences, Westermann's concept of a Sudan language group is highly relevant in the present context. Most importantly, he explicitly identified (1911: 2) a connection between languages of West Africa on the one hand and adjacent languages of Central and partly East Africa on the other hand.

From an empirical perspective, too, he anticipated at least one feature mentioned above in remarking that labial-velars are typical sounds of his Sudan group (1911: 4, 1935: 132, 1940: 11–12); some other shared features suggested by him, such as properties of prosody, syllable structure, and word order, are also worthy of a more detailed comparison to be carried out in the future.

Finally, he himself remarked on the possible areal nature of some of his shared Sudan features (Westermann 1935: 142–3, 1949: 11–14) and in the end appears to have no longer been convinced of the genealogical hypothesis, which figures at best marginally in his later publications on African linguistic classification (Westermann 1949, 1952; Westermann & Bryan 1952). For example, Westermann (1949: 15–17) explicitly establishes the genealogical relationship between Bantu and the Sudan languages immediately to the west, while excluding Nilotic from the Sudan group and refraining from any genealogical assignment of such earlier alleged Sudan lineages in the north, such as Furan, Kordofanian, Kunama, Nera, and Nubian.[13]

5.3.2   Greenberg's "Nuclear African area"

Another predecessor of the present concept goes back to Greenberg (1959, 1983). He tried to identify "special features of African languages," whereby Africa was intended, at least in the later article (1983: 18, footnote 2), to be restricted to the sub-Saharan part of the continent – an idea which was not further motivated. The invoked linguistic properties range from phonology (clicks, labial-velars, implosives, simple consonant and vowel systems, open syllables, few complex consonants with the exception of nasal clusters, distinctive tone and, added in the 1983 article, labiodentals = labial flaps), over morphology (complex systems of nominal genders and verbal derivation), to semantics (same word for 'meat' and 'wild animal'; same word for 'eat,' 'conquer,' 'capture in game,' and 'have sex'; 'child' expresses diminutives; body-part terms express locative relations and reflexive intensifiers; 'surpass' expresses comparatives).

While Greenberg fails to show that these features single out Africa as a whole against other linguistic (macro)-areas of the world, he observes:

... that various sections of the continent differ in the intensity with which they partake of such common characteristics. There is a large central area in which all of these characteristics are found in most of the languages. This core area consists mainly of the Niger-Congo languages, Songhai, the Central Sudanic subgroup of the Macrosudanic family, and, to a certain degree, the Chad subgroup of Afro-Asiatic. (Greenberg 1959: 24)

It should be borne in mind that Greenberg starts from a genealogical language classification which differs from the one underlying this chapter (see section 5.4.2). He also tends to conceptualize languages of his "central area" as somehow more typical of the continent than those of his "marginal areas," such as northern, southern, and eastern Africa – an idea I am equally reluctant to follow, because it is unclear to me in which sense the "central area" is any more representative for the whole continent than another subarea with a different linguistic profile (see section 5.6). Nevertheless, the characterization of the "central area" in terms of the genealogical lineages participating in it and the geography resulting thereof is virtually identical to that given in section 5.2.7.

5.3.3   The genealogical super-group "Niger-Kordofanian + Nilo-Saharan (NKNS)"

In so far as African linguistics in its more recent history tried to come to grips with linguistic commonalities across the relevant sub-Saharan belt, it shifted back to a basically genealogical interpretation. Not too long after Greenberg (1963) it was proposed that two of his four African super-groups, Niger-Kordofanian and Nilo-Saharan, should be combined into a yet larger genealogically defined unit (henceforth, referred to as NKNS). This approach would imply that the areal isoglosses at issue could largely be explained in terms of inheritance from a common ancestor.

Gregersen (1972) was the first to propose a NKNS grouping, calling it "Kongo-Saharan." His hypothesis is based on (a) alleged similarities between Niger-Kordofanian and Nilo-Saharan in affixes for number and/or gender, pronouns, and various other grammatical morphemes, and (b) a list of approximately eighty lexical series comparing items from up to ten randomly chosen languages from each macro-group. In dealing with relevant languages in the geographically more confined area of Cameroon and the Central African Republic, Boyd (1978) presents a follow-up to Gregersen's hypothesis without coming to a clear conclusion whether similarities are to be explained by inheritance or language contact.

Blench (1995, forthcoming) proposes "Niger-Saharan" as the name for NKNS. He invokes commonalities in the domain of phonology (ATR vowel harmony, labial-velar consonants), morphology (alleged reflexes of Niger-Kordofanian noun class affixes for liquid/mass in Nilo-Saharan, especially in Central Sudanic), and lexicon (about thirty comparative series in which Westermann's 1927 and Mukarovsky's 1976/7 data referring to Greenberg's Niger-Congo are confronted mostly with forms from individual languages subsumed under Nilo-Saharan).

A few other authors have also expressed confidence in an NKNS lineage, for example, Bender (2000: 57) and Dimmendaal (2001c: 148–52); the latter attempting to reconstruct logophoric markers for the proto-language of this group.

5.4   Areal vs. genealogical explanation

Previous research then came up with two basic competing explanations for the linguistic commonalities in northern sub-Saharan Africa, genealogical inheritance from the common ancestor of NKNS (early Westermann, Gregersen, Blench, Bender, Dimmendaal) and language contact (Greenberg). I argue here for a basically areal hypothesis and will call the proposed linguistic entity from now on "Macro-Sudan (belt)."[14] In so doing, I intentionally follow Westermann's terminology, because his early perception that the languages at issue belong somehow together, even if based more on intuition than on empirical facts, deserves recognition. The main arguments against the idea of a genealogical NKNS super-group and in favor of the Macro-Sudan belt hypothesis will be laid out now.

5.4.1   Insufficient evidence for the genealogical hypothesis

A major reason for preferring an areal hypothesis is that the evidence for a genealogical NKNS unit is scarce and does not conform to commonly accepted ways to establish this kind of link between heretofore unrelated linguistic lineages. Thus, it comes as no surprise that the hypothesis has not gathered a substantial following among Africanists. Güldemann (2003a: 376–8) gives a critical discussion of Dimmendaal's (2001c) attempt to reconstruct logophoric pronouns for Proto-NKNS; most objections raised there can be transferred to the overall approach taken by Gregersen and Blench.

The mere *presence* of a structural feature (logophorics, labial-velars, ATR vowel harmony, etc.) clearly does not invoke an NKNS unit; such typological properties, however rare crosslinguistically, can develop independently or be acquired via language contact, so that they do not identify an individual proto-language (cf. Nichols 1996: 48–56).

Also, the alleged correspondences in sound and meaning are largely restricted to lexical items. The essentially probative evidence for genealogical relationship, namely shared systems or subsystems of a grammatical and paradigmatic nature, has not yet been brought forward in any convincing form.

Another major problem for the cases where sound–meaning correspondences are claimed to exist is that the evidence for a certain shared form across NKNS comes invariably from just a small number of individual languages or subgroups. Moreover, the languages or groups occur randomly across the different sets, apparently according to whether they possess a form serving a particular comparison. This situation must be confronted with the enormous number of languages and families subsumed under both Niger-Kordofanian and Nilo-Saharan. According to Grimes (2000), Niger-Kordofanian (called there "Niger-Congo") comprises about 1,500 languages belonging to about ten family-level units; the approximate figures for Nilo-Saharan are 200 languages and twenty families. Against these numbers, it is evidently insufficient to cite putative cognates of a tiny and randomly chosen fraction of the actually existing diversity.

Finally, the traditional principles and techniques of the comparative method or other relevant approaches like diachronic typology are not adhered to. In fact, one gets the impression that they are not viewed as essential for the acceptance of a new genealogical relationship. For example, Gregersen considers "the method of mass comparison [to be] a valid strategy for *discovering* genetic relationships" (1972: 70, italics TG), a view that many linguists might be prepared to agree with; but he admits at the same time that he had "not attempted to work out sound correspondences in support of the K[ongo-] S[aharan] hypothesis" (1972: 77). Up to the present, mass comparison and similar exploratory approaches to the NKNS problem have not been followed by more rigorous attempts to substantiate/prove the hypothesis, that is, attempts which follow more or less the standard procedures of historical-comparative reconstruction and are based on more extensive and systematically chosen data.

5.4.2   *The genealogical diversity of the area*

If entertaining an areal hypothesis, the distribution of the linguistic similarities should not correspond to the distribution of language groups defined by genealogical relationships; i.e. isoglosses should recurrently cut across such linguistic boundaries. So the area constituted by certain features should display a good amount of internal genealogical diversity. It is clear that an answer to this question for the Macro-Sudan belt is to a certain extent a function of the underlying genealogical classification of African languages.

I have pointed out that the NKNS hypothesis cannot be accepted for the time being, because the evidence does not meet the common standards of historical linguistics. By the same token, I prefer not to follow the widely accepted African classification by Greenberg (1963).[15] Rather, the present study is oriented toward low-level units which already are, or obviously can be, established on the basis of the presently available data by historical-comparative work and similar techniques. In the present classification I have followed for convenience Nichols' (1992: 24–5) ideal concepts of "family" and "stock." As a result, Greenberg's (1963) more speculative super-groupings Khoisan, Nilo-Saharan, and Niger-Kordofanian are broken down into more acceptable component groups. In particular, the fact that Nilo-Saharan has not yet been substantiated by sufficient evidence from within the framework of historical-comparative research leads to a far larger number of families to be reckoned with. Also, as mentioned above, the present concept of the stock-level unit Niger-Congo is conceived of narrowly in that the families Kordofanian, Mande, Atlantic, Dogon, and Ijoid are not recognized as established members (not implying thereby that none of them will turn out to be a valid member in the future).[16]

Under this approach, the Macro-Sudan belt is genealogically highly heterogeneous.[17] Even if one disregards several isolate languages in the area like Pre, Mpre, Laal, and Jalaa, which have not yet been classified conclusively with a larger group (Williamson & Blench 2000: 36; Kleinewillinghöfer 2001), it would still involve in the order of nine independent linguistic lineages: Atlantic; Mande; Dogon; Songhay; Afroasiatic (with Chadic); Ijoid; Narrow Niger-Congo (with the five families Kru, Gur, Kwa, Benue-Congo, and Adamawa-Ubangi); Central Sudanic (with the two families Bongo-Bagirmi and Moru-Mangbetu); and Eastern Sudanic (with Nilotic). Moreover, it must be taken into account that Central Sudanic and, even more so, Narrow Niger-Congo are internally diverse, which adds to the genealogical heterogeneity of the Macro-Sudan belt. Indeed, a considerable amount of contact has occurred between families within these larger groups, enhancing the geographical proliferation of certain linguistic features (cf., e.g., Dimmendaal 2001a).

Starting out from Greenberg (1963), the question of the genealogical diversity of the Macro-Sudan belt can still be answered positively, because the area would comprise languages from three of his four super-groups, namely Niger-Kordofanian, Nilo-Saharan, and Afroasiatic. Moreover, the great heterogeneity of the Macro-Sudan belt in the above conservative classification would not really vanish under a more lumping approach, because the super-groups resulting from it would then imply a far greater *internal* diversity and time depth, which again make areal explanations viable.

Even under the most lumping classification involving an NKNS unit, a certain degree of genealogical heterogeneity of the Macro-Sudan belt would have to be admitted, because Chadic is included to a certain extent in the isoglosses, but is genealogically unrelated (cf. also the peripheral involvement of Omotic; see section 5.5 below). Thus, a plausible explanation for the distribution of certain features in Africa would, under any type of available classification, require a certain amount of *areal* argumentation.

5.4.3   Language contact in the Macro-Sudan belt

Another reason for entertaining an areal interpretation is that language contact across boundaries of families is indeed attested widely within the Macro-Sudan belt and can recurrently account for the distribution of individual linguistic features in subareas (see Dimmendaal 2001a for some discussion).

Unfortunately, the almost universal acceptance of Greenberg's (1963) lumping classification for Africa seems to have influenced the research on language contact on this continent in that linguistic convergence processes have rarely been considered as alternatives to Greenberg's empirically weak genealogical affiliations. Therefore, published studies on language contact between families *within* Niger-Kordofanian and Nilo-Saharan remain incidental.

Language contact in the Macro-Sudan belt has, however, received considerable attention when involving lineages that Greenberg viewed as unrelated. Linguistic phenomena in Chadic (Afroasiatic) which are likely to be induced by contact with its genealogically unrelated neighbors from Benue-Congo, Adamawa-Ubangi, and Bongo-Bagirmi have been treated by such important studies as H. Wolff (1959), Hoffmann (1970), E. Wolff and Gerhardt (1977), Jungraithmayr (1980, 1987, 1992/3), and Kleinewillinghöfer (1990). Another focus on linguistic contact between different lineages in the Macro-Sudan belt is the relation between Songhay on the one hand and Mande and Berber (and even Chadic) on the other hand. Considerable convergence between Bongo-Bagirmi and the Banda group of Adamawa-Ubangi is the topic of Cloarec-Heiss (1995). Dimmendaal (1995b, 2001a, 2001b), Wrigley (2001), and Storch (2003) have also addressed language contact in the eastern periphery of the Macro-Sudan belt, namely between Nilotic and its western and southern neighbors from Moru-Mangbetu and, yet further away, Bantu.

5.4.4   The areally defined profile of individual families

The fact that several families concerned are internally diverse with respect to Macro-Sudan features, and this according to the proposed geographical pattern, is another significant fact in favor of the areal approach. That is, member languages of a certain family behave differently according to whether they are located in or close to the area at issue or not. In particular, most of Narrow Bantu, a clear member of Benue-Congo (Narrow Niger-Congo), is located outside the Macro-Sudan belt and does not share most of the above properties to any significant degree, while its relatives in the area regularly have them. There are two different scenarios on how such a situation has come into being. Either Proto-Bantu, which might have been spoken at the southern periphery of the Macro-Sudan belt, possessed a given feature and lost it when expanding outside the area (this would imply that the submerged substratum in the Bantu spread zone played an important role in changing the profile of the family to be) or Proto-Bantu lacked the feature but its daughter languages in or close to the Macro-Sudan belt acquired it through language contact. A scenario of the latter type is largely applicable to most other families which have an ambiguous behavior vis-à-vis a Macro-Sudan belt feature; especially clear cases are found with the peripheral families Chadic and Nilotic.

In the same vein, that families within the Macro-Sudan belt share an overall similar profile can be significant as well, in two respects: it may (a) single them out against other related families which are more marginal to the area and (b) not correlate with their genealogical relationship. A good example in this respect is the behavior of Adamawa-Ubangi and (especially eastern) Benue-Congo: the two families are coherent in terms of geography and areal features, which sets them off against the rest of Narrow Niger-Congo, but they are genealogically not particularly close within this stock.

5.4.5   The profile of the linguistic features defining the Macro-Sudan belt

An areal approach is also favored in several respects by the linguistic profile of the features. First of all, the answer to an important question, namely how likely it is that a given feature is due to inheritance, does not particularly support the genealogical hypothesis. That is, the properties are not inherently stable and thus diagnostic of inheritance from a remote ancestor language (*pace* Blench 1995 regarding ATR vowel harmony and labial-velars). Section 5.2 has shown that, on the one hand, there almost always exist historically unrelated cases of a property occurring outside Africa, or in Africa outside the Macro Sudan belt, which suggests that it can emerge independently. On the other hand, and more important for the present areal hypothesis, the majority of features are evidently transferable by language contact.

It is significant in this respect that an author's evaluation of a feature in terms of stability, transferability, etc., is at times clearly steered by her/his particular approach to language history in Africa. The discussion of ATR vowel harmony provides a telling example in that the relevant studies arrive at historical scenarios which are opposed to each other. Blench (1995), in proposing the genealogical super-group NKNS, needs to argue in favor of feature inheritance and indeed claims against some empirical counterevidence that "vowel-harmony systems are fairly resistant to borrowing" (1995: 90). Hall et al. (1974) and Dimmendaal (2001a) try to account for the same synchronic situation by means of a language-contact explanation; Dimmendaal, who is explicitly dedicated in his article to diffusion of linguistic features in Africa, states that "vowel harmony can be acquired and lost easily" (2001a: 371) and "there is a clear-cut areal dimension to the dichotomy between languages with and those without ATR systems" (2001a: 373).

Another major point is that the isoglosses do not belong to the repertoire of common properties of human languages, which reduces considerably the likelihood of chance occurrence. In fact, most properties are so "quirky" that a language with more than one of them can be easily recognized as an African (or for that matter Macro-Sudan) language. It is the very markedness of the features crosslinguistically that allows one to propose an areal explanation, despite the fairly restricted number of isoglosses and their considerable amount of geographical non-overlap (see section 5.5 below).

Finally, the features are independent of each other in the sense that they concern different linguistic domains, like phonology and morphosyntax, and subdomains thereof. This makes it highly unlikely that one is confronted with a complex of related features in which the presence of one favors the presence of another.

The following can be summarized for the areal hypothesis entertained here. The features listed in section 5.2 may not yet be conclusive proof for the existence of a large convergence and diffusion area across northern sub-Saharan Africa. However, they represent solid empirical evidence in this direction. Moreover, alternative explanations like genealogical inheritance or chance do not seem to provide particularly plausible accounts for the empirical facts. All this justifies a systematic search for more corroborating data for the present idea of the Macro-Sudan belt as a linguistic area.

5.5   Preliminaries to the historical emergence
of the Macro-Sudan belt

In this section, I will address the important issue of how the Macro-Sudan belt might have come into being. I must stress from the outset that I consider it to be unlikely that this question will ever be answered by one specific and unitary historical scenario. Accordingly, I will at this stage not speculate on any correlations between the present findings and data from non-linguistic disciplines like human genetics, archaeology, history, cultural anthropology, etc.

The primary empirical reason for this assumption is the existence of considerable differences in the distribution of individual isoglosses. For one thing, among the six features surveyed above in more detail there is an obvious discrepancy between the last two features (V-O-NEG, labial flaps) on the one hand and the first four features (logophoricity, labial-velars, ATR vowel harmony, S-(AUX)-O-V-X) on the other hand, making it necessary to distinguish between the areal "hotbed" and the Macro-Sudan belt as a whole. But the crosscontinental distributions of the first four isoglosses, too, are not identical with each other. Apart from the varying occurrence of features outside the wider area, they differ especially in their presence or absence in its western and eastern peripheries. Labial-velars extend further west than logophorics in that the families Mande, Kru, and Atlantic as well as northern Bantu are now included. The same observation can be made for ATR vowel harmony, but in addition this feature is also found more frequently in the east; particularly, it extends far into the otherwise peripheral Eastern Sudanic groups Nilotic and Surmic. For S-(AUX)-O-V-X, it can be observed that its area is far less compact in that languages in the center and the east, viz. the entire Bongo-Bagirmi family and great parts of Adamawa-Ubangi, do not seem to display it.

Clearly, these differences potentially pose a problem for an areal hypothesis. I would argue, however, that this problem is only relevant under a particular assumption, namely that the area arose in a single historical process. As soon as one starts from the hypothesis that the features did not spread simultaneously and/or from the same source, the picture is no longer incompatible with an areal explanation, because differences in the boundaries of somehow related isoglosses are not an unknown phenomenon in other research of linguistic geography like, for example, dialectology.

The justification for the Macro-Sudan belt is twofold. First, all features cluster within the same broad region of the African continent, while being rare or absent outside it. Second, despite considerable differences, the clustering pattern has in a more abstract sense a robust geographical commonality. The northern and southern boundaries of the Macro-Sudan belt apply to the different features regularly and thus seem to be more or less stable; movements across them appear to be associated with a change in profile on the part of the linguistic population (cf. the cases of Chadic and Bantu with regard to the presence or absence of features). As opposed to this, the eastern and western extensions of isoglosses are subject to considerable variation. This suggests that linguistic features seem to predominantly undergo historical expansion in an eastward and/or westward direction. That is, the overall historical dynamics within the area has an east–west rather than a north–south trajectory. Moreover, the existence of a particularly homogeneous nucleus, the "hotbed," can be interpreted as a possible innovation area that repeatedly radiates into the periphery with variable scope along this horizontal axis.

In section 5.1 I have given a rough outline of the Macro-Sudan belt. In so doing, I have referred to non-linguistic, geographical concepts: the Sahara–Sahel marking the northern boundary and the Atlantic Ocean and the Congo Basin the southern boundary. Since the distribution of linguistic features correlates with these geographical entities, I venture the hypothesis that the Macro-Sudan belt is primarily the result of geographical factors which have been relevant for a sufficiently long time period.

This means that it was not the mere presence or absence of contact between different linguistic populations that shaped the Macro-Sudan; in principle, conditions for contact situations of any kind (cultural exchange, group migration, intermarriage, long-range feature diffusion, etc.) can be assumed to exist almost everywhere. The crucial point is that relatively stable geographical macro-areas differ according to their conditions for human subsistence: heterogeneity between vs. homogeneity within areas. Thus, the impact of population contact across boundaries tends, over a long time span, to be lower vis-à-vis contacts not involving such boundaries.

With respect to the Macro-Sudan, its northern and southern limits were, relatively speaking, a greater barrier for population exchange/movement or the flow of individual features associated with populations, while these processes tended to be facilitated along the west–east trajectory. In other words, stable geographical factors have been constantly reinforcing migration and contact patterns in this part of Africa along a west–east axis, independently of the individual historical processes.[18] At the same time, the effects of these processes did not encroach considerably on neighboring areas like the Sahara–Sahel, the Congo Basin, and the Ethiopian Plateau, nor were similar processes in or emerging from these parts of Africa capable of obliterating the geographical integrity of the Macro-Sudan belt (see, however, below regarding its eastern boundary).

It should be recognized that the Macro-Sudan belt in the conceptualization proposed here may not be entirely comparable to linguistic areas such as the Balkans, South Asia, Meso-America, etc.; these are usually smaller and the shared features seem to be more closely associated with concrete historical processes like the spread of a particular language family, previous presence of a common linguistic substratum, or a certain period of sociopolitical unity, probably under one dominant linguistic population. Future research must show whether the differences between these classical sprachbunds and the macro-area entertained here are of a qualitative nature or rather of degree.

The idea of an area that did not emerge as the result of accidental historical factors, but rather of long-term geographical integrity can also account for the considerable difference regarding the eastern and/or western extensions of linguistic isoglosses. The degree to which the western and eastern peripheries, or areas yet further east, are affected by an individual feature would depend on the impetus and scope of the concrete historical process(es) responsible for its spread and maintenance. As a corollary, considerable distributional differences between features would thus indicate that they did not emerge under the same historical circumstances.

A particular point should in fact be made regarding the eastern limit of the Macro-Sudan. Compared to the other boundaries, it is certainly the least well defined. On the one hand, the Nilotic and Surmic families, which are in general outside the area, partake in a more regular way in one important isogloss, ATR vowel harmony, so that in this case recent and peripheral contact with Macro-Sudan languages cannot be held responsible for their involvement. On the other hand, there are several cases where individual languages in southwestern Ethiopia (all from Omotic) and in the Nuba Mountains in the Sudan (from different lineages) share a certain Macro-Sudan feature. These are not adjacent to the area, but separated from it by languages which are predominantly from Nilotic and Surmic. It is important in this context that these two families are newcomers in the area (cf. Dimmendaal 1998b: 17–20). If one assumes that in colonizing their present territory they replaced languages which were typologically akin to the Macro-Sudan type, two things could find a potential explanation. First, the languages in southwestern Ethiopia and the Nuba Mountains with Macro-Sudan features might be the relics of a greater eastward extension of this area at some earlier point in time. That is, there may have been an uninterrupted connection between these zones and the Macro-Sudan of today, which became submerged by the spread of Nilotic and Surmic. Second, the last two linguistic populations would have incorporated a certain amount of Macro-Sudan features from the defunct substrate languages; this could explain the wider presence of ATR vowel harmony in them.

It is of course important to answer for each Macro-Sudan feature the question of its ultimate origin and subsequent proliferation. Güldemann (2003a: 382–3) gives a rough outline for the possible emergence of the modern distribution of logophoricity in Africa, thereby stressing that different kinds of explanations must be taken into account, namely (i) language-internal innovation, (ii) genealogical inheritance, and (iii) contact-induced acquisition. The gist of the scenario for logophoricity is that it is likely to have been innovated at least once in some early language state of Narrow Niger-Congo and/or Central Sudanic, that it expanded and consolidated in a geographically far wider area due to divergence processes in these lineages, and that it spread still further to languages of other families by way of contact interference; at the same time, languages with the feature, when moving out of the Macro-Sudan belt, were prone to losing it.

Such an interaction of the three factors can also be expected for the other Macro-Sudan features. The historical scenarios entertained for some of them do in fact follow similar lines of argumentation. This concerns particularly one point: Central Sudanic and even more so Narrow Niger-Congo, or parts thereof, are given key roles in the large-scale proliferation of a feature. Compare in this respect Greenberg (1983: 4–11) for labial-velars, Gensler and Güldemann (2003) for S-(AUX)-O-V-X, and Greenberg (1983: 11–12) and Olson and Hayek (2003: 174–8) for labial flaps. So it is quite likely that these two lineages had a generally decisive role in the shaping of the modern profile of the Macro-Sudan belt.

However, the enormous time depth involved confronts us with an important problem regarding the search for a *synchronically* attested source language (group). It cannot be excluded *a priori* that early language forms of such expanding groups as Narrow Niger-Congo and Central Sudanic colonized zones where a certain property was already established as an areal feature, including lineages that have been obliterated in the meantime. Certainly, it is preferable to be able to identify the ultimate origin of a feature in a concrete source. However, without any solid evidence, the primary gain of projecting a modern lineage into the very remote past is that it makes a historical scenario more graspable; it does not make the scenario more probable.

5.6   The Macro-Sudan belt and historical linguistic
research in Africa

I have tried to present evidence that a large belt in northern sub-Saharan Africa forms a linguistic macro-area that has been shaped by geographical conditions that were fairly stable over a long time span. The evidence for this hypothesis consists of linguistic features which are diagnostic first of all because of their markedness both crosslinguistically and on the African continent, not so much because of their number or their entirely similar distribution. If the identification of an areal entity "Macro-Sudan belt" can be substantiated by future research, this has consequences for linguistic research in Africa as a whole.

For one thing, it is bound to change the general outsider perception of the linguistic profile of this continent. There is a strong tendency, most clearly brought out by Greenberg (1959, 1983), to present some of the linguistic properties of the Macro-Sudan belt as typical for Africa in general and thus establishing *the* African language type. This is due to several factors. In purely geographical terms, the area at issue constitutes a large and central part of the continent. Even more important seems to be the fact that it hosts numerically the large majority of African languages as well as most of the larger African language families. A third factor is that the spread zone formed by Bantu, another major portion of African languages with a huge distribution, is historically related to the Macro-Sudan belt. Since this group is a genealogical off-shoot of Benue-Congo within the Macro-Sudan, it shares some traits with the languages of this area, thus increasing the impression that some relevant features are "pan-African" (cf., e.g., Greenberg 1983: 12–18 regarding 'meat' = 'animal' and 'surpass' > comparative periphrasis). Nevertheless, that the implicit equation of the continent with the Macro-Sudan belt is misleading is already prefigured by Greenberg himself when he asks (1983: 3–4) and in fact answers (1959: 24; see the quote in section 5.3.2) the following question: "Are the traits which seem most particularly African on a worldwide basis concentrated within certain areas within Africa itself?" If, as argued here and elsewhere, the features are not of continental, but rather of sub-areal relevance, i.e. just typical of the Macro-Sudan belt, they cannot be taken to characterize Africa as a whole.

There is another way of looking at African languages with a Macro-Sudan bias, namely viewing sub-Saharan Africa as a linguistic area (cf., e.g., Greenberg 1983 and Wald 1994: 294–5). This is related to a long scientific tradition – originating outside linguistics, but corroborated to a certain extent by linguistic evidence – to separate northern Africa from its adjacent zones further south. The factual linguistic distinctness of this part of Africa has both genealogical and areal aspects, namely the different character of the dominating Afroasiatic stock and the possible existence of other, partially adjacent macro-areas, for example, the so-called "Chad–Ethiopia" zone (see Heine 1975; Güldemann 2005). In any case, even the more narrow conception of sub-Saharan Africa as an areal unit is inappropriate because it still includes large territorial portions in the east and south whose typological profiles differ markedly from that of the Macro-Sudan belt. As a general conclusion, I would venture therefore that what has heretofore been viewed to be a "typical" African language should rather be called more concretely a Macro-Sudan language; this acknowledges the fact that other important areal groups of African languages are not of this type.

On the other hand, the case of the Macro-Sudan and its conceptual pre-decessors seems to reveal that a biased research approach can have serious consequences for the range of interpretations entertained for a given set of empirical findings. That is, as in many other parts of the globe, historical linguistics in Africa has for a long time started from the assumption that divergence processes are the paradigm scenario of language history and has thus considered convergence merely as a corrective when the former fails to explain the facts. This approach culminated in Greenberg's (1963) lumping classification into just four genealogical super-groups, which has become the received wisdom, but is shaky in many respects. *Pace* Dimmendaal (2001a: 388), who has claimed for African linguistics in general that "areal diffusion did not obscure the original genetic relationship," I would argue that com-parisons over larger geographical zones – such as Westermann's pioneer work on the "Sudansprachen" – quite often detected linguistic commonalities of an alleged genealogical nature, which may well turn out after a more rigorous analysis to be mediated by areal phenomena (if they are not of a more universal nature). So the virtually unchallenged acceptance of Greenberg's genealogical scheme has in my view deprived African linguistics of some of its potentially most interesting fields of areal-linguistic research. This is not confined to the Macro-Sudan belt, but also seems to apply to other entities whose proposed shared features, as far as they are real, were and/or still are approached mostly in genealogical terms like Khoisan, Nilo-Saharan, and Tucker's (1967a, 1967b) Erythraic, just to mention a few cases.

Finally, if areal-linguistic relations in Africa were addressed in the past, scholars worked, a few exceptions like Greenberg and Heine aside, with a micro- rather than macro-perspective. Accordingly, the cataloguing of the continent as a whole in terms of linguistic geography and the more precise definition of identified macro-areas is still in an exploratory stage. An apparent misconception resulting from the lack of a clearer picture for the entire continent is directly relevant for the Macro-Sudan belt as discussed here: it collides with what has, implicitly or explicitly, been conceived of as a viable research object of areal linguistics on the continent, namely West Africa, characterized roughly as the zone south of the Sahara from Senegal to

Cameroon. The geographical profile of the features treated in this chapter does not provide evidence for West Africa as a well-defined linguistic area. In fact, most properties have their very core distribution around the border between West Africa in the geographical sense and zones further east, attesting to an uninterrupted areal connection across this alleged boundary.

In general, I hope that the present chapter – however preliminary its findings may still be – has shown that non-genealogical explanations may provide feasible accounts of the emergence of Africa's linguistic profile and thus will help to create a more balanced research approach regarding linguistic divergence and convergence processes on this continent.

6   The Tanzanian Rift Valley area

Roland Kießling, Maarten Mous, and Derek Nurse

6.1   Introduction

The Rift Valley area of central and northern Tanzania is of considerable interest for the study of language contact, since it is unique in being the only area in Africa where members of all four language families are, and have been, in contact for a long time, having had linguistic interaction of various intensity at various points in time, which is reflected by convergence in parts of their grammatical structures (see map 6.1). The modern languages that took part in this linguistic contact are the West Rift languages of Southern Cushitic (Iraqw, Gorwaa, Alagwa, and Burunge), the Datooga dialects of Southern Nilotic, some Bantu languages of the F zone (Nyaturu, Rangi, Mbugwe, and maybe Nilyamba, Isanzu, and Kimbu), and Sandawe and Hadza, the Khoisan languages of eastern Africa. Actually, in the absence of any unambiguous indication that Hadza is genetically linked to Khoisan, it is better to be considered a linguistic isolate; see Sands (1998). The fact that the languages involved come from different, genetically unrelated families makes this area very promising for the study of language contact in that similarities between languages have five possible explanations: (i) universal properties, (ii) chance, (iii) borrowing or diffusion, (iv) retention, or (v) parallel development (Aikhenvald & Dixon 2001). All studies of language contact have to deal with factors (i) and (ii), but in our case it is, in principle, straightforward to tease out "similarities due to inheritance among genetically related languages" (iv) from "similarities that are due to language contact" (iii); moreover, the factor of parallel development, (v), due to a shared inner dynamic or drift is much less likely to occur between unrelated languages.

The linguistic history of the relevant groups is known to different degrees. Thus, while West Rift Cushitic (Kießling 2002a; Kießling & Mous 2003a) and Southern Nilotic (Ehret 1971; Rottland 1982) are fairly well studied, the linguistic history of the Bantu languages of the area is less well known, despite the recent monumental work by Masele (2001); on the one hand this is due to the inherent difficulties of subclassification within Bantu (see Schadeberg 2003) and on the other hand because the Rangi-Mbugwe community seems to be one

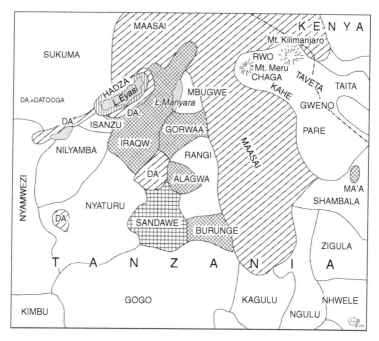

Map 6.1 The languages of the Tanzanian Rift Valley area

of the first Bantu arrivals in Tanzania and its position within the rest of East
African Bantu is unclear; see Nurse (1999) and Masele and Nurse (2003) for
discussion. Elderkin (1989) is devoted to the genetic connection of Sandawe
with Central Khoisan but the time depth is enormous, as is the geographical
distance, and in the absence of intermediate stages, it is often difficult to
determine whether Sandawe features are inherited or not. For Hadza this is
simply impossible since it is an isolate; see Sands (1998) for a full discussion of
the failure to link Hadza with other languages genetically.

The Tanzanian Rift Valley is an area with a long period of contact, with
unstable power relations, in which the directions of influence changed over
time and probably without ever having had one dominant language for the
whole area over an extensive period of time. All but Datooga have been in that
area for a long time. The ancestors of the Hadza and Sandawe, the earliest
linguistically recognizable groups, have probably been present for at least
several millennia; the ancestors of the Southern Cushites entering some 3,000
years ago, followed by the Bantu approximately 2,000 years ago, the Southern
Nilotes being late-comers having arrived in the area 500 to 1,000 years ago.
This scenario is based on the various studies by Ehret (1998, 1974). The East

Table 6.1 *The languages and their genetic classification*

Language	Genetic classification
Hadza	Isolate
Sandawe	East African Khoisan
Datooga	Southern Nilotic, Nilotic, Nilo-Saharan
Iraqw	Iraqwoid (PIRQ), Northern West Rift (PNWR), West Rift (WR), Southern Cushitic, Cushitic, Afroasiatic
Gorwaa	Iraqwoid (PIRQ), Northern West Rift (PNWR), West Rift (WR), Southern Cushitic, Cushitic, Afroasiatic
Alagwa	Northern West Rift (PNWR), West Rift (WR), Southern Cushitic, Cushitic, Afroasiatic
Burunge	Southern West Rift (PSWR), West Rift (WR), Southern Cushitic, Cushitic, Afroasiatic
Nyaturu	Bantu F32, Niger-Congo
Rangi	Bantu F33, Niger-Congo
Mbugwe	Bantu F34, Niger-Congo
Marginal members of the area:	
Nilyamba	Bantu F31, Niger-Congo
Isanzu	Bantu F31, Niger-Congo
Kimbu	Bantu F24, Niger-Congo
Nyamwezi	Bantu F22, Niger-Congo
Sukuma	Bantu F21, Niger-Congo

Rift Southern Cushitic languages Asax and Qwadza are not taken into account in this chapter, because they became extinct before a useful grammatical description could be made. The same is true for the Southern Nilotic languages Sawas and Sarwat (or Omotik) that we know from oral traditions (Berger & Kießling 1998). Ehret (1998) posits, solely on the basis of loanword evidence, now extinct Southern Cushitic communities closer to Lake Victoria, which he names Tale and Bisha.

The language communities in the Tanzanian Rift Valley differ among each other in many ways. There always have been differences in size. It is assumed that the Hadza community of hunter–gatherers has been constant in size of around 500 people. The settled mixed-farming Cushitic communities were probably significantly larger than this. Among them, the Iraqw have been expanding dramatically over the last centuries, welcoming many outsiders, forming a real open immigrant society and now numbering more than half a million speakers. Their closest relatives, the Gorwaa, only number a few thousand speakers. The hunter–gatherers (Hadza, Sandawe) and the settled agriculturalists (the Cushitic and the Bantu peoples) were confined to certain areas, in contrast to the cattle nomads such as the Datooga and the Maasai. Prestige and power were superficially related to the mode of economy, with cattle nomads feeling themselves to be superior to agriculturalists and agriculturalists superior to hunter–gatherers. The dominance of the cattle nomads in times of conflict is not only related to their ability to move with their wealth but also to the difference in their social organization, with strong clan ties and age grades.[1] Power relations were not stable over time; for example, the scales of power between the Iraqw and the Datooga shifted several times (see Kießling 1998b for a detailed analysis); similarly, the Alagwa are presently under pressure from the Rangi, but during colonial times the prestige of the Alagwa king was high enough for him to become paramount chief of the whole area including the Rangi. Interaction between the various communities occured for various reasons: for trade; because of intermarriage; by acceptance of individuals extradited from their community; due to recurrent immigration of individuals and their families sometimes linked to a shift in mode of economy; and by long-standing long-distance trade partnerships between families. There have probably always been various patterns of bilingualism and language shift of smaller and larger groups. There is no indication that there ever was a dominant lingua franca in the area. Swahili, which has this role now, was a very late newcomer; for example, Iraqw oral tradition claims that there was only one interpreter for Swahili during the German administration. In many respects the area was a refuge area.

6.1.1   Shared features

As the languages in our contact zone come from different families they also represent widely different language types. In terms of basic word order, the Cushitic languages and Sandawe are SOV,[2] the Bantu languages are SVO and Datooga (Southern Nilotic) is VSO. Still, in some respects there is inherited structural similarity between the languages under study despite their genetic diversity: verbal derivation and verbal inflection is by suffixation in Bantu, Cushitic, Nilotic, and Sandawe; there is inflection before the verb in Bantu, Datooga, and West Rift Southern Cushitic, and optionally in Sandawe (this developed into our feature G1; see section 6.2.3). The languages inherited very different tone systems; the Cushitic languages came with a pitch-accent system with distinctions in the final syllable(s) only and few if any lexical distinctions. The role of tone in Southern Nilotic must have been much more prominent, on the morphosyntactic as well as on the lexical level.[3] Sandawe has a tone system in which the domain is larger than the word and tone has important syntactic functions; the Bantu languages came with a system of two tones with both lexical and grammatical functions and with tone-spreading rules. There are (and were) major differences in the phonetic nature of the consonant systems, in particular with Sandawe and Hadza having their characteristic clicks and the

Cushitic languages their pharyngeal sounds. Number of nouns is not expressed in Sandawe; Bantu languages, however, express nominal number in their noun class systems, and both Cushitic and Nilotic have complex derivational suffixation systems for expressing nominal number.

The members of this contact zone share to varying degrees several linguistic features that cut across genetic boundaries. In agreement with Campbell, Kaufman, and Smith-Stark (1986), our approach is what they call historicist, that is, we do not merely look for features of similarity but limit ourselves to those that can be explained by contact. In order to make the case stronger we concentrate on non-universal and non-trivial features. Apart from a set of common lexical items, this shared stock comprises phonological features such as the presence of a lateral fricative, ejectives, and a phonological contrast of two voiceless dorsal obstruents; the absence of voiced fricatives; morphological, morphosemantic, morphosyntactic features such as proclitic verbal inflectional morphemes for tense; verbal plurality; marking of the direction of a process, event or action in relation to a deictic center on the verb; head marking of the goal or terminal endpoint of a process, event or action; a tense system that has more than one past and at least one future tense; a subjunctive suffix -*e*(*e*); a preverbal irrealis (future or optative) *laa*; a link between the spatial concepts of 'in' and 'under'; metonymic use of 'belly' for expressing emotional concepts; and purely syntactic features such as infinitive–auxiliary order; head-initial noun phrase order; spatial relations by postpositions and enclitics; grammaticalization of body-part nouns as relational nouns (prepositions).[4]

There is also a large set of shared lexical items. A number of these have connections far outside the area we are dealing with here. We mention only a few as illustration; see (1). In the remainder of the chapter we concentrate on phonological and grammatical features.

(1) A number of shared lexical items in the Tanzania Rift Valley area

'bull, big male animal': Iraqw *yaqamba*, Alagwa *yaqamba*, Burunge *yaqamba*, Nilyamba *nzagamba*, Nyaturu *njaghamba*, *nzagaamba*, but also Sukuma: *yagambá*, *nzagaamba* and widespread in West Tanzania, and Central Kenya languages.

'ram': Iraqw *gwanda*, Burunge *gondi*, Alagwa *gwandu*, Datooga *lagweenda*, Mbugwe *ŋoondi*; but also Sukuma *goondi*, Mbugu *igonji* 'sheep,' Nata *ŋɔndi* 'sheep,' etc.

'boys': Iraqw *masomba*, Alagwa *masomba*, Asax *msumbe*, Nyaturu *nsuumba*, Nilyamba *msumba*, Mbugwe *lemusomba* 'slave,' but also Sukuma *sumba*.

'milk': Nilyamba *masu(n)su*, Rangi *masu(n)su*, Iraqw *maso'o* 'first milk after a cow has calved.'

'beehive': Proto-West Rift **mariinga*, Rangi *muriŋga*, Nilyamba *mlinga*, Bianjida-Datooga *mèrèeŋjáandà*; but also Yaaku *merengo*, Mogogodo-Maasai *mɛrán*.

6.1.2   Interpretation

In terms of historical interpretation, there is a complex picture of mutual linguistic contacts of varying intensity at several points in time, the rough lines of which are summarized as follows.

First, there is diffusion of structural features from a West Rift Southern Cushitic source to some Bantu languages, as is evidenced by OV characteristics in Mbugwe and Rangi; by a phonological opposition of two dorsal obstruents in Nyaturu; by a concentration of non-auxiliary inflectional morphemes for tense and clause type indication in a preverbal clitic cluster. This last feature has also spread to Datooga. There are two possible alternative scenarios: either Datooga and the Bantu languages in question were once used extensively by groups of bilingual West Rift speakers, or considerable sections of the Datooga and Bantu communities in question were once bilingual in a West Rift language, probably Proto-West Rift or a predecessor.

Secondly, there is diffusion of structural features from Datooga to the Iraqw subgroup of West Rift: the grammaticalization of body-part nouns as relational nouns on their way to become prepositions, the linkage of the spatial concepts of 'in' and 'under', the metonymic use of 'belly' for expressing emotional concepts. This is probably the result of shifting Datooga speakers imposing Datooga semantic structures onto the Iraqw group.

Thirdly, there is a Bantu imprint on Burunge (and Alagwa), reflected by the innovation of three tenses with future reference, by the preverbal hortative in *laa*, and by a progressive reanalysis of the nominal gender system on a semantic basis[5] as well as clearer convergence of grammatical gender and sex.[6] This is the result of bilingualism in Rangi (and Swahili) among Burunge speakers and the dominant status of Rangi (and Swahili).

In addition, several features link West Rift with Sandawe and Hadza which seems to reflect an ancient contact; it is not obvious in which direction the shared features have been transferred.

A full list of shared features can be found in tables 6.5 and 6.6. The most salient and important features are discussed in some detail in section 6.2; the remainder is briefly discussed in 6.2.10. In section 6.3 we summarize the interpretation of these features in terms of language contact and we offer possible historical scenarios for the language contact.

6.2   Common features

6.2.1   Lateral fricative and affricate (P1)

The lateral fricative is present in the phonological systems of Hadza and Sandawe. It is also present in all modern West Rift Southern Cushitic languages and can be reconstructed for Proto-West Rift. It is not present in modern Datooga, but as supported by the evidence from Omotik, it has to be reconstructed at least for the Proto-Omotik-Datooga period, maybe for Proto-Southern Nilotic. Rottland (1982: 233) reconstructs a second lateral *L* for Southern Nilotic next to *l* on the basis of comparative series, *l* in Proto-Kalenjin, *sh* in Common Datooga, and *y* or *ɬ* in Omotik. The presence of a lateral fricative in the now extinct Omotik suggests a lateral fricative as the most likely phonetic realization of this proto-phoneme *L, as Heine (1973) proposes. Its genetic status within wider Nilotic is not clear. If it turns out to be a Southern Nilotic innovation (possibly under Southern Cushitic influence), this must have occurred outside the Central Tanzanian contact zone. The heart of the Omotik-speaking area was far from our contact area. Therefore it is beyond the scope of this chapter to try to set up links between the Southern Nilotic lateral fricative and the lateral sounds in Cushitic.

It is safe to assume that the West Rift Cushitic languages had two lateral consonants – *ɬ* and *tɬ'* next to the lateral approximant *l* – when they arrived in the area. These laterals must have spread to Sandawe, since Central Khoisan, or Khoe, is reconstructed without these lateral consonants (Vossen 1997a). Thus, the assumption is that Sandawe acquired them through external influence. Cushitic loans into Sandawe containing laterals are given in (2).[7]

(2) Transfer of laterals from West Rift to Sandawe

tɬ'ùpé 'smash, hit something wet' from PWR *tɬ'up* (v) 'smash'; cf. PEC
    d'₁uf- 'close, shut'
tɬ'úùng 'arm' from PWR *tɬ'ubaʕa* (m) 'upper arm'; cf. Afar *d'abʕe* 'armpit'
tɬ'ìbà'é 'squeeze' from PWR *tɬ'ibiʕ* (v) 'push'; cf. PEC *d'₁iib-* 'squeeze'
    (Borana Oromo *d'iiba* 'push')
tɬ'wâang 'rain' from PWR *tɬ'ubay* (m) 'rain'; cf. Proto-Sam *d'oobo* 'dip in;
    mud'
k'áatɬ'à 'something cut off and thrown away, garbage' from PWR *quutɬ'* (v)
    'cut up, cut into pieces'; cf. PEC *k'ad'₁-* 'cut', Shinassha *k'ùt* 'cut'
ɬàá 'goat' from PWR *ɬee* (n.sg.f) 'cow'; cf. PEC *shaʕ-* 'cow', *lo* 'cattle'
tɬ'ók'òndò 'mud' from ALBU *tɬ'oqoondú* (m) 'wet cow dung'
tɬ'ák'átó 'Grant's gazelle' from PWR *tɬ'aaqataa* (f) 'impalas'

tɬ'ùngù 'clouds' from PWR**tɬ'aangwa* (f) 'fog, mist'
ɬúbárà ~ ɬùúbà 'foam' from PWR *ɬubari (n) 'foam'
ɬùfé 'be swollen (from eating too much)' from PWR *ɬuf (v) 'swell, be swollen'
ɬáarà 'rubbish like fallen leaves' from PWR *ɬaaraħí (f) 'grain stalks'
ɬàɬángè from PWR *ɬangaɬaangáy (m) 'chameleon'
ɬà'é 'sting, stab, hurt' from PWR *ɬaħ (v) 'hit, hurt'
ɬá'tô 'fallow field' from ^{ALBU}... *ɬá'tô* 'fallow field' from ᴬᴸᴮᵁ**ɬa'ay* 'naked, nudity'
ɬá'ato 'glade' from PWR *ɬaʕa (f) 'wilderness, uncultivated land'
xòóɬà 'scratch' from ᴾᴵᴿᵠ*xooɬ (v) 'grind'
tɬáná 'horn'; cf. Burunge *tɬ'aana* 'upper leg, thigh'
ɬébérà 'mixing stick'; cf. Burunge *ɬubisay* 'twirl'
ɬebee 'fin'; cf. Burunge *ɬabi* 'rib'
aɬee 'tree (sp.)'; cf. Burunge *'aɬaw* 'Euphorbia candelabrium'
k'ìtɬ'é 'get angry'; cf. Iraqw *qitɬ'* 'endure'
ɬak'e-e 'be similar'; cf. *ɬaaqaat* 'be similar'

Hadza is an isolate and thus it is difficult to say anything about the origin of lateral consonants in this language. There is no difference in pronunciation between the laterals in Hadza and in the West Rift languages; the Hadza lateral affricate is ejective, as in West Rift. Edenmyr, who is presently researching the Hadza language, has recently presented a study of lexical similarities between Hadza and neighboring languages (2003). Examples are taken from this study. Some of the Hadza words containing lateral consonants have cognates in Iraqw or West Rift, but the direction of borrowing is hard to determine. We have positive external Cushitic evidence for only one of these, that is the Hadza word *tɬu'a* 'to hit a person' which must be borrowed from a West Rift language since Proto-West Rift (and Iraqw) **tɬ'up* 'to smash' is cognate with Proto-Eastern Cushitic **d'₁uf-* 'close, shut.' In the case of Proto-West Rift **tɬ'ooma* (f) 'mountain; temple' and Hadza *tɬ'oma-ko* 'head,' the direction of the metaphor 'mountain' to 'head' (cf. Swahili 'head' < 'termite mound' (see Nurse & Hinnebush 1993: 632) suggests borrowing into Hadza. Two words are also shared with Sandawe: Iraqw/ Gorwaa (not West Rift) *tɬ'arangw* 'flour, dust,' Hadza *tɬalá-* 'dust,' Sandawe *tɬàràang* 'dust'; and Proto-West Rift *ɬubari* 'foam,' Hadza *ɬupa-* 'foam,' Sandawe *ɬúbárà ~ ɬùúbà* 'foam.' Hadza has the ejective affricate for only one word where West Rift has the lateral fricative: Proto-West Rift *ɬupis 'to drill, twirl,' Hadza *tɬipi* 'to twirl, stir.' Some additional examples of Hadza–West Rift Southern Cushitic cognates are: Proto-West Rift *hiinɬaw 'to remember,' Hadza *'eslawi* 'to remember', Proto-West Rift **ɬa'* 'love, like,' Hadza *ɬa'a* 'love something, like'; finally Iraqw *ɬanu* 'python,' Hadza *ɬanó* 'python.'

Contact between Hadza and West Rift is probably old. Presently Iraqw is the only West Rift language that is situated close to the Hadza area, but the Iraqw have only fairly recently inhabited that area and it is not really adjacent; in fact there is very little contact. The linguistic evidence does not exclude the possibility that the Hadza–Southern Cushitic contact was at an earlier level than present-day Iraqw. In fact, the two words that are also shared with Sandawe, i.e. 'dust' and 'foam' would suggest that.

The laterals in Southern Cushitic (the lateral fricative ɬ and the ejective lateral affricate tɬ') have been claimed to be Afroasiatic retentions on the basis of parallels with laterals in Chadic, see Dolgopolsky (1987), Orel and Stolbova (1995: xiv, xix), Ehret (1995: 394), Takács (2003). If Southern Cushitic is a primary branch of Cushitic, this view does not pose any problems in accounting for the laterals in Southern Cushitic; Proto-Cushitic inherited them from Proto-Afroasiatic and Proto-Southern Cushitic from Cushitic. The number of proposed cognates with laterals in both Southern Cushitic and Chadic or Semitic languages is however limited and the validity of the reconstruction of lateral fricatives and affricates for Proto-Cushitic unresolved. There is, however, a growing amount of evidence that Southern Cushitic is in fact not a primary branch of Cushitic but part of Lowland Eastern Cushitic; see Tosco (2000a) for the most up-to-date overview of the issues in Cushitic subclassification. Given the present uncertainty of the subclassification of Cushitic, it is a matter of debate what level these laterals can be reconstructed to. The ejective lateral affricate in Rift corresponds to $*d'_1$ in Proto-Lowland Eastern Cushitic; the lateral fricative corresponds to $*l$ in PEC and occasionally to $*sh$; see Kießling and Mous (2003a: 36–7). Proto-Eastern Cushitic l corresponds to d, ɬ, and l in Proto-West Rift and is lost in certain roots in the second/third consonant position. If we take Tosco's (2000a) proposal as a point of reference we could argue that the common ancestor of Southern and Lowland East Cushitic had two proto-phonemes that correspond to the lateral consonants in Southern Cushitic. Either Southern Cushitic acquired the lateral pronunciation, or the rest of Eastern Cushitic lost it; the choice is far from self-evident. In Ma'a, for example, a number of instances of present-day lateral consonants are clearly innovations. The same correspondence of ɬ with sh exists for newly formed lateral fricatives in Ma'a. Blench (1996) suggests that the ejective lateral affricate is so rare worldwide that it may be a trace from a former language spoken by early inhabitants, to which we can add that the ejective affricates tɬ' and ts' of the area are acoustically quite close to clicks, and click imitation may have played a role in the presence of these sounds in our contact area. There is, however, no concrete evidence to substantiate this suggestion.

If the lateral pronunciation of these sounds was an innovation then it must have happened prior to the entry of the present-day Cushitic peoples into our area. There are several attestations of lateral fricatives and affricates outside our area. Laterals (the fricative and the ejective affricate) are present in both West Rift and East Rift (Qwadza and Aasáx), and outside Rift Southern Cushitic also in Dahalo, in Pre-Ma'a[8] and in former stages of the Taita-Bantu languages and most probably in the now extinct Taita-Cushitic language(s); see Mous (2003a) for evidence on Pre-Ma'á and Taita-Cushitic. Thus it is unlikely that the presence of a lateral fricative and affricate in West Rift Southern Cushitic can be attributed solely to contact with Hadza.

The presence of a lateral fricative and/or affricate in Sandawe and Hadza is at least partly due to transfer from West Rift Southern Cushitic.[9] It can be attributed to transfer of lexical items to these languages. The lexical items involved are varied and include non-cultural basic vocabulary. The contact must have been quite intense but need not have involved bilingualism or language shift. It must have continued over a prolonged period of time as the transfer of Southern Cushitic words into Sandawe is from several earlier stages of the Cushitic languages. Whether the lateral fricative and affricate in Southern Cushitic is original or not is beyond the scope of this chapter since it is irrelevant for our contact area.

6.2.2   *Phonological contrast of two voiceless dorsal obstruents (P3)*

The languages in our area that display this feature have a phonemic contrast of an unmarked voiceless dorsal obstruent *k* vs. a marked one which might have phonetic realizations ranging from ejective stop *k'*, uvular stop *q*, ejective uvular stop *q'* to uvular fricatives, voiceless χ or voiced ʁ. All modern West Rift languages share a phonological opposition of a voiceless velar stop *k* vs. another voiceless dorsal which is realized as a plain uvular *q* or as a uvular ejective *q'* and which is reconstructed at the Proto-West Rift level (Kießling & Mous 2003a) as part of its common Cushitic inheritance. Both Hadza and Sandawe have an opposition of a voiceless velar stop *k* vs. a voiceless velar ejective *k'* which can not be dismissed as a recent innovation in either of them. An opposition of this kind is neither part of the common Bantu inheritance nor is it reconstructed for Southern Nilotic. Yet, our contact zone has two members of these groups that come up with this feature: Datooga and Nyaturu.

As regards Datooga, all the modern dialects display an opposition of plain *k* vs. another dorsal phoneme which has a broad variety of phonetic realization from uvular stop *q* to voiceless uvular fricative χ, voiced uvular fricative ʁ, or even voiced uvular stop *G* (Rottland 1982: 153). Rottland (1982: 232) demonstrates how this contrast arose at the Pre-Datooga level as the result of a split of the original proto-phoneme **k*. This split was conditioned by the ATR quality of surrounding vowels with original **k* being retained in [+ATR] environment and shifted to the uvular in [−ATR] environment, as shown in (3).

(3) Datooga: split of Pre-Datooga *k under ATR influence (Rottland 1982: 232)

$*k > k > g$ / [+ATR]   Proto-Southern Nilotic *kæcæt 'arrow'
                                       > Datooga *gaad*
     $> q$ / [−ATR]   Proto-Southern Nilotic *kaat 'neck'
                                       > Datooga *qaad*

This explanation of the mechanisms of the innovation in terms of purely internal factors raises the question of why exactly Datooga should have undergone such an isolated development within Southern Nilotic. There are two related motives that might be viewed as triggers to this process: (i) the external model of a Cushitic language, maybe Proto-West Rift; (ii) the split may be a strategy of compensation for the reduction of the inherited Nilotic ten-vowel system to seven vowels in Datooga.

In both cases, the internal development of an opposition of two voiceless dorsals in Datooga developed under Cushitic influence. The most likely scenario is this: the main actors of this change were West Rift speakers shifting to Datooga and imposing their Southern Cushitic habits of pronunciation onto the Pre-Datooga language in two ways: simplifying a – by Cushitic standards unnecessarily complex – system of ten contrastive vowels by eliminating the ATR contrasts in the high and low vowels, approximating a Cushitic ideal of five contrastive vowel qualities. At the same time they must have taken the internally developed allophonic variation of *k under ATR influence as the primary token of the ATR contrast, reinforcing and phonemicizing this familiar contrast as a result of the loss of vowel distinctions. In this way, the split of *k appears to be a partial reanalysis of vowel harmony cast in a Cushitic mould.

On the Bantu side, the only language to innovate a phonological contrast of *k* vs. *ʁ* is Nyaturu (Olson 1964). The voiced uvular fricative is a regular reflex of Proto-Bantu *g. Proto-Bantu *k, on the other hand, remains predominantly *k* in Nyaturu; though some instances have shifted to *g*, *x*, and *γ*, the details of this are not clear. Thus, the phonemic opposition of Nyaturu *k* vs. *ʁ* is a fairly recent innovation inspired by external models, either West Rift or Datooga or both. The probability is rather with Datooga, since only Datooga *q* has a range of phonetic realization which also encompasses [ʁ]. Also the fact that it is only Pre-Nyaturu *g which is affected by the shift to the uvular and not *k confirms the point that Datooga must have been the external model, since due to the internal Datooga voicing shift *k > g, the modern Datooga morpho-phonemic alternation (triggered by ATR) is between *g* and *q*, but not between *k* and *q*.

Table 6.2 *Preverbal clitic cluster of Proto-West Rift (Kießling 2002a: 411)*

Sentence type	Subject	Object	Case	Tense
*Ø parataxis	*ta subject indefinite	*ni O1	*ri comitative / instrumental	*-Ø present
*gV oblique subordinate	*na subject focus	*ku O2MSG	(*sa benefactive)	*(g)aa past
	*ha S1/2	*ki O2FSG		*in persistive-perfect
	*hi S3	*gu O3MSG		sequential (category reconstructed but not form)
	*ni S3.collective	*ga O3FSG		
	*ni S1.subordinate	*gi O3PL ~ O3N		
	*ta S2.subordinate	*haanti O1PL		
		*kunu ~		
		*huunku O2PL		
		*ti reflexive		

6.2.3 Preverbal clitic cluster for tense, subordination, sequentiality, focus (G1)

The outstanding syntactic feature of Proto-West Rift and its modern successors is that they have a distributed predicative syntax, i.e. "verbal functions are divided over the verb and an obligatory sentence-building word" (Mous 2001a: 125), a preverbal clitic cluster that is syntactically independent to a certain extent. This syntactic independence of the preverbal clitic cluster is manifest in its separability from the verb. In West Rift the preverbal clitic cluster takes over a variety of functions, such as coindexing subject and non-subject, indicating case value of non-subjects, tense, clause type (subordination), sequentiality, focus. Table 6.2 presents the minimal system of proclitic markers reconstructed for Proto-West Rift.[10] Although in principle an inherited feature from Proto-Eastern and Southern Cushitic (there are structural parallels in Omo-Tana languages of Eastern Cushitic; see Mous 2006), it must be recognized that, in a wider Cushitic perspective, West Rift has considerably expanded the preverbal clitic cluster.

The success story of this preverbal clitic cluster still continues since all the modern West Rift languages have extended this complex in their own way, e.g. by fusion of conjunctions and adpositions, in Iraqw conditional, concessive, goal case.

Table 6.3 *Preverbal clitic cluster and finite verb in Nyaturu (Olson 1964; reanalysis in Nurse 2000a)*

1	2	3^a	subject	tense	verb stem	aspect
ní (subordination)	*náa* (FP)	*qàá* (sequential)	[...]	*a-* (FP)		*-íe* (PF)
	ájà (NP)	*kíɪ* (persistive)		*á-* (non-FP)		*-aa* (HAB)
	nàa (NF)			*qʊ-* (FUT)		*-a* (neutral)
	~ *árì*					
	ìkwí (F2)					

^{a} The markers in slot 3 can take optional subject prefixes.

Preverbal clitic clustering of this type is neither a typical Nilotic feature nor is it characteristic of the predecessors of East African Bantu languages. However, the contact zone has languages from both groups that display incipient preverbal clitic clustering, i.e. Nilyamba (F31) and Nyaturu (F32) on the Bantu side and Gisamjanga from the Datooga cluster (most probably also in the other Datooga varieties, e.g. Barabaiga).

Nyaturu (Olson 1964; Nurse 2000a) has a verbal inflectional system which is typically Bantu in its core, i.e. the verb is modified by inflectional prefixes for subject agreement and tense and by inflectional suffixes for aspect. Nyaturu, however, deviates from the Bantu prototype in that it has a clustering of clitics of non-verbal origin in preverbal position, predominantly used for tense functions (near past *ája*, far past *náa*, near future *naa*, far future *ìkwí*), but also for subordination and sequentiality. These markers are listed in columns 1–3 of table 6.3. The examples in (4) present them in use, preverbal clitic cluster underlined, (4b) illustrating the separability of the preverbal clitic cluster from the inflected verb.

(4) Nyaturu preverbal clitic cluster

a.   <u>ní</u>   <u>náa</u>   <u>a-kíɪ</u>   u-qʊ-righiRya ...
    SUB   FP   3SG-PERS   3SG-PROG-speak
    'while she was still speaking ... ' (Nurse 2000a: 523)
b   <u>ní</u>   <u>ɪ-kíɪ</u>   njololo   í-na-kʊnkʊa ...
    SUB   9-PERS   cock   9-NEG-crow
    'when the cock had not yet crowed ... ' (Nurse 2000a: 523)

Slots 2 and 3 are most interesting. Slot 2 reveals that – on top of the tense system encoded in verbal affixes – Nyaturu has innovated a secondary tense system (used as a frame for the core verb) comprising a near past *ájà*, a far past *náa*, a near future *nàa*, a far future *ìkwí*. Slot 3 suggests that Nyaturu seems to have extracted original Bantu aspect prefixes, such as the indicators of subsequent action, *qàá* (Swahili *ka-*), and the persistive, *kíı* (Swahili *ki-*), from the verb into a preverbal clitic position. It looks as if Bantu material has been used to build a system of preverbal clitics, encoding Bantu categories in a Southern Cushitic frame. Some of the preverbal clitics, though, are not obviously Bantu in origin: far past *náa*, a near future *nàa*, a far future *ìkwí*. Far past *náa* in Nyaturu is a past inflected form of the copula *ni*. This is of course strange in a Bantu context. But in the case of West Rift speakers switching to Nyaturu they would have had no problem with adding *-aa* to a preverbal clitic cluster base that is a copula; this is exactly what speakers of West Rift languages do with a suffix for past tense that has *-aa* as allomorph. Near future *naa* could come from the West Rift subject focus selector *na* (see table 6.2); *ìkwí* has no parallel in West Rift Southern Cushitic. The structural deviation from Bantu standards and the approximation to the West Rift model is evident from (i) the tendency to shift inflectional markers into a preverbal constituent which is syntactically independent of the verb, and (ii) the selection of the semantic categories concerned: subordination, tense, sequentiality. In this scenario, the ancestors of the Nyaturu (and possibly also Nilyamba and Kimbu), a group originally speaking a Sukuma/Nyamwezi type of language, moved into a territory occupied by West Rift speakers. The two interacted over centuries, involving bilingualism of West Rift speakers in Pre-Nyaturu, transforming it and producing these verbal innovations (and also innovations at other linguistic levels).

As regards the alternative explanation on the lines of internal development of these preverbal clitic cluster features via fusion from auxiliary plus main verb structures, we would be looking at processes akin to what Harris and Campbell (1995: 172–94) call clause fusion. In the examples below, the starting point is constructions consisting of strings of two verbs, the last being a main verb, while those preceding are auxiliaries, usually, but not always, forms of 'be.' In morphological terms, there are two possible results. In one, auxiliary and lexical verb fuse by deleting redundant prestem material from the main verb. Here the grammatical information carried by the auxiliary is grafted onto the lexical verb. In the other, the structure of the lexical verb is maintained intact, while the auxiliary is reduced to the status of a particle, clitic, or prefix carrying the relevant grammatical information.

The first type can be illustrated initially via Swahili. In contemporary Northern Swahili of northern Kenya, this reduction is possible:

(5) tw-a-li   tu-ki-imba >   tw-a+li+ki-imba
    we-PAST-be   we-PROG-sing >   we-PAST+be+PROG-sing
    'We were singing'

where the coreferential subject of the main verb is deleted. Other constructions and reductions of this kind have been possible for centuries in Northern Swahili; see Miehe (1979: 219) and Nurse (1982: 106).

Sukuma works similarly. It has several possible reductions of the type:

(6)   [d-aa-líí   dʊ́-gá-gʊ́l-aga] >[d-aa-lʊ́ʊ́-gʊl-aga]
       we-PAST-be   we-PAST-buy-PROG
       'We were buying'

in which the coreferential subject and the prestem -ga- of the main verb, and the final vowel of the auxiliary are all deleted. Sukuma has several single word forms such as the one on the right, the prestem markers all having a lengthened vowel: -lɪɪ progressive, -lʊʊ as above, -taalɪ persistive, -yʊʊ future imperfective, -ʊʊ subsecutive, etc. Sukuma speakers are aware of the historical reduction process in some of these cases, in others not.

The second type can be exemplified in several eastern Bantu languages. The examples in (7) are taken from southern Tanzania (Guthrie's G50 languages: tones unmarked):

(7) a.   tw-a-li   tw-i-gula.
          we-FP-be   we-PROG-buy
          'We were buying, would have bought'
    b.   ali   tw-i-gula
          PAST   we-PROG-buy
          'We were buying, would have bought'

Here it can be seen that the coreferential subject of the auxiliary is deleted, tense and 'be' fuse, leaving a particle of unvarying shape, simply referring to past (the exact status of *ali* is not clear). (8) presents a more complicated example from Kerewe, a language spoken on Lake Victoria:

(8) a.   tw-aa-li-ga   tu-li baalimu
          we-PAST-be-IPF   we-be teachers
          'We were/used to be teachers'
    b.   liga tuli baalimu.
          'We were/used to be teachers'

In this example, the subject marker is deleted, along with the past-tense marker, leaving a particle of unvarying shape. It can have two different tonal shapes, then indicating two different past times. Again from Kerewe G60:

(9) a.   tu-sa   ku-gula
          we-come   to-buy
          'We are going to buy'

b. saa   tu-gula
    FUT   we-buy
    'We will buy'
c. saa   tu-va   tu-gus-ile
    FUT   we-be   we-buy-PERF
    'We will have bought'

In (9a) *sa* 'come' is used as subject-marked auxiliary before an infinitive, in
(9b) it is reduced to a bare particle marking future, and (9c) shows it before a
string of auxiliary and main verb.

(10) a. tw-a   tw-i-gula
         we-a   we-PROG-buy
         'We buy regularly'
     b. tw-aa tw-i-gul-a
         'We buy sometimes'

These constructions apparently consist of auxiliary plus main verb. While the
structure of the main verb is clear, the auxiliary seems to contain subject
marker and what must once have been a prestem tense–aspect marker but
with the auxiliary itself deleted. The mechanism leading to the long vowels in
(9b,c) and (10b) is not clear.

In (8–10) we see auxiliary reduction processes that lead to particles, and
particles lead to clitics and prefixes. These can be shown in Sukuma, where B.
Masele (p.c.) suggests that the first auxiliary reduces to the simple and
unvarying prefix *ı-* on the second verb (it could also be the main verb). Thus:

(11) a. d-aa-lí   d-áá-bííza   dʊ-líí-gʊla   > ı-d-áá-bííza dʊ-líí-gʊla
         we-PAST-be we-PAST-be we-ing-buy   'We were just buying...'

Having outlined the possibilities, we can now examine the data from Nyaturu (Nilyamba, and Kimbu). As we have seen, Nyaturu has a preverbal
complex with three components; #*ní-* (relativizer), followed by a tense slot
with four members (*náa* FP, *ája* NP, *naa / ári* NF, *ìkwí* FF), followed by what
might loosely be called an aspect slot, with two members (*-kíı* persistive, *-qàá*
subsecutive). The nature of the cohesion of the three components of the preverbal complex is unclear, and the members of the last slot can optionally carry
subject markers.

While the data for Kimbu and Nilyamba is much sparser, it is solid enough to
provide some generalities. Neither language has a preverbal complex, in the
sense of Nyaturu. While Nyaturu and Nilyamba (and possibly Kimbu) do have
the initial relativizer #*ni-*, neither Nilyamba nor Kimbu has any visible trace of
the third, aspect slot, and the evidence for the second, tense, slot is tenuous. In

this second slot Kimbu and Nilyamba have Far Past #*alɪ* which might be a reduced form of the Sukuma/Nyamwezi *-alɪ* 'past + be.' The Nyaturu evidence for this shape is shaky; in one Nyaturu dialect it is said to carry the same function as (low-toned) *nàa* Near Future in the main dialect. But it is high-toned *náa* in this second dialect which means Far Past: maybe this is a mistake in the data? Furthermore this *ali=ari* is not unique to our languages, being widespread in the meaning Far Past in many eastern Bantu languages, as can be seen in the examples in (7) and (8), taken from languages adjacent and to the southwest of our target languages.

Similarly with other parts of the preverbal complex. Nyaturu (*ája*) and Nilyamba (*aza*) have a cognate preverbal Near Past, which probably derives from "past+come," a common enough form of grammaticalization, but not attested in Kimbu or Sukuma/Nyamwezi. Finally, Nilyamba and Kimbu have a Persistive morpheme *-kyali-*, which can plausibly be analyzed as *-kɪ*+past+be. While this *-kɪ-* might relate to the *kíɪ* "persistive" of Nyaturu, it should be noted that Nyaturu *-kɪɪ* comes in the final preverbal slot, not the initial one, and that this *kɪ(ɪ)* is not attested in Sukuma/Nyamwezi.

All this detail can be summarized thus. We would like to see a solid set of categories and morphology in Nilyamba and Kimbu similar to those that occur in the Nyaturu preverbal complex. While there are minor similarities, and maybe some shared innovations, the evidence for such a set is simply not there, and its absence is unlikely to be due to lacunae in the data.

On the other hand, in order to prove the preverbal clitic cluster to be an internal development, it would also be necessary to demonstrate reasonably that the Nyaturu preverbal complex is a reduction of structures inherited from the earlier link with Sukuma/Nyamwezi. It should be possible to show that Sukuma/Nyamwezi has the auxiliary structures that could have been fused to produce something like what we find in the preverbal complex in Nyaturu. Sukuma/Nyamwezi is very rich in auxiliary structures. We have counted several dozen structures, most involving two verbs, a few involving three. Further, as suggested in (5) and (10), Sukuma/Nyamwezi does fuse auxiliary and main verbs. But with a few exceptions, all Sukuma/Nyamwezi auxiliaries are forms of 'be' (either *-lɪɪ* or *-ɓiiza*). They do not resemble the morphemes exemplified in (4). And considering the reduction processes current in Sukuma/Nyamwezi, indeed, considering any reduction processes, it is hard to imagine how most of the components of the Nyaturu preverbal complex might derive from anything in contemporary or older Sukuma/Nyamwezi.

The evidence does not support the hypothesis that the preverbal complex can be directly derived from inherited structures. It suggests strongly the adoption of the basic preverbal structure, or at least large parts of it, from a neighboring West Rift language. The structure itself can be interpreted as a transfer, the constituent morphemes are a mixture of inherited and transferred items, the grammatical categories are probably inherited. In other words, we have an alien structure expressing inherited categories and using a mixture of transferred and inherited morphemes of sometimes irregular shape. Earlier Nyaturu seems to have taken an alien structure to express familiar categories, using a mixture of inherited and transferred morphemes. This suggests two possible scenarios. Either Nyaturu, or one form of Nyaturu, was once used by a group of bilingual West Rift speakers, or the Nyaturu, or a section of the Nyaturu, were once bilingual in West Rift or one of its predecessors.[11]

Gisamjanga Datooga (which might be representative of Datooga in general) also has a preverbal clitic cluster, comprising four proclitic structural slots in front of the verb, as shown in table 6.4 (columns 1–4). Again, we find the categories of sequential, future, persistive, and subordination among those marked by proclitics.

The Gisamjanga Datooga examples in (12) and (13) illustrate the separability from the verb of the future and the sequential proclitic.

(12) Preverbal clitic cluster separated from verb by adverb (relative clause)

qwàjâp	hílóogà	qòohâat	héedá	jàa	ʃíɲádà
S3.erect	cattle.enclosure	S3Sg:increase	place	FUT.REL	evening

gwállà	nòoga
S3.sleep.at	goats

'They built a cattle enclosure to increase the room for the goats and sheep to sleep at night' (Berger 1935/36)

(13) Preverbal clitic cluster separated from verb by adverb (relative clause)

ák-àjà	gábá	síisí	gùurs-á	òorjéedàa-ɲi
SEQ:AFF-FUT	every	person	call:APPL-3	son-POSS.3SG

'then everyone will call his son' (Berger 1935/36)

Hadza shows a similar clustering of preverbal clitics for tense and subject person in the sequential (Berger 1943; Wagner 1988; Bonny Sands, p.c.). Their clitic status is manifest in (14), where the cluster is separated from the verb by direct objects.

(14) Hadza: preverbal clitic complex separated from the verb by a direct object

a.
yamo	ts'okwanàko	eláta …
SEQ.3MSG	giraffe	create

'he also created the giraffe…' (Berger 1943: 102f.)

b.
yamo	séseme	élā…
SEQ.3MSG	lion	create

'The lion was also created …' (Berger 1943: 103)

Table 6.4 *Preverbal clitic cluster and finite verb in Gisamjanga Datooga*

Subordination	Polarity	Tense 3	Tense 2	Tense 1	Subject	Verb stem	Object
ámà temporal relative	G affirmative- indicative[a]	Ø unmarked	Ø unmarked	Ø unmarked	aa- / da- 1SG		-aan 1SG
ág sequential	m negative- indicative	àjá future	gùdù persistive	nì- perfect affirmative	í- 2SG		-ini ~ -ey 2SG
íi conditional	àdà negative- subjunctive			i- present negative	(G)a- / Ø 3SG		Ø 3SG
					èe- / si- 1PL		-ɛɛsa 1PL
					oo- 2PL		-ɛɛgwa 2PL
					ée- / si- 3PL		Ø 3PL

[a] This morphophoneme indicates the alternation of the phonemes *g* and *q*.

In Sandawe, the movable person–gender–number marker (Elderkin 1989: 25ff.) bears some similarity to the preverbal clitic cluster in the other languages. It can move from the end of the verb position to the end of the constituent preceding the verb (object, adjunct) and as well to constituents preceding that constituent, compare (15a and b).

(15) a. nâm   sòmbà   thímé-sù̱.
        Nam   fish   cook-3FSG.IRR
        'She will cook Nam's fish' (Eaton 2002:92)

    b. ijo: ^{n}|iniŋ-sa   ‖a:
        mother   corn-3FSG   plant
        'The mother planted corn' (Kagaya 1990: 2, 4 quoted in Eaton 2002: 92)

The function of the position of the person–gender–number marker is pragmatic (focus). Thus the preverbal clitic cluster has the following characteristics in common with West Rift and Nyaturu: (i) there is inflection including subject marking separate from the verb, (ii) cliticization is to the left; (iii) the preverbal clitic cluster has focus function (not in Nyaturu).

The differences with the preverbal clitic cluster in the other languages are that the person–gender–number marker in Sandawe does not express tense–aspect nor does it receive tense–aspect clitics, and that the Sandawe person–gender–number marker does not have a fixed position. In the Khoe languages the person–gender–number markers (which seem cognate) are *nominal* suffixes which can be attached to verbs in order to nominalize them (Güldemann & Vossen 2000). Sandawe's option of detaching and preposing the person–gender–number marker is not too distinct from the behavior of person–gender–number markers in other Khoisan languages where they are often repeated in the same sentence. Although the structures of the preverbal clitic cluster in West Rift and Sandawe are similar to some extent, the differences are important enough not to assume contact influence. Both West Rift and Sandawe inherited the feature, and the expansion of the preverbal clitic cluster in West Rift can not be considered to be under influence of Sandawe because Sandawe shows much more limitation in the variety of categories that is expressed in this preverbal clitic cluster. At most, the structural similarity of the neighboring languages may have reinforced this feature in both.

A historical interpretation can be given as follows. The preverbal innovation of Bantu tense categories in Nyaturu with Bantu morphemes on the basis of a Southern Cushitic syntactic pattern points to a period of massive language shift, Southern Cushitic speakers shifting to Nyaturu and imposing their syntactic patterns on the Bantu language. Similarly, speakers shifting from West Rift to Pre-Datooga must have been responsible for the import of West Rift structures into Datooga. This scenario is suggested by the fact that in the elaboration of preverbal clitic clusters no markers seem to have been transferred directly; it is, rather, inherited material that has been reassembled (sequential and persistive in Nyaturu) or internally motivated developments of grammaticalization from inherited lexemes have been set into motion (future and persistive in Datooga). The similarity with structures in Sandawe is coincidence. The similarities with Hadza can only be judged properly once a full description of Hadza is available.

6.2.4   Verbal plurality (G2)

The category of verbal plurality[12] in the sense of a "plural stem" is an areal phenomenon of this contact zone, linking the West Rift languages of Southern Cushitic (Alagwa, Burunge, Gorwaa, Iraqw) with Southern Nilotic (Datooga) and Sandawe. All these languages display an alternation of singular vs. plural verbal stem, triggered by the number feature in one of the core arguments of the predication, and which operates independently of plural agreement or plural concord as accomplished by inflectional morphemes which combine person, gender, and number marking. Whereas the category of "pluractional" is so common in Africa that it is not a good indicator for language contact, this is decidedly different for the feature of "plural stem," which is quite rare.

In Southern Cushitic, five verbal derivational suffixes together form an inflectional system to mark the plurality of the subject or the object, depending on the transitivity of the verb. This situation has been reconstructed for the Proto-West Rift stage (Kießling 2002a: 315ff.), but within Cushitic as a whole it seems to be unique. The suffixes in question are the durative *-im, the continuative *-it, the frequentative that operates an initial reduplication *CV-, the progressive and the intensive that operate suffixal reduplications *-VVC and *-aaC, respectively. They stand in quasi-complementary distribution whose semantic rationale has become blurred.

(16) Alagwa: plural stem formation by durative derivation in -im in saapis 'move over' vs. saapimis, triggered by plurality of the object

a. ?ana   a-na   saapis   faʕa
    1SG   S1/2-PERF   move:SG:1SG   porridge
    'I have moved over a portion of porridge'
b. handaaʔ   a-na   saapis-an   faʕa
    1PL   S1/2-PERF   move:SG-1PL   porridge
    'We have moved over a portion of porridge'
c. handaaʔ   a-na   saapimis-an   faʕoo
    1PL   S1/2-PERF   buy:PL-1PL   porridges
    'We have moved over portions of porridge'

(17) Burunge: plural stem formation by durative derivation in *-im* in *hatʃ'is* 'fill' vs. *hatʃ'imis*, triggered by plurality of the object

a. ʔana   ha   hatʃ'is-ḁ   yakwa
   1SG   S1/2   fill:SG-1SG:IPERF   calabash
   'I fill a calabash'
b. ʔana   ha   hatʃ'imis-ḁ   yakwaku
   1SG   S1/2   fill:PL-1SG:IPF   calabashes
   'I fill the calabashes'

(18) Iraqw: plural stem formation by intensive derivation in *-aaC* in *hats'miis* 'fill' vs. *hats'maamis*, triggered by plurality of the object (Mous n.d.: 14)

a. ʔaníŋ   a   tʃupitoʔó-r   hats'miis
   1SG   S1/2   bottle-F   fill:SG:1SG:IPF
   'I am filling a bottle'
b. ʔatén   tʃupa   a-na   hats'maamíis
   1SG   bottle   O:3:FSG:-PAST   fill:PL:1SG:IPF
   'I filled the bottles'

Apart from these derivational strategies of forming plural stems, West Rift marginally also uses suppletive verb stems to mark this category: *gaas* 'kill,' plural *tsuʕ*, *gwaaʔ* 'die,' plural *qatɬ* ∼ *kakaʕ*.

(19) Burunge: alternation of suppletive stems *gwaaʔ* 'die' (SG) vs. *kakaʕ* (PL), triggered by plurality of the subject

a. qwaɬara   yáa   gwaaʔ-i̥
   doctor   S3:PAST   die:SG-3MSG:PFV
   'The doctor died'
b. qwaɬeeri   yáa   kakaʕir-i̥
   doctors   S3:PAST   die:PL-3MSG:PFV
   'The doctors died'

(20) Burunge: alternation of suppletive stems *tɬ'aatɬ'af* 'cut down, fell' (SG) vs. *tlaaq* (PL), triggered by plurality of the object

a. dandiray   ha-gu   tɬ'aatɬ'af-an-ḁ   xa'imo
   1PL   S1/2-O3MSG   cut.down-1PL-IPF   tree
   'We cut down a tree'
b. dandiray   ha-gi   tɬ'aaq-an-ḁ   xa'i
   1PL   S1/2-O3PL   cut.down:PL-1PL-IPF trees
   'We cut down trees'

The Gisamjanga dialect of Southern Nilotic Datooga (Kießling 1998a) uses a suffix *-ay(een)*, *-ac(een)*, probably cognate with the Proto-Nilotic frequentative marker ∗*-cVn* (Reh 1991), for deriving a plural stem. In (21b) the plural stem is ambiguous, it may indicate that the action is repeated several times while applied to the same object or that it is applied to a variety of different objects. In (22b), however, the plural stem is obligatory because of the plurality of the direct nominal object.

(21) Gisamjanga Datooga: alternation of stems ŋud 'pierce' (SG) vs. ŋuday (PL), triggered by plurality of the object

a. náa-ŋùcị
    S1SG:PF-pierce:1SG
    'I have pierced him (once)'
b. náa-ŋd-àyị
    S1SG:PF-pierce-PL:1SG
    'I have pierced him (several times)' ∼ 'I have pierced them'

(22) Gisamjanga Datooga: alternation of stems lood 'pull out' (SG) vs. loot (PL), triggered by plurality of the object

a. lôodạ   ŋûtạ
    pull.out:IMP.SG   spear
    'Pull out the spear!'
b. lóotà   ŋútkâakạ
    pull.out:PL:IMP.SG spears
    'Pull out the spears!'

In Gisamjanga Datooga the plural stem also has a holistic idea, as illustrated by the contrast of *rad* 'tie (one body part)' and *raday* ∼ *rat* 'tie (the whole body)':

(23) Gisamjanga Datooga: alternation of stems rad 'tie' (SG) vs. raday ∼ rat (PL)

a. náa-ràcị
    S1SG:PF-tie:1SG
    'I have tied him (partially, e.g. one of his arms)'
b. náa-rád-ày
    S1SG:PF-tie-PL:1SG
    'I have tied him (entirely, i.e. all of his body)'

These semantic specializations of a Nilotic verbal derivational suffix (Reh 1991) have not been reconstructed for the Proto-Nilotic period and must be seen as a Southern Nilotic, probably Datoogan innovation.

Sandawe also has the category of the plural verb stem (Kießling 2002b). Actually this language lacks any means of nominal number marking, plurality of the core participants of a predication being *exclusively* marked on the verb, either by deriving a plural stem by the plural stem suffix *-waa* or by replacing the singular stem by a suppletive plural stem. The morphosyntactic conditioning of these plural stems reflects an ergative-like pattern in that intransitive verbs are marked for the plurality of the subject, whereas transitive verbs tend to be marked for the plurality of the patient object, not that of the subject. Besides this rather inflectional type of plural marking, there is another more derivational type which could be labelled "pluractional," following Newman (1980, 1990), in that it indicates a plurality of action, mostly repetition.

(24) Sandawe: plural stem formation by *-waa* in ŋ‖óo[wé] 'milk' (SG) vs. ŋ‖óo-wâa (PL), triggered by the plurality of the direct object

a.   ʔùmbù-s   ŋ‖óo-wé
     cow-S1SG:PERF   milk-SG
     'I have milked a cow'

b.   ʔùmbù-s   ŋ‖óo-wâa
     cow-S1SG:PERF   milk-PL
     'I have milked cows'

(25) Sandawe: plural stem formation by *-waa* in tɬʼáak^{h}w[é] 'uproot' (SG) vs. tɬʼáak^{h}ú-wáa (PL), triggered by the plurality of the direct object

a.   ŋ!î̠-s   tɬʼáak^{h}w-é
     root-S1SG:PERF   uproot-SG
     'I have torn out a root'

b.   ŋ!i̠i̠-s   tɬʼáak^{h}ú-wáa
     root-S1SG:PERF   uproot-PL
     'I have torn out roots'

(26) Sandawe: plural stem formation by *-waa* in màntʃà 'eat' (SG) vs. màntʃà-wàa (PL), triggered by the plurality of the direct object

a.   tʃí   dìyá-s   màntʃà-a
     I   egg-S1SG:PERF   eat-SG
     'I have eaten an egg'

b.   tʃí   dìyá-s   màntʃà-wàa
     I   egg-S1SG:PERF   eat-PL
     'I have eaten eggs'

(27) Sandawe: alternation of suppletive verb stems *tɬàas* 'die' (SG) vs. *ɬàaté*
(PL) 'die', triggered by the plurality of the subject

a. ŋ|èmésée   tɬàas-â
    man   die:SG-S3MSG:PERF
    'A man has died'

b. ŋ|òmósóo   ɬàaté   [. . . ɬàat-â?a̰]
    people   die:PL   [. . . die:PL-S3PL:PERF]
    'People have died'

It is not clear whether the plural stem category in Sandawe is to be regarded
as a Khoisan inheritance. Suppletive plural stems are found in Northern
Khoisan (Bernd Heine and Christa König, p.c.) and in Southern Khoisan. The
situation in Hadza is not clear.

Regarding the historical interpretation, it seems that pre-Sandawe is the
source of the spread of the feature of verbal plurality to the West Rift Southern
Cushitic languages and to Southern Nilotic Datooga. In both language groups,
West Rift Southern Cushitic and Southern Nilotic, there is no specific need for
it, since a differentiation of number in the nominal arguments of the verb is
already taken care of by the complex morphological apparatus of nominal
plural and singulative derivation. Since this is different in Sandawe, which
lacks a number distinction in nouns, it must be suspected that the strategy of
head marking the number of verbal arguments on the verb itself was spread
together with its principal conditioning factors originating from a Sandawe
predecessor to the neighboring languages of the area. In this context it should
also be noted that the Sandawe iterative marker *-im* is very close – formally as
well as semantically – to the common West Rift Southern Cushitic verbal
extension for the durative **-im* (Kießling 2002a: 296), as it is in its modern
reflexes in Alagwa (16) and Burunge (17).

The descriptions of the Bantu languages of the area occasionally mention the
common Bantu habitual or pluractional marker *-aga*, *-anga*, though it is not
clear if it takes over functions comparable to the plural stem. This needs further
investigation.

6.2.5   The category of ventive marking (G3)

The presence of the category of ventive marking entails that there is a marker
(verbal affix or clitic) for indicating that the event or action is directed towards
a pre-established deictic center.

Datooga has an opposition of a centrifugal (andative, itive) vs. centripetal
(ventive) markers in verbal derivation (Rottland 1982: 184) as part of its
Nilotic heritage (Rottland 1983; Dimmendaal 1981; Reh 1996).

Although paralleled in Somali (Tosco 1997: 96; Saeed 1999: 126; Bourdin 2006), this kind of directional marking on the verb does not seem to be typical of Cushitic languages. All modern West Rift languages, though, come up with a verbal proclitic ventive marker which is reconstructed as *ni for PWR (Kießling 2002a: 368). It is suspected that the development of this verbal category is a structural transfer from a Southern Nilotic source. The long form of the ventive suffix in Southern Nilotic contains an n (-aan or -n). But this suffix was well integrated in lexical verbal morphology. We do not propose a direct borrowing of form *and* function. At most the similarity in form (the presence of n) may have helped the emergence of a independent ventive marker in West Rift. A possible source of the proclitic ventive marker is the first-person singular pronoun *ani*. Sandawe has a ventive morpheme that is almost identical in form, n^i; see (28). There is no comparative evidence to show that this suffix is inherited in Sandawe. Khoe languages have derivational suffixes that express direction (Vossen 1997a: 354) but no obvious cognates with ventive n^i. One option is transfer from Sandawe into West Rift, but if the concept was indeed a result of Datooga influence as we suggested above, the transfer of the form from Sandawe to West Rift at the times when Datooga was influential is unlikely. Transfer from West Rift to Sandawe is also unlikely in view of the difference in position: verbal suffix in Sandawe, preverbal clitic in West Rift. The similarity in form and function is best regarded as chance.

(28)   *thàá-n^i -kò*   'run to this place' (Steeman 2003)
        thàá-ko   'run away'

The marker *ni* in the preverbal clitic complex in Nyaturu, see table 6.3 above, is similar in form but different in function. At most, one could suggest that the frequent use of proclitics in *n* in Cushitic facilitated the use of a Bantu copula *ni* as a proclitic in the preverbal clitic complex in the Nyaturu speech of former Cushitic speakers.

There is no information on Hadza for this feature. The concept is an early Southern Nilotic influence on West Rift. In West Rift the first-person singular pronoun has been remolded into this function; while the function itself was taken from Southern Nilotic. This suggests Southern Nilotic speakers shifting to West Rift. Sandawe inherited or acquired the ventive suffix n^i independently.

6.2.6   *Two or more past tenses (G5); one or more future tenses (G6)*

Tense is typically a highly differentiated category in Bantu languages in general. Meeussen's (1967: 109) reconstruction of Proto-Bantu includes two morphemes with past reference, *a-* (recent or hodiernal) vs. *á-* (hesternal), but at the same time he observes that both markers are usually embedded in a three-way system of pasts with a contrast of hodiernal vs. hesternal vs. distant. Systems with at least three degrees of past reference are widespread in Eastern Bantu, e.g. Nyamwezi (Maganga & Schadeberg 1992: 103), Gogo (Cordell 1941), Sukuma (Batibo 1985; Olson 1964), and Rangi (Oliver Stegen, p.c.).

Cushitic languages typically express only aspect and have no morphological tense system. In spite of this genetic predisposition, all the modern West Rift languages have developed tense systems with two pasts. A twofold past system has been be reconstructed for Proto-West Rift (Kießling 2002a: 375ff., 413f.), operating on the basis of a contrast of preverbal clitics *in* for persistive vs. *gaa* for past. The ultimate origin of both morphemes is unclear; the tendency of past *gaa* to reduce to *aa* in most of the modern West Rift languages is considered to be a convergent development to conform to the Bantu past prefixes *a-* and *á-* in neighboring languages such as Nyaturu (Olson 1964; Nurse 2000a). Proto-Northern West Rift (Iraqw, Gorwaa, Alagwa) has even developed another past by fusion of *(i)n* plus *(g)aa* to *naa*, closely paralleled by Nyaturu verbal proclitic *náa* for far past, but their position in the preverbal clitic complex does not correspond. The development of two pasts in Proto-West Rift is considered a Bantu substrate, and the subsequent innovation of the *naa* past in Proto-Northern West Rift is an indication of prevailing Bantu impact.

Datooga has two tenses with a past-reference component, i.e. perfect and persistive, both of which do not seem to be inherited from Proto-Southern Nilotic (Rottland 1982: 177ff.). The perfect tense is marked by the allomorphs *n-*, *si-*, and *i-* (origin unclear), whereas the persistive in *gudu* can be traced back internally to a periphrastic construction with the verb 'finish.' Here too we have to assume Bantu structural influence due to a Bantu substrate.

In addition to tense distinctions in the past, various languages of our contact zone also introduced a tense system that has at least one non-analytic future tense. Proliferation of morphologically distinct future tenses is also a feature typical of many Bantu languages. Some Bantu languages accommodate up to four different future tenses, e.g. Gogo (Cordell 1941: 50). In the contact zone, Sukuma and Nyamwezi have three futures, Kimbu has two, Nilyamba, Nyaturu, Rangi, and Mbugwe have one. These numbers include morphologically discrete futures, they do not include present tenses functioning as futures.

Cushitic languages do not normally mark tense at the morphological level. No tense marker, let alone future, has been reconstructed for Cushitic. Proto-West Rift also had no morphological marker for future reference, but among the modern West Rift languages Burunge stands out as having innovated three futures marked by the preverbal clitics *aa* for near future, *oo* for prospective, and *maa* for distant future. It is not only the categories that must be considered Bantu influence here, but also the form of the prospective morpheme at least, since it is closely paralleled by the future **o-* of the Ruvu Bantu group (Gogo, Luguru, Zaramo, and others; see Nurse & Philippson 1975: 9). There is a

remarkable parallel involving form and function between tense markers of
Burunge and Nyaturu: Burunge low tone *aa* marker is paralleled by Nyaturu
near future *naa*, and Burunge high-tone *áa* marker for past is paralleled by
Nyaturu far past marker *náa*.

Datooga has a future tense marked by the allomorphs *aj-* and *ija-* (Rottland
1982: 177f.) which is not inherited from Proto-Southern Nilotic and must be
considered a Datooga innovation, all the more since there is evidence that the
future paradigm originated in a periphrastic construction involving a reduced
auxiliary verb plus subordinate main verb. Although the prior auxiliary verb
has not been identified internally so far, the separability and combinatory
potential of the future marker points to its prior syntactic independence (see
examples (12) and (13) and the subordinate status of the main verb is clear
from the presence of the hortative marker *da-* for 1SG subjects (29a) in the
future paradigm (29b), in contrast to the non-subordinative marker *aa-* for 1SG
in the present (29c) and perfect paradigms (29d)).

(29) Datooga subordinative morphosyntax of the future tense

a. qáa-múʊs-cí   **dá**-lâc   fùáandá   qùuwâaŋdạ
    1SG-can-1SG   1SG:SJN-cut   string:CON   bow
    'I can cut the bow-string'

b. gày-**dá**-lâc   fùáandá   qùuwâaŋdạ
    FUT-1SG:SJN-cut   string:CON   bow
    'I will cut the bow-string'

c. q-áa-làj-ì   fùáandá   qùuwâaŋdạ
    DECL:AFF-1SG-cut-1SG   string:CON   bow
    'I cut the bow-string'

d. n-áa-làj-ì   fùáandá   qùuwâaŋdạ
    PF-1SG-cut-1SG   string:CON   bow
    'I have cut the bow-string'

All sources seem to suggest that Sandawe and Hadza encode neither past- nor
future-tense reference at the morphological level. The innovation of past-
tense morphology in West Rift and Datooga reflects a Bantu substrate. Bantu
speakers shifted to West Rift languages at different stages in the history and
to Datooga, introducing the tense distinctions using inherited material.
Burunge was influenced in particular by Nyaturu.

6.2.7   Preverbal hortative laa (G8)

The preverbal hortative in *laa* is an intruiging puzzle. It is new in Burunge and
Alagwa, and it is absent in the Bantu languages of the contact zone, but it

occurs in various other Bantu languages in Tanzania where it is a clear innovation.

Within Eastern Bantu there is a future marker *laa-* which does not go back to Proto-Bantu. It occurs in between 15 percent and 20 percent of the Savanna Bantu languages, in a broad swathe from all around Lake Victoria down through Sukuma/Nyamwezi/Kimbu and Gogo and southwestern Tanzania and finally into Zambia. So it is probably an innovation in Eastern Bantu. It is long (where the languages have a length contrast), and it is predominantly low-toned (although tonally it behaves strangely in Sukuma and Nyamwezi at least, not undergoing or blocking otherwise regular tone shift; Maganga & Schadeberg 1992: 104f.). All around Lake Victoria it refers predominantly to near future but in Sukuma/Nyamwezi and all languages further south it refers predominantly to middle or far past.

Within West Rift, Burunge and Alagwa have innovated a preverbal clitic *la* for optative, probably by internal grammaticalization of an adverbial *lo'i* 'truly,' which does not exclude the possibility that this innovation might have been inspired by the external Bantu model. Burunge and Alagwa do not form a genetic unit and a preverbal clitic for optative has no parallel in the rest of Cushitic. Thus we are either dealing with two independent phenomena, or, more likely, a transfer of the grammatical element *la* from Burunge to Alagwa or the other way around. In view of the fact that there is massive lexical transfer from Burunge to Alagwa (Kießling 2002a: 450, Kießling and Mous 2003a: 30), the most likely scenario is one in which Burunge developed this marker, with or without external influence from Bantu, and Alagwa borrowed it from Burunge in the period where many Burunge women entered Alagwa society; see Kießling (2002: 480ff). If the contact is specifically with Burunge and thus relatively late, Gogo is the best candidate for the Bantu source. However, care should be exercised about the source, because the contact may have occurred earlier, before the language communities were in their current locations, which would allow other languages, such as Sukuma/Nyamwezi, as possible sources. The problem of the origin of preverbal marker *laa* in Eastern Bantu remains, but lies outside our contact zone.

We have not found any indication for a preverbal marker *laa* with hortative or similar functions in Datooga, Sandawe nor Hadza. Evidence for such a marker in Sandawe or Hadza would be of interest for the puzzle of the source of this marker in Eastern Bantu. The present level of description of these two languages does not allow us to exclude such a possibility.

Despite the remarkable uniformity in form and the clear innovative character of this feature, both in Bantu and in Cushitic, it is not unlikely that we are dealing with parallel independent developments.

6.2.8   Grammaticalization of body-part nouns as preposed relational nouns (G13)

The development of body parts to (spatial relational nouns acting as) pre-positions is a common grammaticalization path among (African) languages; see Heine (1989) for an overview. Thus an expression like 'back:of table' comes to function as 'on the table.' This happened in several languages in the Tanzanian Rift Valley. These developments are interrelated.

Like many other Nilotic languages, Datooga uses body-part nouns such as *ùhùudà* 'head,' *jèedà* 'belly,' *bàdáydà* 'back,' and *qùutà* 'mouth' as relational nouns for encoding spatial concepts such as 'on top of,' 'in; under,' 'behind,' and 'beside, at the edge of,' respectively. They may combine with genuine pre-positions in complex constructions of preposition + relational noun + noun.

(30) Datooga: preposition + relational noun + noun

     àbà   jèedá   bêegạ
     in   in   water
     'in the water'

In sharp contrast to the West Rift norm[13], the Iraqw/Gorwaa subgroup has grammaticalized body-part nouns for expressing spatial concepts to a considerable extent (Kießling 2002a: 422ff.). Thus pre-Iraqw *daanda* 'back,' *gura'a* 'belly,' and *'afa* 'mouth' have acquired the general meanings 'on top of,' 'in; under,' and 'beside, at the edge of,' respectively. They even tend to cluster in bundles of up to three relationals, as illustrated in (31), and are well on their way to being grammaticalized as prepositions, reflecting a progressive trend away from postpositional marking of spatial relations (still prevailing in modern Burunge to some extent) towards prepositional marking. This kind of reinforcement of prepositions is symptomatic of a more general trend in West Rift towards head-initial order, as is already manifest in head-initial order within NPs. Syntactic position and conceptual models must be viewed as reflecting a Datooga substrate, probably originating in a large number of Datooga speakers shifting to pre-Iraqw and imposing Datooga syntactic and semantic structures onto pre-Iraqw. We have not observed similar developments in Hadza, Sandawe, and the Bantu languages of our area.

(31) Iraqw: preposition + relational noun + noun

     garmaa   i-ri   ʕakúut   baráa   gurúu   geendariyaandi
     boy   S3-SEQ   fall:3MSG.PFV   in   in   baobab
     'The boy fell into the (hollow) baobab tree'

In addition to the development of body parts into prepositions, there is also the specific link of the spatial concepts of 'in' and 'under' in a single polysemous lexeme (G14), which points to the fact that both concepts are derived from a single model, i.e. the belly of a quadruped which unites the inside notion by virtue of the obvious fact of digestion (Heine 1989:91; Heine & Kuteva 2002) and the under notion by virtue of the fact that the belly of a quadruped always faces downwards, being at the same time the most salient part of the body in an arch-like shape formed by the quadruped's legs, chest, and belly. This quadruped model is relevant for its cultural implications, since it tends to form the basis of spatial conceptualization in societies that are based largely on cattle rearing and keeping.[14]

In Datooga, grammaticalization of the body-part noun *jéedà* 'belly' links the spatial concepts of 'in' and 'under,' reflecting the bovimorphic conceptual model, i.e. spatial relations are construed on the basis of the model of a quadruped, probably a cow, given the enonomic and cultural eminence of cattle keeping in Datooga society. In contrast to the West Rift norm, the Iraqw/ Gorwaa subgroup developed from the body-part nouns **daanda* 'back' and **gura'a* 'belly' abstract relational nouns for 'on top of' and 'in; under,' respectively (Kießling 2002a: 422ff.). This innovation is a semantic imprint left by Datooga speakers shifting in large numbers to Pre-Iraqw.

Although the development of prepositions from body-part nouns is very common in general and in Africa in particular, this feature is still a solid sign of Datooga influence on Iraqw on the basis of the specificity of the bovimorphic model, of the development of prepositions in an OV language, and on the basis of the fact that it runs counter to the norm in Southern Cushitic languages which tend not to use body parts for spatial relations.

6.2.9   *The semantic extension of 'belly' for emotional concepts*

The noun *gura'a* 'belly' came to be used in Pre-Iraqw in compounds expressing emotional concepts such as 'belly-bitter' > 'forget,' 'belly-rise' > 'feel pity' (G15), etc.; see Kießling (2002: 428f.). The model for this may be seen in Datooga which utilizes the noun *jéedà* 'belly' on the syntactic level for expressing emotional concepts, metonymically encoding the experiencer of the emotion as its perceived locus.

(32) Datooga

ánìiní	qw-âak	jéedàa-nyu
1SG	S3-eat	belly-POSS.1SG

'I am upset' (lit. 'I my belly hurts / bites / pinches / eats')

6.2.10   *Other features*

In the following we present briefly a number of features that some of the languages of our contact zone have in common but that are less good candidates for the definition of our contact zone for various reasons. For some of these features it is not clear whether the similarity is due to contact (P2, P4, G4, G7); some of these features are interrelated (G10, G11, G12); some of them are not worked out in enough detail (P4).

P2 *Ejectives*. Ejectives are inherited phonemes in the West Rift group of Southern Cushitic as well as in Sandawe and Hadza. Both the ejective affricates of West Rift are genetically linked to glottalic voiced alveolar stops in Eastern Cushitic. It is possible that there was influence from Hadza or Sandawe on the development of the pronunciation of these inherited glottalic consonants in West Rift. Glottalic consonants do not occur in Bantu, nor in Datooga.

P4 *Absence of voiced fricatives*. All languages of the area, except for the Bantu languages, lack voiced fricatives. This voice asymmetry in the fricatives in West Rift may have been inherited; Proto-Eastern Cushitic has been reconstructed with voiceless *f*, *s*, and *sh*, and one voiced fricative *z*; West Rift, however, only has *f*, *s*, *ɬ*, *x*, x^w, *ħ*, and *h*, and no voiced fricative.[15] Sandawe has *f*, *s*, *ɬ*, *x*, and *h*, and no voiced fricative. For Sandawe too this asymmetry seems to be inherited since voiceless fricatives are far more common than voiced fricatives in Khoisan (Vossen 1997a). Proto-Bantu has been reconstructed without strident fricatives (Schadeberg 2003), but many Bantu languages have developed strident fricatives, both voiced and voiceless, through spirantization and language contact. In our contact area, Rangi (Stegen 2002), Mbugwe (Mous 2004), and Nyaturu (Olson 1964) lack *z*; Nilyamba has no voiced fricatives with the exception of *z* in nasal compounds (Dempwolff 1915), while Nyamwezi (Maganga & Schadeberg 1992) has both *v* and *z*. We cannot show that the lack of *z* of the Bantu languages in the region must be attributed to influence from the surrounding languages, but it is conceivable that pronunciation habits of Sandawe or West Rift speakers shifting to Bantu languages played a role. The similarity between Sandawe and West Rift in asymmetry of voice in the fricatives cannot be shown to be due to contact since for both this seems to be inherited, at least to some extent.

P5 *seven-vowel system*. The Bantu languages of zone F, except F10 and F23, have inherited a seven-vowel system. Neither Sandawe and Hadza nor West Rift share this feature; they all have a system that operates with only five distinctive vowel qualities. Datooga is remarkable since it has reduced the inherited Proto-Southern Nilotic ten-vowel system to a system of seven vowels, seemingly converging towards Bantu zone F standards, which might be interpreted as pointing to a period in Datooga language history characterized by shifting Bantu speakers imposing their phonological habits onto Datooga. In section 6.2.2 we suggested that this reduction in the Datooga vowel system is linked to the phonemicizing of realizations of the dorsal obstruent under the influence of West Rift speakers. Under that analysis the Bantu influence is not needed as an explanation and the feature is directly linked to feature P3. In a way the seven-vowel system of the Bantu zone F languages also provides an example of a remarkable lack of contact influence. Given the fact that many Bantu languages developed a five-vowel system, why not Rangi, Mbugwe, Nyaturu with all these five-vowel languages around them: Cushitic, Sandawe, and Hadza? We disregard this feature.

G4 *The category of an applicative.* Languages with this feature use a verbal affix or clitic as a head-marking strategy to indicate the semantic role of goal, recipient, or benefactive arguments to the verb. As part of its common Nilotic heritage, Datooga marks the goal and recipient case role by the verbal suffix -*s* ("applicative," Rottland 1982: 184). This category is paralleled by the applicative suffix in Bantu. So a head-marking strategy of goal or recipient arguments of the verb is part of both Nilotic and Bantu heritage. This is different in Cushitic, since a verbal marker of goal or recipient arguments has not been reconstructed at the Cushitic level. However, the West Rift languages have innovated a verbal proclitic marker for exactly this function (indication of goal / recipient / benefactive case), which developed via verbal attraction and cliticization of the preposition **sa* 'to, for, because of' (Kießling 2002: 367f.). This innovation must have taken place approximately around the West Rift level, since different West Rift languages have grammaticalized the very same preposition in different slots within the preverbal clitic complex. All in all, this internal development seems to be inspired by external models, either Bantu or Datooga, probably Datooga, since in that case the development is strongly favored by the accidental homophony of the marker in *s* in both groups. Sandawe has an applicative in *k*.

G7 *Subjunctive suffix -ʾe(e).* A verbal suffix **-ʾé* ∼ **-ʾée* for the subjunctive mood is a genuine Bantu inheritance and has been reconstructed in this form for Proto-Bantu (Meeussen 1967: 112). It is present in the F zone, e.g. Nyamwezi (Maganga & Schadeberg 1992: 104, 128ff.) has an optative in -(*e*)*é*. A suffix **-ʾee* for the subjunctive has also been reconstructed for Proto-West Rift (Kießling 2002a: 360, 378), on the basis of modern Burunge (Kießling 1994), of relics in the poetic register of Iraqw, and of relics in imperative suffixes of Alagwa. On the one hand, this subjunctive suffix may be an early Bantu transfer into Proto-West Rift or Pre-West Rift, especially in the light of the parallel in the tonal effects triggered by the suffix: in Bantu and in Proto-West Rift the suffix makes all preceding tones in the verb low. On the other hand, the suffix might be related to an Omo-Tana (Cushitic) suffix -*ee* which shows up in the potential paradigm of the Somali verb (Saeed 1999: 92) and in the optative paradigm of Rendille prefix verbs (Pillinger & Galboran 1999: 43). To add to this picture, the first-person optative in Sandawe is -'*è* (Sander Steeman, p.c.). In a way it is the best feature for the contact area in that it shares both common form and function and is present in three of the language families. At the same time it is posssible that it is inherited in all three families and that brings the similarity down to coincidence. One could argue, however, that the presence of the subjunctive *-é* in Bantu has helped the preservation of optative *-e* in the West Rift languages, and possibly Sandawe. In a similar vein, Watkins (2001:53) suggests that the rich repertory of laryngeals in the different Semitic languages with which Hittites and Luvians were in contact "contributed to a favourable ambience for their conservation, wholly or in part, in Anatolia into the first millennium."

G9 *OV characteristics. infinitive + auxiliary (verb finality).* All modern West Rift languages display to some extent OV characteristics in their syntax. Iraqw and Gorwaa have rigid SOV order and prepose the verbal noun / infinitive to the auxiliary, whereas Alagwa and Burunge – somewhat less rigid as regards OV characteristics – display a pragmatically conditioned variation of OV ~ VO. Nevertheless, finality of the verb must be viewed as a genuine Cushitic feature inherited from Proto-West Rift and even beyond. The transition to SVO in both Alagwa and Burunge must be attributed to Bantu influence. Regarding the position of the auxiliary in periphrastic constructions, however, both languages retain the original head-final order VN + AUX.

(33) Iraqw: periphrastic future: VN + *aw* 'go' (Mous 1993: 267)

makay	i	ma'á	wahúngw	ay-á'
animals	S3	water:CON	drinking:CON	go:3-PL

'The animals will drink water'

(34) Alagwa: periphrastic future: VN + *kaw* 'go'

ningi	taysí	'ibitina	kay
SEQ.S3	there	staying	go:3MSG

'And he went to stay there'

Verb-finality is not part of the general Bantu inheritance. Even though two Bantu languages of the area, Mbugwe (Mous 2000) and to a somewhat lesser extent Rangi (Nurse 1979, 2000a: 525), display OV characteristics in that they put the verbal noun or infinitive in some compound tenses in front of the fully inflected auxiliary, resulting in syntactic structures like S-infinitive–Auxiliary–O illustrated in (34).

(35) Mbugwe: infinitive + auxiliary in present-progressive (Mous 2000: 472)

ora	ko-kéndé	wáre
15:eat	1PL-PRES.PROG	ugali

'We are eating food'

In Rangi, two tenses are involved, the general future and the incipient future. In both cases the auxiliary is of Bantu origin. In Mbugwe, four tenses are involved: present progressive, future, habitual, and past imperfective. For most of them, the Bantu origin of the auxiliary is beyond doubt. The present progressive *kénde* is a special case, since it seems to involve no simple reordering of syntactic constituents, but morphological reanalysis of structures due to phonological similarity. In both cases, Rangi and Mbugwe, the "counteruniversal rise of infinitive-auxiliary order" must be regarded as structural transfers from a West Rift source. For Mbugwe, Mous (2000) even claims a definite recent Iraqw substrate, possibly also of Gorwaa. For Rangi, the age and exact source is not clear. The presence of this feature in both languages might suggest that the structure of the paradigms common to both languages goes back to an older contact of Pre-Rangi-Mbugwe to Proto-West Rift.

SVO characteristics. Head-initial noun phrase order (G10); prepositions (G11); SVO word order (G12). Although genetically predisposed towards a head-final order, as adhered to in Central Cushitic and Highland East Cushitic, the West Rift languages have head-initial order within noun phrases, i.e. possessed precedes possessor in genitival constructions, adjective and numeral following their head noun, innovated prepositions dominating over inherited postpositions. This must be considered substrate influence from Bantu or Southern Nilotic/Datooga, both SVO typologically. Sandawe does not share this feature, in that it generally preposes modifiers to their modified heads, e.g. SOV order, possessor preceding possessed in genitive constructions (Elderkin 1991), however, numerals and demonstratives do occur after the noun in Sandawe. This structural influence on the Cushitic languages cannot be attributed to a single source.

6.3   Historical conclusions

All the features, their origin, and distribution are summarized in tables 6A and 6B in the appendix to this chapter. From these tables it is evident that there are bundles of features from different sources defining different subgroupings of languages, and this reflects the nature of our language area with shifting contact siuations and new languages coming in. Only three of these constituting features come close to a universal distribution within the Tanzanian Rift Valley area: the preverbal clitic complex (G1), verbal plurality (G2), and head-marking of goal (G4). There is a central bundle of features defining the West Rift languages, Sandawe, Datooga, Nyaturu, and possibly Nilyamba as one area all sharing the following features: contrast of two voiceless dorsal obstruents (P3, source: Proto-West Rift); a preverbal clitic complex for tense, subordination, sequence, and focus (G1, source: Proto-West Rift); verbal plurality (G2, source: Sandawe); presence of an applicative verbal extension (G4, source: East African Bantu or Pre-Datooga); at least two past morphemes (G5, source: East-African Bantu); at least one future tense morpheme

Table 6.5 Features of the Tanzanian Rift Valley area according to language families[a]

	Bantu	Southern Cushitic	Southern Nilotic	Sandawe / Hadza
P1 lateral frikative /ɬ/	–	*PWR	*PSN> /ʃ/	*Sandawe Hadza*
P2 ejective obstruents	–	*PWR	–	**Sandawe Hadza**
P3 contrast of /k/ vs. /q/	Nyaturu (Pre-Datooga)	*PWR	<WR	**Sandawe Hadza**
P4 no voiced fricatives	–	*PWR	**Pre-Datooga**	**Sandawe Hadza**
(P5 7-vowel system)	**Bantu (F zone)**	–	> Datooga	–)
G1 preverbal clitic complex	> Nyaturu	*PWR	> Datooga	*Hadza*
G2 verbal plurality	?	> *PWR	> Datooga	**Sandawe**
G3 applicative	*EAB	> *PWR	**Pre-Datooga**	?
G4 ventive	*EAB	> *PWR	**Pre-Datooga**	*Sandawe*
G5 ≥ 2 past tense	*EAB	> *PWR > *PNWR	> Datooga	?
G6 ≥ 1 future	*EAB	> Pre-Burunge	> Pre-Datooga	?
G7 subjunctive -ee	*EAB	> *PWR	–	Sandawe
G8 laa for irrealis	*EAB (future)	*PSWR (optative)	–	?
G9 infinitive + auxiliary order	> Rangi, Mbugwe	*PWR		?
G10 head initial NPs	*EAB	> *PWR	**Pre-Datooga**	*Hadza*
G11 prepositions	*EAB	> *PIRQ < Pre-Datooga	**Pre-Datooga**	?
G12 SVO	*EAB	> *PSWR	–	*Hadza*
G13 body-part nouns > prepositions	?	> *PIRQ	**Pre-Datooga**	?
G14 polysemy 'in' and 'under'	?	< PIRQ	**Pre-Datooga**	?
G15 'belly' in emotional concepts	?	< PIRQ	**Pre-Datooga**	?

[a] Tables 6.5 and 6.6 bring together in a single display all the grammatical features found so far in the Tanzanian Rift Valley area with an indication of their distribution across linguistic boundaries along with a shorthand historical interpretation in terms of genetic status (inherited vs. transferred). Bold indicates that the language (group) has inherited the feature; > indicates that the feature has been carried over through contact; italics indicate that it is unclear whether the feature is inherited or acquired through contact.

Table 6.6 *Features of the Tanzanian Rift Valley area and membership index of individual languages*

	PIRQ	AL	BU	San-dawe	Hadza	F32	F31	F33/34	Datoo-ga	Swa-hili	Maasai	Oromo
P1 lateral fricative /ɬ/	+	+	+	+	+	−	−	−	−	−	−	−
P2 ejective obstruents	+	+	+	+	+	−	−	−	−	−	−	+
P3 contrast of /k/ vs. /q/	+	+	+	+	+	+	−	−	+	−	−	+
P4 no voiced fricatives	+	+	+	+	+	−	−	−	+	−	+	−
G1 preverbal clitic complex	+	+	+	+	+	+	+	−	+	−	−	−
G2 verbal plurality	+	+	+	+	?	?	?	?	+	−	−	−
G3 applicative	+	+	+	+	?	?	?	?	+	−	+	−
G4 ventive	+	+	+	+	+	+	+	+	+	+	+	−
G5 ≥ 2 past tenses	+	+	+	−	−	+	+	+	+	+	−	−
G6 ≥ 1 future	−	−	+	−	+	+	+	+	+	+	−	−
G7 subjunctive -ee	+	−	+	+	+	+	+	+	+	+	−	−
G8 *laa* for irrealis	−	−	+	+	−	−	−	−	−	−	−	−
G9 infinitive + auxiliary order	+	−	+	?	?	−	−	+	−	−	−	+
G10 head initial position in NPs	+	−	+	+	+	+	+	+	+	+	+	+

G11 prepositions	+	+	+	−	+	+	+	+	+	+	+	−
G12 SVO	−	+	+	−	+	+	+	+	+	+	−	−
G13 body-part nouns > prepositions	+	+	+	?	?	?	?	?	+	−	+	−
G14 polysemy of 'in' and 'under'	+	−	−	?	?	?	?	?	+	−	?	−
G15 'belly' for emotional concepts	+	−	−	+	?	?	?	?	+	−	?	−
Membership index on the basis of all features	16/20 = 80%	16/20 = 80%	17/20 = 85%	11/18 = 61%	10/15 = 67%	9/13 = 69%	8/13 = 62%	8/13 = 62%	15/20 = 75%	7/20 = 35%	6/18 = 33%	4/20 = 20%
Membership index on the basis of the bundle of 7 core features	6/7 = 86%	6/7 = 86%	7/7 = 100%	5/7 = 71%	5/6 = 83%	6/7 = 86%	5/6 = 83%	4/6 = 66%	7/7 = 100%	4/7 = 57%	2/7 = 29%	2/7 = 29%

(G6, source: East African Bantu); and finally head-initial NPs (G10, source East African Bantu or Pre-Datooga). This constitutes a strong bundle of features because all of them involve changes and are specific enough to be reliably attributed to contact and not to universal tendencies or chance. In spite of the locality and partial typological countercurrency of most of these developments, some broad general trends are observed: transition to head initial order (G10, G11, G12; but countercurrent: G9), and the transition to head marking of syntactic relations (G1, G2, G4).

We calculated the degree of similarity by establishing for every member of the contact zone, and on the basis of the number of shared areal features, an index that indicates the relative centrality or peripherality of the languages in question (see table 6B in the appendix). We added Swahili (Bantu), Maasai (Nilotic), and Oromo (Cushitic) as control languages from outside our contact zone. This index ranges from a minimum of 61 percent (Sandawe) and 62 percent (Nilyamba, Rangi, Mbugwe) up to a maximum of 85 percent (Burunge). The three control languages confirm the validity of the language area with indices of 20 percent (Oromo), 33 percent (Maasai), and 35 percent (Swahili). The West Rift languages display most of the areal features. The lacunae in the documentation of Hadza, Isansu, and Nilyamba still pose a serious problem, causing some distortion of the results.

With the exception of features (G7) and (G8), which constitute direct transfer of morphemes, all index features are isomorphisms, i.e. convergences in syntactic structures and semantic categories where at least one member of the contact zone innovated structures or categories on the basis of an external model, using internal morphological material. This points to contact scenarios which are characterized by multilingualism and massive language shift (Thomason & Kaufman 1988: 95f.) within settings of shifting political, economical, and cultural dominance.

We were able to identify the ultimate source of most features discussed here.[16] The list in (35) brings together in one display the trends of contact-induced change according to sources.

(35) Source-wise overview of contact-induced innovations in the Tanzanian Rift Valley:
Pre-Sandawe
> PWR, Pre-Datooga
   verbal plurality (G2)
Proto-West Rift
> Pre-F31/32, Pre-Datooga
   preverbal clitic complex (G1)
   contrast of two voiceless dorsal obstruents (P3)

> Pre-F33/34
  infinitive + auxiliary (G9) [< Proto-Iraqw/Gorwaa]
East African Bantu
  > Proto-West Rift
  two pasts (G5)
  subjunctive -ee (G7)?
  > Proto-Southern West Rift / Pre-Burunge
  future (G6)
  SVO (G12)
  > Pre-Datooga
  future (G6)
Pre-Datooga
  > Proto-West Rift, Sandawe
  head-marking the direction of a process in relation to a deictic center (G3)
  > Proto-Iraqw/Gorwaa
  grammaticalization: body-part nouns > prepositions (G13)
  link of the spatial concepts 'in' and 'under' (bovimorphic model) (G14)
  metonymic use of 'belly' in the expression of emotional concepts (G15)

In historical terms, this results in a complex picture of mutual linguistic contacts of varying intensity at several points in time, the rough lines of which are summarized as follows:

(i)   Spread of structural features from a West Rift source to some Bantu F languages and to Datooga. This includes the emergence and rise of a preverbal clitic complex (G1) in Nyaturu and Datooga, the development of a phonemic opposition of two voiceless dorsal obstruents (P3) in Nyaturu and Datooga. These facts point to a scenario of language shift from Proto-West Rift or one of its predecessors to Pre-Datooga and Pre-Nyaturu, where the shifting bilinguals imported these West Rift features into the Bantu and Nilotic target languages. The emergence of head-final order of infinitive plus auxiliary (G9) in some periphrastic tenses in Mbugwe and Rangi happened at a later stage under influence of the individual West Rift languages.

(ii) Steady Bantuization of Proto-West Rift, Proto-Southern West Rift, then Burunge (Alagwa) and a marginal Bantuization of Pre-Datooga. The Bantuization of Pre-Datooga is reflected in the innovation of a synthetic future tense (G6) and possibly in the reduction of a former ten-vowel system to seven vowels (P5). The Bantu imprint on Proto-West Rift is represented by the innovation of two synthetic tenses with past reference (G5) and the retention of a subjunctive in -ee (G7). Possibly the general trend in West Rift towards head-initial order within the NP (G10) must also be attributed to Bantu influence. In a subgroup of West Rift, in Proto-Southern West Rift, and later on in Burunge, the Bantu influence intensified considerably, as manifest in the change of basic word order to SVO (G12), and the innovation of three tenses with future reference in Burunge (G6). Evidence of Bantuization has also been detected in the progressive reanalysis of the nominal gender system of Proto-Southern West Rift on a semantic basis through the increasing affinity of neuter gender to the semantic category of plural, accomplished by reanalysis of neuters with singular reference as masculine and by reanalysis of masculine and feminine plural markers as neuter and through a clearer convergence of grammatical gender and sex, accomplished by the elaboration of paired singulatives, masculine and feminine, for animal referents.

(iii) Diffusion of structural and semantic features from Pre-Datooga into Proto-West Rift and, later on a broader scale, into the Iraqw/Gorwaa subgroup of West Rift. These include the introduction of a morphological expression of the direction of event or action in relation to a deictic center (G3) in Proto-West Rift, the grammaticalization of body-part nouns to prepositions (G13) with concomitant linking of the spatial concepts 'in' and 'under' following the bovimorphic model (G14) and the metonymic use of the body-part noun 'belly' for the experiencer in expressing emotional concepts (G15) in Proto-Iraqw/Gorwaa. This bundle of features must be a semanto-syntactic imprint of Datooga on Proto-West Rift, later Proto-Iraqw/Gorwaa, left by shifting Pre-Datooga bilinguals. The sociohistorical background of the latter line is discussed in detail in Kießling (1998b).

(iv) Only one feature has been attributed to a Pre-Sandawe source, namely verbal plurality (G2), which must have spread to Proto-West Rift and to Datooga by mediation of shifting Pre-Sandawe speakers, generalizing semantic concepts of derivational markers pre-existent in those languages for inflectional purposes.

(v) In addition, there are several features, exclusively phonological ones (P1, P2, P4), that tie up West Rift with Sandawe and Hadza and which seem to reflect an ancient contact predating all the other contacts identified so far, since it is not obvious in which direction the shared features have been transferred, if transfer has actually happened at all.

Some of these features point beyond the Tanzanian Rift Valley area, e.g. the lateral fricative (P1). On the Southern Nilotic side, the only member in the area, Datooga, deviates, since it does not have a lateral fricative. Closely related Omotik, however, has a lateral fricative and on this basis it has been reconstructed for Proto-Southern Nilotic (Rottland 1982: 233). If this was a Southern

Nilotic innovation within Nilotic inspired by Southern Cushitic influence, it must have taken place far north of the Tanzanian Rift Valley area, at the time of the Proto-Southern Nilotic period. This suggests that the Tanzanian Rift Valley might be a secondary contact zone and area of retreat where linguistic groups from genetically different backgrounds came together at various points in time, converging in various aspects of their structures, while part of these convergences might also be traced back to primary contacts at places outside the contemporary scene of contact. This could also mean that the Tanzanian Rift Valley area is a residual zone resulting from a contraction of a formerly much larger area of contact. The Tanzanian Rift Valley area has been coined "das abflusslose Gebiet" in the early German literature (e.g Luschan 1898), denoting the fact that no rivers stream out of the area. Also linguistically our sprachbund acts like an *abflussloses Gebiet*.

7   Ethiopia

Joachim Crass and Ronny Meyer

7.1   Introduction

The Ethiopian Linguistic Area (ELA) is the most famous linguistic area in Africa. It is the only linguistic area of this continent mentioned and (sometimes) discussed to a certain extent in general works dealing with language contact and areal linguistics (e.g. Masica 1976; Thomason 2001b; Thomason & Kaufman 1988). Most scholars dealing with Ethiopian languages refer to this area as the "Ethiopian Language Area" (Ferguson 1970, 1976; Sasse 1986; Hayward 1991; Zaborski 1991, 2003; Tosco 1994b; Crass 2002). This term, however, is problematic in several respects:

(a) The English translation of what is called in German *Sprachbund* is *linguistic area, convergence area,* or *diffusion area* (Campbell 1994: 1471). The term linguistic area is used by most of the authors dealing with such areas (e.g. Masica 1976; several papers written by Emeneau, collected in Dil 1980; Thomason 2001b).
(b) At least partly, the area includes Eritrea, which was a province of Ethiopia until it became an independent state in 1993.
(c) A certain number of features are found beyond Ethiopia and Eritrea in languages spoken in the neighboring countries Djibouti, Somalia, Sudan, and even beyond.

Some scholars have taken these facts into account, at least to some extent. Hayward (2000b: 623) uses the term "Ethio-Eritrean Sprachbund" and Zaborski (2003) proposes "North East African Language Macro-Area." Despite the fact "that the overlap [of features] into neighboring regions is minimal", Bender (n.d.: 4) stresses that "[n]ow we must modify it to 'Ethiopia-Eritrean Area,' in view of recent political history." In the present chapter, the term Ethiopian linguistic area (ELA) is used in order to account for the fact that language area is not the commonly used term in areal linguistics and that the core of the area is Ethiopia.

According to Grimes (2000: 109), eighty-two languages are spoken in Ethiopia. Most of them belong to three language families of the Afroasiatic phylum, namely Semitic, Cushitic, and Omotic. A number of languages in the west and southwest belong to different families of the Nilo-Saharan phylum and are therefore not genetically related to the languages of the Afroasiatic phylum.

According to a widely accepted view, Semitic-speaking peoples arrived in the Horn of Africa at the end of the first millennium BC by crossing the Red Sea after having left their homeland on the Arabian peninsula. They migrated into the area of today's Ethiopia and Eritrea and underwent extensive linguistic and extralinguistic influence by Cushitic-speaking peoples (Ullendorff 1955). A contradicting view considers Ethiopia to be the original homeland of Semitic-speaking people (Hudson 1977; Murtonen 1967). This view is based on the assumption that the linguistic diversity among Semitic languages in Ethiopia is much greater than elsewhere.

7.2   Research history

Leslau (1945, 1952, 1959) and Moreno (1948) describe the influence of Cushitic languages on Ethio-Semitic languages. The first to claim the existence of a linguistic area in "Ethiopia and the various Somalilands" was Greenberg (1959: 24). He is of the opinion that this area is characterized by "relatively complex consonantal systems, including glottalized sounds, absence of tone, word order of determined followed by determiner, closed syllables, and some characteristic idioms." According to Heine (1975: 41f.), who deals with word-order typology, Ethiopia is part of "probably the largest convergence area in Africa, stretching in a broad belt from the Lake Chad region in the west to the Red Sea and the Indian Ocean in the east."

Ferguson (1970, 1976) was the first to describe the ELA in more detail. Ferguson (1976), with an extended database and improvements and corrections, is still the reference work; it will therefore, be the starting point in our analysis of features. Ferguson discusses 8 phonological and 18 grammatical features on the basis of 18 languages, including Arabic and English. He argues that the "languages of Ethiopia constitute a linguistic area in the sense that they tend to share a number of features which, taken together, distinguish them from any other geographically defined group of languages in the world" (Ferguson 1976: 63f.). He stresses that "some of these shared features are due to genetic relationship ... , while others result from the process of reciprocal diffusion among languages which have been in contact for many centuries."

Zaborski (1991: 124) criticizes Ferguson's selection of languages and features. He argues that the languages are "rather random[ly] selected" and that "most of the alleged areal features are not really areal but of common genetic origin." Hayward (2000b: 623) is of the opinion that a number of Ferguson's features are "characteristic of most languages of this region" of which he considers five to be "very widespread." Some contributions deal with only one areal feature: Appleyard (1989) discusses relative verbs in focus constructions; Tosco (1994b) deals with case marking; and Tosco (1996) with extended verb paradigms in the Gurage-Sidamo subarea, one of the subareas of the ELA proposed by Zaborski (1991).

Tosco (2000b) denies the existence of the ELA because of the genetic relatedness of Ethio-Semitic and Cushitic languages, the unilateral diffusion from Cushitic to Ethio-Semitic and the occurrence of features in related languages, which do not belong to the ELA. Four recent papers, namely Bender (2003), Crass (2002), Crass and Bisang (2004), and Zaborski (2003) favor the existence of a linguistic area. Bender (2003) argues against Tosco (2000b) and tries to extend the ELA by testing a number of Nilo-Saharan languages using a selection of Ferguson's features. Crass (2002) discusses two phonological features in detail; in Crass and Bisang (2004) the discussion is extended to features such as word order, converbs, and ideophones verbalized by the verb 'to say.' Zaborski (2003) presents the most extended list, including twenty-eight features which he considers to be valid for a macro-area including Ethiopia, Eritrea, Djibouti, Somalia, and parts of Sudan, Kenya, and even Tanzania and Uganda. Finally, Hayward (1991) deals with patterns of lexicalization shared by the three Ethiopian languages Amharic (Semitic), Oromo (Cushitic), and Gamo (Omotic). According to Hayward (1991: 140), these lexicalizations reinforce "the very real cultural unity of Ethiopia" (see also Hayward 2000b).

The ELA is considered to be composed of several subareas. Leslau (1952, 1959) describes change in Ethio-Semitic languages induced by contact with neighboring Highland East Cushitic languages. Sasse (1986) deals with the Sagan area in the southwest of Ethiopia, and Zaborski (1991: 125ff.) gives a list of seven subareas being composed of "smaller contact and interference units" which he extends to nine by adding a Kenyan and a Tanzanian subarea (Zaborski 2003: 64).

7.2.1   Phonological features

Ferguson's phonological features are listed in table 7.1.

Ferguson's list has been criticized in most of the later publications. Zaborski (1991: 124, footnote 3) considers only P3 and "with reservations" P2 to be "really areal." Zaborski (2003: 62) lists four phonological features. Besides P3 and P6, Zaborski argues that "labialized consonants are frequent [and that] some palatalized consonants are innovations." Tosco (2000b: 341ff.) is of the opinion that P1, P2, P3, and P5 are genetically inherited within Afroasiatic, that P4, P7, and P8 are restricted to one or two language families, and that P6 is widespread in both Afroasiatic and Nilo-Saharan. According to Bender (n.d.), P2 and P6 are typological features, P5 is too limited and P8 "is vacuous because consonant clusters are rare." P1, P3, P4, and P7, however, are "fairly

Table 7.1 *Phonological features (Ferguson 1976: 65ff.)*

P1	/f/ replacing /p/ as the counterpart of /b/
P2	Palatalization of dental consonants as a common grammatical process in at least one major word class
P3	The occurrence of ejectives (in Ferguson's terminology: *glottalic consonants*)
P4	The occurrence of an implosive /d'/
P5	The occurrence of pharyngeal fricatives
P6	The occurrence of consonant gemination
P7	The occurrence of central vowels being shorter in duration than the other vowels
P8	The occurrence of an epenthetic vowel (in Ferguson's terminology: *helping vowel*)

idiosyncratic and easy to check." Hayward (2000b: 623) explicitly mentions only one phonological feature, namely P6.

Crass (2002) discusses P3 and P5 in detail. Both features being genetically inherited in Afroasiatic, Crass argues that occurrence (of ejectives) and non-occurrence (of pharyngeal fricatives) can be considered areal features. Reconstructions of different stages of proto-languages of Afroasiatic show that ejectives were lost over the course of time (cf. Crass 2002: 1683ff.). In recent times, however, ejectives were reimported into most of the languages via contact. For Proto-Highland East Cushitic, for example, only one ejective is reconstructed, namely the velar ejective. In most of the modern Highland East Cushitic languages, however, four ejectives occur as phonemes, namely the dental, the postalveolar affricate, the velar, and to a smaller extent the labial ejective (Hudson 1989: 11). In the Agaw languages (Central Cushitic), ejectives occur predominantly in loanwords from Amharic and Tigrinya and their phonemic status is problematic (cf. Appleyard 1984: 34f.). The reasons for the non-occurrence of pharyngeal fricatives in most Central Ethiopian languages are unclear. The non-occurrence may be due to language contact or due to language-internal change. Tosco (2000b: 343) supports Crass's idea in briefly mentioning that the non-occurrence of pharyngeal fricatives "could identify a smaller 'central Ethiopian area' ... in which pharyngeal consonants are either dropped or reduced."

This short summary shows that the views concerning the phonological features vary considerably. Only in three cases is there clear agreement among scholars, namely between Crass and Tosco concerning the non-occurrence (or loss) of pharyngeal fricatives in Central Ethiopia, between Crass and Zaborski concerning ejectives, and between Hayward and Zaborski concerning consonant gemination. In several other cases, agreement can be postulated: Hayward (2000b: 623) mentions that "Ferguson listed a number of very obvious linguistic typological features, that were characteristic of most languages of this region." Bender (2003: 31) considers all features except P5 and

Table 7.2 *Grammatical features (Ferguson 1976: 69ff.)*

G1	SOV word order
G2	Subordinate clauses precede main clauses
G3	The occurrence of converbs
G4	The occurrence of postpositions
G5	Quotation marked by the verb 'to say' (in Ferguson's terminology: *quoting clauses*)
G6	Compound verbs ... consisting of a noun-like or interjection-like "pre-verb" plus a semantically colorless auxiliary, commonly the verb 'to say'
G7	The occurrence of a negative copula
G8	Singular used with numbers
G9	Possessive suffixes identical or nearly identical with object suffixes added to the verb
G10	Masculine/feminine gender distinction in the second and third person singular of pronouns and verbs
G11	The subject prefixes of the 2MSG and the 3FSG marking a certain tense are identical but contrast with subject suffixes forming other tenses
G12	Many words consist of a consonantal skeleton carrying the lexical meaning and a pattern of vowels carrying the grammatical meaning
G13	Reduplication for forming intensive verbs and plurals of adjectives
G14	Plural formation by change of the pattern, e.g. ablaut, so-called broken plurals
G15	An independent and a subordinate form of the imperfective
G16	Plural nouns agree with a feminine singular adjective, verb or pronoun
G17	The imperative of the verb 'to come' is formed either from "a totally different stem ... or with an exceptional formation"
G18	The unmarked form of a noun is not singular in number but plural or collective

P7 to be "nearly universal among Ethio-Semitic, Cushitic and Omotic languages ..."

7.2.2   Grammatical features

Ferguson's grammatical features are listed in table 7.2.

Zaborski (1991: 124f.) considers G1 to G6 to be areal features and G7 to G18 to be of genetic origin. Furthermore, he adds two features, which are areal in his view, namely (a) adjectives precede substantives and (b) main verbs precede auxiliaries.

Hayward (2000b: 623) is of the opinion that the features G1, G3, G6, and G15 are "very widespread." According to Bender (2003, n.d.) G2, G3, G4, and G9 "are implicational consequences of SOV order," G13 and G18 are "too typological" and G10 to G12, G14 and G16 are Afroasiatic "especially Semitic idiosyncrasies." G7 "looks like a good choice but turns out ... to be inadequately defined." Bender seems to consider G1, G5, G6, G8, G15, and G17 to be candidates of areal features.

Hayward (1991) and Tosco (2000b) correctly stress that G2 and G4 have a relation to G1 and therefore cannot count as individual features. In this context, Campbell (1994: 1471) raises the question of the weight of "a trait so central to the grammar" when it is counted only as a single feature. G3, which, in contrast to Bender's opinion, is not related to G1 (cf. Bisang 2001), is found in an area exceeding the ELA (cf. Azeb & Dimmendaal 2006a). Tosco (2000b) considers G3, G5, G6, G8, G13, and G15 to have spread into Semitic languages due to Cushitic influence. The features G11, G12, and G14 are strongly "Semitic-biased" and G17 and G18 are Afroasiatic features.

The large list presented by Zaborski (2003: 62f.) contains features of different quality concerning their areal status. Unfortunately, in most of the cases Zaborski simply names the features without any discussion. A number of features correlate with the basic SOV word order. Examples are:

(a) Dependent clauses precede main clauses.
(b) Main verbs precede auxiliary ones.
(c) Adjectives precede nouns which they define.
(d) Possessor (genitive) precedes the possessed.

Other features are trivial or represent frequent grammaticalizations such as:

(e) Relative clauses are frequent.
(f) Cleft sentences are frequent.
(g) Postpositions start functioning as new case endings.

However, there are three interesting features which need further study. These are:

(h) Subject is in the oblique case (marked nominative).
(i) Quoting clauses and a lack or at least limited use of indirect speech.
(j) Considerable number of different 'to be' auxiliary verbs.

7.2.3 Lexical features

Hayward (1991) distinguishes three categories of lexicalizations, which he exemplifies with data on Amharic, Oromo, and Gamo. These categories are:

(a) Single-sense lexicalizations
(b) Lexicalizations with two or more distinct senses
(c) Lexicalizations involving similar derivations

The first category comprises "single-sense lexicalizations of typically indigenous concepts," the second category lexicalizations "showing inter-linguistic matching across the three languages," and the third category lexicalizations with a "similar (parallel) 'derivational pathway'." To the first category belong mainly nouns such as lexical items for seasons of the year, categories of terrain, categories of dung/excrement, super-categories for birds, types of borrowing (loan of money, loan of objects to be returned), and skin color classification of people of the region. Furthermore, this category includes the suppletive imperative of the verb 'to come' (Ferguson's feature G17) and particles with the meaning 'Take this!' which have no obvious etymological relationship to a verb. The second category, namely lexicalizations with two or more distinct senses, is predominantly comprised of verbs and some nouns. Examples:

(a) The respective verbs with the basic meaning 'hold, catch' have the secondary meaning 'start, begin.'
(b) The respective verbs with the basic meaning 'play' have the secondary meaning 'chat.'

The third category includes verbal derivations, compound verbs (Ferguson's feature G6), possessive constructions including two NPs, and idiomatic expressions. Examples for verbal derivations are the causative of the verb 'want' having the meaning 'need,' the causative of the verb 'enter' having the meaning 'marry' and the causative of the verb 'pass the night' having the meaning 'administer.' Compound verbs are 'become silent,' 'hurry up,' and 'jump up suddenly.' Possessive constructions including two NPs have a word-by-word meaning and a metaphorical meaning. Examples are 'son of man/people' having the meaning 'mankind, human being' and 'land of man/people' with the meaning 'foreign country.' Idiomatic expressions are 'regain/recover control, take courage' being composed of the noun 'heart' and the verb 'return (intransitive),' and 'catch cold,' of which the noun 'cold' is the subject and the experiencer the object of the verb 'catch.'

7.3   Proposed new features

This chapter deals with a number of morphological and syntactic similarities in several Ethio-Semitic and East Cushitic languages.[1] The investigated languages are the Ethiosemitic languages Gumär, Muher (both Gunnän-Gurage), Wolane, and Zay (both East Gurage) and Amharic (for the classification, see Hetzron 1972: 119). Furthermore, the Highland East Cushitic languages K'abeena (for the classification, see Crass 2001) and Libido and the Lowland East Cushitic language Oromo (West Central variety) have been considered. The languages Gumär, Muher, Wolane, Zay, K'abeena, and Libido belong to the Highland East Cushitic/Gurage subarea, a linguistic area located in the south of central Ethiopia. The eastern border of the area is formed by the northern Rift Valley lakes. Amharic and Oromo are spoken in many parts of Ethiopia. Amharic is the lingua franca in towns (Meyer & Richter 2003); Oromo is the major language in east, south and west Ethiopia.

We consider the similarities, presented by means of recently collected data, to be possible candidates for areal features of the ELA.[2] This is due to the fact that Oromo and Amharic occur widespread in Ethiopia and may have caused the spread of at least some of these features into other languages. However, to prove this, a representative sample of Ethiopian languages must be investigated.

A considerable number of the features presented could have evolved through grammaticalization. However, this does not mean that one should presume they must be excluded as contact-induced features. Especially in the case of rare or unattested grammaticalizations, contact-induced language change is one possible way of explaining the similarities (cf. Bisang 1996; Heine 1994; Heine & Kuteva 2003).

7.3.1   *Morphological features*

In this section we discuss three morphemes which have a number of functions depending on the status of the constituent they are attached to. These multi-functional morphemes occur in almost all languages investigated.

7.3.1.1   Ablative > comparative   The grammaticalization of the ablative case marker to a marker of the standard in comparative constructions is attested in many languages of the world (Heine & Kuteva 2002: 30). In Amharic, the ablative case is marked by the prefix *kä-* (see (1a)), in K'abeena by the suffix *-cci* being preceded by a long vowel which depends on the morphology of the noun (see (1b)). In Zay the ablative marker *bä-* is prefixed not only to the head noun but also to its modifier (see (1c)).

(1) a. Amharic
   shash   yä-gäzzahu-t   kä-zzicc   setyowa
   scarf   REL-buy.PFV.1SG-DEF.M   ABL-this   woman.DEF.F

   näw
   COP.3MSG

   b. K'abeena
   sitira   hi'riyoommiihu   ta   manc-oocc-eeti
   scarf.ACC   buy.PFV.1SG.NOM   this   woman-ABL-COP

   c. Zay
   shashi   yoohäbhiiy   bä-ytaatey
   scarf   REL.buy.PFV.1SG.DEF.M   ABL-this

   bä-seet-ittii.
   ABL-woman-DEF.F.COP.3MSG
   'It is from this woman that I bought the scarf'

In (2), the ablative marks the standard in comparative constructions.

(2) a. Amharic

yä-'ityop'ya	bunna	kä-lelocc	agärocc	bunna
GEN-Ethiopia	coffee	ABL-other.PL	country.PL	coffee

yïsshalall
be.better.IPF.3MSG.AUX.3MSG

b. K'abeena

'itoop'yaa	k'aawwu	gu'ma	baadi	k'aaww-iicci
Ethiopia.GEN	coffee.NOM	all	country.GEN	coffee-ABL

k'ohanu
be.better.IPF.3MSG

c. Zay

yä-t'oo'bä	bunä	bä-liilä	däbïr	bunä
GEN-Ethiopia	coffee	ABL-other	country	coffee

yïräbïnaa
be.better.IPF.3MSG.AUX.3MSG.DC
'Ethiopian coffee is better than the coffee of [all] other countries'

This grammaticalization occurs in all languages of our sample except Wolane, where, instead of the ablative morpheme *bä-* ~ *bi-*, the morpheme *tä-* is used to mark the standard in a comparative construction.

(3) a. Wolane

shaashi	yä-wähäb-ku	bibbi	mishtï-n
scarf	REL-buy.PFV-1SG	ABL.this	woman-COP.3MSG

'It is from this woman that I bought the scarf'

b. Wolane

'itobyä	k'awa	tä-gänäccä	geccä	k'awa
Ethiopia	coffee	COMP-other.PL	country.PL	coffee

yït'ä'ïl-an
be.better.IPF.3MSG-AUX.3MSG
'Ethiopian coffee is better than the coffee of [all] other countries'

The fact that this kind of grammaticalization is typical of Ethiopia and the fact that it is found rarely elsewhere in Africa are discussed by Zelealem and Heine (2003: 56ff.). However, one has to admit that the category case is restricted in Africa mainly to languages spoken in Ethiopia and adjacent countries. Therefore, the areal occurrence of the ablative in comparative construction is not surprising.

7.3.1.2 Ablative > 'since' temporal > real conditional The ablative case marker can be grammaticalized also to a marker of 'since' temporal clauses (Heine & Kuteva 2002: 35). Haspelmath (1997: 66ff.), who deals with this grammaticalization process in detail, calls the marker of a 'since' temporal clause "posterior durative marker." This grammaticalization process is attested in all investigated languages except Oromo, which possesses conjunctions to mark 'since' temporal and real conditional clauses. In (4), identical morphemes occur in the functions of ablative markers and 'since' temporal clause markers. In addition, the ablative morpheme *kä-* in Amharic has the function of a comitative marker whereas in Zay the comitative is marked with a different morpheme.

(4) a. Amharic

kä-järmän	kä-mätt'ahu	zare	wär
ABL-Germany	POST-come.PFV.1SG	today	month

kä-samïnt	honwall
COM-week	be.CNV.3MSG.AUX.3MSG

b. K'abeena

jarman-iicci	ameeccoomm-iicci	kabare	'agana
Germany-ABL	come.PRF.1SG-POST	today.GEN	month.ACC

saaminta	'ikko
week.ACC	be.PRF.3MSG

c. Zay

bä-järmän	bä-mät'aah^w	'awji	wär
ABL-Germany	POST-come.PRF.1SG	today	month

tä-saamït	haanämmaa
COM-week	become.PRF.3MSG.FC.CONV.AUX.3MSGDC

'It is five weeks ago today since I came from Germany'

The ablative marker also occurs with adverbs to express posteriority, as illustrated in (5). This fact can be considered to be a grammaticalization step linking the function of the morpheme as ablative marker on nouns and as a marker for 'since' temporal clauses.

(5) a. Amharic

kä-tïlantïnna	jämmïro	bunna
ABL-yesterday	begin.CNV.3MSG	coffee

täwäddwall
be.expensive.CNV.3MSG.AUX.3MSG

b. Kabeena

ber-eecci	k'aawwu	t'e'yo
yesterday-ABL	coffee.NOM	be.expensive.PFV.3MSG

c. Zay

bä-taashnä	jiimäräm	bunä
ABL-yesterday	begin.CNV.3MSG	coffee

c'aamämmaa
be.expensive.FC.CNV.3MSG.AUX.3MSG.DC
'Since yesterday coffee is expensive'

In all languages except Muher and Gumär, both Gunnän-Gurage languages, the function of the ablative morpheme is further used to mark real conditional clauses.

(6) a. Amharic

c'at	kä-k'amku	ïnk'ïlf
Khat	CND-chew.PFV.1SG	sleep

ay-wäsdä-ññ-ïm
NEG-take.IPF.3FSG-1SG.O-NEG

b. K'abeena

c'aata	k'ama'yoomm-iicci	'ossuti
Khat.ACC	chew.PFV.1SG-CND	sleep.NOM

'affaa-'e-ba
hold.IPF.3FSG-1SG.O-NEG

c. Zay

c'aat	bä-k'aamuh	'ay-aamuuk'te-ño
Khat	CND-chew.PFV.1SG	NEG-let.sleep.IPF.3MSG-1SG.O.DC

'If I chew khat, I cannot sleep'

Although this grammaticalization process does not occur in the Gunnän-Gurage languages, it might be attested for the East Gurage languages Wolane and Zay. However, it is not clear whether the conditional marker in East Gurage developed out of the ablative morpheme. Hetzron (1977: 54f.) mentions that the ablative in some Ethio-Semitic languages merged with other markers of local relations. Therefore, the morphological identity of the real conditional marker and the ablative in the East Gurage languages may be due to merging of different case markers into the prefix *bä-*. This merging did not happen in the investigated Gunnän-Gurage languages.

The grammaticalization from a 'since' temporal to a real conditional marker is not listed in Heine and Kuteva (2002) and seems not to be well attested in the languages of the world. Therefore, it is possible that this grammaticalization evolved or was reinforced due to contact.

7.3.1.3 Simile > complementizer > purpose   The source of this grammaticalization process is a similative marker, i.e. a morpheme which indicates that the marked entity is similiar or identical to the standard. This marker first grammaticalizes into a complementizer (Heine & Kuteva 2002: 273f.) and subsequently into a marker of purpose clauses (Heine & Kuteva 2002: 91). While the grammaticalization of a similative marker into a complementizer is attested in many languages of the world, this does not hold true for the grammaticalization into a marker of purpose clauses. Both grammaticalizations occur in all investigated languages. The languages Libido, Muher, and Oromo illustrate these processes. In (7) the morphemes -*iso* (Libido), -*häma* (Muher), and *akka* (Oromo) have the function of a similative marker:

(7) a. Libido
      gamta'n-iso   joor   luwi   beekk'ee
      theft-SIM   bad   thing   not.exist.3MSG

   b. Muher
      yä-lebaa-häma   t'ïfwä'e   yännä
      GEN-thief-SIM   bad.thing   not.exist.PFV.3MSG

   c. Oromo
      akka   hattummaa   gadhee-n   hin-jir-u
      SIM   theft   bad-NOM   NEG-exist-IPF.3MSG
      'There is nothing as bad as theft'

In (8), the respective morphemes mark complement clauses.

(8) a. Libido
      'abbiyyi   soodu   waaraa-'iso
      Abbiyya.NOM   tomorrow   come.IPF.3MSG-CMPL

      macc'eesoommoo
      hear.PERF.1SG

   b. Muher
      abbäbä   nägä   yïbäsa-häma
      Abbebe   tomorrow   3MSG.come.IPF-CMPL

      sämmahum   ba
      hear.PFV.1SG.CNV   AUX.past.3MSG

   c. Oromo
      Abbabaa-n   akka   bor
      Abebe-NOM   CMPL   tomorrow

      dhuf-u   dhaga'eera
      come-IPF.3MSG   hear-PFV.1SG.CNV.AUX.1SG
      'I heard that Abbiyya/Abebe will come tomorrow'

Finally, these morphemes mark purpose clauses in all investigated languages as illustrated in (9). In Oromo, however, a purpose clause is marked additionally by the suffix -*VVf*, which is used with nouns to mark the dative.

(9) a. Libido

'ati	'aggaa-'iso	k'aawanni	buuro
2SG.NOM	drink.IPF.2SG-PURP	coffee.LOC	butter.ACC

'aagisso'o
add.PFV.3FSG

b. Muher

dähä	tïtk'äw-häma	bä'awawe	k'ïb
2MSG	drink.IPF.2MSG-PURP	LOC.coffee.DEF	butter

gäffattïm
add.PFV.3FSG.DC

c. Oromo

akka	ati	dhugduuf	buna-tti
PURP	you.2SG.NOM	drink.IPF.2SG.PURP	coffee-LOC

dhadhaa	dabaltee-tti
butter	add.PFV.3FSG.CNV-AUX.3FSG

'She added butter to the coffee for you to drink it'

According to Heine and Kuteva (2002: 91) the "directionality proposed here [i. e. the grammaticalization of a complementizer to a marker of purpose clauses] has not yet been established beyond reasonable doubt. More data to substantiate this hypothesis are required." The data presented here show that the grammaticalization of a complementizer to a marker of purpose clauses is more frequent than it has been considered to be. However, the overall rarity makes it reasonable to consider the occurrence in all these languages to be due to language contact.

Furthermore, the fact that the grammaticalization of a similative marker to a marker of purpose clauses exists in all three Cushitic languages indicates that this feature is more common in Cushitic than Hetzron (1972: 129, footnote 11) supposes. He considers the morphological identity between a similative marker and the marker of a purpose clause to be an early Agaw influence on Ethio-Semitic. However, Hetzron does not discuss the grammaticalization from a similative marker to a complementizer, which we consider the linker between the grammaticalization of a similative into a purpose clause marker.

7.3.2   Syntactic features

In this section we deal with six syntactic features. The first three concern copula constructions,[3] namely the categories prospective/intentional, the benefactive focus and the fact that copulas differ considerably in main and subordinate clauses.

7.3.2.1   Prospective and intentional   These two categories are discussed together because they are expressed by similar constructions in six languages, and in two languages they are even identical. The prospective is an aspectual, the intentional a modal category. Both refer to future events. If the occurrence of the event is considered to be definite or beyond doubt, the prospective is used. According to Comrie (1976: 64), the prospective is a form "where a state is related to some subsequent situation, for instance where someone is in a state of being about to do something." If the speaker indicates that he/she will do something in the future, the intentional is used instead. Both categories are expressed by a copula construction. Prospective and intentional are distinguished morphosyntactically in all languages except Libido and Oromo. While the predicative, i.e. the predicate without the copula morpheme, consists of a verbal noun in the prospective, the intentional is marked by a subordinate verb form.

Concerning the prospective aspect, two different constructions must be distinguished. In K'abeena the verbal noun is marked with the dative, while Ethio-Semitic languages use a verbal noun with possessive suffixes. However, the position of the copulas differ. In Wolane (and in the other East Gurage languages), the copula precedes possessive suffixes, in Muher and in most of the other Ethio-Semitic languages it follows possessive suffixes.

(10) a. K'abeena
     'ani   timhirtita   shuuliihaati
     1SG.NOM   study.ACC   finish.VN.DAT.COP

    b. Muher
     zïndrä   ädi   tïmhïrt-ïddi   wäfj-ïddi-n
     this.year   1SG   study-POSS.1SG finish.VN-POSS.1SG-
                                   COP.3MSG

    c. Wolane
     yihä   tïmïrt-eyä   c'eresot-än-eyä
     1SG   study-POSS.1SG   finish.VN-COP.3MSG-POSS.1SG
     'I am about to finish my studies (this year)'

The intentional construction contains a subordinate clause in the predicate position. Different types of subordinate clauses must be distinguished. In Amharic and East Gurage an imperfective verb marked with the prefix *l-* is used, which also marks purpose clauses or the dative case. In the Gunnän-Gurage languages the intended action is marked by the locative morpheme *-ät* suffixed to the imperfective verb. In K'abeena, the predicative is a converb which usually marks purpose clauses.

(11) a. K'abeena
     hokkoppaati   'intotaa-ti
     afternoon.snack.ACC   eat.CNV.PURP.1PL-COP

    b. Muher
     yorar   nïbäyän-ät-ïn
     late.afternoon   eat.IPV.1PL-LOC-COP.3MSG

    c. Wolane
        mäksäs   lï-llbälnä-n
        afternoon.snack   PURP-eat.IPF.1PL-COP.3MSG
        'We intend to eat our afternoon snack'

Remarkable is the situation in Oromo and Libido. As mentioned earlier, both languages do not distinguish morphologically between intentional and prospective. Oromo expresses both categories by a construction consisting of a verbal noun in the dative case followed by the copula.

(12) Oromo
    a. prospective
        nuyi   barumsakeeña   t'umuruu-f-i
        1PL.NOM   study.POSS.1PL   finish.VN-DAT-COP
        'We are about to finish our studies'

    b. intentional
        nuyi   laak'ana   ñaaccuu-f-i
        1PL.NOM   lunch   eat.VN-DAT-COP
        'We intend to eat lunch'

Furthermore, Oromo has an additional construction to express the prospective. This construction contains a noun with possessive suffixes.

(13) Oromo
    ani   barumsa   t'umuruu   koo-ti
    1SG.NOM   study   finish.VN   POSS.1SG-COP
    'I am about to finish my studies'

This construction is identical to the prospective construction in the Ethio-Semitic languages. Therefore, it may have developed in Oromo due to contact with these languages. Libido expresses intentional and prospective by a copula construction with a converb in the predicate position. This strategy is identical to the intentional construction in K'abeena.

(14) Libido
    a. prospective
        losano   guullena-tte
        study.ACC   finish.CNV.1SG-COP
        'I am about to finish my studies'

    b. intentional
        hurbaata   'intena-tte
        dinner.ACC   eat.CNV.1PL-COP
        'We intend to eat lunch'

In conclusion, the languages which have a morphological distinction between intentional and prospective use a subordinate verb to express the intentional, and a modified noun to express the prospective. Oromo and Libido, however, choose one out of the two strategies – either a subordinate verb (Libido) or a case-marked verbal noun (Oromo) – to express both categories.

7.3.2.2   Benefactive focus   All languages have a construction consisting
of a predicate involving a converb of the respective verb 'to say' followed
by a copula. The verb 'to say' has two internal arguments, namely a noun
phrase in the dative case and a complement clause. The dative noun
phrase refers to an emphasized beneficiary of the event described by the
complement clause.

(15) a. Amharic
ïne   yämmïtaggälä-w   l-antä   biyye
1SG   REL.struggle.IPF.1SG-DEF.M   DAT-2MSG   say.CNV.1SG

näw
COP.3MSG

b. K'abeena
'ani   'app'amaammiihu   kesaa-ni-ma
1SG.NOM   struggle.IPF.1SG.NOM   2SG.DAT-too-after.all

yiyee-ti
say.CNV.1SG-COP

c. Libido
'ani   gubamaammooki   keesa
1SG.NOM   struggle.IPF.1SG.NOM   2SG.DAT

yee-tte
say.CNV.1SG-COP
'That I am struggling is for the sake of you'

7.3.2.3   Different copulas in main and subordinate clauses   All languages
of our sample have different copula constructions in main and subordinate
clauses. A copula with agreement markers for the subject occurs in the main
predication of all investigated Ethio-Semitic languages except Zay. In the
Cushitic languages, however, agreement is more restricted.

(16) a. Amharic
ïssu   astämari   näw
3MSG   teacher   COP.3MSG

b. Gumär
hut   astämari-w
3MSG   teacher-COP.3MSG

c. K'abeena
'isu   rosisaanco-ha
3MSG.NOM   teacher.ACC-COP.M
'He is a teacher'

In subordinate clauses, a fully inflected verb with the meaning 'to live, to
become' is used in the function of a copula. This holds true for all languages,

i.e. also for Zay. The respective verb occurs in the perfective aspect but refers to a present or future event.

(17) a. Amharic

t'ïru	dañña	yä-honä	säw ...
good	judge	REL-be.PFV.3MSG	person

b. Gumär

wähe	dañña	yä-härä	säb ...
good	judge	REL-be.PFV.3MSG	man

c. K'abeena

maat'aaree	'ikkoo	mannu ...
wise.ACC	be.PFV.3MSG.REL	person.NOM

'A person who is wise / a good judge ...'

7.3.2.4 Experiential perfect According to Comrie (1976: 58), the "experiential perfect indicates that a given situation has held at least once during some time in the past leading up to the present." In all investigated languages this category is expressed by a construction which consists of the verb 'to know' in the main clause and its complement expressed by a converb clause. The event, which was experienced by the subject, is encoded in the converb clause.

(18) a. K'abeena

'ameerikaani	'orooteeni	kasseenta-'i?
America.LOC	go.CNV.2PL	know.PRV.2PL-Q

'Have you ever been to America?'

'ee,	'ameerikaani	'oroo'ni	kansoommi
yes	America.LOC	go.CNV.1PL	know.PFV.1PL

'Yes, we have been in America'

b. Oromo

ameerikaa	deemtan-i	beektuu?
America	go.PFV.2PL-CNV	know.IPF.2PL.Q

'Have you ever been in America?'

eeyee,	ameerikaa	deemnee	beekna
yes	America	go.PFV.1PL.CNV	know.IPF.1PL

'Yes, we have been in America'

c. Wolane

'amarikan	hedkum-ani	tïcluw-ahum?
America	go.PFV.2PL-CNV	know.IPF.2PL-AUX.2PL

'Have you ever been in America?'

'aw,	'amarikan	hedï-nä	yïclïnan
yes	America	go.PFV-1PL.CNV	know.IPF.1PL.AUX.3MSG

'Yes, we have been in America'

7.3.2.5   Exist > 'have' possessive > obligation   The grammaticalization of the verb 'to exist' to a marker of possessive 'have' constructions (Heine & Kuteva 2002: 127f.) can be linked with the grammaticalization of possessive 'have' constructions to a marker of obligation (Heine & Kuteva 2002: 243f.) to the chain exist > 'have' possessive > obligation. This grammaticalization chain is attested in all languages except Libido and Oromo.

'Have' possession is expressed by suffixing object agreement markers to the respective verb 'to exist' as exemplified in the sentences (19b) to (21b). In order to express obligation, an additional morpheme is suffixed to the verb in Ethio-Semitic languages. In K'abeena, however, there is no morphological difference between possession and obligation. The two categories are distinguished only by the word class of the subject. If it is a noun, possession is expressed, if it is a verbal noun, obligation is expressed.

(19) Amharic
    a. Existence
        ahun   wuha   allä
        now   water   exist.PFV.3MSG
        'Now there is water'

    b. Possession
        yantä   yahïl   lïjj   allä-ññ
        GEN.2SG   size   child   exist.PFV.3MSG-1SG.O
        'I have a child of the same age/size as yours'

    c. Obligation
        mähed   allä-bbï-ññ
        go-VN   exist.PFV.3MSG-OBL-1SG.O
        'I have to go'

(20) Zay
    a. Existence
        ahu   mäy   alä-n-u
        now   water   exist.PFV.3MSG.-FC-DC
        'Now there is water'

    b. Possession
        yähaatä-naah   bäwu   alä-ñ
        GEN.2MSG-FC.size child   exist.PFV.3MSG-1SG.O
        'I have a child of the same age/size as yours'

    c. Obligation
        shäggär   woheedaat-ïn   alä-bi-ño
        Addis Ababa   go.VN-FC   exist.PFV.3MSG-OBL-1SG.DC
        'I have to go to Addis Ababa'

(21) K'abeena
    a. Existence
        teesu   wuu   yoo
        now   water.NOM exist.PFV.3SG/PL
        'Now there is water'
    b. Possession
        kii   bikku   c'uulu   yoo-'e
        2S.GEN   size.NOM   child.NOM   exist.PFV.3SG/PL-1SG.O
        'I have a child of the same age/size as yours'
    c. Obligation
        'oro'-u   yoo-'e
        go-VN.NOM   exist.PFV.3SG/PL-1SG.O
        'I have to go'

In Libido, only the grammaticalization from the verb 'to exist' to 'have' possession is attested. Obligation is expressed by the verb 'be necessary.' Furthermore, Libido does not possess object agreement suffixes on the verb. Therefore, the possessor is marked by a personal pronoun in the dative case (see (22b)).

(22) Libido
    a. Existence
        kaaru   wa'i   yooko
        now   water.NOM exist.PFV.3SG
        'Now there is water'
    b. Possession
        kaa   k'at'i   beeti   'eessa   yooko
        2SG.GEN size.NOM child.NOM 1SG.DAT exist.PFV.3MSG
        'I have a child of the same age/size as yours'
    c. Obligation
        'ani   ba'immi   hasisaako
        1SG.NOM   go-VN.NOM be.necessary.PFV.3MSG
        'I have to go'

In Oromo the situation is completely different. Neither of the grammaticalizations is attested. 'Have' possession is expressed by a verb with the meaning 'to have':

(23) Oromo
    a. Existence
        bishaan-ni hamma   jir-a
        water-NOM   now   exist-IPF.3MSG
        'Now there is water'
    b. Possession
        ijjoollee   amma-kee-n   qab-a
        child   as.much.as-POSS.2SG-FC.1S have-IPF.1SG
        'I have a child of the same age/size as yours'

Obligation is either expressed by the verb 'to have' or by a construction
involving the verb 'to exist' and a personal pronoun in the ablative case.
Neither of the constructions is commonly accepted.

(24) Oromo
 Obligation
 a. ? deemuu-n   qab-a.
   go.VN-FC.1SG have-IPF.1SG
 b. ? deemuu-n   na-irra   jir-a
   go.VN-NOM   1SG.O-ABL exist-IPF.3MSG
   'I have to go'

More often the simple imperfective is used which may have the semantic
implication of obligation.

(25) Oromo
 Obligation
 n-an   deem-a
 FC-FC.1SG   go-IPV.1SG
 'I will go'

7.3.2.6 Past > apodosis of an irrealis conditional clause A further
grammaticalization process involves the past marker. Beside its function to
express tense, it is used to mark irrealis conditional clauses. In all investigated
language the past marker occurs in the apodosis of an irrealis conditional clause.

(26) Gumär
 a. Past
  b-abba-nä   bet   k'e
  LOC-father-POSS.1SG house   wait.IMP.2SG.1SG.O

  bahu-m   ambwär-hu   banä?
  say.PFV.1SG-CNV   NEG.go.PFV-1SG AUX.PAST.3MSG
  'Didn't I leave, saying to you: "Wait in my father's house!"'?'
 b. Irrealis condition
  tramäna zïrab   tanzänäbä
  yesterday rain   SUB.NEG.rain.PFV.3MSG

  ïhïn   nïdïrgnä   banä
  corn   thresh.JUS.1PL AUX.PAST.3MSG
  'If it had not rained yesterday we would have threshed corn'

(27) Oromo
 a. Past
  mana   abbaa   kooti-tti   na
  house   father.GEN POSS.1SG.GEN-LOC 1SG.O

dheegi	siin	jedhee-n
wait.IMP.2SG	2SG.O.INST	say.PFV.1SG.CNV-FC.1SG

turee?
AUX.PAST.1SG.Q
'Didn't I tell you to wait for me in my father's house?'

  b. Irrealis condition

osso	kaleessa	bokkaa-n	hin-roobne
if	yesterday	rain-NOM	NEG-rain.PFV

sila	t'aafii	tuma-na	turre
IRR	tef	thresh-IPF.1PL	AUX.PAST.1PL

'If it had not rained yesterday we would have threshed tef'

(28) K'abeena
  a. Past

'anniɨi	bokkooni	'agar'e
father.GEN	house.LOC	1SG.O.wait.IMP.2SG

yiyehe	'oro'yoommi-kk'i-ba-indo?
say.CNV.1SG.2SG.OBJ	go.PFV.1SG-AUX.PAST-NEG-Q

'Didn't I leave, saying to you: "Wait in my father's house!"?'

  b. Irrealis condition

bereta	t'eenoo	'ubboba'ikkaani
yesterday	rain.NOM	rain.PFV.3MSG.NEG.SUB

t'aafaa	'udunnaammi-kk'i
tef.ACC	thresh.IPF.1PL-AUX.PAST

'If it had not rained yesterday we would have threshed tef'

When no adverb indicates tense, a past or a non-past interpretation of the sentence is possible. The sentences in (i) are irrealis conditional clauses, the sentences in (ii) hypothetical conditional clauses.

(29) a. Amharic

zïnab	bayzänb		t'ïru	näbbär
rain	CND.NEG.rain.IPF.3MSG		good	AUX.PAST.3MSG

    (i) 'It would have been good if it had not rained'
    (ii) 'It would be good if it did not rain'

  b. K'abeena

t'eenoo	'ubbo-ba'i-kkaani	t'uma-ha-kk'i
rain.NOM	fall.PFV.3MSG-NEG-CND	good-COP.M-IRR

    (i) 'It would have been good if it had not rained'
    (ii) 'It would be good if it did not rain'

The usage of past markers in the apodosis of an irrealis conditional clause is a rare grammaticalization. Very often past markers occur in the protasis of a conditional clause, e.g. in English. According to Fleischman (1989: 4f.) the

Table 7.3 *Possible new features of the ELA*

	K'abeena	Libido	Oromo	Amharic	Zay	Wolane	Gumär	Muher
Morphological features								
Ablative > comparative	+	+	+	+	+	−	+	+
Ablative > 'since' temporal	+	+	+	+	+	+	+	+
'Since' temporal > real conditional	+	+	−	+	+	+	−	−
Simile > complementizer	+	+	−	+	+	+	+	+
Complementizer > purpose clause	+	+	+	+	+	+	+	+
Syntactic features								
Prospective and intentional as separate categories	+	−	−	+	+	+	+	+
Experiential perfect	+	+	+	+	+	+	+	+
Benefactive focus	+	+	+	+	+	+	+	+
Different copulas in main and subordinate clauses	+	+	+	+	+	+	+	+
Exist > 'have' possession	+	+	−	+	+	+	+	+
'Have' possession > obligation	+	−	−	+	+	+	+	+
Past > marker of irreal conditional clauses in the apodosis	+	+	+	+	+	+	+	+

"relationship between PAST tense and non-actuality has been widely acknowledged in the linguistic literature." With regard to conditional clauses the "scalar
view of time and probability ... may be inferred ... The greater the likelihood
that a situation will be realized, i.e. the closer to 'reality' the speaker perceives it
as being, the closer to 'now' (= PRESENT) will be the tense used to represent it;
similarly, the lesser the likelihood ascribed by the speaker to the situation, the
further in the direction of past will be the tense used to represent it." However,
the "typical" place for a past marker in bi-clausal conditional sentences is the
protasis of hypothetical or contrary to fact conditions. The use of the past tense
for the apodosis seems to be quite rare (Fleischman 1989: 6f.). A possible
explanation for the occurrence of past markers in the apodosis in certain languages is given by James, cited from Fleischman (1989: 6): "James (1982)
suggests that the apodosis is the more hypothetical, whence more irrealis, of the
two clauses. The protasis ... sets up an imaginary world where X is the case.
The fact that it is an imaginary world means that we are already one step away
from reality ... Under the condition 'given X, Y,' a further logical step is
required for the realization of Y, which, being contingent on X, is therefore more
hypothetical and further removed from reality than X."

The relative rareness of the occurrence of past markers in the apodosis in the
languages of the world leads to the assumption that in the case of Amharic and
K'abeena language contact is one possible explanation.

7.4   Summary

Most of the features discussed occur in all investigated languages, as illustrated
in table 7.3. In Amharic, K'abeena, and Zay all the features are attested.
Wolane, Gumär, and Muher lack one feature, Libido lacks two; and Oromo
lacks five features.

The new features that are proposed in this chapter support the assumption
that Ethiopian languages indeed form a linguistic area, and they enlarge Ferguson's (1976) number of features considerably. Since Amharic and Oromo
are lingua francas in most parts of Ethiopia, we expect contact-induced spread
of at least some of these features into languages spoken in other parts of the
country to have played some role. However, the current number of investigated
languages and features is too small to propose a definite conclusion. Furthermore, most of the investigated languages are spoken in the Highland East
Cushitic/Gurage subarea. Therefore, further research on the occurrence of the
features in languages of other parts Ethiopia is necessary.

8 The marked-nominative languages of eastern Africa

Christa König

Africa is a continent where grammaticalized case systems are a rare phenomenon. Of the roughly 2,000 languages there are only a few with grammaticalized case, probably less than one-tenth of all African languages. Of the two basic case systems, (nominative/)accusative and ergative(/absolutive) distinguished worldwide, the latter hardly occurs in Africa, and the former accounts for less than one-third of all African case languages. The majority of African case languages, that is, roughly two-thirds, belong to the so-called marked-nominative type. Elsewhere in the world, marked-nominative systems are virtually non-existent.

African case languages show an areal and genetical distribution: Afroasiatic and Nilo-Saharan are primarily the phyla with case languages. Eastern Africa is a region with a high concentration of case languages in general and of marked-nominative languages in particular. In the border region of Uganda, Kenya, Ethiopia, and Sudan, marked-nominative languages are nearly the only type of case-marking languages to be found. Neighboring marked-nominative languages may belong to different phyla, namely Afroasiatic or Nilo-Saharan. In this chapter it is argued that marked-nominative systems are at least to some extent an areal phenomenon.

8.1 Introduction

Marked-nominative case systems stand out against other types of case systems, their defining property being that in such systems the nominative case is functionally marked vis-à-vis the accusative case (see section 8.2.1 for more details).

In the relevant literature, the phenomenon of marked-nominative languages has been recognized mostly from the perspective of each regional philology: Cushitists, Berberologists, and Niloticists all have looked at the phenomenon within their own language subgroup. One result of this more narrow inspection is terminological confusion: one and the same phenomenon receives two or more different labels, or one label is used to refer to different phenomena. So far there is no general treatment of this language type.

The concern of this chapter is this particular type of case marking, which is found mainly in eastern and northeastern Africa. There are also a few marked-nominative systems outside eastern Africa, namely in Berber languages. Furthermore, it has been claimed more recently that Bantu languages spoken in Angola and Zambia have developed a tonal case system out of a former definite marker (see Blanchon 1998; Schadeberg 1986, 1990; Maniacky 2002 for details). The profile of the accusative in these Bantu languages in fact shows similarities to the accusative found in marked-nominative languages of eastern Africa. Nevertheless, the western Bantu languages and the Berber languages are excluded here on the following grounds. First, these languages exhibit some structural properties not found in eastern Africa. In Bantu it is unclear whether the languages concerned really are case languages. Some scholars present alternative hypotheses according to which the tonal distinctions are triggered by a certain position in the clause, namely the first position after the verb. Second, if these languages are case languages, it remains unclear which of the two forms is morphologically unmarked: in most, though not in all, works it has been argued that the accusative is derived from the nominative (Maniacky 2002; Schadeberg 1986, 1990; Blanchon 1998). According to our definition of marked-nominative this would be a problem.

Within Berber there are languages which in addition to marked nominative also have split-S systems, typically expressed by bound pronouns but sometimes also by nouns (Aikhenvald 1995). This never occurs in marked-nominative languages of eastern Africa. Berber languages also constitute a different type of marked nominative than the one found in eastern Africa.

The second reason for excluding western Bantu and Berber languages from discussion here is of a geographical nature. Both are spoken several thousand kilometers away from the eastern African marked-nominative area and there is no conceivable historical link between the two language areas (see König, 2006, forthcoming for an analysis of these Bantu and Berber languages).

The chapter is organized as follows. The typological features of marked-nominative languages are described in section 8.2, which also illustrates these features with examples from two neighboring but genetically unrelated languages, which are the East Nilotic language Turkana and Dhaasanac, a Lowland East Cushitic language. Section 8.3 provides an overview of the languages that have a marked-nominative system and deals with the question of whether the distribution of marked-nominative languages is genetically or areally motivated, and in section 8.3.3 I speculate on how such unusual systems could have developed. Finally, some conclusions are drawn in section 8.4.

8.2   The nature of marked-nominative languages

Before describing the structure of marked-nominative systems, a note on terminology may be useful. Such systems are also called "extended ergative"

(Dixon 1994: 66f.). With regard to the case labels used for marked-nominative systems, none of the established terms is entirely satisfactory. In eastern Africa the morphologically unmarked form has often been called "absolute" or "absolutive," irrespective of whether an accusative or a marked-nominative system is involved (König 2006). "Subject case" is an additional term proposed for the nominative in marked-nominative systems, e.g. by Sasse (1984a). I will use the term accusative when dealing with a case covering the syntactic function O, and nominative when dealing with a case covering A and S (see below). In order to be consistent, I have changed some of the glosses found in the literature. All case forms are glossed, including the morphologically unmarked ones.

8.2.1   Characteristics

In order to define typical features of a marked-nominative language, it is necessary to illustrate briefly how prototypical case systems can be described. Case systems are distinguished with regard to the three basic syntactic functions as defined by Dixon (1994: 62ff.) and others, namely S, the intransitive subject function, A, the transitive subject function, and O, the transitive object function. In an accusative system (accusative in short), S and A are treated the same and simultaneously differently than O. In an ergative system, S and O are treated the same and simultaneously differently than A. These patterns are illustrated in figure 8.1. The case that covers A in an accusative system is called the nominative[1] and the case covering O the accusative. The case that covers A in an ergative system is called the ergative and the case covering S and O the absolutive. Furthermore, the nominative of an accusative system is typically the morphologically unmarked form,[2] functionally the unmarked form, and the form used in citation. The absolutive of an ergative system on the other hand is typically the morphologically unmarked form, the functionally unmarked form, and the form used in citation.

With "morphologically unmarked" I mean zero realization (or marking), and "morphologically marked" accordingly means that there is some formal exponent expressing case. "Functionally unmarked" means being used in a wide range of different contexts and/or functions. "Functionally marked" means being used in a few functions only. The morphologically unmarked form is sometimes called "basic form." The morphologically marked form is derived from the morphologically unmarked form by adding some extra element. The morphologically unmarked form is shorter and/or underived vis-à-vis the morphologically marked form.

Marked-nominative languages are a mixture of both systems, as pointed out by Dixon (1994: 64f.): the pattern of A, S, and O is identical to that in accusative languages, namely A and S are treated the same and simultaneously differently than O. However, the accusative in marked-nominative languages

254   Christa König

S = intransitive subject function
A = transitive subject function
O = transitive object function

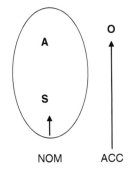

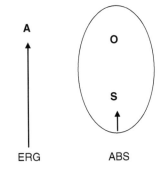

NOM   ACC   ERG   ABS

Accusative system   Ergative/(Absolutive) system
Nominative = morphologically unmarked   Absolutive = morphologically unmarked
          = functionally unmarked   = functionally unmarked
          = used in citation   = used in citation

Figure 8.1 Definitional characteristics of case systems

is the morphologically unmarked form, at least typically (see below); it is used in citation, and is functionally the unmarked form. The nominative on the other hand is the morphologically marked form in a marked-nominative system; A, i.e. the transitive subject, is therefore encoded by the morphologically marked form. Marked-nominative languages share this feature with ergative systems.

In accusative languages, the nominative is encoded typically in a morphologically unmarked form but there are some languages where both case forms, nominative and accusative, are equally morphologically marked; two subtypes therefore need to be distinguished among the accusative languages.

In a similar fashion, two subtypes of marked-nominative languages are to be distinguished with regard to the morphological markedness of nominative and accusative: Type 1 (the most common one), in which the accusative is the morphologically marked form and the nominative the morphologically unmarked form, and type 2, in which both case forms, nominative and accusative, are morphologically marked. In type 1 of marked-nominative languages, the accusative is morphologically unmarked, functionally unmarked, and used in citation. In type 2, the accusative is morphologically marked, functionally unmarked, and used in citation.

In sum, marked-nominative languages are defined thus: a marked nominative language is present when at least two cases are distinguished, namely an accusative covering O, and a nominative covering S and A. The accusative must be the functionally unmarked form; it is the default case, that is, the case which is used with the widest range of functions. If one of the two cases is derived from the other, it must be the nominative which is derived from the accusative and never the other way round.

Prototypically, the accusative covers functions such as citation form, nominal predicate, and O. In addition, indirect objects, possessee, nominal modifiers, modified nouns, nouns headed by adpositions, peripheral participants introduced by verbal derivations, topicalized and/or focused participants, and S and A before the verb may be covered by the accusative. The accusative is the morphologically unmarked form in type 1 languages; in type 2 languages, both cases are morphologically marked.

8.2.2   Case studies

In order to illustrate how marked-nominative systems work, I will now present data from two typologically contrasting and genetically unrelated languages. These languages are Turkana, an East Nilotic language of the Nilo-Saharan phylum, and Dhaasanac, an East Cushitic language of the Afroasiatic phylum. What the two have in common is that they are spoken in the same general area west and north of Lake Turkana in Kenya and Ethiopia (see map 8.2).

8.2.2.1   Turkana   The basic constituent order of Turkana is VS/VAO, that is, the language has a verb-initial syntax. The marked-nominative system is expressed by tone. In general, two tones are distinguished: high tone (left unmarked) and low tone (marked with a grave accent). Seven cases are distinguished: accusative, nominative, genitive, instrumental, locative 1 (encoding location and destination), locative 2 (like an ablative), and vocative. All cases are marked by tone. All modifiers within a noun phrase are case-inflected, except for demonstratives (Dimmendaal 1983b: 264ff.). The nominative is the only case that is encoded by a distinct tonal morpheme, namely by low tone. The genitive, the two locatives, and the vocative are encoded by fixed tonal patterns. The nominative is derived from the accusative by a floating low tone (see Dimmendaal 1983b: 261). The accusative (called "absolute" by Dimmendaal) is identical with the basic form, which is also used in citation. The nominative encodes A (see *a-pà* 'father' in (1a)), S (see *a-wuyè naga*ˋ 'this home' in (1b)), and S in copula clauses with a copula (1d). Beyond citation, the accusative encodes O (cf. *a-k-ìmuj* 'food' in (1a)), nominal predicates (1c)–(1e), S in non-verbal clauses without a copula (1e), additional participants being introduced by verbal derivation. This applies to the valency-increasing devices *-akì*, called dative by Dimmendaal (1983b), similar to an applicative (1f), and to the causative *ite-* (1g). With the dative extension, direct and indirect objects (IO) occur in the accusative (1f). With the causative, the agent and the patient occur in the accusative and the causee in the nominative (1g).

Furthermore, the accusative encodes S and A under certain conditions: first, if used before the verb, second in passive-like constructions, and third in so-called subjectless clauses.

There is a rule, which I propose to call "No case before the verb," which applies in Turkana, meaning that – irrespective of the case function involved – in preverbal position only one case form occurs, namely the morphologically unmarked one (see König 2006 for details). This rule applies to all verb-initial and verb-medial languages of eastern Africa, verb-final languages being excluded for obvious reasons. In languages with a basic verb-initial order like Turkana, a participant placed preverbally encodes pragmatic functions, such as topic or focus. Core participants before the verb appear in the unmarked accusative case irrespective whether they serve as S, A (1h) or O (1i). In an AVO word order, the case distinction is neutralized.

In passive clauses, called impersonal active by Dimmendaal (1983b: 65), S occurs in the accusative,[3] as 'milk' in (1j) or 'we' in (1k). The construction with a demoted subject is mixed: in crossreference, the bound verbal pronoun does not agree with the demoted subject, but instead, it invariably refers to the third-person by means of the prefix è-. Thus in (1j), where S refers to first person plural, è, the third person pronoun, is used on the verb. S is treated like O, occurring in the accusative. Nevertheless, the meaning of the clause is impersonal. The construction in (1j) goes back to a concept like 'he/it drank milk,' meaning 'the milk was drunk.' In other Nilotic languages, such as Maa, a similar construction is used (Heine & Claudi 1986: 79–94).

Dimmendaal argues that clauses like (1l) are "subjectless," which is suggested by the fact that the only free-standing noun phrase expressed occurs in the accusative. It is possible to add a nominative participant such as 'thing'; however, this construction is not much liked by the Turkana (Dimmendaal 1983b: 73). In expressions of emotion, the experiencer is often not expressed as the subject but as the object of the clause. In non-verbal clauses with a copula, S is encoded differently than S in non-verbal clauses without a copula (cf. (1d) and (1e)).

(1) Turkana (East Nilotic, Nilo-Saharan)

a. è-sàk-ì   a-pà   a-k-ìmuj   V A O
   3-want-A[4]   father.NOM   food.ACC
   'Father wants food' (Dimmendaal 1983b: 263)

b. è-jɔk̀   a-wuyè̀   nagà   V S
   3-good   home-NOM   this
   'This homestead is nice' (Dimmendaal 1983: 263)

c. ŋɪ-dè̀   omwɔnì   N. PRED
   children.ACC   four
   'There are four children' (Dimmendaal 1983b: 74)

d. mèèrɛ̀   a-yɔ̀ŋ   ɛ-ka-pɪl-a-nɪ̀   COP SN.PRED
    not   I.NOM   witch.ACC
    'I am not a witch' (Dimmendaal 1983b:75)

e. a-yɔŋ̀   ɛ-ka-pɪl-a-nɪ̀   S N.PRED
    I.ACC   witch.ACC
    'I am a witch' (Dimmendaal 1983b:75)

f. to-dyak-akɪ̀   ŋesì   ɪ-tʊanɪ̀   a-torobʉ́   V A IO O
    3-divide-eDAT   3SG.NOM   person.ACC   chest.ACC
    'He shared the chest with the person' (Dimmendaal 1983b:70)

g. à-ìte-lep-ì   a-yɔ̀ŋ   ŋèsì   a-kàal   V CAUS AGENT O
    1-CAUS-   1SG.NOM   3SG.ACC   camel.ACC
    milk-A
    'I will have her milk the camel' (Dimmendaal 1983b:200)

h. è-kìle   lò   pɛ-ɛ̀-à-yɛn-ì   ŋa-kɪrɔ̀   ŋuna   k-ɪdaɾ   A V O
    man.ACC   this not-3-PAST-   matters.ACC   those   3-wait
                         know-A
    'This man, not knowing about these problems, waited ... ' (Dimmendaal
    1983b: 408)

i. ɛ-maànik   ŋoɾ   kI-gɛlɛ̀m-ɪ   O V A
    bull.ACC   that   we-castrate-A
    'That bull we castrated' (Dimmendaal 1983b: 409)

j. ɛ̀-à-mas-ɪ̀   ŋa-kilè
    3-PAST-drink-V   milk.ACC
    'The milk was drunk' (Dimmendaal 1983b: 132)

k. è-twa-kì-o   (sùà)
    3-dead-PL-A-V   we.ACC
    'We (people) will die' (Dimmendaal 1983b: 133)

l. k-à-bur-un-iɾ̀   a-yɔŋ̀   (i-bóre)
    t⁵-1SG-tire-VEN-A   1SG.ACC   (thing.NOM)
    'I am tired' (Dimmendaal 1983b: 73)

To conclude, Turkana is a marked-nominative language of type 1. The
accusative encodes O, IO, S, and A in preverbal position, S in passive clauses,
S in subjectless clauses, S in non-verbal clauses without a copula, participants
introduced by valency-increasing devices, nominal predicates, and it is used as
the citation form. The nominative encodes S and A in post-verbal position
only. The accusative is morphologically and functionally the unmarked case, as
can be seen in the fact that it covers a wide range of different functions.

8.2.2.2 Dhaasanac While Turkana is verb-initial, the Lowland East
Cushitic language Dhaasanac is an AOV/SV, that is, a verb-final language.

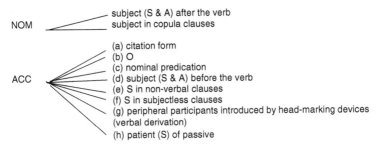

Figure 8.2 Functions covered by the nominative and accusative cases in Turkana

Furthermore, Tosco describes it as an accent language, distinguishing between "accented words," which are, according to him, high-tone (marked by an acute accent) and "unaccented words," which are non-high-tone (left unmarked) (Tosco 2001: 38–9). In accordance with this analysis, most nouns are unaccented (see below). One may wonder why the accented noun always has high tone, but, for our purposes it is not crucial whether Dhaasanac is a tone or an accent language.

All nouns are uttered in two different ways, either in the so-called "context form," that is, in fluent speech (Tosco 2001: 65), or in the form used in isolation, that is, before a pause, in slow speech, or in isolation. The context form can be derived from the isolation form basically by the deletion of the terminal vowel. The latter is largely meaningless, except for some cases, e.g. when -*u* for masculine and -*i* for feminine nouns are used (Tosco 2001: 65). The noun may consist of the stem plus a formative or a suffix: the latter is a derivational element such as singulative or plural; the former is a meaningless invariant ending[6]. The term "basic form" is used by Tosco on the one hand as an equivalent to absolutive (when opposed to subject case), and on the other hand as an equivalent to stem (when opposed to extended noun) (cf. Tosco 2001: 65ff. and 94ff.).

S, A, and O are crossreferenced on the verb by clitics. There are two different sets of pronouns. One set encodes S and A preverbally, and the other set encodes O postverbally. The crossreferencing subject pronouns look like shortened versions of the selfstanding nominative pronouns. The crossreferenced object pronouns look like shortened versions of the selfstanding accusative pronouns. Interestingly, crossreference is defective, in that first and second singular subject, as well as first-person inclusive, and third-person (singular and plural) object are not cross referenced.

Case is expressed by accent shift or through suffixes (Tosco 2001: 93). Three cases are distinguished: accusative, called either the absolutive or basic form by Tosco, nominative, called subject case by Tosco, and genitive.

The accusative is the morphologically unmarked form and it is identical with the so-called basic form. In the accusative masculine, monosyllabic nouns are throughout accented, feminine nouns are throughout unaccented, and so are most plural forms. In addition, the so-called extended nouns (see above), which are either derived forms or forms which bear a meaningless ending (a formative), are mostly unaccented (Tosco 2001: 39). The nominative is derived from accented accusative forms by lowering the accent (high tone) (Tosco 2001: 94). With non-accented (non-high-tone) accusative nouns, the nominative is only "latent," as Tosco calls it (2001: 95). It remains unclear whether in the latter the nominative is identical with the accusative (Tosco 2001: 97).[7] Genitive is expressed by a suffix -íet and the high tone of the accusative is lowered, e.g., cár 'snake.ACC' caríet 'snake.GEN' (Tosco 2001: 97). Many nouns however do not take the genitive suffix; instead, they take the form which is called the isolation form – that is, the form without loss of the terminal vowel. It is possible that the isolation form constitutes a case form of its own, namely the only unmarked form of the language. Consequently, all remaining forms, including the accusative, would be derived forms.

The unmarked form is used in restricted contexts only and with certain nouns only, such as presenting a possessor (cf. (2j) and (2k)). In the Kuliak language Ik, spoken to the west of the Dhaasanac area, the situation is strikingly similar: all nouns of the language are expressed in what Tosco would call either the isolation form or the context form. The context form can be derived from the isolation form by the loss of final phonemes, either a vowel or consonant plus vowel. The isolation form has relics of occurrences, such as possessor in possessee–possessor construction, or in objects of imperative clauses. Therefore it is claimed in König (2002) that the isolation form has the value of a case form, called the oblique case. In table 8.1, the different labels are illustrated with the Dhaasanac noun ʔáað 'sun.'

Case is encoded only once in the noun phrase: just the last element of a noun phrase undergoes lowering when used in the nominative (see table 8.1 and example (2i)). Table 8.2 gives an overview of a few case forms in Dhaasanac. Selfstanding pronouns are case-inflected differently than nouns, either by suppletive stems or by derivation. The accusative forms seem to be derived from the nominative forms by the suffix -ni, which according to Tosco (2001: 211) is found on subject pronouns of neighboring languages such as Oromo. There is no accusative form for the third person. With regard to the pronoun-building pattern, selfstanding pronouns do not match the general pattern of marked-nominative languages, in that in this pattern it is not the accusative which is the morphologically unmarked form but the nominative. Functionally, however, the selfstanding pronouns match the general pattern of marked-nominative languages as the accusative is used as the default form with the

Table 8.1 *Case terminology in Dhaasanac*

Tosco	Proposed here	Example 'sun'
Form in isolation	Oblique = basic form	ʔáaðu
Absolutive = Basic form	Accusative	ʔáað
Subject case	Nominative	ʔaað
Genitive	Genitive	ʔaaðíet

Table 8.2 *Examples of case forms in Dhaasanac (Tosco 2001: 96–7)*

ACC	NOM	Meaning
múor	muor	leopard
máa	maa	man
ʔárab	ʔarab	elephant
gáal yáb	gáal yab	males (people male)
yú	yáa	I
kúnni	kúo	you (SG)
	ʰé	he, she, it, they
múuni	(ʰé) ké˜ kí	we (INCL)
ɲíini	ɲaaɲi	we (EXCL)
ʔitíni	ʔití	you (PL)

widest range of functions. The irregular behavior of the selfstanding pronouns is in need of explanation.

The accusative covers the following functions (see figure 8.3): citation form (cf. (2a)), O (2b), nominal predicates (2e), topicalized participants (2f), focalized participants (2g), nouns before adpositions (2d), modified nouns (2e), and the possessee in a possessee–possessor order (2j). If the subject is topicalized, the subject slot is filled by the third-person pronoun as a dummy; the selfstanding noun occurs in clause-initial position in the accusative case form (2g). The nominative encodes S (2d) and A (2b), but only if not topicalized (2f), focused (2g), or modified (2e).

Dhasaanac has no passive. There is one pragmatic construction which according to Tosco (2001: 275) is an equivalent of passive clauses, namely a clause with a topicalized left- dislocated object (2l).

(2) Dhaasanac (Lowland East Cushitic, Afroasiatic)

a. múor
    leopard
    'Leopard' (Tosco 2001:95)

b. yú   múor   ʔargi   A O V
    I.NOM   leopard.ACC   see.PERF.A[8]
    'I saw a leopard' (Tosco 2001:95)

c. múor   yú   ʔargi   O A V
    leopard.ACC   I.NOM   see.PERF.A
    'I saw a leopard' (Tosco 2001: 95)

d. min   bie   gaa   ɗoti   S V
   woman.NOM water.ACC   in   run.PERF.B[9]
   'She ran away from the water' (Tosco 2001: 94)

e. máa=ti=a   ɗáasanac   S N.PRED
   man.ACC= that=DET   Dhaasanac.ACC
   'That man is a Dhaasanac' (Tosco 2001:94)

f. múor   ʰé   kufi   S V
   leopard.ACC   3.NOM   die.PERF.A
   'The leopard died; as to the leopard, it died' (Tosco 2001: 95)

g. múor=ru   kufi   S V
   leopard.ACC=FOC die.PERF.A
   'The leopard died' (Answer to the question: Who died?) (Tosco 2001:95)

h. 6íl   caríet   PEE   POR
   house   snake.GEN
   'snake-house'

i. gáal yab   ʰí   koi   cf. gáal yáb 'males'
   people males.NOM   3SG.VERB   eat.PERF.A
   'The males ate' (Tosco 2001: 97)

j. kimiɗɗi   búul   PEE POR
   nest   bird.OBL
   'bird's nest'

k. ɗáa   ʔáaðu   ∼ ʔaaðíet
   side   sun.OBL   sun.GEN
   'West' [the side of the sun] (Tosco 2001: 254)

l. lokoɗ=ci-a   6asau=a   ʃíet   ʰé   koɲɲi   O A V
   skin.ACC=   flat.ACC=DET   fire.ACC 3.NOM   eat.PERF.B
   my-DET
   'The fire burnt my flat hide' ['my flat hide, the fire burnt it', or: 'my flat
   hide was burned by fire'] (Tosco 2001: 275)

To conclude, Dhaasanac is a marked-nominative language of type 1 following Tosco's analysis, or type 2 following my suggestion. Functionally, the
accusative is the case with the broadest range of occurrences and the widest
range of functions; it therefore is the functionally unmarked case. Functions

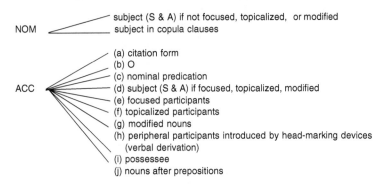

NOM — subject (S & A) if not focused, topicalized, or modified
— subject in copula clauses

ACC
(a) citation form
(b) O
(c) nominal predication
(d) subject (S & A) if focused, topicalized, modified
(e) focused participants
(f) topicalized participants
(g) modified nouns
(h) peripheral participants introduced by head-marking devices (verbal derivation)
(i) possessee
(j) nouns after prepositions

Figure 8.3 Functions covered by the nominative and accusative cases in Dhaasanac

such as citation, nominal predicate, object, topicalized participants, focused participants, and modified nouns are covered by the accusative. The nominative is used only to encode S, and A if neither topicalized, focused, nor modified. If, as I suggest, Dhaasanac does not have three cases, namely accusative, nominative and genitive, but four, namely also genitive plus an oblique, the language would follow type 2. If there is an oblique, this corresponds to the "basic form" of nouns, which is the only morphologically unmarked form. All other cases are derived forms. The accusative is derived from the oblique via vowel loss, and the nominative is derived from the accusative via accent lowering. For a complete list of functions covered by the accusative and the nominative in marked-nominative languages, see König (2006).

8.2.3   Typological generalizations

There are a number of observations suggesting that marked-nominative languages such as Turkana and Dhaasanac stand out typologically as a class of their own. The following is a listing of the most salient properties of these languages; the reader is referred to König (2004, 2006) for more details and evidence.

First, all case languages in eastern Africa with verb-initial or verb-medial word order obey the rule "No case before the verb" (König 2006), which means that in preverbal position only the morphologically unmarked form appears, irrespective of the case function expressed by the relevant participant. In marked-nominative systems the case before the verb is invariably the accusative.

Second, marked nominative occurs essentially only in two of the four language phyla of Africa, namely Afroasiatic and Nilo-Saharan (marked-nominative languages share this feature with African case languages in general; they all belong to these two language phyla); as we observed above, however, there are a few western Bantu languages spoken between Gabon and Angola (see chapter 4, this volume) that distinguish case by means of tone and also seem to follow a marked-nominative pattern (see Blanchon 1998; Schadeberg 1986, 1990; Maniacky 2002).

Third, case expressed by tone appears in marked-nominative languages only; of the 49 marked-nominative languages in my sample, 13 use tone (10 exclusively, 3 in a mixed system by suffixes or tone), but in none of the accusative or the few ergative languages[10] is case expressed by tone.

Fourth, if case is not expressed suprasegmentally by tone or accent shift, it is expressed by suffixes (suffixes are the only tool for case marking used in all African ergative and accusative languages). There are however two exceptions. Berber is one, where there is vowel reduction at the beginning of the noun, which may go back historically to a clitic preceding the noun. Shilluk is the second, where the ergative case is expressed by a prefix (Miller & Gilley 2001).

Fifth, the use of tone as a case marker appears to be genetically determined: it is found especially in the Omo-Tana branch of East Cushitic and in Nilotic languages, in particular in East and South Nilotic languages. Among the Surmic languages, tone is only a minor means for expressing case (it appears only once, or more exactly, only 0.5 times in Tennet: Tennet uses tone and suffixes).

Sixth, marked-nominative languages belong prototypically to type 1. Of the 49 African marked-nominative languages, the majority, namely 35, belong to type 1 with a zero-marked form for the accusative and a non-zero form for the nominative, while only 14 follow type 2, 3 of them only partly so.

Seventh, type 2 languages with an obligatory (rather than an optional) case system are mostly marked-nominative languages. All marked-nominative type 2 languages belong to Cushitic, in particular Highland East Cushitic, and Western Omotic, especially Ometo. In all type 2 languages which encode case by suffixes, case marking is interwoven with gender. Exceptions are Kemantney (Central Cushitic), and Ik (Kuliak), which are both accusative rather than marked-nominative languages. In both languages, there is a mor-phologically unmarked form, in Kemantney with indefinite nouns, in Ik in certain clause types (e.g. imperatives, some copula clauses). Further type 2 languages are the Saharan languages Tubu and Kanuri; both follow an accusative system, but case marking is not obligatory (König 2004).

Eighth, marked-nominative languages follow to some extent a genetically motivated pattern (see the appendix to this chapter). Berber, Cushitic, and

Omotic are the only Afroasiatic families which are marked nominative, and Surmic and Nilotic are the only Nilo-Saharan groups. The languages of the Chadic branch of Afroasiatic have no grammaticalized case systems. Within Cushitic, marked nominative is found in East and North Cushitic only; Central Cushitic has accusative and South Cushitic no case system at all. Within Omotic, Western Omotic, especially Ometo, is marked nominative throughout, while Eastern Omotic is accusative only.

The Berber languages allow for the following prediction: if a Berber language has inflected case, it is marked nominative, and it is either North or South Berber, all East and West Berber languages having lost their marked-nominative system.

Within Nilotic, East and South Nilotic are marked nominative. West Nilotic mostly has no case; but there are two languages with a split marked-nominative system, namely Päri and Jur-Luwo. Both are simultaneously ergative and marked nominative. West Nilotic is the only branch with ergative languages so far found within Africa. The ergative case marker in some clauses functions as an ergative and in others as a marked-nominative case.

Ninth, the presence of marked-nominative languages of type 2 appears to be genetically motivated. These languages are found in Highland East Cushitic and Ometo languages only. Among the Ometo languages, all marked-nominative languages are of type 2, with the exception of Maale (see the appendix).

Tenth, marked-nominative languages occur with all constituent orders. This distribution however appears to be genetically determined: With the exception of Berber, which is verb-initial, all Afroasiatic marked-nominative languages are verb-final. All Nilo-Saharan marked-nominative languages are either verb-initial (East and South Nilotic, Surmic) or verb-medial (West Nilotic, Surmic).

Eleventh, marked nominative is statistically the most common case pattern, not only in eastern Africa but in Africa as a whole. In my sample, there are 49 marked-nominative languages as opposed to 27 accusative languages, and among the latter there are 5 in which case is not obligatorily marked, accusative suffixes being only used in pragmatically marked constituent orders.

8.3   Distribution of marked-nominative languages

Worldwide, marked-nominative languages are a rare phenomenon. The only other part of the world where they are found is among the Yuman languages of California, e.g. Maricopa (Gordon 1986), Diegueño, Jamul Tiipy (Langdon 1970; Miller 2001). Furthermore, the Austronesian language Houailou and the Australian language Malak-Malak are mentioned in the relevant literature (Plank 1985: 302; Mallinson & Blake 1981: 47–8). Therefore, marked nominative is essentially an African feature.

8.3.1   Genetic distribution

Within Africa however, marked nominative is the prevailing system among all
case systems (see below); for its genetic distribution see the appendix. Among
the Cushitic languages, East and North Cushitic are predominantly marked
nominative, whereas Central Cushitic languages are accusative only; there is
no case marking in South Cushitic languages. Within Omotic, the Western
Omotic languages show a concentration of marked-nominative, whereas
Eastern Omotic has accusative systems only. Within Western Omotic languages, the Ometo languages are mostly marked nominative.

In Nilo-Saharan, only two branches have marked-nominative languages,
namely Nilotic and Surmic languages, both being subbranches of Eastern
Sudanic languages. Among the Nilotic languages, East and South Nilotic are
marked nominative. Most West Nilotic languages show no case at all, but
within West Nilotic, the only African languages so far identified as having an
ergative system are found, namely Päri, Jur-Luwo, and Shilluk. The first two
are partly ergative and partly marked nominative. In Päri, the ergative marker,
a suffix -*Cì*, functions in some clauses as an ergative case and in other clauses
as a marked-nominative case (König 2006).

Type 2 marked-nominative languages are found in Highland East Cushitic
and Ometo languages. Within Ometo, the following generalization holds: if an
Ometo language has a marked-nominative system, it belongs to type 2. The
only exception found so far is Maale, which is the only South Ometo language
of my sample.

8.3.2   Areal distribution

As the above features show, marked-nominative languages follow at least to
some extent a genetically motivated pattern. Nevertheless, their distribution
cannot be explained satisfactorily by genetic relationship only; rather, it clearly
exhibits an areal pattering. Map 8.1 shows the distribution of case systems in
Africa. The languages mentioned on the map are identical with the ones listed
in the appendix.[11]

Map 8.2 shows the areal distribution of case languages spoken in the border
region of southern Ethiopia, Kenya, Uganda, and Sudan. Each language is
represented by one spot only and the areal dimension of a language is dis-
regarded. Berber is spoken in a huge area, and some relevant languages or
dialects are listed separately (for some languages it is difficult to determine
their exact location; the map constitutes a first approximation).

Evidence for the presence of areal relationship is of the following kind: first,
marked nominative systems cut across genetic boundaries. Within the border
region of Kenya, Uganda, Sudan, and Ethiopia there are, with few exceptions,

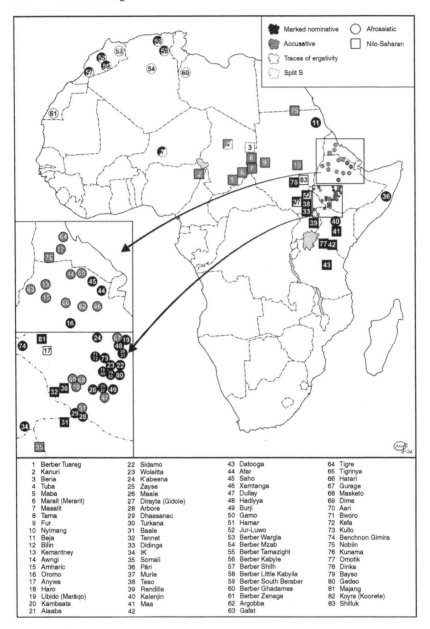

1	Berber Tuareg	22	Sidamo	43	Datooga	64	Tigre
2	Kanuri	23	Wolaitta	44	Afar	65	Tigrinya
3	Beria	24	K'abeena	45	Saho	66	Harari
4	Tuba	25	Zayse	46	Xamtanga	67	Gurage
5	Maba	26	Maale	47	Dullay	68	Masketo
6	Marait (Merarit)	27	Dirayta (Gidole)	48	Hadiyya	69	Dime
7	Masalit	28	Arbore	49	Burji	70	Aari
8	Tama	29	Dhaasanac	50	Gamo	71	Bworo
9	Fur	30	Turkana	51	Hamar	72	Kefa
10	Nyimang	31	Baale	52	Jur-Luwo	73	Kullo
11	Beja	32	Tennet	53	Berber Wargla	74	Benchnon Gimira
12	Bilin	33	Didinga	54	Berber Mzab	75	Nobiin
13	Kemantney	34	IK	55	Berber Tamazight	76	Kunama
14	Awngi	35	Somali	56	Berber Kabyle	77	Omotik
15	Amharic	36	Päri	57	Berber Shilh	78	Dinka
16	Oromo	37	Murle	58	Berber Little Kabyila	79	Bayso
17	Anywa	38	Teso	59	Berber South Beraber	80	Gedeo
18	Haro	39	Rendille	60	Berber Ghadames	81	Majang
19	Libido (Maräqo)	40	Kalenjin	61	Berber Zenaga	82	Koyra (Koorete)
20	Kambaata	41	Maa	62	Argobba	83	Shilluk
21	Alaaba	42		63	Gafat		

Map 8.1 Case in northern and eastern Africa

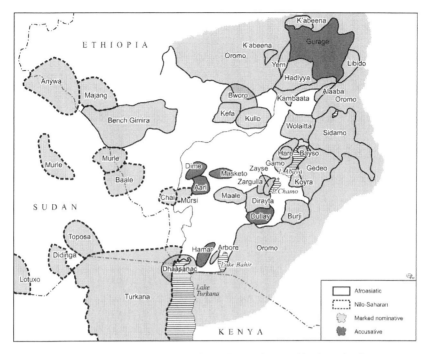

Map 8.2 Areal distribution of case in southern Ethiopia and adjacent areas

only marked-nominative languages. Genetically, they belong to both the Afro-asiatic and the Nilo-Saharan phyla. Within both phyla, they belong to different branches. The following marked-nominative languages are of different genetic origin but spoken in direct neighborhood or even in overlapping areas:

(a) The Nilo-Saharan (NS) Surmic languages Majang, Murle, and Baale are spoken partially in an overlapping area with Bench, an Afroasiatic (AA) Omotic language.

(b) The Nilotic language Turkana (NS) is spoken in an overlapping area with the East Cushitic language Dhaasanac (AA). It is also spoken adjacent to the East Cushitic languages Oromo and Rendille.

(c) The Surmic language Chai (NS) is spoken at river Omo surrounded by Cushitic marked-nominative languages (AA).

The few exceptions in that area which are accusative rather than marked-nominative are Afroasiatic languages, in particular Eastern Omotic languages such as Hamar, Dime, and Aari, as well as Masceto, which is the only Western Omotic language not being marked nominative. The Semitic accusative languages spoken on the northern and the eastern fringes of southern Ethiopia,

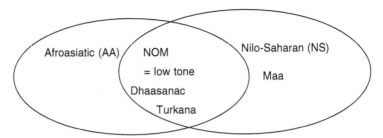

Figure 8.4 A schematic overview of the distribution of low tone for nominative encoding

such as Gurage and Amharic, seem to be without greater influence on the case systems found in their neighborhood (for Gurage see map 8.2, for Amharic see map 8.1). In northern Ethiopia, the situation is different: Semitic accusative languages have influenced Cushitic languages. For example, the Semitic language Amharic has had massive influence on the Central Cushitic language Kemantney (Leyew 2003b) and on the East Cushitic language Dullay (Tosco 1994b: 229). For Tosco, the lack of marked-nominative systems in Central Cushitic as well as in Dullay is the result of areal influence from Ethio-Semitic languages such as Amharic, Tigre, Tigrinya, and Gurage:

Diachronically, the weakness of subject marking is shown in its dismissal in the majority of Agaw (Central Cushitic) languages, in favour of an object marking system presumably borrowed from Ethio-Semitic; and the same development is shown by Dullay, which has apparently given away subject marking and developed object marking. (Tosco 1994b: 229)

Tone or accent shift as a means of deriving the nominative from the accusative also shows an areal distribution. As we saw above, the nominative is marked in Turkana by a spreading low tone. Turkana shares this feature with other Nilotic marked-nominative languages, such as Maa. In the neighboring Cushitic Dhaasanac language, the nominative is also expressed by tone lowering: there is an accent shift from initial high to initial low. In the genetically closely related Cushitic languages Arbore and Bayso, which are not spoken adjacent to Turkana, the marked nominative is not expressed by initial low. Accordingly, it is likely that the Dhaasanac initial low encoding nominative is the result of areal influence rather than of genetic relationship. Since tone lowering is common in East Nilotic but not in Cushitic languages, there is reason to hypothesize that this feature was transferred from Turkana to Dhaasanac. Figure 8.4 shows the areal distribution of this phenomenon.

Thus, I take the fact that neighboring languages that are genetically unrelated and typologically contrastive but share the presence of a marked-nominative system to be strongly suggestive of areal relationship, considering that such a system is rare in Africa and virtually non-existent outside Africa. This hypothesis is strengthened by the following observation: Turkana and Dhaasanac belong to two different language phyla, Nilo-Saharan and Afroasiatic, while other languages genetically closely related to Turkana or Dhaasanac, respectively, are not marked nominative: Lango or Bari are both Nilotic languages like Turkana but have no marked-nominative system, and Dullay or Agaw are Cushitic languages like Dhaasanac but lack a marked-nominative system.

8.3.3   Diachronic observations

There is not much information on the history of marked-nominative systems; the evidence available suggests, however, that these systems have developed more than once, that is, that there are different origins for the marked-nominative case. As is argued in König (2006), possible sources for these markers are definite markers (e.g. in Päri and Berber), topic markers (as in Cushitic; see Tosco 1994b: 231), and agent encodings in clauses with a demoted subject (in Maa). Hayward and Tsuge (1998) claim that in Proto-Omotic marked nominative case has developed out of a former accusative system, and the same development is claimed by Sasse (1984a) for Cushitic. Aikhenvald (1995) argues that in Proto-Berber marked nominative was not yet present, which would be additional evidence for the assumption that marked nominative developed independently in different languages.

Still, as has been hypothesized in the preceding section, areal diffusion must also have been involved in the development of marked-nominative systems in eastern Africa. The question then is who influenced whom, that is: what is the directionality of diffusion? In general, it is plausible that East Cushitic languages influenced East and South Nilotic languages, and not the other way round. First, as has been demonstrated, for example, by Ehret (1974) and Heine et al. (1979), there has been massive East Cushitic influence on East and South Nilotic languages, resulting in lexical and other kinds of borrowing. Second, with regard to number and diversity of marked-nominative systems it is more likely that their origin is to be sought in Cushitic, that is, in Afroasiatic languages and not in Nilo-Saharan languages. The number of Cushitic languages having such a system is much larger than that of Nilotic and Surmic languages: the total number of marked-nominative systems found in Afroasiatic languages is 34 as opposed to 15 in Nilo-Saharan languages.

A third piece of evidence is possibly provided by the fact that there is much more structural diversity in Afroasiatic than in Nilo-Saharan languages: (i) All Nilo-Saharan languages belong to type 1 (see section 8.2.2), while in Cushitic and Omotic, both type 1 and type 2 languages are found. (ii) In Nilotic, the marked-nominative case is expressed by tone (Päri and Jur-Luwo are exceptions), and in Surmic only by suffixes (Tennet uses tone in addition), whereas in the Afroasiatic languages case is expressed by accent shift, suffix, tone, or some combination of these. (iii) The total number of case categories is restricted in Nilotic languages. Except for Turkana, there are only two to three cases, while in the Afroasiatic languages there is as a rule a much larger set of case categories. Furthermore, there are three families within Afroasiatic that have a marked nominative, namely Omotic, Cushitic, and Berber, whereas in Nilo-Saharan, marked nominatives are found only in the Eastern Sudanic branch, to which Nilotic and Surmic belong. These observations might suggest that inflectional case in general and marked-nominative systems in particular are older in Afroasiatic than in Nilo-Saharan languages.

As we observed in the case of Turkana and Dhaasanac, however, there is also one example where there is evidence for an opposite directionality from Nilotic to Cushitic. Contact between these two languages is a recent phenomenon. The Turkana left their former homelands in eastern Uganda only in the first half of the nineteenth century and occupied the semi-deserts east and north of Lake Turkana considerably later; accordingly, contact with Dhaasanac speakers can be hardly older than 150 years.

8.4   Conclusions

To conclude, marked-nominative systems represent a distinct type of case marking which is rarely found among the world's languages, while in eastern Africa they are extremely common, and in Africa this is by far the most prominent case pattern. We saw that all case systems expressed by tone in eastern Africa have a marked nominative. Marked nominative is not restricted to any constituent order; there are verb-initial languages such as Turkana or Maa, verb-final languages such as Dhaasanac or Somali, or verb-medial languages such as Baale and Chai of Surmic. The distribution of marked-nominative languages patterns to some extent with genetic boundaries but, as was shown in the preceding sections, there is also evidence that areal relationship, that is, language contact, must have played some role in its development. There is a high concentration of marked-nominative systems in the border region of Kenya, Uganda, Sudan, and Ethiopia, and the areal distribution of marked-nominative systems in this area cuts across the genetic boundaries that exist between Nilo-Saharan languages of the Nilotic and Surmic subgroups on the one hand, and Afroasiatic languages of the Omotic and Cushitic families on the other. There is some evidence to suggest that the direction of influence was from Afroasiatic to Nilo-Saharan languages; in certain cases, however, such as Dhaasanac and Turkana, it is plausible that at a later stage, areal influence has taken place from the Nilo-Saharan language Turkana to the Afroasiatic language Dhaasanac.

**Appendix: Genetic overview of marked-nominative languages
in eastern Africa**

Note: Non-bold stands for type 1, and bold for type 2 languages. Language
names written with capitals are both ergative and marked nominative.

Afroasiatic
  Berber
    North: Tamazight, Kabyle, Shilh, Little Kabyila: Ait Ziyan, South
    Beraber
    South: Tuareg
  Cushitic
    East: Afar, Dirayta (Gidole)
      Lowland East: Saho, Oromo
        Omo Tana: **Arbore,** Dhaasanac, Rendille, Somali, Bayso
        Highland East: Sidamo, **Alaaba, Kambaata, K'abeena, Libido
        (Marägo)**, Gedeo, Burji, Hadiyya
      North: **Beja**
    Omotic:[12] Western: Ometo: South: Maale
    East: **Haro, Koyra (Koorete),** Zayse
    North: **Gamo, Kullo,** Wolaitta, **Benchnon Gimira**
    Kefoid: **Bworo, Kefa**

Nilo-Saharan

  Nilotic
  West: PÄRI, (ANYWA),[13] JUR-LUWO, SHILLUK, Dinka
    South: Kalenjin: Pokot, Nandi, Sebei, Kipsigis Datooga, Omotik
    East: Maa, Teso, Turkana
  Surmic
    North: Majang
    Southwest: Didinga, Murle, Tennet, Baale
    Southeast: Chai

9   Africa's verb-final languages

Gerrit J. Dimmendaal

9.1   The verb-final type in a crosslinguistic perspective

The position of the verb relative to other constituents within a clause has been claimed by a number of authors to be a predictor of an additional set of syntactic features. Thus, according to Greenberg (1966), verb-initial languages tend to be prepositional rather than postpositional, putting inflected auxiliary verbs before rather than after the main verb; with more than chance frequency, verb-final languages tend to use postpositions, with auxiliary verbs following the main verb. Such inductively based generalizations about the nature of language of course require further analyses and explanations, e.g. in terms of preferred parsing or processing structures for the human mind.

In more recent correlative studies of this type, e.g. by Dryer (1992), a distinction is drawn between phrasal and non-phrasal elements. Whereas phrasal elements, such as subject and object phrases or adpositions appear to follow a more consistent right-branching or left-branching pattern cross-linguistically, the position of non-phrasal categories such as adjectives, demonstratives, negative particles, or tense–aspect markers does not seem to correlate with constituent order type, as argued by Dryer.

Obviously, constituent order is but one of various factors determining the typological portrait of a language, morphological techniques used in expressing syntactic and semantic relations being another important parameter. This latter observation of course is not new; Sapir (1921:120–46) already pointed out that languages may differ considerably in the techniques used for the expression of syntactic relations. The Sapirian typology has been elaborated upon by Nichols (1986, 1992), who also shows that languages may mark dependency relations between categories either on the head or on the dependent constituent; alternatively, both elements may be marked or neither of the two. From the extensive survey by Nichols it also follows that dependent marking at the clausal level tends to favor a verb-final syntax, whereas head-marking tends to favor a verb-initial structure.

We now know that languages may further differ considerably in the way they organize information structure within a clause as well as beyond the clausal or sentential level, e.g. in narrative discourse. In his seminal study of the storyline in a variety of African languages, Longacre (1990) has shown that verb-initial languages in northeastern Africa investigated by him tend to use special subsecutive verb forms in order to enhance the storyline, whereas verb-final languages in the area tend to use converbs (i.e. morphologically reduced verb forms occurring in dependent clauses) for the same purpose.

With these more recent advances in our understanding of language variation, it seems a momentous time to reiterate the question of what constituent order typology is going to bring us, when we try to understand typological variation between languages. Below, I will focus on the question of whether verb-final languages on the African continent manifest a degree of typological consistency that would justify classifying them as exponents of a specific language type. The strategy followed here is the so-called "method of dynamic comparison," as first proposed probably by Greenberg (1969) in one of his ground-breaking articles, involving a combination of intragenetic and intergenetic processual comparison.

In concrete terms, the application of this method below encompasses a comparison between African languages with a presumed verb-final order, first, on an intragenetic basis, in order to arrive at a proper understanding of the synchronic and diachronic variation between languages which are genetically related, followed by an intergenetic comparison, i.e. a comparison between different genetic groupings. To this end, I will investigate so-called verb-final languages belonging to Afroasiatic, Nilo-Saharan, the Ijoid group within Niger-Congo, and, finally, Central Khoisan languages.[1] The somewhat harsh conclusion arrived at below is that, from a typological point of view, "verb-final" languages like the Ịjọ language Izon and the Omotic language Wolaitta in fact have very little in common. Typological similarities between African "verb-final languages" compared below appear to be due, first, to genetic inheritance, second, to areal contact, and as further argued below, to so-called "self-organizing principles" in these languages. Consequently, constituent order typology appears to be of relatively little importance if we try to understand where and how languages differ.

The main purpose of the present contribution, however, is not to present a nihilistic, deconstructionist picture of constituent order typology. As a kind of alternative, I intend to show what (in my view) the more prominent morpho-syntactic and pragmatic properties of these various genetic groupings are. By presenting a typological portrait of these different genetic units, so to speak, I also intend to show what makes these genetic groupings so different from each other. In addition, I aim to focus on specific analytical issues of particular interest, I believe, for a historical understanding of these various genetic groupings, as well as for language typology in general.

9.2   African languages with a presumed verb-final constituent order

In his typological survey of constituent order types on the African continent, Heine (1976) arrived at a fourway division. In addition to the Greenbergian division between VSO, SVO, and SOV languages, Heine established a fourth type involving languages manifesting a variation between SAUXOV and SVO. These latter languages also tend to place the nomen rectum (genitive) before the nomen regens, using postpositions rather than prepositions (similar to many verb-final languages). This type is particularly common in West Africa, more specifically in the Mande area and neighboring zones; see, for example, Kastenholz (2003) for a detailed discussion of the so-called "split-predicate case" in Mande languages, where the verb as a functionally complex category is distributed variously over the sentence. Contrary to the more strict verb-final languages (called type D languages by Heine), for example, the verb precedes (rather than follows) the adverbial phrase or oblique constituents in the split-predicate type (referred to as type B by Heine 1976).

Greenberg (1966)

VSO	SVO	SOV

Heine (1976)

C	A	B	D

In the discussion I will focus on languages for which it has been claimed that the main verb occurs in clause-final or sentence-final position, i.e. on Greenberg's SOV languages, or Heine's type D languages. As illustrated below, the actual identification of so-called verb-final languages as a type is already problematic in many cases, given the amount of freedom for constituent order in these languages. In line with more general traditions in typological research, I am taking "surface structures" at face value, i.e. I do not assume that there may be a disparity between "deep structures" and "surface manifestations" of constituent order. Where variation occurs within a language, one constituent order type may be argued to be more basic to the system on the basis of specific criteria such as frequency of occurrence or other criteria, as argued below. I will refrain, however, from claims about one underlying (deep-structure) order in such cases, as is common in current Generative Grammar, where alternative manifestations of constituent order may be derived through movement rules.

With respect to so-called verb-final (i.e. type D) languages, Heine (1976) draws a distinction between two subtypes, D1 and D2. In the former, the "consistent SOV type," heads systematically follow their modifiers. Thus, not only the object, but also the obliques precede the verb; postpositions are used, and at the noun phrase level, all kinds of modifiers (including the genitival modifier) precede the head noun. In type D2 on the other hand, one finds the order modifier/head at the clause level, but the order head/modifier in the construction of noun phrases: objects and obliques precede the verb, whereas all kinds of noun modifiers follow the noun they modify. As we shall see below, the former (D1) pattern is common in Omotic (Afroasiatic) languages, whereas the latter (D2) is more widespread in Nilo-Saharan languages in the eastern Sahel region, although the two subtypes (modifier–head as against head–modifier) in actual fact are part of a continuum. As pointed out by Dryer (1992), on the basis of a worldwide survey of head/modifier relations at the clausal and phrasal (NP) level, similar discrepancies are found in so-called verb-final languages outside Africa. It is exactly these kinds of disparities between phrases and clauses which motivated Dryer to draw a distinction in his constituent order typology between phrasal and non-phrasal constituents.

9.2.1   Afroasiatic

Some sixty years ago, Leslau (1945) pointed towards a set of properties which appeared to be shared between Ethio-Semitic languages and neighboring groups belonging to the Cushitic branch within Afroasiatic. These properties included phonological, but also morphosyntactic features as well as constituent order, such as a verb-final constituent order. Leslau (1945) further argued that substratum influence (or shift-induced interference and imposition from Cushitic, in more modern terms) lead to this convergence area.[2]

As argued by Tosco (2000), the notion of an "Ethiopian language area" as such is false, given the disparity of typological features found within the country. But the author agrees that SOV constituent order is a good example of an areal feature in fact "attested . . . well outside Ethiopia . . ." (2000: 344). As already observed by Heine (1976), there are also various Nilo-Saharan languages mainly to the west of the Ethiopian region, and extending into Nigeria and Niger, which manifest a similar constituent order pattern.

Over the past thirty years or so, more detailed studies have appeared on Nilo-Saharan and Afroasiatic languages from this region. It seems a momentous time, therefore, to reinvestigate the issue of (basic) constituent order in these languages covering major parts of northeastern and north-central Africa.

When languages are identified as verb-final, the assumption is that the verb occurs in final position in a basic, transitive clause. But is this basic order always obvious? The case of Maale, an Omotic language described by Azeb Amha (2001), shows that languages may allow for a set of alternative constituent orders, each being grammatical given certain pragmatic conditions. The constituent order SOV is fairly common in basic sentences uttered in isolation, as well as in main clauses in connected discourse:

(1) ʔííní   ginʔ-á-ne
     3MSG:NOM   sleep-IPF-AFF:DECL
     'He is sleeping'

(2) ʔííní   salítsi   zér-á-ne
     3MSG:NOM   sesame:ABS   sow-IPF-AFF:DECL
     'He is sowing sesame'

The OSV template is associated with a specific focus structure construction in Maale, whereby the subject carries (assertive) focus:

(3) waas'-ó   táání   láál-é-ne
     water-ABS   1SG:NOM   spill-PF-AFF:DECL
     'I spilled the water'

Whereas the order SOV (and SV in intransitive clauses) is the most frequent order in texts and in elicited material in Maale, alternatives such as OSV, but also SVO or OVS, do in fact occur in connected speech. In other words, postverbal subjects or objects are not excluded. Inversion of subject–verb order is common crosslinguistically as a strategy for expressing presentative focus (see Sasse 1987), as in the following Maale example:

(4) kumm-uwá-se   ʔagínn-á
     fill-IPF:NEG-NEG:DECL   month-NOM
     'It does not last for a month (lit. a month does not fill)'

Interestingly, Maale also allows for SVO as well as verb-initial clauses:

(5) kan-z-i   múʔ-é-ne   ʔaʃk-ó
     dog-DEF-NOM   eat-PERF-AFF:DECL   meat-ABS
     'The dog ate the meat'

(6) múʔ-é-ne   kan-z-i   ʔaʃk-ó
     eat-PERF-AFF:DECL   dog-DEF-NOM   meat-ABS
     'The dog ate the meat'

Verb-initial sentences in Maale are judged to be less appropriate with indefinite or generic arguments (Amha 2001: 238).

In dependent (e.g. adverbial) clauses in Maale on the other hand, the verb obligatorily appears in final position, i.e. the order is either SOV or OSV.

(7) goys'-ó   né   táná   ɗaww-é-to   tá
    road-ABS   2SG:NOM   1SG:ABS   show-   1SG:NOM
                                           PERF-CND

    néé-m   miiʃʃe   ing-andá-ne
    2SG-DAT   money:ABS   give-F:IPF-AFF:DECL
    'If you show me the road, I will give you money'

Given this latter distributional property, as well as the higher frequency of SOV and OSV order (i.e. of verb-final as against other constituent order types) in main clauses, it may be claimed that verb-final order in Maale is more basic to the system than a verb-medial or verb-initial order (Amha 2001: 235ff).

Parallel to constituent order variation at the clausal level, we find variation at the noun phrase level in Maale, although prenominal modifying structures constitute the most common pattern. A demonstrative may precede the head noun in Maale, in which it is only inflected for gender and number. But when following the noun, it takes over all inflectional properties of the noun, i.e. gender, number, and case (Amha 2001: 243). Given these morphological properties and the more independent status of the postnominal demonstrative (which may also be used elliptically in this form, i.e. without a preceding noun), the prenominal modifying order may be argued to be more basic.

Similarly, adpositions in Maale, called "Locative nominals" by Amha (2001: 246), most frequently follow their complements, but they may also precede the latter:

(8)   kan-á   démm-a   bó??-átsí-ko   ?ek'k'-é-ne
       dog-NOM   under-LOC   animal-M-GEN   stand-PERF-AFF:DECL
       'The dog stood under the wild animal'

In terms of frequency, it is more common to find such relational modifiers in a position following the head noun. This criterion, in combination with notions like morphological complexity (as for demonstratives above), may be used as an argument in favor of a modifier–head relation as the more basic, unmarked structure in this Omotic language.

It is important to realize that even relatively closely related languages may differ in the rigidity of their constituent order. Thus, in Wolaitta, which also belongs to the Ometo group within Omotic, post-verbal subjects and/or objects do occur, but they are extremely rare (Azeb Amha, p.c.). Describing such language-internal variation and its link with information packaging in a clause therefore is important, also because existing variation may set the trigger for language change. And here is our first analytical problem when we try to do constituent order typology: the issue of descriptive adequacy. Bender (1991: 92–3), for example, writes that in his data on the Omotic language Aari relative clauses follow the head noun, whereas in the data provided (to Bender) by another linguist (Dennis Tully) relative clauses precede the latter. Fleming (1990: 546) observes with respect to the Omotic language Dime that numerals "usually act like adjectives in following nouns but it is not an obligatory position because numbers may also precede the noun they modify." Hayward (1990: 320) observes that Zayse "in general . . . appears to be a language which fulfills the 'S-O-V' stereotype . . . ; there are many obvious violations of the type when we consider sentences ... These anomalies are a result of the all-important effect of syntactic re-arrangements concerned with focus." Analyzing constituent order in such languages without taking discourse-related effects into account accordingly appears to be rather meaningless.

What one would like to know, both for historical-comparative and for general typological studies, for each and every language that has been claimed to be verb-final is:

(i) How rigid is the order of constituents in fact?
(ii) To what extent are differences in information packaging within a clause or sentence expressed through constituent order?

It has been observed by Van Valin and LaPolla (1997: 213) that flexibility in constituent order points to the adaptation of syntax and discourse structure to each other's demands. The authors draw a comparison between English and Italian in this respect. Constituent order in the former is relatively constrained and focus placement is flexible. In Italian on the other hand, constituent order is rather flexible and focus placement is very constrained. Phrased differently, the focus structure adapts to the rigidity of constituent order in English, by allowing free focus placement. In Italian, however, the syntax adapts to the rigid focus structure "by having constructions which allow focal elements which would normally be prenuclear to occur in a postnuclear position." The Omotic language Maale is similar to Italian, in that constituent order is rather flexible, whereas focus marking is restricted, as pointed out by Amha (2001: 250). But it remains to be determined to what extent this also applies to other Omotic languages. Presumably, genetically related languages may be classified along a continuum in this respect, as is the case with languages in general.

The presence of case marking makes it possible to move constituents around for pragmatic reasons without resulting in considerable ambiguity as to their syntactic function within a clause. But an alternative ordering is *not* required per se, since focus marking may be accomplished other than by means of constituent order change. If focus marking is expressed morphologically, alternation in constituent becomes superfluous, as shown for Haro (Woldemariam 2004). In this Omotic language, any constituent may be focused by way of a suffix or enclitic -*kko*; the latter constituent occurs in the position immediately preceding the verb:

(9) ʔassá-z-i   paráze-ʔinkí-kko   é-wos's-e
     man-DEF:M-NOM   horse:ABS-like-FOC   3MSG-run-AFF:DECL
     'The man runs *like a horse*'

(10) ʔassá-z-i   ittá-na-kko   é-wos's-e
     man-DEF:M-NOM   bad-INST-FOC   3MSG-run-AFF:DECL
     'The man runs *badly*'

(11) ʔés-í   moló   ʔáyk-óra   lábu-kko   ʔé-wudd-ín-e
      3SG:NOM   fish:ABS   hold-PURP   shore:ABS-FOC   3MSG-run-
      'He went down to *the shore* to catch a fish'   AFF:DECL

Haro thus is similar to Maale in that constituent order is rather flexible, whereas focus marking is restricted. But Haro differs from the latter language in that postverbal subjects or objects do not seem to be attested. One reason for this important difference may be the fact that referentiality (e.g. notions like top-icality, definiteness, or focus of attention) is expressed differently in these two genetically related languages. Here, then, we have an initial clearcut instance of the interaction between different grammatical subsystems, in this case between referentiality and the rigidity of constituent order, in a specific language. This issue will be readdressed in section 9.5 below.

The situation for Cushitic appears to be equally diverse. Lowland East Cushitic languages, more specifically those belonging to the Omo-Tana group, Oromoid languages, and the Dullay cluster, appear to be verb-final, using postpositions (rather than prepositions). But nominal modifiers follow, rather than precede, the head noun in these languages, according to our current state of knowledge. It has been argued by Tosco (1993) that this situation in fact goes back to Proto-East Cushitic (except for the position of the demonstrative, which appears to have been prenominal originally).

Highland East Cushitic and Saho-'Afar apparently are "more consistent" verb-final languages, with modifier–head order also at the nominal level. But this situation has been argued by Tosco (1993: 438) to be a later development; the prenominal modifying structure apparently was initiated by adjectives and relative clauses, followed by genitive constructions in these languages.[3] And here we are touching upon a second analytical problem (next to discourse-related investigations) when trying to compare languages typologically. When comparing the position of the adjective relative to the head noun, for example, the assumption often appears to be that the identification of the former as a syntactic category is straightforward. But of course adjectival concepts, i.e. expressions denoting qualities attributed to some noun, may be expressed by way of various syntactic strategies. As shown by Banti (1988: 245) for Cushitic, special verbs, nominal complements with 'be,' genitives, or special adpositions may be used. And the derivational basis of "adjectives" in other language families may be quite different.

Similar problems in crosslinguistic comparisons of course occur when comparing adpositions and their position relative to their complements. A simple dichotomy between prepositional and postpositional languages presents a gross oversimplification of facts. First, there are languages with prepositions as well as postpositions. Moreover, as we saw for Maale, so-called postpositions may also precede the complement noun under certain pragmatic conditions, whereas in other languages the order is more rigid. This variation parallels the relative rigidity for the position of subject and object relative to the verb in some languages, as against "free constituent order" in others. Moreover, these syntactic elements called postpositions by others have been argued by Amha (2001: 246–8) to be relational or locative nouns in a language like Maale. What is more, adpositions may perform a grammatical role in a particular language, or they merely function to specify the search domain for some object ('underneath,' 'on top of'), as in Maale. Adpositional modifiers often share features with, or are derived from, nouns (e.g. expressing body-part terminology) or verbs. They may or may not take case in languages with case-marking systems, or alternatively, they may operate in competition with (peripheral) case markers, as appears to be common in various Omotic languages. Also, adpositions may or may not be used elliptically (or be "stranded", in traditional generative terminology); alternatively, they may cliticize onto verbs, for example when used with pronominal complements, as appears to be common crosslinguistically. Each of these various properties – which do not necessarily present an exhaustive listing of typologically relevant differences between "adpositions" crosslinguistically – may have consequences for their grammatical status in a particular language.

One apparent conclusion to be drawn from the discussion above is that some languages can be identified as strict verb-final languages on the basis of criteria such as morphological complexity, frequency, or some other principle, such as discourse sensitivity, or constituent order in sentences enhancing the storyline. For the same reasons, one may also expect to find languages for which it is not possible to identify a basic constituent order (be it verb-initial, verb-final or otherwise), as the following sections should also help to illustrate.

In the discussion above, I further argued against a lumping analysis of parts of speech when comparing categories between various languages; clearly, we need more subtle scales whether we are dealing with adjectives, adpositions, or any other parts of speech, because the etymological history of such categories as well as their derivational basis synchronically may co-determine their structural behavior. Categories are identified on the basis of constructions in which they occur, as argued by Croft (2001). Such distributional properties also need to be taken into account when comparing linguistic systems.

Third, areal contact – a common factor affecting language structures in multilingual societies, as is typical for most African speech communities – clearly is relevant. So-called verb-final languages like the Ethio-Semitic language Tigre have prepositions, rather than postpositions. It is widely assumed by Semiticists that early Semitic had a verb-initial structure as well as pre-positions. The latter property therefore probably is a retention in Tigre; compare also Tosco (2000), who observes that the further south Ethio-Semitic languages are based within the country, the more "consistent" they are (in Greenbergian terms) with respect to modifier/head relations.[4] This appears to be the case for Amharic, where prepositions like *bä* (for phrases expressing Instrument, Manner, or Malefactive), or *kä* (for Ablative or Source) are combined with the use of postpositions specifying the search domain for objects, as shown by Zelealem Leyew (2003):

(12) a. bä-t'or   'with a spear'
        PREP-spear
     b. bä-säw   lay   'on people'
        PREP-people on

9.2.2   Central Khoisan

Whereas in Greenberg's classification of African languages Khoisan is assumed to constitute a language family or phylum, most specialists these days seem to treat Khoisan as an areal, rather than a genetic grouping, consisting of Central Khoisan (or Khoe), Northern Khoisan (or Ju), Southern Khoisan (or !Ui-Taa), Sandawe, Kwadi, and Hadza; see, for example, Güldemann and Vossen (2000: 102). More recently, it has been argued by Güldemann and Elderkin (forth-coming) that Central Khoisan probably forms a genetic unit with Sandawe and Kwadi. Güldemann and Vossen (2000) also point out that SOV is the dominant constituent order in Central Khoisan as well as Kwadi (2000: 117, 119). The non-Khoe languages on the other hand are claimed to use SVO order with a nominal head-modifier structure "with the important exception of associative constructions where the reverse order modifier-head is found," as pointed out by Güldemann and Vossen (2000: 108).

In one of the rare modern monographs on a Khoisan language, Hagman (1977: 66–7) points out that a transitive declarative sentence like 'Bill was giving the letter to Mary there' has the order 'Bill there Mary letter give' in the Central Khoisan language Nama. The sentence-final verb in Nama may be preceded by a selection of tense–aspect markers. But how common is the SOV order in fact in connected discourse for languages like Nama? Hagman (1977: 107) refers to the SOV order as the "normal" sentence order, i.e. "the order which occurs with the greatest frequency and which can therefore be assumed to be basic ... An important feature of Nama syntax, however, is that it allows for considerable variety in the order of sentence constituents to emphasize or de-emphasize a particular element in the sentence."

Hagman further observes (1977: 108) that interrogative words, as in 'Where are you going' must be initialized; in the corresponding answer 'I am going to the town' the phrase 'to the town' may either precede or follow the verb. The

282   Gerrit J. Dimmendaal

initial position in Nama may be occupied by objects, but also by the verb, if the
latter is in focus (Hagman 1977: 111). This is presumably a manifestation of a
widespread property, Givón's principle of communicative task: fronting of an
information unit is more urgent when the information to be communicated is
either less predictable or important. The inverse process, "finalization" of
deposed subject noun phrases or adverbials, also occurs in Nama, according to
Hagman (1977: 113–14). "Internal scrambling," whereby certain elements
within the sentence are reordered, is another common feature of Nama.
Compare the following sentence from Hagman's description of Nama:

(13) |'apa!namku ke ||'ari   !arop   !naa !nari'opa ke   !xoo
     policemen   DP   yesterday   forest in   thief   DP   caught
     'The policemen caught the thief yesterday in the forest'

According to Hagman (1977: 114), the constituents 'the thief,' 'yesterday',
and 'in the forest' may be permuted in any way to produce an acceptable
sentence, although the verb always appears to occur in final position. Consequently, Nama may indeed be claimed to be a verb-final language, which also
uses postpositions (Hagman 1977: 101–5), although adverbial phrases may
precede or follow the main clause. But for several other Central Khoisan
languages the situation appears to be less clear.
   In his description of ||Ani, Heine (1999) points towards similar
"scrambling" rules for this Central Khoisan language. As pointed out by Heine
(1999: 58), it is hard to tell whether ||Ani has a basic word order. In terms of
frequency of occurrence, VO, with 20 percent of the sample clauses, and OV,
in 24.2 percent, are common, while 33.3 percent are compatible with both;
verb-initial constituent order is attested in 2.5 percent of the narrative discourse
text. As further pointed out by the author (1999: 58), auxiliary verbs over-
whelmingly follow the main verb, but they may also precede the latter. In the
text included in the description, SVO order appears to be quite common.
Compare the OSV order in (13) with the SVO order in (14):

(14) ngú   tí   n||ání-à-gòè
     house 1SG   build-I-FUT
     'I shall build a/the house'

(15) tí   mûn-m̀-tè   xám-má |áú
     1SG   see-3MSG-PRES lion-3MSG   big
     'I see a big lion'

The position of question words relative to the verb suggests that the position
immediately before the verb is used for constituents which are in focus:

(16) há   má-kà   mûn-à-hàn   pǒ   yǐ   yâ   dì   'á
     2FSG   where   see-I-PERF   jackal tree climb   POSS   O
     'Where have you ever seen a jackal climbing a tree?'

‖Ani also has postpositional phrases. These phrases seem to follow the verb, and may themselves be preceded by so-called "secondary postpositions" specifying the search domain (Heine 1999: 47):

(17) ‖á-ɦì   ngú   n≠órón   ká   tìn
      chair   house   back   LOC   stay
      'The chair is behind the house'

(18) ‖á-ɦì-hɛ́   ɦì   oanà   tìn
      chair-FSG   tree   LOC   stay
      'The chair is under the tree (lit. the chair is at the tree)'

Adverbial clauses may either precede or follow the main clause (Heine 1999: 22):

(19) tí   khóé-tè   kûn-à-nà   khó-mà   ɦàâ
      1SG   wait-PRES   until   person-MSG   come
      'I wait until he comes'

These various distributional properties suggest that ‖Ani shares properties with Heine's type B, rather than with his type D (i.e. verb-final) languages. But again, it is obvious that here too we are not dealing with one rigid language type. So-called type B languages again differ with respect to rigidity of constituent order. A rather rigid SVO/SAUXOV order with postpositions appears to be common in Central Sudanic languages (see Andersen 1984 for a description of Moru). The order SVO/SAUXOV (in combination with the use of postpositions) is also attested in Western Nilotic languages like Dinka. But as shown by Andersen (1991), Dinka is better characterized as a Topic-V or Topic-AUX language, rather than as a type B language. Any constituent (subject, object, adverb, etc.) may precede the verb or auxiliary verb. Alternatively, the slot preceding the main verb or auxiliary verb may be empty, as when the topic is understood from the context, thereby resulting in a verb-initial structure.

When studying constituent order in narrative discourse in the Central Khoisan language Khoe, e.g. in the texts published by Kilian-Hatz (1999), again it is not obvious that verb-final structures are more basic in any sense than other constituent order types in this language. The common constituent order in clauses enhancing the storyline ("and then x did y . . .") in fact appears to be SVO. But do we gain anything by saying that Khoe is a SVO language?[5] Hardly, it would seem, first because SVO constituent order is not a predictor of a language type, at least not in a statistically significant way; second, such a simple statement would also leave the observed variation with other order types unaccounted for.

There appears to be some evidence for a genetic link between Central Khoisan and Sandawe. With respect to Sandawe, Dalgish (1979: 274) has claimed that SOV word order is more prevalent statistically. But Dobashi (2001: 57–8) points out that this language "allows any possible word order . . . restricted by agreement." The latter, so-called nominative clitic, is a marker which agrees with the subject in gender, person, and number, and may appear on the verb or the object:

| (20) | iyoo | \|nining'-sa | \|\|aa |
| | mother | maize-3FSG | plant |

(21)	||aa-sa	|nining'-sa	iyoo
	plant-3FSG	maize-3FSG	mother
	'Mother planted maize'		

The final example is also grammatical without the suffix -sa appearing on the object noun 'maize.' Alternatively, SVO, OSV, OVS, and VSO may occur in Sandawe.

In languages with relatively rigid constituent order it may indeed be possible, on the basis of such criteria as distribution, frequency, or morphological complexity, to identify a basic constituent order (of the type identified by Heine 1976). But for languages in which constituent order is largely governed by pragmatic principles, this may not be a very useful exercise. From a descriptive as well as from a theoretical point of view, it would be more enlightening, first, to list the different order types, second, to describe the pragmatic conditions under which these appear, and, third, to identify the coding mechanisms for these alternative ways of information packaging.

9.2.3   Nilo-Saharan

In their highly informative survey of languages of northeastern Africa, Tucker and Bryan (1966) pointed out that in a series of language groups in this area the verb in main clauses tends to occur in final position. More specifically, this applies to a series of language groups which these days are commonly held to be members of the Nilo-Saharan family, stretching roughly along a west–east axis geographically: Saharan, Maban and Mimi, Tama, Fur, Nyimang, Nubian, Nara, and Kunama.

Today, these various Nilo-Saharan groups, classified as type D languages by Heine (1976), only constitute a geographically contiguous area to a certain extent. It is important to note, however, that virtually no other language types are represented in this area. Moreover, the relative isolation of these language groups geographically today, in particular in the central and eastern Sahel region, is most likely an outcome of the gradual desertification of the region over the past 5,000 years, a process which appears to have forced people to retreat towards more mountainous regions where there was still water available, such as the border area between Sudan and Chad. Most likely, a former tributary of the Nile, the Wadi Howar or Yellow Nile, which flowed from western Chad towards the Nile roughly between the third and the fourth cataract (Pachur & Kröpelin 1987), provided the geographical conditions for this areal contact zone between regions east of the Nile and the zones towards the west. There is solid archaeological evidence that this region indeed constituted a diffusional zone for various cultural traits, such as pastoralism and the use of Leitband pottery traditions (see Jesse 2000; Keding 2000). The numerous typological traits shared between the Ethiopian Afroasiatic languages and the Nilo-Saharan languages stretching from northern Ethiopia and Eritrea all the way towards Chad would therefore seem to present an additional piece of evidence for such an ancient contact zone. (See also Amha & Dimmendaal 2006a.)

In his survey of constituent order types in Africa, Heine (1976) pointed out that the Nilo-Saharan groups in this area are typologically similar to Afroasiatic groups in Ethiopia, more specifically Cushitic, Omotic, and Ethio-Semitic. Not only do these various groups share the same word order type, according to the author, they also use case markers and postpositions in order to express predicate frames, with adverbial clauses preceding main clauses.[6] From the map with areal nuclei in Heine (1976) it is clear that the author assumed that these Nilo-Saharan languages acquired these typological properties (associated with type D in Heine's typology) through areal diffusion from the Ethiopian Afroasiatic zone. But it is also possible that the diffusion went in the other direction, given the fact that this phenomenon is also widespread in Nilo-Saharan groups that are distantly related to each other.

As already discussed above (and as illustrated on map 9.1), the current distribution of these Nilo-Saharan groups is partly diffuse. Thus, one of the languages sharing the predominantly verb-final syntax, postpositions, and the extensive use of case marking is Nyimang, a language spoken in the Nuba Mountains and surrounded by Kordofanian languages, i.e. by Niger-Congo languages which are genetically and typologically distinct from the Nilo-Saharan languages.

Case marking is a prominent feature of Nyimang, as table 9.1 helps to show (data collected by the present author). Nyimang appears to be a fairly strict verb-final language. But again, the relatively poor descriptive state of this language at present prevents us from making more firm claims on clausal structures in this respect. This caution also applies to nominal phrases. Rather characteristically for Nilo-Saharan as a whole, verb-final languages such as Kanuri (Saharan), Bura Mabang (Maban), Fur, Kunama, or Eastern Sudanic languages such as Dongolese Nubian or Nyimang, appear to put nominal modifiers such as adjectives and demonstratives after the head noun. But even closely related languages like Nyimang and Afitti appear to differ in terms of head–modifier relations at the nominal level. Thus, Tucker and Bryan (1966: 252) observe an

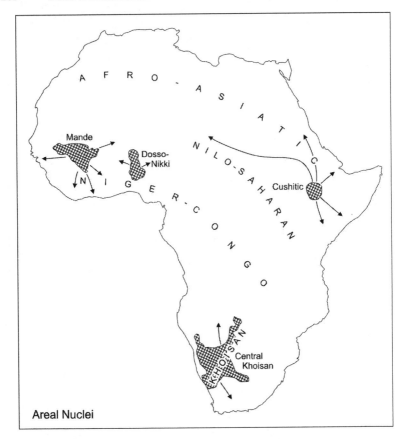

Map 9.1 Typological zones (based on Heine 1976)

order possessor–possessed for Nyimang, but Afitti apparently also allows for
possessed–possessor order.

As is common in Nilo-Saharan languages in the Wadi Howar region – i.e. in
the typological zone identified by Heine (1976), and including subgroups such as
Fur, Kunama, Nubian, or Tama – nominative case is morphologically unmarked
in Nyimang, whereas accusative case is marked; in this respect these languages
differ from case-marking Nilo-Saharan groups further south, such as Berta,
Nilotic, and Surmic, which are characterized by a morphologically marked
nominative and zero marking for accusative. Examples from Nyimang:

(22)   ɛ̀n   élê-wò   t̪wēèn
        3SG:NOM   milk-ACC   bring
        '(S)he is bringing milk'

Table 9.1 *Case marking in Nyimang*

Nominative	Zero marking
Accusative	-ɔ/o, -wo, tone
Dative	-ɪ/i
Locative	-ʊ, , -aʊ, -V
Instrumental/Comitative	-ɛy, -V
Similative	-ɪl
Genitive	-ʊ, -u

(23) àì   ɲìŋānŋ-ɛ́ì   mɔ̀
     1SG:NOM   sun-INST   rise
     'I got up at sunrise'

(24) àì   bâ   kw-àʊ̀   kà
     1SG:NOM   TA   field-LOC go
     'I am going to the field'

(25) àì   bâ   Màhmūd-īl   tɔ̀wúrʊ́   nɛ̄ɛ̀
     1SG:NOM   TA   Mahmud-SIM   tall   be
     'I am taller/fatter than Mahmud'

Similative case (as against a comparative construction involving the verb supersede, surpass), as in (25), is typical as a possession-marking strategy for a variety of languages in northeastern Africa (Leyew & Heine 2003). As shown by these examples, Nyimang also allows for specific tense–aspect–mood markers to occur in second position, between the subject and the object. In this respect, this language is reminiscent of Heine's type B language.

From a typological point of view, Nyimang is similar to Nubian languages in the Nuba Mountains. Typologically similar systems, to some extent involving cognate case-marking morphemes, are further attested in Nilo-Saharan languages northwest and northeast of this area.[7] Saharan language groups in the border area between Sudan and Chad (with an extension into Chad and Nigeria for the Saharan languages) as well as Fur (plus Amdang), the Maban and Taman group, and Nubian languages spoken along the Nile, plus Nara and Kunama, appear to employ similar morphosyntactic properties. Thus, in Tama extensive case marking occurs, distinguishing nominative, accusative, locative, ablative, instrument, comitative, and genitive.

(26) Khàmís-!íŋ   dá!fá   nék
     Khamis-ACC   pay   do
     'pay Khamis'

(27) Khàmís-gí   nʊ́ʊ!ná-ŋá
     Khamis-COM   1SG.come-PERF
     'I came with Khamis'

288 Gerrit J. Dimmendaal

(28) Jàzíírέr-!ín   nʊ́ʊ!ná-ŋá
      Jazira.SPEC-ABL   1SG.come-PERF
      'I came from Jazira'

(Data on Tama from Dimmendaal, to appear. The exclamation marks in these examples represent tonal downstepping.)

As observed for Central Khoisan above, case marking is not necessarily a property of so-called verb-final African languages. This property in combination with a number of additional morphosyntactic features further discussed in section 3 below, as found in Nyimang and other Nilo-Saharan languages such as Tama, is consequently explained best as an instance of contact-induced change or areal diffusion. Whether this diffusion was initiated by Afroasiatic languages in the area, or whether, alternatively, the Nilo-Saharan languages were the cause of the areal diffusion of these properties into Afroasiatic remains to be determined on the basis of future historical-comparative work on these language phyla.

In order to illustrate the maximal typological contrast between African languages that have been claimed to have a basic verb-final syntax, the Ijoid languages, spoken in the Niger delta of southern Nigeria, are discussed next.

9.2.4   Ijoid

Though classified as a member of the Benue-Congo branch within Niger-Congo by Greenberg (1963), subsequent research has made it clear that the Ijoid cluster in the Niger Delta (Nigeria) occupies a more isolated position genetically within this phylum. Today, it is assumed that the Ijoid cluster constitutes an earlier split-off from Niger-Congo (see Williamson & Blench 2000: 18).[8]

The Ijoid cluster appears to be untypical for Niger-Congo as a whole in a number of respects, e.g. in that its members show gender distinctions with third-person singular pronouns between masculine, feminine and neuter.[9] The Ijoid cluster probably is closely related to Defaka, another verb-final language in the area described by Jenewari (1983). An example from the latter language:

(29) Bomá   Gogó   píníma
      Boma   Gogo   beat.TA
      'Boma beat Gogo'

Jenewari (1977) has described the Ijoid language Kalaḅarị in considerable detail. From the evidence available through this study, this language appears to have a fairly strict verb-final syntax:

(30) ini   wámina   sịnm̃
      they   us   call.FAC
      'They called us'

(31) ọ   dukų́m̄   bẹbẹ́ẹ̄   wá   múba
      he   permits   if   we   go.FUT
      'If he permits us, we shall go (there)'

Postpositional phrases also appear to precede the main verb:

(32) ori   ásárị̣   bị́ō   émí-∅-ī
      he   Asarị̣   inside be.somewhere-GEN-NSM
      'He is in Sari'

(33) ori   ogie   kẹ́   anị   pẹlẹ́m̄
      he   knife PNM   it   cut.FAC
      'He cut it with a knife'

Adverbial phrases expressing reason or time tend to occur before the main verb, but time adverbials may also appear after the latter (Jenewari 1977: 151–3).

(34) o   bote   só   wá   yé   fị́m̄
      he   come.COMPL   after   we   thing   eat.FAC
      'After he had come, we ate'

Apart from the definiteness marker or the quantifier, all modifiers (including relative clauses) precede the head noun in Kalabarị:

(35) Inị   álábọ́   bé   fị-∅   yé   mē   bẹ́lẹ́máárị
      they chief   the   die-FAC   NOML   the   converse.GEN
      'They are conversing about the death of the chief'

The nominalization of complement phrases, as in the example above, in fact appears to be common in Kalabarị:

(36) o   bọ́-∅   boto   a   nimi-∅-áā
      he   come-FAC   NOML   I   know-FAC-not-NSM
      'I don't know if he came'

(37) míē   ∅   a   kẹ́ẹ̄   bo-∅   yéē
      this.thing   COP   I   PNM   come.FAC   thing.NSM
      'This is the thing/what I came with'

Subject pronouns appear in three different sets in Kalabarị. One set clearly is used for emphasis or focus. Compare the marker *a* for 'I' in the examples above with the following marker for first person singular, *iyẹrị́:*

(38) Iyẹrị́   anị   yém̄
      I   it   do.FAC
      '*I* did it'

But there is an additional set of (non-emphatic) pronouns which are to be used with certain tense–aspect forms apparently. Compare the first-person singular form *arị* in (39) with the short form *a* in (40):

(39)   arị   íyé   érịm̄
         I   you   see.FAC
         'I saw you (SG)'

(40)   a   ḅóḅa
         I   come.FUT
         'I shall come'

The short form in Kalaḅarị may indeed be a prefix (or proclitic), rather than a free pronoun. As pointed out by Creissels (2000: 238), pronominal markers presented as free markers in the description of various West African languages may in fact be bound markers (affixes or clitics). Consequently, a reanalysis of the Kalaḅarị data would imply that there is a certain degree of head marking at the clausal level in this Ijoid language as well, e.g. crossreferencing for subjects on the verb.

9.3   The grammatical coding of constituency and dependency relations

The morphosyntactic coding of syntactic relations, whether through dependent-marking strategies such as case or through head-marking strategies such as verbal morphology is a property which should also be part of a synchronic typology, next to constituent order and categorization, given its potential consequence for the structural behavior of constituents. In an interesting survey of the Kalahari Basin as an object of areal typology, Güldemann (1998) investigated a variety of structural features, following Nichols' (1992) worldwide survey of morphosyntactic coding strategies. Güldemann investigated the head/dependent marking type (at the phrasal as well as the clausal level), complexity (morphological marking), alignment (e.g. neutral, accusative, ergative, active), clausal word order, inclusive/exclusive pronouns, inalienable/alienable possession, noun classification as well as valency changes in the Kalahari Basin. Table 9.2 summarizes some of the findings emerging from this comparison, also in relation to Africa as a whole as well as universally.

The subcontinental area favors head marking at the clausal level and verb medial order, as pointed out by Güldemann (1998: 19). But what these figures further show is a tremendous internal diversity of the Kalahari Basin in terms of head marking and dependent marking. This divergence in turn is indicative of an ancient residual zone, where distinct families apparently coexisted for a considerable period of time.

In Central Khoisan languages like Khwe, there is a rich inventory of head marking on verbs, more specifically of verbal derivational suffixes including

Table 9.2 *Head marking and dependent marking in the Kalahari Basin*

Feature	Feature value	Kalahari Basin	Africa	World
Head/dependent	head	67 (50)	16	35
	double/split	17 (25)	21	30
	dependent	17 (25)	63	34
Word order	verb-initial	0 (0)	5	14
	verb-medial	83 (75)	37	20
	verb-final	17 (25)	47	53
	(split/free)	0 (0)	10	11

The figures in brackets are the respective percentages when Khoisan languages like ǂHoa and !Xoo are excluded from the set as separate genetic units.

causative, applicative, comitative, locative, passive, reflexive, and reciprocal (Kilian-Hatz, 2006). Compare:

(41) tí   tcá   à   djà-ró-mà-à-tè
     1SG   2MSG   O   work-II-APPL-I-PRES
     'I work for you'

(42) tí   yaá-o-à-tè   tí   wécan-nà
     1SG   come-LOC-I-PRES   1SG   friend-3C:PL
     'I go right up to my friends'

Most languages which are predominantly dependent marking at the clausal level (e.g. by using case marking) tend to have some degree of head marking, e.g. in that they use crossreference markers for core syntactic notions such as subject (and/or object) on the verb, as shown by Nichols (1986). This also seems to apply to Ijoid languages, as argued above. Consequently, the absence of this type of head marking (for subject and/or object) in Central Khoisan languages is typologically significant. Absence of obligatory subject marking on the verb is also characteristic for the non-Khoe languages (Bernd Heine, p.c.). Within the Nilo-Saharan phylum on the other hand, subject marking, and to a lesser extent object marking, is very common, as table 9.3 helps to show.

However, within this phylum there is an interesting correlation between constituent order and dependent-marking versus head-marking strategies. Whereas so-called verb-final Nilo-Saharan groups tend to have extensive case-marking systems, language groups with other dominant constituent order types, e.g. Nilotic or Surmic, which are verb-initial or verb-second, manifest a decrease in peripheral case marking and an increase in head marking at the clause level (compare also Dimmendaal, 2005). For example, Nilotic and Surmic languages usually distinguish between nominative (or ergative) and absolutive, with only one peripheral case marker covering location, instrument, and other roles. Corresponding to this reduction in dependent marking,

Table 9.3 *Dependent marking in Nilo-Saharan*

Language group	Constituent order	Periph. case*	ProSu	ProOb
Saharan	V-final	yes	yes	yes
Maban	V-final	yes	yes	yes
Fur	V-final	yes	yes	no
Kunama	V-final	yes	yes	yes
Eastern Sudanic				
Nubian	V-final	yes	yes	no
Tama	V-final	yes	yes	no
Nyimang	V-final	yes	no	no

* Peripheral case: Dative, Instrument, Locative, Ablative, Genitive.

one observes an increase in head marking on the verb, e.g. bound markers for semantic roles such as dative, instrumental, location, or direction. In Dimmendaal (2006) it is argued that in Nilo-Saharan groups like Nilotic and Surmic we see a drift away from dependent marking at the clausal level as well as a slant towards head marking on the verb. And, as argued in the same contribution, the typological shift appears to be related historically to a shift in constituent order, since the verbal strategy is common in Nilo-Saharan, more specifically in Eastern Sudanic, groups which are not verb-final.

In spite of the fact that the marking of more peripheral semantic roles such as location or instrument does not appear to be attested in the so-called verb-final Nilo-Saharan or Afroasiatic languages, it cannot be claimed that this is a property of verb-final languages in general. Köhler (1981: 503) points out with respect to the Central Khoisan language Khoe (Kxoe) that among the many verbal derivational markers, there is a marker -'*o* expressing a directive-inessive. The marking of direction on verbs is also attested, for example, in Ijoid languages. Compare Izon (data from Williamson & Timitimi 1983), which uses a directional suffix -*mǫ́* with inherently intransitive verbs in order to incorporate a notion of path or direction:

(43)   arǐ   kịmị-bí   wẹnị-mŏ-mị
         ISG   man-DF   walk-DIR-TA
         'I walked towards the man'

Alternatively, when the verb is already transitive, a serial verb 'take' is used in order to host the original object in Izon:

(44)   arǐ   aruụ-bí   akị   tǐn   kaka-mŏ-mị
         1SG   canoe-DF   take   tree   tie-DIR-TA
         'I moored the canoe to a tree'

Accordingly, the virtual absence of this verbal strategy in Nilo-Saharan languages with a verb-final syntax and its emergence in Nilo-Saharan groups which are not verb-final, such as Nilotic or Surmic, is nothing but an incidence of family-specific historical fact.

The actual system of head marking on the verb, whether involving core or peripheral semantic roles, always depends on the specific history of a language or language family, with internal as well as external (contact) factors determining the direction of change. There is thus absolutely no uniformity in this respect between languages that may indeed be claimed to share a verb-final syntax.

Languages putting the verb in final position may also differ considerably as to the way in which they express complex clausal relations. Nevertheless, there seems to be at least one non-trivial morphosyntactic phenomenon which does seem to be related to constituent order phenomena, namely verbal compounding. This latter aspect, as argued in section 9.5, would seem to follow from the "self-organizing principles" of these languages. Before moving into this common and widespread morphosyntactic property of so-called verb-final languages, however, I will investigate one additional property of languages with this proclaimed syntactic configuration, showing again how different such languages can in fact be from each other from a typological point of view.

9.4   Beyond the clause level

In an important study on the structure of narrative discourse, Longacre (1990) has shown that African languages may differ considerably with respect to the expression of the storyline in narrative discourse. A common pattern in so-called verb-final languages of northeast Africa involves the use of converbs, i.e. of morphologically reduced finite verbs occurring in dependent clauses.

Traditionally, converbs have been referred to by way of a variety of other terms, e.g. as participles or gerunds. But these labels would seem to represent a typical translation-oriented nomenclature rendering the pseudo-literal translation of the form into European languages, rather than recognizing its true form and function. Crosslinguistically, converbs tend to share two important characteristics (as established by Haspelmath & König 1995). First, such verb forms are morphologically distinct from main verbs, which tend to carry the maximum number of inflectional properties, or from other dependent verb forms, e.g. those occurring in adverbial clauses. Second, the semantic range covered by these converbs includes (an adverbial type of) modification, and the expression of event sequences. These properties are illustrated mainly for Omotic languages in table 9.4.

Omotic languages differ as to whether coreferential (logophoric) versus disjunctive reference marking for subjects is distinguished on converbs. In

Table 9.4 *Inflection of main verbs and converbs in Omotic*

Omotic	Converb	Main verb
Wolaitta	gender + number for subject	gender + number, aspect
Aari	person + number for subject	tense, aspect, person, number
Bench	tense, aspect, person + gender for subject	tense, aspect, person, gender
Maale	no marking for tense, aspect, person or gender; one marker for subject	aspect

Maale, where the verb has a rather reduced morphological structure compared to most other Omotic languages, this distinction is nevertheless marked, as shown by the following examples from Amha (2001):

(45) ʔízí   mís'-ó   tík'-áʔʔo   makiin-aa
      3MSG:NOM   tree-ABS   cut-CNV   car-LOC

     c'aan-é-ne
     load-PERF-A:DECL
     'Having cut the wood, he loaded it on a car [sequential]'

(46) ʔízí   mís'-ó   tík-ém   núúní   makiin-aa
      3MSG:NOM   wood-ABS   cut-CNV   1PL:NOM   car-LOC

     c'aan-é-ne
     load-PERF-AFF:DECL
     'He having cut the wood, we loaded it on the car [disjunctive reference]'

Omotic languages differ as to whether the common distinction between masculine and feminine gender is maintained as an inflectional property in converbs. Wolaitta uses a suffix *-a(da)* on the converb when the corresponding subject is feminine, and a suffix *-i(di)* for masculine subjects. In Maale, only one type of marker is found, *-i* (historically the masculine form) regardless of gender; Dime has generalized the feminine form, *-a*.

As pointed out by Van Valin & LaPolla (1997: 448), "[t]he traditional contrast between subordination and coordination seems to be very clearcut for languages like English and its Indo-European brethren, but when one looks farther afield, constructions appear which do not lend themselves to this neat division." Unlike coordinated clauses, clauses containing a converb could not stand on their own as independent clauses, e.g. because the latter lack a modality marker, nor do converbs carry aspect in languages like Maale. In this sense, converb clauses are dependent, but they are distinct from subordinate clauses in that the latter again require aspect markers as well as specific modality markers which are formally distinct from the indicative marker on main verbs; in other words, both the main clause and the subordinate (adverbial) clause may carry their own illocutionary force. Consequently, Amha (2001) has argued in her analysis of Maale that converb constructions in this Omotic language indeed involve a third type of nexus relation, namely co-subordination, rather than coordination or subordination.

Converbs are also common in a variety of Nilo-Saharan languages (Amha & Dimmendaal 2006a; see also map 9.2). The very same languages manifest additional typological similarities to Afroasiatic languages in Ethiopia, such as the common use of verb-final structures, case marking, postpositions (or postnominal modifiers), and the frequent use of 'say' constructions and other types of verbal compounding amongst others. For example, in their analysis of the Saharan language Beria (also known as Zaghawa), Crass and Jakobi (2000) have shown that the converb in this language represents a morphologically reduced finite verb which is used in order to express a sequence of events.

(47) áī   bágárá égī nɔ́ɔ́g-ɛ   gēnīr   júgí
     1SG friend my visit:1SG-CNV village:DAT/LOC go:1SG:PERF
     'I went (in)to the village to visit my friend'

Clauses with converbs usually are part of a continuum involving dependency relations, with subordination on the one hand, and coordination at the other end of the continuum. This may be further illustrated with examples from the Omotic language Wolaitta, which uses a distinct set of suffixes on verbs, reflecting different degrees of cohesion between the clause containing the verb and the main clause (see table 9.5).

The short forms -a and -i in Wolaitta occur as optional variants of the converb markers -ada and -idi. However, with lexicalized compounds in Wolaitta, i.e. with idiomatic converb plus main verb constructions, the short variants are obligatory; lexical compounding in Wolaitta and other languages in the area is further discussed below in section 9.5. (For a more detailed account of verbal compounding and converb constructions in Wolaitta and other languages in northeastern Africa, see Amha & Dimmendaal 2006b.)

Examples illustrating the use of these markers:

(48) ʔá   na-at-a   kaass-ádá   zinʔ-is-ausu
     3FSG:NOM   child-PL-ABS play:TR-CNV   lie down-CA
                                            US-3F:SG:IPERF
     'She brings the children to bed after having played with them'

(49) ʔá   na-at-a   kaass-ídí   zinʔ-is-iisi
     3MSG:NOM   child-PL-ABS play:TR-CNV   lie down-CAUS-
                                            3MSG:PERF
     'He brought the children to bed after having played with them'

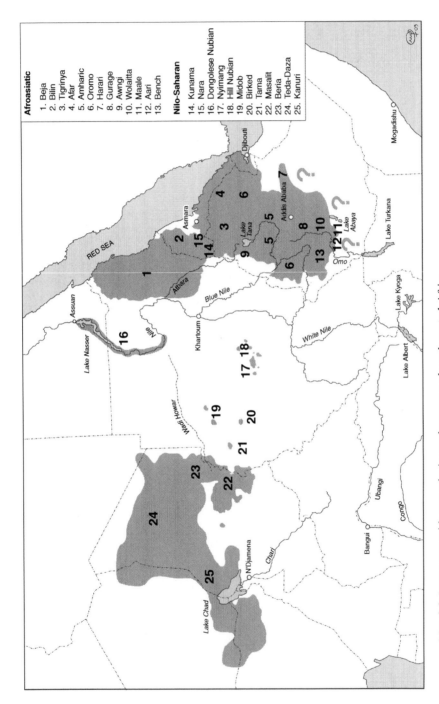

Afroasiatic

1. Beja
2. Bilin
3. Tigrinya
4. Afar
5. Amharic
6. Oromo
7. Harari
8. Gurage
9. Awngi
10. Wolaitta
11. Maale
12. Aari
13. Bench

Nilo-Saharan

14. Kunama
15. Nara
16. Dongolese Nubian
17. Nyimang
18. Hill Nubian
19. Midob
20. Birked
21. Tama
22. Masalit
23. Beria
24. Teda-Daza
25. Kanuri

Map 9.2 Languages with converbs in northeastern and north-central Africa

Table 9.5 *Clausal cohesion markers in Wolaitta*

	Feminine	Masculine
lexicalized converb plus main verb constructions	-a	-i
freely generated converb constructions	-ada	-idi
simultaneous clauses with coreference	-aíddá	-iíddí
simultaneous clauses with switch reference	-íʃin(i)	
temporal/causal clauses	-ín(i)	

As shown by these examples, converb constructions are commonly used in order to express a sequence of actions. A distinct set of (gender-sensitive) markers are used in Wolaitta in order to express simultaneous events. There are two types of simultaneous clauses: "same-subject simultaneous clauses" and "different-subject-simultaneous clauses." In same-subject simultaneous clauses, the subject of the dependent verb and that of the main verb are coreferential with each other.

(50) ʔas-at-í   harg-iíddí   ʔoott-óson
      person-PL-PL:NOM   be sick-SIM:PL   work-3PL:IPF
      'The people work while they are sick'

(51) miʃir-íyá   kátta   gaac'c'-aíddá   yet't'-ausu
      woman-F:NOM   grain:ABS   grind-SIM:F   sing-3FSG:IPF
      'The woman sings while grinding grain'

The converb in these examples shows agreement with the subject, which is its obligatory controller (i.e. the same-subject converb cannot take its own subject). By contrast, example (52) contains a clause ('while the woman grinds grain') which is more adverbial in nature. Unlike the dependent verb in same-subject simultaneous clauses such as (51), it has its own overt (disjunct) subject, itself non-coreferential with the subject of the main verb. This latter feature is also reflected in the fact that gender distinctions between masculine and feminine subjects in the respective clauses are not expressed, i.e. the simultaneous event markers are invariable.

(52) miʃir-íyá   kátta   gaac'c'-íʃin   bitan-ee   k'er-eesi
      woman-F:NOM   grain:ABS   grind-SIM   man-M:NOM   wood:ABS

      mítta
      split-3MSG:IPF
      'The man splits wood while the woman grinds grain'

Example (53) contains a verbal suffix *-ín(i)* indicating temporal adverbial clauses; this latter type often corresponding to causal clauses in English.

(53) táání   kúnd-íni   ʔí   táná   dent-iísi
     1SG:NOM   fall-DS:CNV   3MSG:NOM   1SG:O   raise-3MSG.PERF
     'I having fallen, he helped me to stand up'

Adverbial clauses in Wolaitta of the type above are in paradigmatic contrast
with other clausal types, e.g. those expressing condition:

(54) mi ʃir-íý   kátta   gaac'c'-íkko   bitan-ee   mítta
     grain:ABS   grind-CND   man-M:NOM   wood:ABS   woman-F:NOM

     k'er-eesi
     split-3MSG:IPERF
     'If the woman grinds grain, the man splits wood'

Whereas verb concatenation or serialization as such is also common in Central
Khoisan languages, it would seem that from a typological point of view this
strategy is to be distinguished from the converb plus main verb construction
illustrated for Wolaitta above, itself characteristic of a variety of Afroasiatic
and Nilo-Saharan languages in the area. Contrary to Omotic and other northeast African languages, there appears to be no formal indexing for conjunctive
versus disjunctive reference between subjects of dependent versus main
clauses in Central Khoisan; moreover, switch reference as found in these
Afroasiatic and Nilo-Saharan languages, does not appear to be a part of the
verb concatenation system in Central Khoisan languages, as shown next.

In his description of the Central Khoisan language ‖Ani, Heine (1999: 77)
uses the label "converb" with quotation marks in reference to specific reduced
clauses headed by a marker *ko* or *yo*. From the examples presented by Heine
(1999:77–9) it would seem that the distributional and functional properties of
constructions with such markers in ‖Ani are indeed rather different from
converbs in Afroasiatic or Nilo-Saharan languages. Firstly, in all cases in ‖Ani
coreference appears to be involved. Second, the so-called converb may also co-
occur with verbs in main clauses apparently, e.g. imperative verb forms. Third,
the use of these particles occurs next to a strategy whereby a sequencing of
events is expressed without the obligatory use of either of these markers, as
shown by the narrative discourse text (Heine 1999: 87–111).

(55) ǂx'oa- ra   ko   kun
     go.out-II   CONV   go
     'Go away!'

In ‖Ani, the so-called converb marker is apparently a free morpheme, which
need not be adjacent to the verb with which it co-occurs.[10]

Verb concatenation or serialization is a characteristic property of Central
Khoisan languages in general. One of the most detailed analyses of clause
chaining in such a language is Kilian-Hatz (2006) on Khoe. As shown by the

author, there are different degrees of interlacing between clauses in this
Central Khoisan language, manifested in the degree of independent reference in
terms of tense, aspect, negation, modality, subject, or object marking. Tense,
aspect, mood as well as negation is suffixed to the last verb (verbs may not be
separately marked for TAM). Note also that the object may follow the verbal
complex.

(56) tí   ǁ'ám-á |x'ṹ-ŋya-á-tè   córò-hὲ   ὲ
     1SG   beat-II   kill-NEG-I-   monitor-   O
                                 PRES   3FSG
     'I don't beat the monitor to death'

Verbs may not be separately passivized in Khoe, the passive marker being
suffixed to the last verb. Also, transitive verbs may share the direct object role
or have different objects, and the verbs are or are not contiguous. With same
object constructions the object precedes or follows the verbal complex.

Verb serialization in languages like Khoe appears to cover a range of event
structures. Semantically, such additional verbs may serve to express manner,
movement ('come, arrive'), as well as position ('stand', 'sit', 'lie'). In addition,
the Aktionsart of a verb may be modified this way, e.g. in order to express a
continuous, proximative ('be about to'), or inchoative meaning. In contrast to
the converb constructions of Afroasiatic and Nilo-Saharan languages discussed above, such concatenations of verbs in Khoe do not inflect for person.
Compare again the the following examples from Kilian-Hatz (2006):

(57) xàmá   té-ɛ́   gàrà-á-tè   thám̀   à
     3MSG   stand-II   write-I-PRES   letter   O
     'He writes a letter in standing'

(58) xàmá   kyãĩ-a   ǁám̀-à-tè
     3MSG   be.nice-II   feel-I-PRES
     'He feels well'

(59) cṹṹ-a   n⧺ũ-a-xu-cù
     hurry-II   sit.down-II-COMP-2FSGVOC
     'Sit down quickly!'

Comparative constructions are also rendered through the same strategy of verb
serialization in Khoe. Whereas in the northeastern African region comparatives tend to be formed by way of a separate (similative) case marking, Khoe
uses the more common African pattern, by way of the verb 'surpass,' *ngyέέxu*
(or, alternatively, the verb 'overpower,' *ngóéngoɛ*)

(60) ǁgὲɛ-khòè-djì |í-è-ǁòè   kx'á-khòè-ǁùà   á   ngyέέxu-a
     female-person-3FPL   sing-I-HAB   male-person-3MPL   O   surpass-II
     'Women sing better than men'

300 Gerrit J. Dimmendaal

Treis (2000) also presents a classification of complex sentence structures in the Central Khoisan language Khoe, focusing on the dependency marking morphemes -*ko* and *no*, and using a variety of criteria, such as the occurrence of independent subject and object reference, and the use of independent operators such as tense–aspect, modality, illocutionary force, and negation in the clauses together forming a complex sentence. The author uses a framework inspired by Role and Reference Grammar (Van Valin & LaPolla 1997), thereby distinguishing between different types of junctures, e.g. nucleus and core. On the basis of a careful screening of the various criteria listed above, Treis (2000: 93) concludes that complex clauses with -*kó* mainly, but not exclusively, belong to the nucleus juncture type, i.e. to a construction type in which core arguments are shared:

(61) kx'éí   tí |'é 'à ‖gù-á-xu-à-kò   n|góá-à-gòè
      first 1SG fire O light-II-COMP-II-CONV cook-I-FUT

      kx'óxò 'à
      meat   O
      'First I will light the fire, and then I will cook meat'

In a minority case, core juncture, characterized by independent argument reference, is involved. Clauses involving the conjunction *no* on the other hand represent a looser type of complex clause formation in Khoe, involving core juncture; in the latter case, each of the clauses may itself contain a nucleus juncture, as in the following example (Treis 2000: 94):

(62) wámda-mà   kyãá-kó   kṹũ nò   xàmá xàvána
      springhare-2MSG run-CONV   go   CONJ 3MSG again

      xàmá‖héí
      3MSG pull
      'When the springhare moves, he pulls [again]'

According to Treis (2000: 62), the marker -*kò* in Khoe is used primarily with same-subject constructions. However, the same formative is compatible with different subject constructions, as attested through a number of examples. What appears to be crucial to the Central Khoisan system, however, is adjacency of the two verbs. The explicit crossreferencing system in Omotic languages would seem to make such a condition superfluous in this latter genetic grouping. Interestingly, however, whenever verbs are adjacent in languages from the various genetic groupings discussed here, they start to interact semantically, leading to verbal compounding and to lexicalization and idiomaticization, as shown in section 9.5 below.

In languages discussed in this chapter, the categorial distinction between nouns and verbs is usually evident on distributional as well as on formal (morphological) grounds.[11] Thus, in a prototypical Omotic language the finite verb is inflected for tense, aspect, negation, and modality, whereas a noun is inflected for gender, number, case, and definiteness, although not all of these inflectional features are necessarily present in all forms at all times. At the same time, one may observe a transgression of these categorial boundaries under specific syntactic and semantic conditions, in that verbs may take specific peripheral case markers such as the dative. This property is best known from Omotic and Cushitic languages. (We do not know at present whether the same property is attested in any of the Nilo-Saharan languages discussed above.) Compare the following example from Maale (Amha 2001: 186):

(63) ʔííní   [ʔízá   ʔamʔó   ʃanc-ó-m]
      3MSG:NOM   3FSG:NOM   coffee:ABS sell-ABS-DAT
      bookk-ó   dákk-é-ne
      market-ABS   send-PERF-AFF:DECL
      'He sent her to the market to sell coffee'

In order to express a purposive meaning, Maale uses a dative case marker. As the purposive clause involves a verb, and as dependent clauses in Maale are always verb-final, the case marker is attached to this final constituent as a phrasal affix; the absolutive case marker is present as well, as peripheral case markers such as the dative, locative, or instrumental are always based on the absolutive form in Maale.

The presence of case markers in the Afroasiatic and Nilo-Saharan languages discussed here expressing these types of symbolic relations makes the use of conjunctions or other devices for the expression of complex clause relations, as attested in Ijoid or Central Khoisan languages, superfluous.

9.5   Below the clause level: the role of self-organizing principles

According to Greenberg (1963), verb-final languages tend to be predominantly suffixing, rather than prefixing. This property is indeed common in Omotic languages, which, as we saw above, are probably the best representatives of modifier–head languages, on the African continent, with both derivational and inflectional suffixes following the root. But the picture is far more diverse in other African language groups with a predominantly verb-final constituent order; in Nilo-Saharan, for example, verbal prefixes marking pronominal subjects or causatives are common. But there is one morphosyntactic property which does seem to emerge independently in these languages, namely verb compounding.

As pointed out by Westermann (1911: 61) in his survey of "Sudanic" languages, it is common in, for example, Nubian (now classified as Nilo-Saharan) to concatenate verbs or verbal roots as a lexical process, resulting

in verb forms which in German tend to be expressed with markers such as
weg- or *hin-* (i.e. *wegtragen* 'carry away,' *hinlegen* 'put down'). Some
sixty-five years later, Masica (1976) pointed out that this property is
common in many verb-final south-Asian and central-Asian languages, as
well as in the Ethiopian area. And, as illustrated below, verbal compounding is also common in other African languages with a predominantly
verb-final syntax. In order to illustrate the nature of this type of construction, I will first present a more detailed analysis of one Omotic language, Wolaitta, followed by a comparison with genetically related as well
as unrelated languages.

From a formal point of view, Wolaitta verbal compounds are best treated as
a specialized (lexicalized) type of converb plus main verb construction.
Wolaitta uses a number of converb markers, as shown above, alternating for
gender (masculine versus feminine) as well as for coreferential versus switch
reference marking. In the compound type the subject of the converb and the
main verb are always identical; the converb in such cases is marked by either *-a*
(feminine) or *-i* (masculine). Moreover, objects never intervene between
converb and main verbs in verbal compounds. An example:

(64) Ɂí   ba   keett-aa   [baizz-í   Ɂekk-iisi]
      3MSG:NOM   LOG   house-M:ABS   sell-CNV   take-3MSG:PERF
      'He sold his house'

There is also a prosodic clue that the converb plus main verb constitute a
lexical unit in Wolaitta, because the main verb does not carry a high-tone pitch
accent (65), as would be the case in a freely generated converb plus main verb
construction (66):

(65) Ɂí   maay-úwa   meec'c'-ídí   míc'c'-iisi
      3MSG:NOM   cloth-M:ABS   wash-CNV   hang-3MSG:PERF
      'Having washed the cloth, he hung it up'

(66) bitánee   Ɂoós-uwa   wurs-ídí   ʃemp-eési
      man:NOM   work-M:ACC   finish-CNV   rest-3MSG:IPF
      'Having finished work, the man is resting'

We thus observe a discrepancy in Wolaitta between the grammatical and the
phonological word in the case of verbal compounds. Interestingly, however,
the prosodic structure of the latter is identical to that of nominal compounds in
Wolaitta, where there is also one high pitch only within the phrase, rather than
each word or stem having its own pitch accent (Amha 1996:133).

It is useful in Wolaitta to distinguish between symmetrical and asymmetrical compounding. In both types the main verb bears the full range of
inflectional information (person, number, gender, tense–aspect, modality) as
well as negation of verbs. With the former symmetrical type the converb and

the main verb may be argued to contribute an equal amount of semantic information, as with 'be too tight', lit. slap-hold, below.

(67) hage   súre   néna   bak'k'í   ʔoyk'-iisi
      this.M   trousers:NOM   2SG:ABS   slap-CNV   hold-3.
                                                             MSG.PF
      'These trousers are too tight for you'

With the so-called asymmetrical type on the other hand, the main verb is selected from a closed set, whereas the converb is freely generated. Although formally it is clear that the converb is a dependent verb form with asymmetrical (as well as with symmetrical) verbal compounds, the main verb appears to modify the meaning of the preceding converb, more specifically the Aktionsart, in the case of asymmetrical compounds. These main verbs may also occur as an independent main predication. (For a full list of asymmetrical verbs in Wolaitta, see Amha & Dimmendaal 2006b.)

(68) hargánc-íya   ʔaáʔʔ-á   wóʔʔ-aasu
      patient-F:NOM   pass-CNV   descend-3FSG:PERF
      'The patient (F) turned over'

(69) márz-iya   ʔúy-ídí   haík'k'-i   ʔagg-iisi
      poison-ACC   drink-CNV   die-CNV   give up-3SG:PERF
      'Having taken the poison, he died instantly'

(70) siy-í   ʔak'-ibeenna
      hear-CONV   spend.the.night-3M:PERF:NEG:DECL
      'He did not hear receptively'

It is also common in Wolaitta to form lexical compounds with a verb 'say,' as in the following example:

(71) bay-í   g-iisi
      disappear-CNV   say-3M:PERF
      'He suddenly disappeared'

Wolaitta uses 'say' in combination with intransitive verbs, whereas transitive verbs are combined with a verb 'do':

(72) fúttu   g-   'to come, to appear unexpectedly'
      k'órc'u   ʔoott-   'to swallow something quickly'

'Say' constructions are mentioned as an areal feature of Ethiopian languages by Ferguson (1970). But the same property is in fact widespread in the typological zone to which Wolaitta and other Afroasiatic as well as Nilo-Saharan languages belong, as pointed out above. The prosodic clue for the composite structure of such constructions does not necessarily involve tonal reduction. In the Nilo-Saharan language Nyimang, a language with three register tones, the verb root 'say' alternates for vowel harmony, depending on whether the preceding verb root or ideophonic adjective contains [−ATR] or [+ATR] vowels, showing that 'say' is phonologically bound:

(73)   ɗùnā̄ŋ-šèè
       bow-say
       bend'
       'bow, bend'

(74)   jèrjèr-šɛ́ɛ̄
       IDEO-say
       'scatter'

Interestingly, verbal compounding is not a prominent property of all languages belonging to this typological zone in northeastern Africa, in spite of the fact that they commonly appear to have converb plus main verb constructions. In Haro, which also belongs to the Ometo group within Omotic, only compounds with 'say' appear to be common. As argued above, the verbs from the so-called asymmetrical set in Wolaitta affect the Aktionsart (or "derivational aspect") of verbs. In Haro, these symbolic functions are expressed through other strategies, e.g. the use of manner adverbs. This latter language also has a more extensive system of tense–aspect as well as modality marking than Wolaitta does. The presence of these properties would seem to make the use of asymmetrical compounding in Haro superfluous.

Verbal compounding is also common in Nilo-Saharan languages with converbs; see Ch. and M. le Coeur (1956) on the Saharan language Teda, or Armbruster (1960) on Dongolese Nubian, or Tucker and Bryan (1966: 344), as well as Bender (1996: 34–5, et passim) on Kunama. Bender (1996: 36) also makes reference to compound verbs in Kunama, which differ from converb plus main verbs in that the former "act like a single verb, i.e. they take person/number and T[ense]M[ood]A[spect] affixes like single verbs. Converbs . . . are subordinate verbs marked for TMA . . . "

Verbal compounding also appears to be attested in Ijoid languages. Jenewari (1977: 535) discusses so-called "auxiliary verbs" in Kalaḅarị which seem to affect the Aktionsart expressed by the preceding verb. For example, the verb 'complete, finish,' which is a derived form consisting of a root *fá-* plus a causative marker *-mā*, may be combined with verbs in order to express totality:

(75)   o   si   fámāmrị
       he   be.bad   finish.GEN
       'He is becoming totally bad'

(76)   ọ   mangị   lámām̄
       he   run   reach.FAC
       'He ran very well'

From the existing data on Ijo it is not clear to what extent transitivity, more specifically the presence of coreferential objects, plays a role, since all examples appear to be with intransitive verbs.

Kilian-Hatz (2006) discusses verbal compounds in Khoe involving motion verbs as the first component. Unlike other types of serial verbs forming a complex predicate, verbal compounds are necessarily contiguous in Central Khoisan languages like Khoe:

(77) cɛ́ɛ-ɛ-xùú
take-I-leave
'take away' (xuu 'leave')

(78) yáa-a- ‖õã
climb-I-go.down
'climb down' (high tone on oa)

(79) mũũ-a-ã
see-I-know
'understand, realize, recognize (high tone on nasal vowels)

(The epenthetic vowel, harmonizing with the preceding root vowel, is a transitivity marker.)

Another domain where lexicalization appears to have taken place in Khoe (to such an extent that the verbs from the closed list may be considered derivational suffixes, according to Kilian-Hatz 2006) is with two verbs affecting Aktionsart ('leave' and 'remain') and valency ('distribute to'):

(80) xuu 'leave' -xu 'do completely, be done already'
ei 'remain' -ei 'firmly, tightly, well'

We thus observe in language after language that grammaticalized ways of expressing meaning may emerge from the semantic interaction between adjacent verbs if coreferential subjects (or agents) are involved, and if no other constituent (e.g. an object) intervenes. These latter conditions presumably set the switch for semantic interaction between the main verb and the adjacent dependent verb. The emergence of verbal compounding accordingly would seem to follow from so-called self-organizing principles. Verbal compounding in languages of northeastern Africa as well as southern Asia shows that such systems may emerge independently of each other. Accordingly, one may observe the emergence of parallel structures between languages without either genetic inheritance or areal diffusion being necessarily involved. This process, where the organization of a system spontaneously increases without this increase being controlled by an external system (e.g. the environment) is known as "self-organization" in the natural sciences. One may consequently observe the emergence and development of verbal compounding as new, complex structures taking place in and through the system itself, i.e. from internal or self-organizing principles; the linguistic parallel to the external or environmental factor would be areal contact with other languages. This is not to say that constructions require adjacency in order to build a complex predicate, since morphological coindexing or a fixed order may accomplish the same. But in the absence of such properties, adjacency is the more likely trigger for semantic interaction. The semantic range covered by such verbal compounds will virtually never be identical even between closely related languages, as we saw for Wolaitta and Haro above. Whether such specialized uses emerge and become conventionalized or grammaticalized would seem to depend on the frequency with which such collocations are used. This in turn would seem to be related to the question to what extent other construction types (e.g. manner adverbs, tense–aspect markers) may render the same meaning. Clearly, then, interaction with other grammatical subsystems determines the productivity of verbal compounding and the lexicalization of such structures.

9.6   Extending the typology or accepting the limits of typological research?

In a somewhat destructive spirit, I have dissolved the concept of verb-final languages as a type, not out of intention, but because this seems to be the only logical conclusion to be drawn from descriptions of so-called verb-final languages in Africa which have become available after the seminal contribution by Heine (1976).

First, I observed that there is an important difference typologically between languages in their degree of rigidity with respect to constituent order. I observed a similar problem with respect to so-called type B languages, some of which indeed follow a strict SVO/SAUXOV order, whereas in other languages the preverbal position may be occupied by any constituent. Similarly, so-called verb-initial languages differ with respect to rigidity of constituent order. In Nilotic languages like Nandi, which allows for postverbal scrambling, any syntactic constituent may occur immediately after the verb, the actual order being governed by pragmatic principles. But the position immediately after the verb is used for focused elements (Creider & Creider 1983). In the Nilotic language Turkana, on the other hand, the syntactic order is far more rigid and focus marking is less strict than in Nandi, i.e. not fixed with respect to one position within the sentence (Dimmendaal 1983b).

Of course, the same kind of variation in terms of constituent order can be observed between languages which have been claimed to be basically SVO languages. Compare the following examples from the Bantu language Rundi, which is usually characterized as an SVO language. But, as shown by Ndayiragije (1999), there are various alternatives possible:

(81) ábâna   ba-á-ra-nyôye   amatá
      2:children   2-PAST-AFF-drink:PERF   milk
      'Children drank milk'

(82) amatá   y-á-nyôye   abâna
      milk   S-PAST-drink:PERF   2:children
      'Children (not parents) drank milk'

(83) pro_{exp}   ha-á-nyoye   amatá   abâna
                   16-PAST-drink:PERF   milk   children
      'Children (not parents) drank milk'

For the same reason, i.e. because syntactic order may be governed entirely by information structure, it may be impossible to determine a basic constituent order, or it may be claimed that OVS is the basic order, as for a number of Western Nilotic languages (Andersen 1988; Reh 1996; Miller & Gilley 2001). The important descriptive task to be addressed when analyzing such languages is the question to what extent syntax adapts to discourse structure or vice versa, and the question which (morphosyntactic and/or constituent order) strategies these languages use in order to accomplish such interactions.

Second, when studying parts of speech from a crosslinguistic perspective, we again observe rather dramatic differences. Whereas the categorical distinction between noun and verb appears to be fundamental to all of the languages and language groups discussed here (though not necessarily to other African languages), it is also clear that the status of these categories in a specific language is determined by the constructions in which they may occur. The structural behavior of a verb in a verb-final Omotic language is not the same as in a verb-final Ijoid or Central Khoisan language, as argued above, and these differences are far from trivial. They relate to inflectional properties of verbs and their syntactic behavior; the central status of case marking (as a dependent-marking strategy) in Omotic for the expression of semantic relations, for example, also has its impact upon the behavior of finite verbs. Alternatively, the conceptual and etymological link between nouns and adpositions, or instead, between verbs and adpositions, may have consequences for the structural behavior of these respective categories synchronically (Bernd Heine, p.c.).

Third, at the clausal level we are in need of more subtle representations than the traditional, and somewhat outdated, coordination–subordination distinction, regardless of the type to which a particular language may belong. This latter position has, of course, been argued for extensively by Van Valin and LaPolla (1997).

On the basis of the dynamic (intragenetic and intergenetic) comparison, I arrive at the following conclusions: where typological similarities can be observed between Africa's verb-final languages, these are due not to some presumed universal typological principle, but rather to genetic inheritance on one hand and to areal diffusion on the other. The typological link between Nilo-Saharan languages in the eastern Sahel region and Afroasiatic languages of Ethiopia is probably explained best along these lines. In addition, what we perceive of as a language type or a Gestalt appears to be due to so-called self-organizing principles of languages; the interaction between different sub-systems (adjacency and subsequent semantic interaction between constituents; absence of alternative strategies in a language) may indeed result in typologically similar phenomena. This applies to verbal compounding, for example, which may emerge independently without one having to assume genetic inheritance or areal contact.

Even if we accept the old descriptivist attitude that every language is unique in its structure, this does not imply that one's approach to language description and analysis is necessarily naïve. Knowledge about crosslinguistic variation is indeed an important heuristic device in describing and analyzing hitherto undescribed or poorly described languages. And there are still many such languages on the African continent waiting to be investigated in more detail along these lines.

The success of future investigations in language typology would seem to depend on the question to what extent we succeed in showing how linguistic subsystems in a specific language interact. Obviously, such an understanding is accomplished best through in-depth comparative studies of languages which are closely related genetically, in tandem with intergenetic comparisons. It is only through such a dynamicization of subtypologies that one may arrive at an ultimate understanding of the portrait of a language as well as of important similarities or differences in the organizational structure of languages.

Notes

1 INTRODUCTION

1 In a more technical format, this tool for identifying instances of contact-induced transfer has been described in the following way: "If there is a linguistic property x shared by two languages M and R, and these languages are immediate neighbors and/or are known to have been in contact with each other for an extended period of time, and x is also found in languages genetically related to M but not in languages genetically related to R, then we hypothesize that this is an instance of contact-induced transfer, more specifically, that x has been transferred from M to R" (Heine & Kuteva 2005: 1.4.6).

2 Since the Hadza language of Tanzania has basic VSO order, one might say that all three word-order types are found within the Khoisan phylum. However, Hadza's genetic position is controversial; as we will see in chapter 6, there are good reasons to treat it as a genetic isolate.

3 We are ignoring here the fact that verb-final negation is also found in the fourth phylum, Khoisan: the Central Khoisan language Khwe places its negation marker *bé* at the end of the clause. The reason for ignoring Khoisan is that it does not appear to be genetically or areally related to the Niger-Nile belt of verb-final negation.

4 There is a partial exception: the Central Khoisan language ‖Ani is reported to lack subject agreement on the verb but to commonly exhibit object agreement (Voßen 1985).

2 IS AFRICA A LINGUISTIC AREA?

1 We are grateful to Felix Ameka, Joachim Crass, Gerrit Dimmendaal, Ludwig Gerhardt, Tania Kuteva, Martine Vanhove, Derek Nurse, Marie-Claude Vandame, and Erhard Voeltz for valuable comments and information on the subject matter of this chapter. Our gratitude is also due to the roughly fifty colleagues who have provided us with valuable data on a wider range of African languages.

2 In a number of works discussing linguistic areas, Joseph (1983) is cited as the primary reference work, or at least as one of the primary works on the Balkan sprachbund. However, while this work constitutes the most detailed study on the sprachbund, it deals essentially only with one linguistic property making up this area.

3 For a critical review, see Tosco (2000b).

4 Cf. also the following statement according to which areal linguistics "deals with the results of the diffusion of structural features across linguistic boundaries" (Campbell et al. 1986: 530).

5 "This term 'linguistic area' may be defined as meaning an area which includes languages belonging to more than one family but showing traits in common which are found not to belong to the other members of (at least) one of the families" (Emeneau 1956: 16, n. 28).

6 It is possible that the presence of gender systems in the Eastern Nilotic languages (Maa, Teso-Turkana, Lotuxo, Bari) is the result of language contact with Cushitic languages, but the evidence on this issue is far from conclusive.

7 According to Mike Cahill (p.c.), "perhaps 20 languages of Papua New Guinea have labial-velar stops, including Kate, Dedua, Kube, Ono, Fulumu, Amele, as well as Yeletnye, which uniquely not only has /kp, gb/, but also phonemic post-alveolar /tp, db/ as well." Furthermore, he adds that Santa Ana of the Solomon Islands has /gb/.

8 Greenberg (1983:16) says, however, that this is not always so: "The most conspicuous exception is the Grasslands languages where the form *bep* or the like is found in many languages with the meaning 'meat' while the *nama* root survives as 'animal.' "It would seem that this fact does not invalidate the hypothesis of a directionality 'meat' > 'animal'; rather, it might suggest that – for whatever reasons – an earlier meaning 'meat' received a new form of expression.

9 This is to express our gratitude to all our colleagues who have contributed to the survey.

10 "In these maps the demarcation lines, called isopleths, mark off areas with languages displaying the same number or *plethora* of features, but not necessarily the same features" (van der Auwera 1998: 260).

3 AFRICA AS A PHONOLOGICAL AREA

We would like to thank a number of colleagues for their generous help in responding to queries and contributing language data, in particular Derek Nurse, Gerrit Dimmendaal and Mohamed Elmedlaoui, as well as Zygmunt Frajzyngier, Tom Güldemann, and Larry Hyman for reading and sending comments on the final draft version. We give special thanks to Raphaël Kaboré and the Bibliothèque Africaine of the Université de Paris 3, whose resources greatly aided us in compiling data on lesser-known languages.

1 The term "Sudanic languages" is used here and below as a convenient shorthand for "languages spoken in the Sudanic belt," and does not refer to any presumed genetic grouping. *Sudan* as a geographical term enjoys a long tradition, predating later linguistic adaptations. The term *Sudanic* in this historical sense is not to be confused with *Sudanese*, referring to the land and people of the Republic of the Sudan, nor with *Central Sudanic* and *East Sudanic*, designating genetic subunits of the Nilo-Saharan language family.

2 We identify languages in terms of the traditional Greenberg-derived classification for convenience, though not all its proposals are accepted by all scholars. In particular, many specialists prefer to treat the "Khoisan" languages as a grouping of as many as five unrelated families.

3 The full database draws on the (mostly non-Bantu) African phoneme systems collected in UPSID (UCLA Phonological Segment Inventory Database, Maddieson & Precoda 1989), the Bantu phoneme systems collected in Nurse and Philippson (2003), and a variety of other published sources. All non-African languages are drawn from UPSID. We regret that space limitations preclude our citing sources for all language data mentioned in this survey. Standard sources have been used whenever they were available to us, and the best reliable sources were used otherwise.

4 Shona, a Bantu language spoken in Zimbabwe.

5 Amele, a language of Papua New Guinea, and Iai, a Malayo-Polynesian language spoken on Ouvéa Island in New Caledonia.

6 Alphanumeric codes such as S10 refer to Guthrie's system of Bantu language classification, as updated and amplified by Maho (2003). We follow the current preference for referring to Bantu languages without their prefixes, e.g. Ganda rather than Luganda, Swahili rather than Kiswahili. In citing languages here and below we use the following conventions:"X/Y" indicates alternate names for the same language, "X-Y" indicates closely related languages or members of a dialect chain (exception: Diola-Fogny is a single member of the Diola cluster), and dialect names precede language names: Dendi Songay, Owere Igbo.

7 An exception to this generalization occurs in the variety of Ma'di described by Blackings and Fabb (2003), where the prenasalized stop [m(ŋ)gb] begins with labial closure; the existence of a velar closure is reported as uncertain.

8 It is mainly in languages which lack voiced stops that we find /kp/ to the exclusion of /gb/. Excluding such languages, Cahill (1999) finds that languages having [gb] alone outnumber those with [kp] alone by a significant margin. One consideration that might explain such a trend is the occasional tendency for labial-velar stops to have implosive realizations, as in the case of the Nigerian languages Idoma, Isoko, and Igbo (Ladefoged 1968; Ladefoged & Maddieson 1996); implosives are of course normally voiced.

9 Our sources include Richardson (1975), Guthrie (1967–71), Tylleskär (1986–7), Mutaka and Ebobissé (1996–7), Grégoire (2003), and Mangulu (2003), among others.

10 Guthrie (1967–71: vol. 3, 303–4, vol. 4, 16), Nurse and Hinnebusch (1993: 171–3).

11 Our sources are Schachter and Fromkin (1968), Le Saout (1973), Bentinck (1975), Singler (1979), Capo (1981, 1991), Bole-Richard (1983a,b, 1984), Ihionu (1984), Creissels (1994), and Clements and Osu (2005), to which we have added languages drawn from inventories in Bole-Richard (1985), Maddieson (1984), and Cohn (1993a,b). The zone in question is a sprachbund, characterized by a complex of other features such as a strong tendency toward monosyllabism, "horizontal" (that is, front–back) root harmony, three or more distinctive tone levels, and certain "lax" question markers. We discuss the latter two features in sections 3.3.2 and 3.3.3.

12 Our transcriptions are phonemic; stops are voiced intervocalically.

13 Languages like Yoruba or Kikuyu, with one high vowel series, two mid vowel series and constraints requiring consecutive mid vowels to be of the same height, have also been described as having ATR harmony. In such systems, unlike those with two series of high vowels, [−ATR] is usually the active value, at least in African languages (Casali 2003). See below for illustrations from Kikuyu.

14 Phonemic voiceless implosives have also been reported, though without phonetic data, in the Gur language Bwamu (Manessy 1960), the Atlantic language Seereer-Siin (McLaughlin 1992–4), the Edoid language Isoko (Elugbe 1989a), and the Kwa language Ebrié (Bole-Richard 1983b).

15 The implosive /ɓ/ was described for Zulu at the beginning of the last century by Meinhof and Doke, but appears to have shifted to a voiced explosive /b/ since then in at least some contemporary varieties of Zulu (see references and discussion in Clements 2003).

16 Many other "effluxes" are best analyzed not as features at all, but as independent segments, forming clusters with clicks just as they do with non-clicks. See Traill (1993) and Güldemann (1999) for further discussion.

17 Plain voiced stops are recent innovations in Zulu; see Clements (2003).

18 In some P-less Bantu languages, *p* survives as the second member of a prenasalized cluster *mp*. However, this cluster does not qualify as a P-sound in the sense assumed here.

19 Areas in which Proto-Bantu **p* is usually retained (though sometimes only as a reflex of **mp*) are the northwest (zones A–C), the center-east (zones G, M, N, P, as well as Shona S10), the southwest (zone R), and the southeast (the Nguni group S40). For fuller discussion of eastern Bantu languages see Nurse (1999: 22, 40) and especially Nurse (1979: 393–452), where the facts are set out in detail.

20 Maddieson (2003b) speculates that P-lessness in African languages might be related, among other factors, to "the impact of cosmetic modification of the lips, once practiced among a number of the peoples of the Sahel, the northern rain forest, and the Ethiopian highlands." This hypothesis would not explain why the great majority of African languages lacking /p/ have other labial stops such as /b/, /kp/, and /m/.

21 Note that **p* is reconstructed for Afroasiatic as a whole (Hodge 1994).

4 AFRICA AS A MORPHOSYNTATIC AREA

1 More recently, it has been found that at least one Central Sudanic language, Lendu, has remnants of a former case system. Lendu distinguishes, by way of tonal inflection, between peripheral roles expressing direction as against location, as argued by Kutsch Lojenga (2004).

2 There is no consensus on the terms to be used in the description of case contracts of this type. A case form distinct from the quotation or designation form of nouns and used for both S and A is most of the time called "nominative case" (which departs from the traditional use of this term, since the extra-syntactic use in a function of pure designation is essential in the traditional notion *nominative*), but some authors prefer "ergative case" or "subject case." For a case form identical to the extra-syntactic designation form of nouns and used for objects, but not for subjects, the terms "absolutive case," "nominative case," and "accusative case" can be encountered: the first two terms are equally well motivated from an etymological point of view, but their choice departs from current practice, according to which nominative applies to the designation form of nouns in systems in which this form is also used for A and S, whereas absolutive applies to the designation form of nouns in systems in which this form is also used for O and S; the choice of *accusative* is consistent with the syntactic distribution of case forms in systems of the "marked-nominative" type, but does not

account for the use of the same form in the extra-syntactic function of pure designation and in the syntactic role of object.

3 This is at least the way Amharic and Tigre are most often described. However, as indicated in Frajzyngier and Shay (2003), the accusative case marking in Amharic is used even with nouns overtly marked as indefinite; such a marking is required when the object, for whatever reason, does not occur in preverbal position.

4 On the basis of this condition, bound or "weak" pronouns attached to words that do not necessarily have a particular syntactic relation with the noun phrase they substitute for, are not *pronominal markers* (for example, weak pronouns behaving as second position clitics).

5 In the first person plural, a distinction between 'we including you' and 'we excluding you' sporadically occurs in several groups of African languages. As a rule, additional distinctions in the third person are encountered in languages with a gender system in which identical distinctions are involved in the agreement between nouns and modifiers. With gender systems of the Niger-Congo type (traditionally referred to as "noun class systems"), gender distinctions are found in the third person only. In gender systems based on the sex distinction, gender distinctions may be found in the second person too. In Khwe (or Kxoe, Central Khoisan) there is a gender distinction based on sex, expressed by the so-called PGNs (person–gender–number markers), which even in first person dual and plural show gender distinctions. Note that the correlation between "nominal gender" and "pronominal gender" is not absolute: one may encounter languages either with gender-like distinctions in pronouns and/or pronominal markers only, or with gender distinctions manifested at the level of the relation between the noun and its modifiers that do not extend to pronouns and/or pronominal markers. For example, Wolof has noun class distinctions at the noun phrase level, but these distinctions do not manifest themselves in the variations of free pronouns or of subject and object markers. Conversely, Zande is devoid of any gender distinction at the noun phrase level, but in the third person, the free pronouns and subject markers have different forms for masculine human, feminine human, and non-human animate and inanimate.

6 This historical slant appears to be common crosslinguistically. Compare, for example, Dixon (2002) for similar observations on the historical development of pronouns in cyclic fashion in Australian languages.

7 At least in some languages, there is a relation between the choice of this element and morphological variations of the verb. Historically, at least some of these "predicative markers" may originate from auxiliary verbs, but synchronically, most of them show no evidence of a verbal status. It is also worth noting that sometimes (but not always) their phonological interaction with the context suggests analyzing them as bound to the last word of the subject noun phrase, or to the first word of the verb phrase; but this is not directly relevant to the present discussion.

8 Contrary to what occurs in Hausa with other morphemes analyzed as prepositions, however, phrases introduced by *wa/mV-* can be stranded, i.e. *Audu* may be fronted under conditions of focus or relativization, leaving the bare marker *wa* in situ (Newman 2000: 276–87).

9 Note however that Maale has also double object constructions with some verbs, for example with a verb meaning 'feed (somebody with something)' (Amha 2001: 207).

10 Morphological variations of the verb coding valency changes are dealt with in section 4.3.5.

11 The prototypical function of passives is backgrounding of agent, as argued by Shibatani (1985). The prototypical function of antipassives appears to be backgrounding of patients or goals (semantic roles typically associated with objects crosslinguistically), which tend to have a generic, non-referential meaning in such constructions. From an aspectual point of view, antipassive verbs typically describe a non-punctual activity without a perceptible onset or conclusion (Cooreman 1994). Consequently, the focus of attention in such constructions is directed towards the occurrence of a specific verbal event viewed as incomplete.

12 In most descriptions of Southern Bantu languages, such forms are misleadingly called "participles".

13 Decausative verb forms assign a patient-like role to their subject, but, in contrast with passive forms, do not imply the existence of an agent triggering and/or controlling the process. From a general linguistics point of view, this is a particular variety of middle voice, but in most descriptions of African languages in which such a voice occurs, it is either not clearly distinguished from a true passive voice, or referred to by terms (such as "neuter") that do not identify it as a voice at all. The following example from Tswana illustrates the distinction between passive and decausative:

(i)   a. mààí   á-tʰùb-íl-w-è   (kí   ŋwàná)
         6:egg   S3:6-break-ANT-PSV-ANT   by   1:child
         'The eggs were broken (by the child)'

      b. mààí   á-tʰúb-èχ-ílè
         6:egg   S3:6-break-DECAUS-ANT
         'The eggs broke'

14 Optional applicatives promote obliques to the status of direct object, whereas obligatory applicatives make it possible to mention participants that cannot be mentioned at all in the construction of the same verb in the non-applicative form. In the languages of the world, optional applicatives seem to be more common than obligatory applicatives, but this is not the case for African languages and, in particular, for Niger-Congo languages, in which obligatory applicatives are much more common than optional applicatives.

15 See the survey of verb serialization in a crosslinguistic perspective presented in Aikhenvald and Dixon (2006).

16 Several authors working in a typological perspective explicitly restrict the use of the term *serial verb* to such constructions, but descriptive grammars of many languages make a much wider use of this term. Very often, descriptive grammars mention the existence of "serial constructions" without discussing their syntactic nature, and without even providing data that would make it possible to know whether they are dealing with serial constructions in a narrow sense or in a wider sense.

17 However, among Chadic languages, the gender distinction is not general, and it appears that it is not associated with geographical distribution, as present today, or with genetic subgrouping. Two languages, Gidar and Mina, belonging to the same branch, Central Chadic, and spoken in adjacent areas, differ in that Gidar has a two-gender system in nouns and pronouns and Mina has no gender distinction in either nouns or pronouns.

18 The two-gender distinction of Eastern Nilotic has been claimed to be areally induced by contact with East Cushitic.

19 Historically, the origin of nominal class affixes is not established, but some specialists consider the hypothesis that they originated as derivational morphemes to be the most plausible.

20 Some languages provide evidence that definite articles may originate from possessives too.

21 When the bound nature of these morphemes is recognized, they are often classified as "clitics"; but they are often simply designated as adpositions in descriptive grammars that do not recognize them explicitly as bound forms.

22 Descriptions of Berber languages make a different use of the term *construct form* or *construct state*: in descriptions of Berber languages, this term does not apply to a form of head nouns triggered by the presence of certain modifiers, but to a case form determined by the syntactic role of the noun phrase, irrespective of its internal structure.

23 This does not apply to languages that have optional applicatives, or to languages that have applicative forms of the verb that depart from the most typical ones in requiring the term they license to be constructed as the complement of an adposition.

24 The idea is that, in such languages, noun phrases corresponding to the object of finite verb forms precede nominalized verb forms, since they are treated as their genitival modifier; consequently, with complex verb forms consisting of an auxiliary verb and a nominalized form of the main verb, the noun phrase corresponding to the object of a finite verb form precedes the nominalized form of the main verb. Subsequently, the decategorialization of the auxiliary verb leads to the reanalysis of such constructions as involving a finite verb form preceded by a noun phrase in object function. There are, however, other plausible scenarios, for example the syntacticization of a pragmatically driven constituent order of the type observed in Basque or in Hungarian, in which the main constraint is that discursively salient constituents (in other words, topicalized and focalized constituents) must precede the verb, whereas the default position of constituents devoid of discursive salience is after the verb.

25 Note, however, that, in some Chadic VS languages, the SV order is available only for subject topicalization or subject focus.

26 Constructions that combine a focus particle and a movement of the focalized constituent to the left edge of the sentence may be suspected to result from the grammaticalization of cleft-type constructions, and they are not always easy to distinguish from them.

27 According to Andersen (2002), Dinka has a very uncommon distinction between two locative cases: allative and inessive-ablative (crosslinguistically, allative-inessive vs. ablative is much more common).

28 The possible existence of the same phenomenon in some Chadic languages has already been mentioned (see section 4.2.3.2).

5 THE MACRO-SUDAN BELT: TOWARDS IDENTIFYING A LINGUISTIC AREA IN NORTHERN SUB-SAHARAN AFRICA

I am grateful to Knut Finstermeier (Max Planck Institute for Evolutionary Anthropology Leipzig, media department) for drawing the maps. Thanks go also to Nick Clements, Stefan Elders, Orin Gensler, Jeffrey Good, Bonny Sands, and the editors of this book for valuable comments on drafts of this chapter.

1 Francophone specialists call this family "Sara-Bongo-Bagirmi."

2 A genealogical unit "Narrow Niger-Congo," which is on the higher-order level of a stock, rather than a family, will be assumed here, though, and includes Kru, Gur, Kwa, Benue-Congo, and Adamawa-Ubangi. This is quite comparable to a concept first developed by Stewart 1976 and Bennett and Sterk (1977) called there "Volta-Congo" and "Central Niger-Congo," respectively. While nothing in the discussion hinges on this choice, I will stick to Greenberg's usage of "Niger-Kordofanian," "Niger-Congo," etc. The main reason is that it is unclear to me which of the post-Greenbergian classificatory and terminological proposals will eventually prevail.

3 They are Bendor-Samuel (1989) for families assigned to Niger-Kordofanian (called there Niger-Congo), Schadeberg (1981) for Kordofanian, Nurse and Philippson (2003) for Bantu, Hayward (1990) for Omotic, Dimmendaal and Last (1998) for Surmic, and Serzisko (1989) for Kuliak.

4 I am indebted to Azeb Amha for information on Omotic, to Tucker Childs on Atlantic, to Christopher Culy on Dogon, to Ursula Drolc on the Cangin group of Atlantic, to Stefan Elders on Adamawa and Gur, to Raimund Kastenholz on West Mande, to Ulrich Kleinewillinghöfer on Adamawa and Central Gur, to Maarten Kossmann on Berber, to Maarten Mous on Cushitic and Kru, to Kay Williamson on Ijoid, and to Ekkehard Wolff on Chadic.

5 There is a fourth fragmentation zone indicated in the maps. It is located further south in north-central Tanzania, centering in the basin of the Lakes Eyasi and Manyara. This is dealt with by Kießling, Mous, and Nurse (this volume chapter 6) under the term "Tanzanian Rift Valley area."

6 There is an isolated case in Bantu of labial-velars originating in labialized velars, namely in Mijikenda spoken in Kenya and Tanzania. I do not assume this to be related historically to the area at issue.

7 Dryer assumes for some relevant western Bantu languages a geographical link to Central Africa, which is not obvious to me. Güldemann (1996, 1999) presents evidence that negation reinforcement is a recurrent phenomenon in Bantu. In the scenario at issue here (see Güldemann 1996: 256–8), the inherited negative verb prefixes of Bantu are supplemented by postverbal negative intensifiers, which can be independent or bound to the verb. If the functional load is transferred from the older prefix to the innovated gram and the prefix becomes lost subsequently, the resulting order can be V-O-NEG.

8 Semantically, this special pronoun is first person inclusive dual. This is why it tends to be associated with dual number (cf. Creissels 2000: 247). This is inadequate, however, because these languages usually do not display a third number category in the more diagnostic noun morphology; the isolated "dual" pronoun rather reflects a special conceptual organization of personal pronouns. See Corbett (2000: 166–9) for a brief introduction and Cysouw (2003) for a typological survey of this property.

9 Güldemann (2004) reconstructs a minimal-augmented system for the common ancestor language of the Khoe family and Kwadi in southern Africa; its modern descendents no longer display it.

10 According to Köhler (1975: 156, 162), the term was originally coined by Carl Meinhof.

11 These two and a number of other northern languages subsumed under the Sudan group (*inter alia* entire families like Saharan, Maban, and Furan) probably

participate in another linguistic macro-area and thus should be kept apart (see Heine 1975: 41–3, who proposed to call this the "Chad–Ethiopia area," and Güldemann 2005 for more discussion).

12 However, Westermann (1927) focused on a more coherent subset of his Sudan group and compared this to Bantu. In so doing, he laid the foundation for Narrow Niger-Congo as a genealogically defined group and for its historical-comparative reconstruction.

13 His article had been presented orally in 1948. It is not surprising, then, that Westermann (1952) had no difficulty with agreeing on these and other points with Greenberg's (1949/50/54) classification.

14 I intentionally do not use the form "Sudanic," because in light of the research tradition in the past this evokes precisely the notion I want to exclude from the concept entertained here. That is, the form with the adjective ending -ic is associated in general with genealogically intended entities and in particular has been and/or still is used for language families proposed in the relevant area (cf. "Macrosudanic," "Central Sudanic," "Eastern Sudanic"). In particular, Greenberg's term "Macrosudanic" (as in the quote in section 5.3.2) is related to the present "Macro-Sudan belt" in terms of research history and the terminology associated with it; it is obviously inspired by the earlier terminology that ultimately goes back to Westermann's use of "Sudan" with respect to African language classification. However, as a concept, Greenberg's "Macrosudanic" denotes something different, namely the core of what was to become in his 1963 classification the "Nilo-Saharan" *language family*. Hence, my "Macro-Sudan" and Greenberg's "Macrosudanic" must not be confounded.

15 I do not repeat here the numerous objections to Greenberg's methodology and treatment of empirical data in genealogical language classification. Suffice it to say that all his major proposals, i.e. on Africa (1963), the Pacific (1971), the Americas (1987), and Eurasia (2000–2), met with serious criticisms by the respective specialists. His African work remains a remarkable scholarly achievement, because it managed to do away with some classification criteria that had previously hampered the success of several promising hypotheses. However, the fact that his all-encompassing scheme of just four super-groupings in Africa has been widely accepted, instead of being rejected or even ignored, is to a large extent due to the state of research African linguistics happened to be in at the time of his proposals; it cannot be taken as proof for the viability of his approach (cf. Thomason 1994; see Güldemann forthcoming b for Greenberg's failure to make a plausible case in Africa for a Khoisan unit).

16 Even the present breakdown into reference/sample groups cannot always ensure that one is confronted with a proven genealogical entity. For example, Atlantic is not viewed by (all) specialists as a coherent lineage and reference could have been made to the North and South groups separately (cf. Wilson 1989; Childs 2001); Adamawa-Ubangi could just as well be split up into its two primary components or yet more entities (cf. Kleinewillinghöfer n.d.); the Senufo group might have been taken out of Gur, etc.

17 The enormous genealogical diversity of the area has been recognized previously. For example, Dalby (1977) has coined the term "Sub-Saharan Fragmentation Belt" for "a zone of extreme linguistic complexity extending from Senegal to

Ethiopia and Northern Tanzania." While his area is far more inclusive, its core is clearly what I call here the "Macro-Sudan belt."

18 To be sure, concrete historical processes can sometimes be observed in attested migrations along this trajectory, for example, the west–east expansion of the Ful along the Sahel. The basic idea entertained here is compatible with a concept developed by Diamond (1999: chapter 7) regarding human history in general, in particular with respect to the considerable differences between continental areas (thanks to J. Good for pointing this out to me). Diamond concludes that the historical dynamics on a continent is decisively determined by the orientation of its geographical axis in the sense that it "affected the rate of spread of crops and livestock, and possibly also of writing, wheels, and other inventions" (1999: 176), i.e. spreads are facilitated in an east–west trajectory, but inhibited in a north–south direction (see also Diamond 1999: 399–400 for the relevance of this general factor in Africa). This principle can equally be held responsible for the formation of larger subcontinental areas like that proposed here.

6 THE TANZANIAN RIFT VALLEY AREA

1 In contrast to certain Eastern Cushitic-speaking people, e.g. the Oromo, there are no signs of age-group organization among the West Rift Cushitic people.

2 Sandawe is claimed to be a free-word-order language (Dalgish 1979, but see Eaton 2002 for a detailed discussion).

3 In spite of the total lack of tonological reconstructions at the Southern Nilotic level, recent investigations into Datooga tonology (Kießling 2001) make it clear that tone distinguishes major syntactic categories such as case forms of nouns and tense–aspect oppositions in verbs. Creider and Creider (1989a, 1989b, 2001) report four phonemic tones for closely related Nandi, and comparison to Eastern and Western Nilotic makes it clear that a more complex system of at least two level tones plus two contour tones is part of the Nilotic heritage.

4 Other candidate features are: preverbal fusion and inflection of conjunctions; morphological opposition of a common marker of first- and second-person arguments vs. a marker for third-person arguments; the tonal marking of genitival constructions on the preceding possessed noun (anti-genitive).

5 This is realized by an increasing affinity of neuter gender to the semantic category of plural, accomplished by reanalysis of neuters with singular reference as masculine, and reanalysis of masculine and feminine plural markers as neuter. The second development is most drastic, as becomes clear in a simple calculation. Nouns in West Rift fall into three agreement classes: masculine, feminine, and neuter. For derived nouns, the agreement class is not a lexical property, but a property of the derivational suffix, e.g. the plural marker. Calculating the ratio of plural markers that assign neuter class against those that assign non-neuter classes (masculine or feminine), PWR has a ratio of 1.6 (i.e. 61% vs. 39%), PIRQ slightly less 1.4 (i.e. 58% vs. 41%), whereas in PSWR the ratio rises sharply to 3.5 (i.e. 78% vs. 22%) (Kießling 2002a: 147–8). This indicates a process of "degrammaticalization" of the neuter agreement class in PSWR, i.e. a process of reanalysis semantically motivated by the plural feature.

6 This is accomplished by the elaboration of paired singulatives, masculine and feminine, for animal referents (Kießling 2002a: 162, 241). Thus, PWR and PIRQ

frequently come up with number oppositions where a plural or collective form of a noun pairs with a single singulative which is either masculine or feminine, but denoting both male and female single referents. In this PWR and PIRQ could be seen to tolerate a mismatch of the grammatical category of gender/agreement class and the semantic category of sex. Burunge and, to a lesser extent, also Alagwa tend to remove this mismatch by innovating a singulative counterpart which pairs with the original singulative and narrows down its former broad denotational range, a masculine singulative for male referents contrasting with a feminine singulative for a female referent. Thus PWR *tsawadu* 'waterbucks' pairs with the single masculine singulative *tsawadimo* ~ *tsawadumo* which denotes a single waterbuck of either sex. Burunge, however, innovated *cawadiya* 'female waterbuck,' narrowing down the meaning of *cawadimo* to 'male waterbuck,' which had the effect of making the categories of grammatical class/gender and sex reference match.

7 There is one case where the transfer is more likely to be in the other direction: Sandawe *bútɬi* 'red' transferred into ^{ALBU}*butɬi* (ideo) 'blood-red.'

8 For discussion of the inclusion of Dahalo in Eastern Cushitic see Tosco (1992). Mous (1996, 2003) provides ample evidence that the original Cushitic language that the Ma'a people once spoke was Eastern rather than Rift Southern Cushitic.

9 However, the existence of laterals in these languages in itself cannot be accounted for by transfer from Cushitic; both Hadza and Sandawe have a richer inventory of laterals when compared to West Rift and display an opposition between the ejective and non-ejective lateral affricate.

10 In addition, subject, aspect, mood, negation, and yes/no questions are marked by suffixes on the verb.

11 There are parts of the scenario which need more explanation and there are some gaps in our knowledge: (i) Sukuma/Nyamwezi have four past and three future categories, Nyaturu three pasts and one future. Yet the Nyaturu preverbal complex has a different system, two futures and two pasts, mostly consisting of unidentifiable morphemes. Where has this parallel system come from? (ii) While the preverbal structure as a whole has come from West Rift, there are some parallels between Nyaturu, Nilyamba, and Kimbu, parallels whose origin does not seem to lie in the Sukuma/Nyamwezi connection.

12 This morphophoneme indicates the alternation of the phonemes *g* and *q*.

13 From a general semanto-syntactic point of view, the term "verbal plurality" can be understood to relate to three different phenomena:

   (a) subject and/or object agreement or concord where a set of inflectional markers encode the number feature along with person and – if relevant – class features of the core participants of the predication;

   (b) plural stem formation where a derivational or suppletive alternation of verbal stems encodes the number of one of the core participants of the predication; this marking strategy comes on top of the agreement;

   (c) pluractional marking where a derivational or suppletive alternation of verbal stems indicates semantic plurality, relating to some kind of iteration of the action or event encoded in the verb, independent of the plurality of core participants of the predication.

The rigid distinction of both terms, "pluractional" vs. "plural stem," has been set up by Newman (1980: 13) in discussing the phenomenon in Chadic languages to keep apart the "derived plural verb stems denoting semantic plurality" (Newman 1990: 53) from "the inflected plural form of a verb required by a conjugational concord system (where agreement is either with the subject in a nominative system or with the patient in an ergative system)" which is called "plural stem." "Although pluractional verbs sometimes relate to plurality of a nominal argument in the sentence (e.g. subject, direct object, even indirect object), the essential semantic characterisation of such verbs is almost always plurality or multiplicity of the verb's action" (Newman 1990: 53f.).

14 Proto-West Rift rather had abstract relational nouns, grammaticalized geomorphological nouns and postpositions for expressing spatial relations.

15 Carlin and Mous (1995) argue against this quadruped model as explanation of the use of 'belly' for 'in' and 'under' and suggest "outside/inside" as a model instead; Reh (1999) develops this alternative of "tactile outside" as a central concept but links it again to the animal model if the body-part noun 'back' is used.

16 Leaving aside the voiced pharyngeal in West Rift which is analyzed as a plosive.

17 The exceptions are head marking of goal (G4) and prepositions (G11). In both cases it is clear that external influence must have stimulated an internal innovation in Proto-West Rift, but it is hard to decide whether the instigators were Bantu or Datooga, since both bring the required feature. Subjunctive -ee (G7) and irrealis *laa* are possibly independent developments. The source of the seven-vowel system (P5) in Datooga is not certain. The SVO typological characteristics (G10, 11, 12) have two possible sources (East African Bantu, Pre-Datooga). The direction of influence is unclear for the features lateral fricative (P1), ejectives (P2), absence of voiced fricatives (P4).

7 ETHIOPIA

1 The data of these languages were collected between March 2002 and September 2004. Crass, who initiated the research on this topic, provided the data on Amharic, K'abeena, and Libido; Meyer the data on Gumär, Muher, Wolane, Zay, and Oromo. We want to thank all our informants, namely Abubakr Sherifo (Muher), Debela Goshu and Eyob Keno (Oromo), Mengistu Teklemariam (Amharic), Mubarek Mudesir (K'abeena), Temesgen Woldemedhin (Zay), Wondimu Aregga (Gumär), Worjamo Birru (Libido) and Zeynu Alemar (Wolane). We crosschecked the data on Amharic with Girma A. Demeke (Addis Ababa) during his stay in Mainz from October to November 2003. Girma provided us with some additional data on Amharic for which we are grateful to him.

2 This research has been supported by the German Research Foundation (Deutsche Forschungsgemeinschaft) within the Collaborative Research Centre 295 *Cultural and linguistic contacts: Processes of change in North Eastern Africa and West Asia* (Sonderforschungsbereich 295 *Kulturelle und sprachliche Kontakte: Prozesse des Wandels in historischen Spannungsfeldern Nordostafrikas/Westasiens*). We want to thank Gerrit Dimmendaal and Bernd Heine for defining their position concerning the areal status of some features. We are also indebted to Walter Bisang, Bernd Heine, and Yvonne Treis for comments on earlier versions of this chapter.

3 Ethio-Semitic languages differ considerably in regard to copula morphemes in present-tense nominal clauses (cf. Crass, Girma, Meyer & Wetter 2005). The usage

of various inflected copula morphemes (particles and pronouns) and uninflected particles is very common. Zay does not possess a present-tense copula; instead, the declarative sentence marker and the focus particles are used (cf. Meyer 2002). However, we treat both constructions as copula clauses.

8 THE MARKED-NOMINATIVE LANGUAGES OF EASTERN AFRICA

1 Note that there are different uses of the term nominative in the literature. I will use the nominative only when the relevant case marker covers S and A.
2 As Dixon points out, "if any case has zero realization it will be nominative" (Dixon 1994: 62).
3 Note, however, that Dimmendaal (1983: 132) says that the nominative (called absolute by him) is used.
4 A = aspect marker, V = verb elsewhere, here probably voice, even if not in Dimmendaal's abbreviations.
5 k- glossed as 't' stands for object pronoun marker.
6 For a complete list of all noun classes see Tosco (2001: 70, table 1).
7 "Subject case" is glossed "SUBJ" only when realized through lowering of the accent (high tone) of a basic form. It is not glossed when "latent," i.e. on all unaccented (not high-toned) nouns (see Tosco 2001: 95).
8 The abbreviations A and B refer to two verb classes which behave differently with regard to inflexion or derivation (see Tosco 2001: 112).
9 See the preceding note.
10 The only ergative languages so far found in Africa are Päri, Jur-Luwo, and Shilluk.
11 Kalenjin is an exception. On the map it appears only once, while in the genetic overview, four different dialects are listed.
12 Classification according to Fleming (1976).
13 Anywa is put into parentheses as it is not entirely clear whether Anywa has a case system (see Reh 1996). Traces of ergativity are definitely present with regard to constituent order and bound pronouns.

9 AFRICA'S VERB-FINAL LANGUAGES

The present chapter was written as part of a typology project on Participant marking in African languages, which was made possible on the basis of grant number HE 574/31–1 from the DFG (the German National Science Foundation). Special thanks are due to Azeb Amha, who provided extensive information on the structure of Omotic languages, and to Bernd Heine for comments on an earlier draft of this chapter. Data on Nyimang were gathered by the present author in the Sudan as part of the SFB research project 389 "ACACIA," also financed by the DFG; the financial support for this fieldwork is gratefully acknowledged here. I would also like to express special thanks to Al-Amin Abu-Manga and Leoma Gilley from the Institute of African and Asian Studies, University of Khartoum, for making this research possible. The help provided by the principal informant for Nyimang, Mahmoud Mousa Tawor, is also gratefully acknowledged here. I would also like to thank the principal informant for Tama, Mahmoud Išmail.

1 Apart from the language groups introduced above, a number of languages belonging to the Atlantic branch within Niger-Congo appear to have a verb-final syntax (Wilson 2007). However, because data on these Atlantic languages are rather limited and inconclusive, they are not further discussed here.

2 In his typological survey of verb-final south Asian languages, Masica (1976) suggested that Ethiopia may form an extension of the "Indo-Altaic" verb-final bond in this respect.

3 The Omo-Tana language Bayso is also apparently turning into a "more consistent" head-final language, also at the nominal level. Tosco (1994a) attributes this modification to areal influence from neighboring Highland East Cushitic languages.

4 The inverse pattern, a verb-initial syntax with postpositions, or more properly, postnominal modifiers, is attested in Surmic (Nilo-Saharan) languages in the southern Sudan. Here, the verb-initial pattern appears to be an innovation (Dimmendaal 1990c).

5 Treis (2000: 10) also points out that verb-final ordering is dominant in Khoe, with SVO, OVS, and VSO occurring as alternatives.

6 One additional property attested in these Nilo-Saharan and Afroasiatic languages involves the use of so-called converbs, which are further discussed below in section 4.

7 The verb systems of languages in this area are also similar typologically, involving the frequent use of light verbs ('do,' 'put,' etc.) preceded by a nominal, adjectival or adverbial complement, as in example (26) from Tama.

8 According to Erhard Voeltz, the Ijoid languages and Defaka may be more closely related to the Mande branch within Niger-Congo.

9 The masculine from appears to be cognate with the widespread Niger-Congo (and Nilo-Saharan) third-person pronoun (Dimmendaal 2001).

10 Kilian-Hatz (1999) treats the cognate *â* morpheme in Khoe as a bound marker. These differences possibly reflect differences between these related languages with respect to the morphosyntactic status of this marker.

11 For a fascinating study on an African language, more specifically a member of the Jukunoid group within Niger-Congo, Hone, where the categorial distinction between nouns and verbs is obliterated to some extent, the interested reader is referred to Storch (forthcoming).

References

Aboh, Enoch O., Katharina Hartmann & Malte Zimmermann (eds.) forthcoming. *Focus Strategies: Evidence from African Languages (Niger-Congo, Afro-Asiatic, West-Atlantic)*. Trends in Linguistics – Studies and Monographs. Berlin: Mouton de Gruyter.

Abu-Manga, Al-Amin, Leoma Gilley & Anne Storch (eds.) forthcoming. *Insights into Nilo-Saharan Language, History and Culture*. Nilo-Saharan, 23. Cologne: Rüdiger Köppe.

Aikhenvald, Alexandra Y. 1995. Split ergativity in Berber languages. *St. Petersburg Journal of African Studies* 4: 39–68.

1996. Areal diffusion in northwest Amazonia: the case of Tariana. *Anthropological Linguistics* 38: 72–116.

2002. *Language Contact in Amazonia*. New York: Oxford University Press.

Aikhenvald, Alexandra Y. & Robert M. W. Dixon 2001a. Introduction. In Aikhenvald & Dixon (eds.), pp. 1–26.

(eds.) 2001b. *Areal Diffusion and Genetic Inheritance: Problems in Comparative Linguistics*. Oxford: Oxford University Press.

(eds.) 2006. *Serial Verb Constructions: A Cross-linguistic Typology*. Oxford: Oxford University Press.

Akinlabi, Akinbiyi (ed.) forthcoming. *Proceedings of the Fourth WOCAL (Rutgers)*. Cologne: Rüdiger Köppe Verlag.

Amberber, Mengistu 2000. Valency-changing and valency-encoding devices in Amharic. In Dixon & Aikhenvald (eds.), pp. 312–32.

Ameka, Felix 2003. Prepositions and postpositions in Ewe (Gbe). In Sauzet & Zribi-Hertz (eds.), pp. 41–67.

Ameka, Felix K., Nicholas Evans & Alan Dench (eds.) 2006. *Catching Language: The Standing Challenge of Grammar Writing*. Trends in Linguistics. Berlin: Mouton de Gruyter.

Amha, Azeb 1996. Tone-accent and prosodic domains in Wolaitta. *Studies in African Linguistics* 25.2: 111–38.

2001. *The Maale Language*. Leiden: Center for Non-Western Studies.

Amha, Azeb & Gerrit J. Dimmendaal 2005. Depictive secondary predicates and adverbials in Nilotic and Omotic: a typological comparison. In Himmelmann & Schultze-Berndt (eds.), pp. 299–321.

2006a. Converbs in an African perspective. In Ameka et al. (eds.), pp. 393–400, also in Dimmendaal (ed.) forthcoming a.

2006b. Verbal compounding in Wolaitta. In Aikhenvald & Dixon (eds.), pp. 319–37.

Andersen, Henning (ed.) 2003. *Language Contacts in Prehistory: Studies in Stratigraphy*. Amsterdam: John Benjamins.

Andersen, Torben 1984. Aspect and word order in Moru. *Journal of African Languages and Linguistics* 6: 19–34.

1988. Ergativity in Päri, a Nilotic OVS language. *Lingua* 75: 289–324.

1991. Subject and topic in Dinka. *Studies in Language* 15.2: 265–94.

1999. Anti-logophoricity and indirect mode in Mabaan. *Studies in Language* 23.3: 499–530.

2002. Case inflection and nominal head marking in Dinka. *Journal of African Languages and Linguistics* 23: 11–30.

Ansaldo, Umberto 2004. Contact, typology and the speaker: the essentials of language. *Language Sciences* 26: 485–94.

Appleyard, David 1984. The internal classification of the Agaw languages: a comparative and historical phonology. In Bynon (ed.), pp. 33–67.

1989. The relative verb in focus constructions: an Ethiopian areal feature. *Journal of Semitic Studies* 34.2: 291–305.

2001. The verb 'to say' as a verb "recycling device" in Ethiopian languages. In Zaborski (ed.), pp. 1–11.

Archangeli, Diana & Douglas Pulleyblank 1994. *Grounded Phonology*. Cambridge, Mass.: MIT Press.

Armbruster, Charles Hubert 1960. *Dongolese Nubian*. Cambridge: Cambridge University Press.

Armstrong, Lilias E. 1967. *The Phonetic and Tonal Structure of Kikuyu*. London: Dawsons of Pall Mall.

Asher, Ron E. (ed.) 1994. *The Encyclopedia of Language and Linguistics*. Oxford: Pergamon Press.

Auwera, Johan van der 1998. Revisiting the Balkan and Meso-American linguistic areas. *Language Sciences* 20.3: 259–70.

Bakker, Peter & Maarten Mous (eds.) 1994. *Mixed Languages: 15 Case Studies in Language Intertwining*. Amsterdam: Institute for Functional Research into Language and Language Use (IFOTT).

Banti, Giorgio 1988. "Adjectives" in East Cushitic. In Bechhaus-Gerst & Serzisko (eds.), pp. 205–59.

Bascom, William R. & Melville J. Herskovits (eds.) 1959. *Continuity and Change in African Cultures*. Chicago: University of Chicago Press.

Batibo, Herman 1985. *Le kesukuma*. Paris: Editions Recherche sur les Civilisations.

Baumann, Hermann (ed.) 1975. *Die Völker Afrikas und ihre traditionellen Kulturen, Teil 1: Allgemeiner Teil und südliches Afrika*. Studien zur Kulturkunde, 34. Wiesbaden: Franz Steiner.

Baumann, Hermann, Richard Thurnwald & Diedrich Westermann (eds.) 1940. *Völkerkunde von Afrika*. Essen: Essener Verlagsanstalt.

Baxter, William H. 1992. *Handbook of Old Chinese Phonology*. Berlin: Mouton de Gruyter.

Bearth, Thomas 1999. The contribution of African linguistics towards a general theory of focus: update and critical review. *Journal of African Languages and Linguistics* 20: 121–56.

Bearth, Thomas & Hugo Zemp 1967. The phonology of Dan (Santa). *Journal of African Linguistics* 6.1: 9–29.

Bearth, Thomas, Wilhelm J. G. Möhlig, Beat Sottas & Edgar Suter (eds.) 1994. *Perspektiven afrikanistischer Forschung.* Cologne: Rüdiger Köppe.

Beaudoin-Lietz, Christa, Derek Nurse & Sarah Rose forthcoming. Pronominal object marking in Bantu. In Akinlabi (ed.).

Bechert, J., G. Bernini & C. Buridant (eds.) 1990. *Toward a Typology of European Languages.* Berlin and New York: Mouton de Gruyter.

Bechhaus-Gerst, Marianne 1996. *Sprachwandel durch Sprachkontakt am Beispiel des Nubischen im Niltal: Möglichkeiten und Grenzen einer diachronen Soziolinguistik.* Language Contact in Africa, 3. Cologne: Rüdiger Köppe.

Bechhaus-Gerst, Marianne & Fritz Serzisko (eds.) 1988. *Cushitic – Omotic. Papers from the International Symposium on Cushitic and Omotic Languages, Cologne, January 6–9, 1986.* Hamburg: Helmut Buske.

Beck, David 2000. Grammatical convergence and the genesis of diversity in the Northwest Coast *Sprachbund. Anthropological Linguistics* 42.2: 147–213.

Bender, M. Lionel (ed.) 1976. *The Non-Semitic Languages of Ethiopia.* East Lansing: African Studies Center, Michigan State University.

(ed.) 1983. *Nilo-Saharan Language Studies.* Michigan: African Studies Center.

(ed.) 1989. *Topics in Nilo-Saharan Linguistics.* Nilo-Saharan Linguistic Analyses and Documentation, 3. Hamburg: Buske.

1996. *Kunama.* Munich: Lincom Europe.

(ed.) 1997. *The Nilo-Saharan Languages: A Comparative Essay*, second edition. Munich: Lincom Europe.

1999. *The Omotic Languages: Comparative Morphology and Lexicon.* Munich: Lincom Europe.

2000. Nilo-Saharan. In Heine & Nurse (eds.), pp. 43–73.

2003. Northeast Africa: a case study in genetic and areal linguistics. *Annual Publication in African Linguistics* 1: 21–45.

n.d. Ethiopian Language Area. 1–4. Typescript.

Bender, M. Lionel, J. Donald Bowen, Robert L. Cooper & Charles A. Ferguson (eds.) 1976. *Language in Ethiopia.* London: Oxford University Press.

Bender, M. Lionel, Gábor Takàcs & David L. Appleyard (eds.) 2003. *Selected Comparative-Historical Afrasian Linguistic Studies: In Memory of Igor M. Diakonoff.* Munich: Lincom.

Bendor-Samuel, John (ed.) 1989. *The Niger-Congo Languages.* Lanham, MD: University Press of America.

Bennett, Patrick R. & Jan P. Sterk 1977. South Central Niger-Congo: a reclassification. *Studies in African Linguistics* 8: 241–73.

Benson, T. Godfrey 1964. *Kikuyu-English Dictionary.* Oxford: Clarendon Press.

Bentinck, Julie 1975. Le niaboua, langue sans consonnes nasales? *Annales de l' Université d'Abidjan*, série H, Linguistique 8: 5–14.

Berger, Paul 1935/36. Fieldnotes on Datooga. Unpublished manuscripts.

1943. Überlieferungen der Kindiga mit einem Anhang: ein Jagdbericht. *Afrika* 2: 97–122.

Berger, Paul & Roland Kießling 1998. *Iraqw Texts.* Cologne: Rüdiger Köppe.

Beukema, Frits & Sjef Barbiers (eds.) 2002. *Modality.* Amsterdam, Philadelphia: Benjamins.

326   References

Bisang, Walter 1996. Areal typology and grammaticalization: processes of grammaticalization based on nouns and verbs in east and mainland south east Asian languages. *Studies in Language* 20.3: 519–97.

2001. Finite vs. non finite languages. In Haspelmath et al. (eds.), pp. 1400–13.

Bisang, Walter & Peter Rinderknecht (eds.) 1991. *Von Europa bis Ozeanien – von der Antonymie zum Relativsatz.* Arbeiten des Seminars für Allgemeine Sprachwissenschaft der Universität Zürich, 11. Zurich: University of Zurich.

Bisang, Walter, Thomas Bierschenk, Detlev Kreikenbom & Ursula Verhoeven (eds.) 2004. *Kultur, Sprache, Kontakt.* Kulturelle und sprachliche Kontakte, 1. Würzburg: Ergon.

Blackings, Mairi & Nigel Fabb 2003. *A Grammar of Ma'di.* Berlin: Mouton de Gruyter.

Blake, Barry J. 1987. *Australian Aboriginal Grammar.* Beckenham: Croon Helm.

Blanchon, Jean 1998. Semantic/pragmatic conditions on the tonology of the Kongo noun-phrase: a diachronic hypothesis. In Hyman & Kisseberth (eds.), pp. 1–32.

1999. "Tone cases" in Bantu group B 40. In Blanchon & Creissels (eds.), pp. 37–82.

Blanchon, J. & D. Creissels (eds.) 1999. *Issues in Bantu Tonology.* Cologne: Rüdiger Köppe Verlag.

Blench, Roger M. 1995. Is Niger-Congo simply a branch of Nilo-Saharan? In Nicolaï & Rottland (eds.), pp. 83–130.

1996. Lateral fricatives in Africa and worldwide: explorations in the prehistory of phonemes. Paper read at the Colloquium of African Languages and Linguistics.

forthcoming. Further evidence for Niger-Saharan and the problem of pan-African roots. In Cyffer (ed.) forthcoming b.

Bokamba, Eyamba G. 1976. Question Formation in some Bantu Languages. Ph.D. dissertation, Indiana University.

Bole-Richard, Rémy 1983a. *Systématique phonologique et grammatical d'un parler éwé: le gen-mina du sud-togo et sud-bénin.* Paris: Editions l'Harmattan.

1983b. Ebrié. In Hérault (ed.), pp. 307–57.

1984. Le ngwla, langue sans consonne nasale. *Cahiers Ivoiriens de Recherche Linguistique* 16: 23–35.

1985. Hypothèse sur la genèse de la nasalité en Niger-Congo. *Journal of West African Languages* 15.2: 3–28.

Bolinger, Dwight 1978. Intonation across languages. In Greenberg et al. (eds.), pp. 471–524.

Boretzky, Norbert 1983. *Kreolsprachen, Substrate und Sprachwandel.* Wiesbaden: Otto Harrassowitz.

(ed.) 1996. *Areale, Kontakte, Dialekte, Sprachen und ihre Dynamik in mehrsprachigen Situationen.* Bochum-Essener Beiträge zur Sprachwandelforschung, 24. Bochum: Brockmeyer.

Bourdin, Philippe 2005. The marking of directional deixis in Somali: how typological idiosyncratic is it? In Voeltz (ed.), pp. 13–41.

Boyd, Raymond 1978. A propos des ressemblances lexicales entre languages Niger-Congo et Nilo-Sahariennes. *Etudes comparatives: Oubanguien et Niger-Congo–Nilo-Saharien*, pp. 43–94. Bibliothèque de la SELAF, 65. Paris: SELAF.

Brenzinger, Matthias (ed.) 1992. *Language Death: Factual and Theoretical Explorations with Special Reference to East Africa.* Berlin: Mouton De Gruyter.

Brenzinger, Matthias & Christa König (eds.) forthcoming. *Khoisan Languages and Linguistics: The Riezlern Symposium 2003*. Quellen zur Khoisan-Forschung, 17. Cologne: Rüdiger Köppe.

Bright, William (ed.) 1992. *International Encyclopedia of Linguistics*, vol. 1. New York and Oxford: Oxford University Press.

Brugnatelli, Vermondo (ed.) 1994. *Sem, Cam, Iafet: Atti della 7ª Giornata di Studi Camito-Semitici e Indoeuropei*. Milan: Centro Studi Camito-Semitici.

Burns, Rebecca 1987. The verbal suffix /E/ in Kru. Paper read at the 17th Conference on African Linguistics, Bloomington, Indiana.

Buth, Randall 1981. Ergative word order – Luwo is OVS. *Occasional Papers in the Study of Sudanese Languages* 1: 74–90.

Bynon, James (ed.) 1984. *Current Progress in Afro-Asiatic Linguistics. Papers of the Third International Hamito-Semitic Congress*. Amsterdam and Philadelphia: Benjamins.

Cahill, Michael 1999. Aspects of the phonology of labial-velar stops. *Studies in African Languages* 28.2: 155–84.

Campbell, Lyle 1987. Syntactic change in Pipil. *International Journal of American Linguistics* 53.3: 253–80.

   1994. Grammar: typological and areal issues. In Asher (ed.), pp. 1471–4.

Campbell, Lyle, Terrence Kaufman & Thomas C. Smith-Stark 1986. Meso-America as a linguistic area. *Language* 62.3: 530–70.

Campbell, Lyle & Marianne Mithun (eds.) 1979. *The Languages of Native America: Historical and Comparative Assessment*. Austin: University of Texas Press.

Capo, Hounkpati B. C. 1981. Nasality in Gbe: a synchronic interpretation. *Studies in African Linguistics* 12: 1–43.

   1991. *A Comparative Phonology of Gbe*. Berlin: Foris Publications; Garome: Labo Gbe (Int).

Carlin, Eithne B. & Maarten Mous 1995. The "back" in Iraqw: extensions of meaning in space. *Dutch Studies Published by NELL* 1.2: 121–33.

Casali, Roderic F. 2003. [ATR] value asymmetries and underlying vowel inventory structure in Niger-Congo and Nilo-Saharan. *Linguistic Typology* 7.3: 307–82.

Childs, G. Tucker 1995. *A Grammar of Kisi: A Southern Atlantic Language*. Mouton Grammar Library, 16. Berlin, New York: Mouton de Gruyter.

   2001. What's so Atlantic about Atlantic? Paper presented at the Colloquium on African Languages and Linguistics, University of Leiden.

   2004. It's everywhere! The S-AUX-O-V-OTHER syntagm in Atlantic. Typescript, Portland State University.

Claudi, Ulrike 1993. *Die Stellung von Verb und Objekt in Niger-Kongo-Sprachen: Ein Beitrag zur Rekonstruktion historischer Syntax*. Afrikanistische Monographien, 1. Cologne: Institut für Afrikanistik, Universität zu Köln.

Clements, G. N. 1975. The logophoric pronoun in Ewe: its role in discourse. *Journal of West African Languages* 10: 141–77.

   1991. Vowel height assimilation in Bantu languages. In Hubbard (ed.), pp. 25–64.

   2003. Feature economy in sound systems. *Phonology* 20.3: 287–333.

Clements, G. N. & John Goldsmith (eds.) 1984. *Autosegmental Studies in Bantu Tone*. Berlin: Mouton de Gruyter.

Clements, G. N. & Sylvester Osu 2002. Explosives, implosives, and nonexplosives: the linguistic function of air pressure differences in stops. In Gussenhoven & Warner (eds.), pp. 299–350.

2005. Nasal harmony in Ikwere, a language with no phonemic nasal consonants. *Journal of African Languages and Linguistics* 26.2, 165–200.

Cloarec-Heiss, France 1995. Emprunts ou substrat? Analyse des convergences entre le groupe banda et les langues du soudan central. In Nicolaï & Rottland (eds.), pp. 321–55.

Cohn, Abigail C. 1993a. The status of nasalized continuants. In Huffman & Krakow (eds.), pp. 329–67.

1993b. A survey of the phonology of the feature [±nasal]. *Working Papers of the Cornell Phonetics Laboratory* 8: 141–203.

Comrie, Bernard 1976. *Aspect: An Introduction to the Study of Verbal Aspect and Related Problems.* Cambridge Textbooks in Linguistics. Cambridge: Cambridge University Press.

1983. Switch-reference in Huichol: a typological study. In Haiman & Munro (eds.), pp. 17–37.

(ed.) 1987. *The World's Major Languages.* New York: Oxford University Press.

Connell, Bruce 1994. The structure of labial-velar stops. *Journal of Phonetics* 22: 441–76.

Connell, Bruce & Amalia Arvaniti (eds.) 1995. *Phonology and Phonetic Evidence: Papers in Laboratory Phonology 4.* Cambridge: Cambridge University Press.

Cooreman, Ann M. 1994. A functional typology of antipassives. In Fox & Hopper (eds.), pp. 49–88.

Corbett, Greville G. 1991. *Gender.* Cambridge: Cambridge University Press.

2000. *Number.* Cambridge: Cambridge University Press.

Cordell, Oliver 1941. *Gogo Grammar.* London: Christian Missionary Society.

Cox, Monica 1998. Description Grammaticale du ncam (bassar), langue gurma du Togo et de Ghana. Thèse doctorale, Ecole Pratique des Hautes Etudes, Paris.

Crass, Joachim 2001. The position of K'abeena within Highland East Cushitic. *Afrikanistische Arbeitspapiere* 67: 5–60.

2002. Ejectives and pharyngeal fricatives: two features of the Ethiopian language area. In Yimam et al. (eds.), pp. 1679–91.

Crass, Joachim & Walter Bisang 2004. Einige Bemerkungen zum äthiopischen Sprachbund und ihre Relevanz für die Areallinguistik. In Bisang et al. (eds.), pp. 169–99.

Crass, Joachim, Girma A. Demeke, Ronny Meyer & Andreas Wetter 2005. *Copula and Focus Constructions in Selected Ethiopian Languages.* University of Leipzig Papers on Africa: Languages and Literatures, 25. Leipzig: Institut für Afrikanistik.

Crass, Joachim & Angelika Jakobi 2000. Der Kube-Dialekt des Berio (Zaghawa) im Tschad – eine erste Skizze. *Afrika und Übersee* 83: 3–46.

Creider, Chet A. & Jane T. Creider. 1983. Topic-comment relations in a verb-initial language. *Journal of African Languages and Linguistics* 5: 1–15.

1989a. *A Dictionary of the Nandi Language.* Cologne: Rüdiger Köppe.

1989b. *A Grammar of Nandi.* Hamburg: Helmut Buske.

Creissels, Denis 1979. Les constructions dites possessives, étude de linguistique générale et de typologie linguistique. Thèse de doctorat d'état. University of Paris (Paris 4).

1994. *Aperçu sur les structures phonologiques des langues négro-africaines*, second edition. Grenoble: Editions littéraires et linguistiques de l'Université de Grenoble (ELLUG).

1996. Conjunctive and disjunctive verb forms in Setswana. *South African Journal of African Languages* 16.4: 109–15.

2000. Typology. In Heine & Nurse (eds.), pp. 231–58.

2001. Setswana ideophones as uninflected predicative lexemes. In Voeltz & Kilian-Hatz (eds.), pp. 75–85.

2002. Valence verbale et voix en tswana. *Bulletin de la Société de Linguistique de Paris*, 97. 1: 371–426.

2003a. L'emploi comme auxiliaire du verbe tswana *re* 'dire'. In Stéphane (ed.), pp. 162–85.

2003b. Adjectifs et adverbes dans les langues subsahariennes. In Sauzet & Zribi-Hertz (eds.), pp. 17–38.

2005. A typology of subject and object markers in African languages. In Voeltz (ed.), pp. 43–70.

forthcoming. Indirect objects and datives in African languages.

Croft, William 2001. *Radical Construction Grammar*. Oxford: Oxford University Press.

Culy, Christopher 1994. Aspects of logophoric marking. *Linguistics* 32.6: 1055–94.

Culy, Christopher & Koungarma Kodio 1995. Dogon pronominal systems: their nature and evolution. *Studies in African Linguistics* 23.3: 315–44.

Cyffer, Norbert 2000. Areale Merkmale im TAM-System und in der syntax der saharanischen Sprachen. In Voßen et al. (eds.), pp. 159–82.

(ed.) forthcoming a. *Negation in West Africa*. Typological Studies in Language. Amsterdam: Benjamins.

(ed.) forthcoming b. *Proceedings of the Seventh Nilo-Saharan Conference in Vienna, 2–6 September, 1998*.

Cysouw, Michael 2003. *The Paradigmatic Structure of Person Marking*. Oxford: Oxford University Press.

Dahl, Östen & Maria Koptjevskaja-Tamm (eds.) 2001. *Circum-Baltic Languages: Typology and Contact,* vol. 2: Grammar and Typology. Studies in Language and Companion Series, 55. Amsterdam, Philadelphia: Benjamins.

Dalby, David 1977. *Language Map of Africa and the Adjacent Islands*. London: International African Institute.

Dalgish, Gerard M. 1979. Subject identification strategies and free word order: the case of Sandawe. *Studies in African Linguistics* 10.3: 273–310.

Déchaine, Rose-Marie & Victor Manfredi (eds.) 1997. *Object Positions in Benue-Kwa: Papers from a Workshop at Leiden University, June 1994*. Holland Institute of Generative Linguistics Publications, 4. The Hague: Holland Academic Graphics.

Demolin, Didier 1995. The phonetics and phonology of glottalized consonants in Lendu. In Connell & Arvaniti (eds.), pp. 368–85.

Dempwolff, Otto 1915. Beiträge zur Kenntnis der Sprachen in Deutsch-Ostafrika, 5: Ilamba. *Zeitschrift für Kolonialsprachen* 5: 227–53.

Diamond, Jared M. 1999 [1997]. *Guns, Germs, and Steel: The Fates of Human Societies*. New York and London: W. W. Norton.

Dickens, Patrick 1987. Qhalaxarzi consonants. In Traill & Young (eds.), pp. 297–305.

Dihoff, Ivan R. (ed.) 1983. *Current Approaches to African Linguistics*, vol. 1. Dordrecht: Foris Publications.

Dil, Anwar S. (ed.) 1980. *Language and Linguistic Area: Essays by Murray B. Emeneau*. Stanford: Stanford University Press.

Dimmendaal, Gerrit J. 1981. On verbal derivation in Nilotic: the case of Turkana. In Schadeberg & Bender (eds.), pp. 59–73.

    1983a. Turkana as a verb-initial language. *Journal of African Languages and Linguistics* 5.1: 17–44.

    1983b. *The Turkana Language*. Publications in African Languages and Linguistics, 2. Dordrecht, Cinnaminson: Foris Publications.

    1995a. The emergence of tense marking in the Nilotic-Bantu borderland as an instance of areal adaptation. In Zima (ed.), pp. 29–43.

    1995b. The role of bilingualism in Nilotic sound change. In Dominicy & Demolin (eds.), pp. 85–109.

    1998a. Review: Haspelmath, Martin & Ekkehard König (eds). *Converbs in Cross Linguistic Perspective: Structure and Meaning of Adverbial Verb Forms – Adverbial Participles, Gerunds*. Empirical Approaches to Language Typology, 13. Berlin and New York: Mouton de Gruyter. *Studies in Language* 22.2: 515–20.

    1998b. Surmic languages and cultures: an introduction. In Dimmendaal & Last (eds.), pp. 3–33.

    1998c. A syntactic typology of Surmic from an areal and historical-comparative point of view. In Dimmendaal & Last (eds.), pp. 35–81.

    2000. Number marking and noun categorization in Nilo-Saharan languages. *Anthropological Linguistics* 42.2: 214–61.

    2001a. Areal diffusion versus genetic inheritance: an African perspective. In Aikhenvald & Dixon (eds.), pp. 359–92.

    2001b. Language shift and morphological convergence in the Nilotic area. In Nurse (ed.), pp. 83–124.

    2001c. Logophoric marking and represented speech in African languages as evidential hedging strategies. *Australian Journal of Linguistics* 21.1: 131–57.

    2003. Locatives as core constituents. In Shay & Seibert (eds.), pp. 91–109.

    2005. Head marking, dependent marking and constituent order in the Nilotic area. In Voeltz (ed.), pp. 71–92.

    (ed.) forthcoming a. *Coding Participant Marking: Construction Types in Twelve African Languages*. Amsterdam and Philadelphia: John Benjamins.

    forthcoming b. Turkana datives in a Nilotic perspective. In Voeltz (ed.) forthcoming.

    forthcoming c. Tama. In Dimmendaal (ed.) forthcoming a.

Dimmendaal, Gerrit J. & Marco Last (eds.) 1998. *Surmic Languages and Cultures*. Nilo-Saharan Linguistic Analyses and Documentation, 13. Cologne: Rüdiger Köppe.

Dixon, R. M. W. 1994. *Ergativity*. Cambridge: Cambridge University Press.

    2002. *Australian Languages: Their Nature and Development*. Cambridge: Cambridge University Press.

Dixon, R. M. W. & Alexandra Y. Aikhenvald (eds.) 2000. *Changing Valency: Case Studies in Transitivity*. Cambridge: Cambridge University Press.

Dobashi, Yoshihito 2001. Agreement and word order in Sandawe. *Cornell Working Papers in Linguistics* 18: 57–74.

Doke, Clement M. 1931. *A Comparative Study in Shona Phonetics*. Johannesburg: University of the Witwatersrand Press.

Dolgopolksy, Aron B. 1987. South Cushitic lateral consonants as compared to Semitic and East Cushitic. In Jungraithmayr & Müller (eds.), pp. 195–214.

Dominicy, M. & Didier Demolin (eds.) 1995. *Sound Change*. Amsterdam: John Benjamins.

Drolc, Ursula 2004. A diachronic analysis of Ndut vowel harmony. *Studies in African Linguistics* 33.1: 35–63.

Dryer, Matthew S. 1992. The Greenbergian word order correlations. *Language* 68.1: 81–138.

 forthcoming. Verb-object-negative order in Central Africa. In Cyffer (ed.) forthcoming a.

Durie, Mark & Malcolm D. Ross (eds.) 1996. *The Comparative Method Reviewed: Regularity and Irregularity in Language Change*. New York: Oxford University Press.

Eaton, Helen 2002. The grammar of focus in Sandawe. Ph.D. dissertation, University of Reading.

Ebert, Karen H. 1979. *Sprache und Tradition der Kera (Tschad), vol 3: Grammatik*. Marburger Studien zur Afrika- und Asienkunde, A15. Berlin: Dietrich Reimer.

 1991. Vom Verbum dicendi zur Konjunktion: Ein Kapitel universaler Grammatikentwicklung. In Bisang & Rinderknecht (eds.), pp. 77–95.

Edenmyr, Niklas 2003. Conducting a study of Hadza grammar: aims and methodology, and beyond. Paper read at the Languages of Tanzania workshop, University of Dar-es-Salaam, 25–26 January 2003.

Ehret, Christopher 1974. *Ethiopians and East Africans: The Problem of Contacts*. Nairobi: East African Publishing House.

 1995. *Reconstructing Proto-Afroasiatic (Proto-Afrasian): Vowels, Tone, Consonants and Vocabulary*. University of California Publications in Linguistics, 126. Berkeley: University of California Press.

 1998. *An African Classical Age: Eastern and Southern Africa in World History, 1000 BC to AD 400*. Charlottesville: University Press of Virginia.

Eklo, Alubue Amavi 1987. Le kposso de Tomegbe (Togo). Ph.D. dissertation, University of Grenoble.

Elderkin, Edward D. 1989. The significance and the origin of the use of pitch in Sandawe. Ph.D. dissertation, University of York.

 1991. Clause structure and tone in Sandawe. *York Papers in Linguistics* 15: 93–115.

Elders, Stefan 2003. A survey of distributed predicative syntax in Adamawa-Ubangi. Typescript, University of Bayreuth.

Elugbe, Ben O. 1980. Reconstructing the lenis feature in Proto-Edoid. *Journal of African Languages and Linguistics* 2: 39–67.

 1989a. *Comparative Edoid: Phonology and Lexicon*. Delta Series, 6. Port Harcourt: University of Port Harcourt Press.

 1989b. Edoid. In Bendor-Samuel (ed.), pp. 291–304.

Emenanjo, E. 'Nolue & Ozo-mekuri Ndimele (eds.) 1995. *Issues in African Languages and Linguistics: Essays in Honour of Kay Williamson.* Aba: National Institute for Nigerian Languages.

Emeneau, Murray B. 1956. India as a linguistic area. *Language* 32.1: 2–16.

1980. Bilingualism and structural borrowing. In Dil (ed.), pp. 38–65.

Evans, Nicholas & David Wilkins 1998. *The Knowing Ear: An Australian Test of Universal Claims about the Semantic Structure of Sensory Verbs and their Extension into the Domain of Cognition.* Arbeitspapier 32, Neue Folge. Institut für Sprachwissenschaft, Universität zu Köln.

Ewan, William G. & R. Krones 1974. Measuring larynx movement using the thyroumbrometer. *Journal of Phonetics* 2: 327–35.

Faraclas, Nicholas G. 1989. Cross River. In Bendor-Samuel (ed.), pp. 377–99.

Ferguson, Charles A. 1970. The Ethiopian language area. *Journal of Ethiopian Studies* 8.2: 67–80.

1976. The Ethiopian language area. In Bender et al. (eds.), pp. 63–76.

Feuillet, Jack 2001. Aire linguistique balkanique. In Haspelmath et al. (eds.), pp. 1510–28.

Fiedler, Ines, Catherine Griefenow-Mewis & Brigitte Reineke (eds.) 1998. *Afrikanische Sprachen im Brennpunkt der Forschung: Linguistische Beiträge zum 12. Afrikanistentag, Berlin, 3.–6. Oktober 1996.* Cologne: Rüdiger Köppe.

Fishman, Joshua A., Andrée Tabouret-Keller, Michael Clyne, Bhadriraju Krishnamurti & Mohamed Abdulaziz (eds.) 1986. *The Fergusonian Impact: In Honour of Charles A. Ferguson on the Occasion of his 65th Birthday*, vol. 1. Berlin: Mouton de Gruyter.

Fleischman, Suzanne 1989. Temporal distance: a basic linguistic metaphor. *Studies in Language* 13: 1–50.

Fleming, Harold C. 1976. Omotic overview. In Bender (ed.), pp. 299–323.

1990. A grammatical sketch of Dime (Dim-Af) of the Lower Omo. In Hayward (ed.), pp. 494–583.

Fox, Barbara & Paul Hopper (eds.) 1994. *Voice: Form and Function.* Amsterdam and Philadelphia: John Benjamins.

Frajzyngier, Zygmunt 1977. The plural in Chadic. In Newman & Ma Newman (eds.), pp. 37–56.

1985. Logophoric systems in Chadic. *Journal of African Languages and Linguistics* 7.1: 23–37.

(ed.) 1989. *Current Progress in Chadic Linguistics.* Amsterdam: John Benjamins.

1993. *A Grammar of Mupun.* Berlin: Dietrich Reimer.

1996. *Grammaticalization of the Complex Sentence: A Case Study in Chadic.* Complementary Series to the Study in Language. Amsterdam and Philadelphia: Benjamins.

1997. Grammaticalization of number: from demonstratives to nominal and verbal plural. *Linguistic Typology* 1: 193–242.

2001. *A Grammar of Lele.* Stanford Monographs in African Linguistics. Stanford: CSLI.

2002. System interaction in the coding of modality. In Beukema & Barbiers (eds.), pp. 165–84.

Frajzyngier, Zygmunt & Traci S. Curl (eds.) 2000. *Reciprocals: Forms and Functions.* Typological Studies in Language, 41. Amsterdam and Philadelphia: Benjamins.

Frajzyngier, Zygmunt, Holly Krech & Armik Mirzayan 2002. Motivation for copula in equational clauses. *Linguistic Typology* 6.2: 155–98.

Frajzyngier, Zygmunt & Erin Shay 2002. *A Grammar of Hdi*. Berlin: Mouton de Gruyter.

2003. *Explaining Language Structure through Systems Interaction*. Amsterdam and Philadelphia: John Benjamins.

Fréchet, Anne-Lise 1989. Tons et downdrift: quelques aspects prosodiques du Gungbe de Porto-Novo (Bénin). Mémoire de DEA, Université de Paris 3.

Garvin, P. 1949. Standard Average European and Czech. *Studia Linguistica* 3: 65–85.

Gensler, Orin D. 1994. On reconstructing the syntagm S-Aux-O-V-Other to Proto-Niger-Congo. *Berkeley Linguistics Society (Special Session)* 20: 1–20.

1997. Grammaticalization, typology, and Niger-Congo word order: progress on a still-unsolved problem. *Journal of African Languages and Linguistics* 18.1: 57–93.

Gensler, Orin D. & Tom Güldemann 2003. S-Aux-O-V-Other in Africa: typological and areal perspective. Paper read at the Fourth World Congress of African Linguistics, Workshop "Distributed predicative syntax (S P O V X)," Rutgers University, June 21, 2003.

Gilbers, D. G., J. Nerbonne & J. Schaeken (eds.) 2000. *Languages in Contact*. Studies in Slavic and General Linguistics, 28. Amsterdam and Atlanta: Rodopi.

Gilley, Leoma G. 1992. *An Autosegmental Approach to Shilluk Phonology*. Dallas: Summer Institute of Linguistics and the University of Texas at Arlington.

Gilman, Charles 1986. African areal characteristics: sprachbund, not substrate? *Journal of Pidgin and Creole Languages* 1.1: 33–50.

Givón, Talmy 1988. The pragmatics of word-order: predictability, importance and attention. In Hammond et al. (eds.), pp. 243–84.

(ed.), 1994. *Voice and Inversion*. Amsterdam and Philadelphia: John Benjamins.

Goldsmith, John (ed.) 1995. *Handbook of Phonological Theory*. Cambridge, Mass.: Blackwell.

Gordon, Lynn 1986. *Maricopa Morphology and Syntax*. University of California Publications in Linguistics, 108. Berkeley: University of California Press.

Gordon, Raymond G. 2005. *Ethnologue: Languages of the World*, fifteenth edition. Dallas: SIL International.

Gowlett, Derek 2003. Zone S. In Nurse & Philippson (eds.), pp. 609–38.

Greenberg, Joseph H. 1949/50/54. Studies in African linguistic classification 1–8. *Southwestern Journal of Anthropology* 5.2: 79–100; 5.3: 190–8; 5.4: 309–17; 6.1: 47–63; 6.2: 143–60; 6.3: 223–37; 6.4: 388–98; 10.4: 405–15.

1959. Africa as a linguistic area. In Bascom and Herskovits (eds.), pp. 15–27.

1963. *The Languages of Africa*. Indiana University Research Center in Anthropology, Folklore and Linguistics, Publication 25. The Hague: Mouton.

1966. Some universals of grammar with particular reference to the order of meaningful elements. In Greenberg (ed.), pp. 73–113.

(ed.) 1966. *Universals of Language*. Cambridge, Mass.: MIT Press.

1969. Some methods of dynamic comparison in linguistics. In Puhvel (ed.), pp. 147–203.

1970. Some generalizations concerning glottalic consonants, especially implosives. *International Journal of American Linguistics* 36: 123–45.

1971. The Indo-Pacific hypothesis. In Sebeok (ed.), pp. 807–71.

1978. How does a language acquire gender markers? In Greenberg et al. (eds.), pp. 47–82.

1983. Some areal characteristics of African languages. In Dihoff (ed.), pp. 3–21.

1987. *Language in the Americas*. Stanford: Stanford University Press.

1988. The first person inclusive dual as an ambiguous category. *Studies in Language* 12.1: 1–18.

2000–2. *Indo-European and its Closest Relatives: The Eurasiatic Language Family*. Stanford: Stanford University Press.

Greenberg, Joseph H., Charles A. Ferguson & Edith A. Moravcsik (eds.) 1978. *Universals of Human Language*. Stanford: Stanford University Press.

Gregersen, Edgar A. 1972. Kongo-Saharan. *Journal of African Languages* 11.1: 69–89.

1977. *Language in Africa: An Introductory Survey*. New York, Paris and London: Gordon & Breach.

Grégoire, Claire 1988. An attempt to reconstruct labial consonants in Mande. *Belgian Journal of Linguistics* 3: 103–55.

2003. The Bantu languages of the forest. In Nurse & Philippson (eds.), pp. 349–70.

Griefenow-Mewis, Catherine & Tamene Bitima 1994. *Lehrbuch des Oromo*. Cologne: Rüdiger Köppe Verlag.

Griefenow-Mewis, Catherine & Rainer M. Voigt (eds.) 1996. *Cushitic and Omotic Languages: Proceedings of the Third International Symposium*. Cologne: Rüdiger Köppe.

Grimes, Barbara F. (ed.) 2000. *Ethnologue*, vol. 1: *Languages of the World*, Fourteenth edition. Dallas: SIL International.

Guéhoun, N. Augustin. 1993. Description systématique du dida de Lakota. Ph.D. dissertation, University of Grenoble.

Güldemann, Tom 1996. *Verbalmorphologie und Nebenprädikationen im Bantu: Eine Studie zur funktional motivierten Genese eines konjugationalen Subsystems*. Bochum-Essener Beiträge zur Sprachwandelforschung, 27. Bochum: Universitätsverlag Dr. N. Brockmeyer.

1998. The Kalahari basin as an object of areal typology – a first approach. In Schladt (ed.), pp. 137–69.

1999. The genesis of verbal negation in Bantu and its dependency on functional features of clause types. In Hombert & Hyman (eds.), pp. 545–87.

2001a. *Quotative Constructions in African Languages: A Synchronic and Diachronic Survey*. Habilitationsschrift, University of Leipzig.

2001b. Phonological regularities of consonant systems across Khoisan lineages. University of Leipzig Papers on Africa, Languages and Literatures, 16. Leipzig: Institut für Afrikanistik, Universität Leipzig.

2003a. Logophoricity in Africa: an attempt to explain and evaluate the significance of its modern distribution. *Sprachtypologie und Universalienforschung* 56. 4: 366–87.

2003b. Present progressive vis-à-vis predication focus in Bantu: a verbal category between semantics and pragmatics. *Studies in Language* 27.2: 323–60.

2004. Reconstruction through "de-construction": the marking of person, gender, and number in the Khoe family and Kwadi. *Diachronica* 21.2: 251–306.

2005. Complex predicates based on generic auxiliaries as an areal feature in Northeast Africa. In Voeltz (ed.), pp. 131–54.

forthcoming a. !Xõõ of Lone Tree. In Voßen (ed.) forthcoming a.

forthcoming b. Greenberg's "case" for Khoisan: the morphological evidence. In Voßen (ed.) forthcoming b.

forthcoming c. Preverbal objects and information structure in Benue-Congo. In Aboh et al. (eds.) forthcoming.

Güldemann, Tom & Edward D. Elderkin forthcoming. On external genealogical relationships of the Khoe family. In Brenzinger & König (eds.) forthcoming.

Güldemann, Tom & Manfred von Roncador (eds.) 2002. *Reported Discourse: A Meeting Ground for Different Linguistic Domains.* Typological Studies in Language, 52. Amsterdam, Philadelphia: Benjamins.

Güldemann, Tom & Rainer Voßen 2000. Khoisan. In Heine & Nurse (eds.), pp. 99–122.

Gussenhoven, Carlos & Tomas Riad (eds.) forthcoming. *Tones and Tunes: Studies in Word and Sentence Prosody.* Berlin: Mouton de Gruyter.

Gussenhoven, Carlos & Natasha Warner (eds.) 2002. *Laboratory Phonology 7.* Berlin: Mouton de Gruyter.

Guthrie, Malcolm 1967–71. *Comparative Bantu.* Farnborough, Hants: Gregg International.

Haacke, Wilfrid H. G. 1999. *The Tonology of Khoekhoe (Nama/Damara).* Cologne: Rüdiger Köppe.

Hagège, Claude 1973. *Profil d'un parler arabe du Tchad.* Paris: Paul Geuthner.

1974. Les pronoms logophoriques. *Bulletin de la Société de Linguistique de Paris* 69.1: 287–310.

Hagman, Roy S. 1977. *Nama Hottentot Grammar.* Bloomington: Indiana University Publications.

Haiman, John & Pamela Munro (eds.) 1983. *Switch-reference and Universal Grammar.* Amsterdam and Philadelphia: John Benjamins.

Hajek, John 2005. Vowel nasalization. In Haspelmath et al. (eds.), pp. 46–9.

Hale, Kenneth & David Nash 1997. Lardil and Damin phonotactics. In Tryon & Walsh (eds.), pp. 247–59.

Hall, Beatrice L., R. M. R. Hall, Martin D. Pam, Amy Myers, Stephen A. Antell & Godfrey K. Cherono 1974. African vowel harmony systems from the vantage point of Kalenjin. *Afrika und Übersee* 57.4: 241–67.

Hammond, Michael, Edith A. Moravcsik & Jessica Wirth (eds.) 1988. *Studies in Syntactic Typology.* Amsterdam and Philadelphia: John Benjamins.

Hamp, Eric 1977. On some questions of areal linguistics. *Berkeley Linguistics Society* 3: 279–82.

1979. A glance from here on. In Campbell & Mithun (eds.), pp. 1001–16.

Harris, Alice C. & Lyle Campbell 1995. *Historical Syntax in Cross-Linguistic Perspective.* Cambridge Studies in Linguistics, 74. Cambridge: Cambridge University Press.

Haspelmath, Martin. 1995. The converb as a cross-linguistically valid category. In Haspelmath and König (eds.), pp. 1–55.

1997. *From Space to Time: Temporal Adverbials in the World's Languages.* Munich and Newcastle: Lincom Europa.

1998. How young is Standard Average European? *Language Sciences* 20.3: 271–87.

2001. The European linguistic area: Standard Average European. In Haspelmath et al. (eds.), pp. 1492–1510.

Haspelmath, Martin, Matthew S. Dryer, David Gil & Bernard Comrie (eds.) 2005. *The World Atlas of Language Structures*. Oxford: Oxford University Press.

Haspelmath, Martin & Ekkehard König (eds.) 1995. *Converbs in Cross-Linguistic Perspective: Structure and Meaning of Adverbial Verb Forms – Adverbial Participles, Gerunds*. Berlin: Mouton de Gruyter.

Haspelmath, Martin, Ekkehard König, Wulf Oesterreicher & Wolfgang Raible (eds.) 2001. *Language Typology and Language Universals: An International Handbook*, vol. 2. Handbücher zur Sprach- und Kommunikationswissenschaft, 20.2. Berlin: Walter de Gruyter.

Haudricourt, André-Georges 1954. De l'origine des tons du vietnamien. *Journal asiatique* 242: 69–82.

Hayward, Richard J. 1990. Notes on the Zayse Language. In Hayward (ed.), pp. 210–355.

(ed.) 1990. *Omotic Language Studies*. London: School of Oriental and African Studies, University of London.

1991. À propos patterns of lexicalization in the Ethiopian language area. In Mendel & Claudi (eds.), pp. 139–56.

2000a. Afroasiatic. In Heine & Nurse (eds.), pp. 74–98.

2000b. Is there a metric for convergence? In Renfrew et al. (eds.), pp. 621–40.

Hayward, Richard & Yoichi Tsuge 1998. Concerning case in Omotic. *Afrika und Übersee* 81: 21–38.

Heath, Jeffrey 1978. *Linguistic Diffusion in Arnhem Land*. Australian Aboriginal Studies Research and Regional Studies, 13. Canberra: Australian Institute of Aboriginal Studies.

1999. *A Grammar of Koyraboro (Koroboro) Senni*. Cologne: Rüdiger Köppe Verlag.

Heine, Bernd 1973. Vokabulare ostafrikanischer Restsprachen, Teil II. *Afrika und Übersee* 57: 38–49.

1975. Language typology and convergence areas in Africa. *Linguistics* 144: 26–47.

1976. *A Typology of African Langages Based on the Order of Meaningful Elements*. Kölner Beiträge zur Afrikanistik, 4. Berlin: Dietrich Reimer.

1989. Adpositions in African languages. *Linguistique africaine* 2: 77–127.

1994. Areal influence on grammaticalization. In Pütz (ed.), pp. 55–68.

1997. *Cognitive Foundations of Grammar*. Oxford: Oxford University Press.

1999. *The //Ani: Grammatical Notes and Texts*. Khoisan Forum Working Papers, 11. Institut für Afrikanistik, University of Cologne.

2000. Polysemy involving reflexive and reciprocal markers in African languages. In Frajzyngier & Curl (eds.), pp. 1–29.

Heine, Bernd & Ulrike Claudi 1986. *On the Rise of Grammatical Categories: Some Examples from Maa*. Berlin: Dietrich Reimer.

2001. On split word order: explaining syntactic variation. *General Linguistics* 38.1: 41–74.

Heine, Bernd, Ulrike Claudi & Friederike Hünnemeyer 1991. *Grammaticalization: A Conceptual Framework*. Chicago: University of Chicago Press.

Heine, Bernd & Tania Kuteva 2001. Convergence and divergence in the development of African languages. In Aikhenvald & Dixon (eds.), pp. 392–411.

2002. *World Lexicon of Grammaticalization*. Cambridge: Cambridge University Press.

2003. On contact-induced grammaticalization. *Studies in Language* 27.3: 529–72.

2005. *Language Contact and Grammatical Change*. Cambridge: Cambridge University Press.

2006. *The Changing Languages of Europe*. Oxford: Oxford University Press.

Heine, Bernd & Derek Nurse (eds.) 2000. *African Languages: An Introduction*. Cambridge: Cambridge University Press.

Heine, Bernd & Mechthild Reh 1984. *Grammaticalisation and Reanalysis in African Languages*. Hamburg: Helmut Buske.

Heine, Bernd, Franz Rottland & Rainer Voßen 1979. Proto-Baz: some aspects of early Nilotic-Cushitic contacts. *Sprache und Geschichte in Afrika (SUGIA)* 1: 75–92.

Hérault, Georges (ed.) 1983. *Atlas des langues kwa de Côte d'Ivoire*, vol. 1: *Monographies*. Abidjan: Institut de linguistique appliquée (ILA).

Herbert, Robert K. 1990. The sociohistory of clicks in Southern Bantu. *Anthropological Linguistics* 32.3/4, 295–315.

Hermann, Eduard 1942. Problem der Frage. Nachrichten von der Akademie der Wissenschaften in Göttingen. *Philologisch-Historische Klasse* 3–4.

Hetzron, Robert 1972. *Ethiopian Semitic: Studies in Classification*. Manchester: Manchester University Press.

1987. Semitic languages. In Comrie (ed.), pp. 654–63.

Himmelmann, Nicholaus & Eva Schultze-Berndt (eds.) 2005. *Secondary Predication and Adverbial Modification: The Typology of Depictives*. Oxford: Oxford University Press.

Hodge, Carleton T. 1994. Afroasiatic languages. In Asher (ed.), pp. 50–2.

Hoffmann, Carl 1963. The noun-class system of Central Kambari. *Journal of African Linguistics* 2.2: 160–9.

1970. Ancient Benue-Congo loans in Chadic? *Africana Marburgensia* 3.2: 3–23.

Holm, John A. 1988. *Pidgins and Creoles*, vol. I: *Theory and Structure*. Cambridge: Cambridge University Press.

Hombert, Jean-Marie & Larry M. Hyman (eds.) 1999. *Bantu Historical Linguistics: Theoretical and Empirical Perspectives*. Stanford: Center for the Study of Language and Information.

Hopper, Paul J. 1973. Glottalized and murmured occlusives in Indo-European. *Glossa* 7.2: 141–66.

Houis, Maurice 1974. A propos de /p/. *Afrique et langage* 1: 35–8.

1980. Propositions pour une typologie des langues négro-africaines. *Afrique et langage* 13: 5–47.

1977. Language classification and the Semitic prehistory of Ethiopia. *Folia Orientalia* 18: 119–66.

Hubbard, Kathleen (ed.) 1991. *Proceedings of the 17th Annual Meeting of the Berkeley Linguistics Society: Special Session on African Language Structures*. Berkeley: Berkeley Linguistics Society.

Hudson, Grover 1989. *Highland East Cushitic Dictionary*. Kuschitische Sprachstudien Cushitic Language Studies, 7. Hamburg: Buske.

Huffman Marie K. & Rena A. Krakow (eds.) 1993. *Phonetics and Phonology 5: Nasals, Nasalization, and the Velum*. New York: Academic Press.

Hulst, Harry van der & Norval Smith (eds.) 1982. *The Structure of Phonological Representations*, part 1. Dordrecht: Foris Publications.

Hutchison, John 1981. *A Reference Grammar of the Kanuri Language*. University of Wisconsin, Madison.

Hyman, Larry M. 1982. The representation of nasality in Gokana. In van der Hulst & Smith (eds.), pp. 111–30.

1985. *A Theory of Phonological Weight*. Dordrecht: Foris Publications. (New edition: Stanford, Center for the Study of Language and Information, 2003.)

1999. The historical interpretation of vowel harmony. In Hombert & Hyman (eds.), pp. 235–95.

2003. Segmental phonology. In Nurse & Philippson (eds.), pp. 42–58.

Hyman, Larry M. & Charles Kisseberth (eds.) 1998. *Theoretical Aspects of Bantu Tone*. Stanford: Center for the Study of Language and Information.

Ihionu, Peter U. 1984. Nasality and vowel harmony in Igbo: an autosegmental approach. M.A. thesis, University of Ilorin.

Ikoro, Suanu M. 1994. Numeral classifiers in Kana. *Journal of African Languages and Linguistics* 15.1: 7–28.

1996. *The Kana Language*. CNWS Publications, 40. Leiden: Research School CNWS, Leiden University.

James, Deborah 1982. Past tense and the hypothetical: a cross linguistic study. *Studies in Language* 6: 375–403.

Jenewari, Charles E. W. 1977. Studies in Kalabari Syntax. Ph.D. dissertation, University of Ibadan.

1983. *Defaka: Ịjọ's closest linguistic relative*. Port Harcourt: University of Port Harcourt Press.

Jesse, Friederike 2000. Early Khartoum ceramics in the Wadi Howar (northwest Sudan). *Studies in African Archaeology* 7: 77–87. (Poznań Archaeological Museum.)

Jessen, Michael 2002. An acoustic study of contrasting plosives and click accompaniments in Xhosa. *Phonetica* 59: 150–79.

Jessen, Michael & Justus C. Roux 2002. Voice quality differences associated with stops and clicks in Xhosa. *Journal of Phonetics* 30.1: 1–52.

Johanson, Lars 1992. Strukturelle Faktoren in türkischen Sprachkontakten. *Sitzungsberichte der Wissenschaftlichen Gesellschaft an der Johann Wolfgang Goethe-Universität Frankfurt am Main* 29.5: 169–299. Stuttgart: Franz Steiner.

2000. Linguistic convergence in the Volga area. In Gilbers, Nerbonne & Schaeken (eds.), pp. 165–78.

2002. *Structural Factors in Turkic Language Contacts*. London: Curzon.

Joseph, Brian D. 1983. *The Synchrony and Diachrony of the Balkan Infinitive: A Study in Areal, General, and Historical Linguistics*. Cambridge Studies in Linguistics, supplementary volume. Cambridge: Cambridge University Press.

1992. The Balkan languages. In Bright (ed.), pp. 153–5.

Joseph, Brian D. & Richard D. Janda (eds.) 2003. *The Handbook of Historical Linguistics*. Oxford: Blackwell.

Jungraithmayr, Herrmann 1980. Kontakte zwischen Adamawa-Ubangi- und Tschad-Sprachen: Zur Übertragung grammatischer Systeme. *Zeitschrift der Deutschen Morgenländischen Gesellschaft* 130: 70–85.

1987. Langues tchadiques et langues non tchadiques en contact: problematique. In Jungraithmayr (ed.), pp. 17–33.

(ed.) 1987. *Contacts de langues et contacts de cultures 5: Langues tchadiques et langues non tchadiques en contact en Afrique Centrale (Actes de la Table Ronde franco-allemande, Ivry (France), 8–12 décembre 1978)*. LACITO – Documents, Afrique, 10. Paris: SELAF.

1992/3. On vowel systems in Chadic. *Folia Orientalia* 29: 119–29.

Jungraithmayr, Herrmann & Walter W. Müller (eds.) 1987. *Proceedings of the Fourth International Hamito-Semitic Congress: Marburg, 20–22 September, 1983*. Amsterdam Studies in the Theory and History of Linguistic Science, Series 4: Current Issues in Linguistic Theory, 44. Amsterdam: John Benjamins.

Kaboré, Raphaël & Zakari Tchagbalé 1998. ATR, ouverture et arrondissement vocaliques dans quelques systèmes africains. In Platiel & Kabore (eds.), pp. 467–90.

Kagaya, Ryohei 1990. Jiyu gojun gengo de nogojun seigen: Sandawe go no baai. [Restriction on word order of free word order language: the case of the Sandawe language.] *Journal of Asian and African Studies* 40: 1–12.

1993. *A Classified Vocabulary of the Sandawe Language*. Asian and African Lexicon, 26. Tokyo: Institute for the Study of Languages and Cultures of Asia and Africa (ILCAA).

Karlgren, Bernhard 1960. Tones in archaic Chinese. *Bulletin of the Museum of Far East Art* 32: 113–42.

Kastenholz, Raimund 1987. *Materialien zum Koranko: Glossar Koranko-Deutsch, Texte*. Afrikanistische Arbeitspapiere, Sonderheft 1987. Cologne: Institut für Afrikanistik, Universität zu Köln.

2003. Auxiliaries, grammaticalization, and word order in Mande. *Journal of African Languages and Linguistics* 24.1: 31–53.

Kaye, Jonathan 1981. Implosives as liquids. *Studies in African Linguistics*, supplement 8: 78–81.

Keding, Birgit 2000. New data on the Holocene occupation of the Wadi Howar region (Eastern Sahara/Sudan). *Studies in African Archaeology* 7: 89–104. (Poznań Archaeological Museum.)

Keuthmann, Klaus, Gabriele Sommer & Rainer Voßen (eds.) 1999. *Essays in Honor of Anthony Traill*. Quellen zur Khoisan-Forschung, 17. Cologne: Köppe.

Khabanyane, Khathatso E. 1991. The five vowel heights of Southern Sotho: an acoustic and phonological analysis. *Working Papers of the Cornell Phonetics Laboratory* 5: 1–34.

Kießling, Roland 1994. *Eine Grammatik des Burunge*. Hamburg: Research and Progress.

1998a. Der Pluraktionalis im Datooga. In Fiedler et al. (eds.), pp. 179–96.

1998b. Reconstructing the sociohistorical background of the Iraqw language. *Afrika und Übersee* 81: 167–225.

2001. The marked nominative in Datooga. Paper read at the Max-Planck-Institute of Evolutionary Anthropology, Leipzig.

2002a. *Die Rekonstruktion der südkuschitischen Sprachen (West-Rift): von den systemlinguistischen Manifestationen zum gesellschaftlichen Rahmen des Sprachwandels*. Cologne: Rüdiger Köppe.

2002b. Verbal plurality in Sandawe. *Hamburger Afrikanistische Arbeitspapiere* 1: 59–90.

Kießling, Roland & Maarten Mous 2003a. *The Lexical Reconstruction of West-Rift Southern Cushitic.* Kuschitische Sprachstudien, 21. Cologne: Rüdiger Köppe.

2003b. Cushitic classification from below. Paper read at the East-African Workshop, Lyon, 8–10 May 2003.

Kilian-Hatz, Christa 1999. *Folktales of the Kxoe in the West Caprivi.* Namibian African Studies, 5. Cologne: Rüdiger Köppe.

2001. *Ideophone: eine typologische Untersuchung unter besonderer Berücksichtigung afrikanischer Sprachen.* Habilitationsschrift, University of Cologne.

2003. Serial verb constructions in Khwe. Typescript, University of Cologne.

2006. Serial verb constructions in Khwe (Central-Khoisan). In Aikhenvald & Dixon (eds.), pp. 108–23.

Kisseberth, Charles & David Odden 2003. Tone. In Nurse & Philippson (eds.), pp. 59–70.

Kleinewillinghöfer, Ulrich 1990. Aspects of vowel harmony in Waja and Tangale-Waja common vocabulary. *Frankfurter Afrikanistische Blätter* 2: 93–106.

2001. Jalaa – an almost forgotten language of northeastern Nigeria: a language isolate? In Nurse (ed.), pp. 239–71.

n.d. The northern fringe of the Jos Plateau: a prehistorical contact zone of Benue-Plateau and North Volta-Congo languages. Typescript, University of Bayreuth.

Köhler, Oswin 1975. Geschichte und Probleme der Gliederung der Sprachen Afrikas: von den Anfängen bis zur Gegenwart. In Baumann (ed.), pp. 135–373.

1981. Les langues khoisan. In Perrot (ed.), pp. 455–615.

König, Christa 2002. *Kasus im Ik.* Cologne: Rüdiger Köppe.

2003. Serial verb constructions in !Xun. Typescript, University of Cologne.

2006. Marked nominative in Africa. *Studies in Language* 30. 4: 705–82.

forthcoming. *Case in Africa.* Oxford: Oxford University Press.

König, Ekkehard & Martin Haspelmath 1999. Der europäische Sprachbund. In Reiter (ed.), pp. 111–27.

Koptjevskaja-Tamm, Maria & Bernhard Wälchli 2001. The Circum-Baltic languages: an areal-typological approach. In Dahl & Koptjevskaja-Tamm (eds.), pp. 615–750.

Kouadio, N'guessan Jérémie. 1996. Description systématique de l'attié de Memni. Thèse de doctorat d'état, University of Grenoble.

Krüger, C. J. H. & J. W. Snyman 1986. *The Sound System of Setswana.* Goodwood: Via Afrika.

Kuteva, Tania 1994. Iconicity and auxiliation. *Journal of Pragmatics* 22: 71–81.

1998. Large linguistic areas in grammaticalization: auxiliation in Europe. *Language Sciences* 20.3: 289–311.

2000. Areal grammaticalization: the case of the Bantu-Nilotic borderland. *Folia Linguistica* 34.3–4: 267–83.

Kutsch Lojenga, Constance 1994. *Ngiti: A Central-Sudanic language of Zaire.* Cologne: Rüdiger Köppe.

2003. Bila (D32). In Nurse & Philippson (eds.), pp. 450–74.

2004. The role of tone in Lendu locatives. Paper read at the Seventh Nilo-Saharan Linguistics Colloquium, Khartoum (Sudan). To appear in Abu-Manga et al. (eds.) forthcoming.

Ladefoged, Peter 1968. *A Phonetic Study of West African Languages*, second edition. Cambridge: Cambridge University Press.

Ladefoged, Peter & Ian Maddieson 1996. *The Sounds of the World's Languages*. Oxford: Blackwell.

Ladefoged, Peter, Kay Williamson, Ben Elugbe & A. Uwulaka 1976. The stops of Owerri Igbo. *Studies in African Linguistics*, supplement, 6: 147–63.

Langdon, Margaret 1970. *A Grammar of Diegueño: The Mesa Grande Dialect*. Berkeley: University of California Press.

Larochette, J. 1959. Overeenkomst tussen Mangbetu, Zande, en Bantu-talen. *Handelingen van het XXIIIe Vlaams Filologencongres*, Brussels, pp. 247–48.

Le Coeur, Charles & Marguerite 1956. *Grammaire et textes Teda-Daza*. Dakar: IFAN.

Le Saout, Joseph 1973. Langues sans consonnes nasales. *Annales de l'Université d'Abidjan*, Series H, 6: 179–205.

Leben, William R. 1989. Intonation in Chadic: an overview. In Frajzyngier (ed.), pp. 199–217.

Lefebvre, Claire 1998. *Creole Genesis and the Acquisition of Grammar: The Case of Haitian Creole*. Cambridge: Cambridge University Press.

Leslau, Wolf 1945. The influence of Cushitic on the Semitic languages of Ethiopia: a problem of substratum. *Word* 1.1: 59–82.

1952. The influence of Sidamo on the Ethiopic languages of Gurage. *Language* 28.1: 63–81.

1959. Sidamo features in the South Ethiopic phonology. *Journal of the African and Oriental Society* 79.1: 1–7.

1995. *Reference Grammar of Amharic*. Wiesbaden: Harrassowitz.

Lex, Gloria 2001. *Le dialecte peul du Fouladou (Casamance – Sénégal): Etude phonétique et phonologique*. Munich: Lincom.

Leyew, Zelealem 2003a. Adpositions in Amharic. Paper presented at the Institut für Afrikanistik, University of Cologne.

2003b. *The Kemantney Language: A Sociolinguistic and Grammatical Study of Language Replacement*. Cushitic Language Studies, 20. Cologne: Rüdiger Köppe.

Leyew, Zelealem & Bernd Heine 2003. Comparative constructions in Africa: an areal dimension. *Annual Publication in African Linguistics* 1: 47–68.

Lichtenberk, Frantisek 1991. Semantic change and heterosemy in grammaticalization. *Language* 67.3: 475–509.

Lindau, Mona 1984. Phonetic differences in glottalic consonants. *Journal of Phonetics* 54: 147–55.

Lindsey, Geoffrey A. 1985. Intonation and interrogation: tonal structure and the expression of a pragmatic function of English and other languages. Ph.D. dissertation, UCLA.

Lindsey, Geoffrey A., Katrina Hayward & Andrew Haruna 1992. Hausa glottalic consonants: a laryngographic study. *Bulletin of the School of Oriental and African Studies* 55.3: 511–27.

Lloret, Maria-Rosa 1995. The representation of glottals in Oromo. *Phonology* 12: 257–80.

Longacre, Robert E. 1990. *Storyline Concerns and Word Order Typology*. SAL Supplement 10 (Copyright 1991).

Lord, Carol 1993. *Historical Change in Serial Verb Constructions*. Typological Studies in Language, 26. Amsterdam and Philadelphia: Benjamins.

Luschan, F. von 1898. Beiträge zur Ethnographie des abflusslosen Gebiets von Deutsch-Ost-Afrika. In Werther (ed.), pp. 323–86.

MacNeilage, Peter F. (ed.) 1983. *The Production of Speech*. New York: Springer-Verlag.

Maddieson, Ian. 1977. Universals of tone: six studies. Ph.D. dissertation, UCLA.

1984. *Patterns of Sounds*. Cambridge: Cambridge University Press.

2003a. The sounds of the Bantu languages. In Nurse & Philippson (eds.), pp. 15–41.

2003b. Phonological typology in geographical perspective. In Solé et al. (eds.), pp. 719–22.

2005. Some special consonants. In Haspelmath et al. (eds.), pp. 82–5.

Maddieson, Ian & Karen Precoda 1989. Updating UPSID. *UCLA Working Papers in Phonetics* 74: 104–11.

Maganga, Clement & Thilo C. Schadeberg 1992. *Kinyamwezi: Grammar, Texts, Vocabulary*. East African Languages and Dialects, 1. Cologne: Rüdiger Köppe.

Maho, Jouni 2003. A classification of the Bantu languages: an update of Guthrie's referential system. In Nurse & Philippson (eds.), pp. 639–51.

Mallinson, Graham & Barry J. Blake 1981. *Language Typology: Cross-linguistic Studies in Syntax*. Amsterdam and New York, Oxford: North-Holland.

Manessy, Gabriel 1960. *La morphologie du nom en bwamu (bobo-oulé): dialecte de bon doukuy*. Université de Dakar: Publications de la section de langues et littératures, 4.

1979. *Contribution à la classification généalogique des langues voltaïques: le groupe proto-central*. Paris: Société d'Etudes Linguistiques et Anthropologiques de France (SELAF).

Manfredi, Victor 1997. Aspectual licensing and object shift. In Déchaine & Manfredi (eds.), pp. 87–122.

Mangulu, Motingea 2003. Esquisse de l'egbuta: une langue en passe d'extinction au nord du Congo-Kinshasha. *Studies in African Linguistics* 32.2: 25–98.

Maniacky, Jacky 2002. Tonologie du Ngangela: variété de Menongue (Angola). Ph.D. disseration, Inalco, Paris.

Marchese, Lynell 1983. *Atlas linguistique kru*. Abidjan: Institut Français d'Afrique Noire (IFAN), Université d'Abidjan.

Masala, Carlo (ed.) 2002. *Der Mittelmeerraum – Brücke oder Grenze?* Schriften für Europäische Integrationsforschung, 48. Baden-Baden: Nomos.

Masele, Balla F. Y. P. 2001. The linguistic history of Sisuumbwa, Kisukuma, and Kinyamweezi in Bantu Zone F. Ph.D. dissertation, Memorial University of Newfoundland, St. John's.

Masele, Balla F. Y. P. & Derek Nurse 2003. Stratigraphy and prehistory: Bantu Zone F. In Andersen (ed.), pp. 115–34.

Masica, Colin P. 1976. *Defining a Linguistic Area: South Asia*. Chicago and London: University of Chicago Press.

1992. Areal linguistics. In Bright (ed.), pp. 108–12.

Matras, Yaron 1996. Prozedurale Fusion: grammatische Interferenzschichten im Romanes. *Sprachtypologie und Universalienforschung* 49.1: 60–78.

Maurer, Philippe. 1995. *L'angolar: un créole afro-portugais parlé à São Tomé. Notes de grammaire, textes, vocabulaires.* Kreolische Bibliothek, 16. Hamburg: Buske.

McLaughlin, Fiona 1992–4. Consonant mutation in Seereer-Sin. *Studies in African Linguistics* 23.3: 279–313.

Meeussen, A. E. 1967. Bantu grammatical reconstruction. *Africana Linguistica* 3: 80–122.

1975. Possible linguistic Africanisms. Fifth Hans Wolff Memorial Lecture. Language Sciences, 35. Bloomington: Indiana University.

Mendel, Daniela & Ulrike Claudi (eds.) 1991. *Ägypten im afro-asiatischen Kontext: Aufsätze zur Archäologie, Geschichte und Sprache eines unbegrenzten Raumes. Gedenkschrift Peter Behrens.* Afrikanistische Arbeitspapiere. Sondernummer 1991. Cologne: Institut für Afrikanistik.

Meyer, Ronny 2002. "To be or not to be" – is there a copula in Zay? In Yimam et al. (eds.), pp. 1798–1808.

Meyer, Ronny & Renate Richter 2003. *Language use in Ethiopia from a Network Perspective.* Schriften zur Afrikanistik, Research in African Studies, 7. Frankfurt: Lang.

Miehe, Gudrun 1979. *Die Sprache der älteren Swahili-Dichtung.* Berlin: Dietrich Reimer.

Miller, Amy 2001. *Grammar of Jamul Tiipay.* Berlin: Mouton de Gruyter.

Miller, Cynthia L. & Leoma G. Gilley 2001. Evidence for ergativity in Shilluk. *Journal of African Languages and Linguistics* 22.1: 33–68.

forthcoming. Evidentiality marking in Shilluk.

Mohrlang, Roger 1972. *Higi Phonology.* Studies in Nigerian Languages, 2. Zaria: Institute of Linguistics.

Moravcsik, Edith 2003. A semantic analysis of associative plurals. *Studies in Language* 27.3: 469–503.

Moreno, M. M. 1948. L'azione del cuscitico sul sistema morfologico delle lingue semitiche dell'Etiopia. *Rassegna di Studi Etiopici* 7: 121–30.

Moseley, Christopher & R. E. Asher (eds.) 1994. *Atlas of the World's Languages.* London: Routledge.

Mous, Maarten 1993. *A Grammar of Iraqw.* Cologne: Rüdiger Köppe.

1996. Was there ever a Southern Cushitic language pre-Ma'a? In Griefenow-Mewis & Voigt (eds.), pp. 201–11.

2000. Counter-universal rise of infinitive-auxiliary order in Mbugwe (Tanzania, Bantu F34). In Voßen et al. (eds.), pp. 469–81.

2001a. Basic Alagwa syntax. In Zaborski (ed.), pp. 125–35.

2001b. Ma'a as an ethnoregister of Mbugu. In Nurse (ed.), pp. 293–320.

2003a. *The Making of a Mixed Language: The Case of Ma'a/Mbugu.* Creole Language Library, 26. Amsterdam: John Benjamins.

2003b. Nen (A44). In Nurse & Philippson (eds.), pp. 283–306.

2004. *A Grammatical Sketch of Mbugwe. Bantu F34, Tanzania.* Grammatical Annalyses of African Languages, 23. Cologne: Rüdiger Köppe.

2005. Selectors in Cushitic. In Voeltz (ed.), pp. 303–25.

n.d. Paradigmatic meaning of imperfective aspect in Iraqw. Typescript, Leiden.

344   References

Mukarovsky, Hans G. 1976/7. *A Study of Western Nigritic*, 2 volumes. Vienna: Institut für Ägyptologie und Afrikanistik, University of Vienna.
(ed.) 1987. *Leo Reinisch: Werk und Erbe*. Vienna: Verlag der Akademie.
Murtonen, A. 1967. *Early Semitic: A Diachronical Inquiry into the Relationship of Ethiopic to Other So-called South-East Semitic Languages*. Leiden: Brill.
Mutahi, Karega 1991. Interborrowing between Maasai and Kikuyu. In Rottland & Omondi (eds.), pp. 197–207.
Mutaka, Ngessimo M. 1995. Vowel harmony in Kinande. *Journal of West African Languages* 25.2: 41–55.
Mutaka, Ngessimo M. & Carl Ebobissé 1996/7. The formation of labial-velars in Sawabantu: evidence for feature geometry. *Journal of West African Languages* 26.1: 3–14.
Myers-Scotton, Carol 2002. *Contact Linguistics: Bilingual Encounters and Grammatical Outcomes*. Oxford: Oxford University Press.
Naden, Tony. 1989. Gur. In Bendor-Samuel (ed.), pp. 141–68.
Naït-Zerrad, Kamal. 2001. *Grammaire moderne du kabyle*. Paris: Karthala.
Nau, Nicole 1996. Ein Beitrag zur Arealtypologie der Ostseeanrainersprachen. In Boretzky (ed.), pp. 51–67.
Ndayiragije, J. 1999. Checking economy. *Linguistic Inquiry* 30: 399–444.
Neumann, Sabine (ed) 1999. *Comparing African Spaces*. Frankfurter Afrikanistische Blätter, 11. Cologne: Rüdiger Köppe.
Newman, Paul 1977. Chadic classifications and reconstructions. *Afroasiatic Linguistics* 5.1. Malibu: Undena Publications.
1980. *The Classification of Chadic within Afroasiatic*. Inaugural Lecture, Leiden University. The Hague: Universitaire Pers Leiden.
1990. *Nominal and Verbal Plurality in Chadic*. Publications in African Languages and Linguistics, 12. Dordrecht: Foris.
2000. *The Hausa Language: An Encyclopedic Reference Grammar*. New Haven: Yale University Press.
Newman, P. & R. Ma Newman (eds.) 1977. *Papers in Chadic Linguistics*. Leiden: Afrika-Studiecentrum.
Nichols, Johanna 1986. Head-marking and dependent-marking grammar. *Language* 62: 56–119.
1992. *Linguistic Diversity in Space and Time*. Chicago: University of Chicago Press.
1996. The comparative method as heuristic. In Durie & Ross (eds.), pp. 39–71.
Nicolaï, Robert (ed.) 2001. *Leçons d'Afrique: filiations, ruptures et reconstitutions des langues, en hommage à Gabriel Manessy*. Louvain: Peeters.
Nicolaï, Robert & Franz Rottland (eds.) 1995. *Proceedings of the Fifth Nilo-Saharan Linguistics Colloquium, Nice, 24–29 August, 1992*. Nilo-Saharan Linguistic Analyses and Documentation, 10. Cologne: Köppe.
Nicolaï, Robert & Petr Zima 1997. *Songhay*. Munich: Lincom Europa.
Nougayrol, Pierre 1989. *La langue des Aiki dits Rounga, Tchad, République Centrafricaine: Esquisse descriptive et lexique*. Paris: LACITO.
1999. *Les parlers gula – Centrafrique, Soudan, Tchad: grammaire et lexique*. Paris: CNRS.
Nouguier, Sylvie 2002. Relations entre fonctions syntaxiques et fonctions sémantiques en wolof. Ph.D. dissertation, University of Lyon.

Nurse, Derek 1979. *Classification of the Chaga Dialects: Language and History on Kilimanjaro, the Taita Hills, and the Pare Mountains, with 24 Tables and 3 Maps*. Hamburg: Helmut Buske.

1982. The Swahili dialects of Somalia and the northern Kenya coast. In Rombi (ed.), pp. 73–146.

1994. South meets north: Ilwana = Bantu + Cushitic on Kenya's Tana River. In Bakker & Mous (eds.), pp. 213–22.

1999. Towards a historical classification of East African Bantu Languages. In Hombert & Hyman (eds.), pp. 1–41.

2000a. Diachronic morphosyntactic change in Western Tanzania. In Voßen et al. (eds.), pp. 517–34.

2000b. *Inheritance, Contact, and Change in Two East African Languages*. Sprachkontakt in Afrika, 4. Cologne: Rüdiger Köppe.

(ed.) 2001. *Historical Language Contact in Africa*. Sprache und Geschichte in Afrika (SUGIA) 16/7. Cologne: Rüdiger Köppe.

Nurse, Derek & Thomas J. Hinnebush 1993. *Swahili and Sabaki: A Linguistic History*. University of California Publications, Linguistics, 121. Berkeley and Los Angeles: University of California Press.

Nurse, Derek & Gérard Philippson 1975. The north-eastern Bantu languages of Tanzania and Kenya: a classification. *Kiswahili* 45.2: 1–28.

(eds.) 2003. *The Bantu Languages*. Routledge Language Family Series, 4. London: Routledge.

Odden, David. 1995. Tone: African languages. In Goldsmith (ed.), pp. 444–75.

Ohala, John J. 1984. An ethnological perspective of common cross-language utilization of F0 of voice. *Phonetica* 41: 1–16.

Ohala, John J. & J. Lorentz 1977. The story of [w]: an exercise in the phonetic explanation for sound patterns. *Proceedings of the Annual Meeting of the Berkeley Linguistics Society* 3: 577–99.

Olson, H. S. 1964. *The Phonology and Morphology of Rimi*. Hartford: Hartford Studies in Linguistics.

Olson, Kenneth S. & John Hajek 2003. Crosslinguistic insights on the labial flap. *Linguistic Typology* 7: 157–85.

Oomen, Antoinette 1978. Focus in the Rendille clause. *Studies in African Linguistics* 9.1: 35–65.

Orel, Vladimir E. & Olga V. Stolbova 1995. *Hamito-Semitic Etymological Dictionary: Materials for a Reconstruction*. Handbuch der Orientalistik, 1. Abt., Der Nahe und Mittlere Osten, I, 18. Leiden: Brill.

Oumarou Yaro, Bourahima 1993. Eléments de description du Zarma. Ph.D. dissertation, University of Grenoble.

Oyètádé, B. Akíntúndé & Malami Buba 2000. Hausa loan words in Yorùbá. In Wolff & Gensler (eds.), pp. 241–60.

Pachur, H.-J. & S. Kröpelin 1987. Wadi Howar: paleoclimatic evidence from an extinct river system in the southeastern Sahara. *Science* 237: 298–300.

Pasch, H. 1985. Possession and possessive classifiers in Dongo-ko. *Afrika und Übersee* 68: 69–85.

Payne, Doris, Mitsuyo Hamaya & Peter Jacobs 1994. Active, passive, and inverse in Maasai. In Givón (ed.), pp. 283–315.

Payne, Thomas E. 1997. *Describing Morphosyntax: A Guide for Field Linguists.* Cambridge: Cambridge University Press.

Peng, Long 2000. Nasal harmony in three South American languages. *International Journal of American Linguistics* 66.1: 76–97.

Perrot, Jean (ed.) 1981. *Les langues dans le monde ancien et moderne. Première Partie: Les langues de l'Afrique subsaharienne.* Paris: Editions du Centre National de la Recherche Scientifique.

Pilaszewicz, Stanislaw & Eugeniusz Rzewuski (eds.) 1991. *Unwritten Testimonies of the African Past: Proceedings of the International Symposium held in Ojrzanów n. Warsow on 07–08 November 1989.* Orientalia Varsoviensia, 2. Warsaw: Wydawnictwa Uniwersytetu Warszawskiego.

Pillinger, Steve & Letiwa Galboran 1999. *A Rendille Dictionary Including a Grammatical Outline and an English–Rendille Index.* Kuschitische Sprachstudien, 14. Cologne: Rüdiger Köppe.

Plank, Frans (ed.) 1984. *Objects: Towards a Theory of Grammatical Relations.* London, Orlando: Academic Press.

1985. The extended accusative/restricted nominative in perspective. In Plank (ed.), pp. 269–310.

(ed.) 1985. *Relational Typology.* Berlin, New York and Amsterdam: Mouton de Gruyter.

Platiel, Suzy & Raphaël Kabore (eds.) 1998. *Les langues d'Afrique subsaharienne.* Faits de langues, 11–12. Paris: Ophrys.

Przezdziecki, Marek A. 2005. Vowel harmony and coarticulation in three dialects of Yoruba: phonetics determining phonology. Ph.D. dissertation, Cornell University.

Puhvel, J. (ed.) 1969. *Substance and Structure of Language.* Berkeley and Los Angeles: University of California Press.

Pulleyblank, Edwin G. 1991. *Lexicon of Reconstructed Pronunciation in Early Middle Chinese, Late Middle Chinese and Early Mandarin.* Vancouver: University of British Columbia Press.

Pütz, Martin (ed.) 1994. *Language Contact and Language Conflict.* Amsterdam and Philadelphia: Benjamins.

Ramat, Paolo & Giuliano Bernini 1990. Area influence versus typological drift in western Europe: the case of negation. In Bechert et al. (eds.), pp. 25–46.

Randal, Scott 1998. A grammatical sketch of Tennet. In Dimmendaal & Last (eds.), pp. 219–72.

Raz, Shlomo 1989. Areal features as a further criterion in elucidating the term "Ethiopian Semitic." *African Languages and Cultures* 2.1: 92–108.

Redden, James E. 1979. *A Descriptive Grammar of Ewondo.* Occasional Papers on Linguistics, 4. Carbondale: Department of Linguistics, Southern Illinois University.

Reh, Mechthild 1983. Krongo: a VSO language with postpositions. *Journal of African Languages and Linguistics* 5.1: 45–55.

1991. Frequentative derivation in Anywa: present-day reflexes of a Proto-Nilotic suffix. *Afrika und Übersee* 74: 223–46.

1996. *Anywa Language: Description and Internal Reconstructions.* Nilo-Saharan, 11. Cologne: Rüdiger Köppe.

1999. 'Body', 'back,' and 'belly' – or: on the antonyms of 'inside' and their conceptual sources. In Neumann (ed.), pp. 101–23.

Reiter, Norbert (ed.) 1999. *Eurolinguistik*. Wiesbaden: Harrassowitz.

Renfrew, Colin, April McMahon & Larry Trask (eds.) 2000. *Time Depth in Historical Linguistics*, vol. 1. Cambridge: McDonald Institute for Archaeological Research.

Rialland, Annie 1984. Le fini/l'infini ou l'affirmation/l'interrogation en moba (langue voltaïque parlée au Nord-Togo). *Studies in African Linguistics*, supplement 9: 258–61.

1998. Systèmes prosodiques africains: une source d'inspiration majeure pour les théories phonologiques multilinéaires. In Platiel & Kabore (eds.), pp. 407–28.

2001. Une "ponctuation vocalique" en gulmancema (langue gurma) et les conséquences de sa perte dans une langue proche: le moba. In Nicolaï (ed.), pp. 91–102.

forthcoming. Question prosody: an African perspective. In Gussenhoven & Riad (eds.).

Richardson, Irvine 1957. *Linguistic Survey of the Northern Bantu Borderland*, vol. 2. London: Oxford University Press.

Rombi, M-F. (ed.) 1982. *Etudes sur le Bantu oriental (Comores, Tanzanie, Somalie, et Kenya)*. Paris: Société d'Etudes Linguistiques et Anthropologiques de France.

Roncador, Manfred von 1992. *Zwischen direkter und indirekter Rede: nichtwörtliche direkte erlebte Rede: logophorische Konstruktionen und Verwandtes*. Tübingen: Niemeyer.

Rottland, Franz 1982. *Die südnilotischen Sprachen*. Berlin: Dietrich Reimer.

1983. Southern Nilotic (with an outline of Datooga). In Bender (ed.), pp. 208–38.

Rottland, Franz & Lucia N. Omondi (eds.) 1991. *Proceedings of the Third Nilo-Saharan Linguistics Colloquium, Kisumu, Kenya, August 4–9, 1986*. Hamburg: Helmut Buske.

Saeed, John Ibrahim 1987. *Somali Reference Grammar*. Wheaton, MD: Dunwoody Press.

1999 *Somali*. London Oriental and African Language Library, 10. Amsterdam: John Benjamins.

Sands, Bonny 1998. *Eastern and Southern African Khoisan. Evaluating Claims of Distant Linguistic Relationships*. Quellen zur Khoisan-forschung, 14. Cologne: Rüdiger Köppe.

Sapir, Edward 1921. *Language: An Introduction to the Study of Speech*. New York: Harcourt, Brace & Company.

Sasse, Hans-Jürgen 1984a. Case in Cushitic, Semitic and Berber. In Bynon (ed.), pp. 111–26.

1984b. The pragmatics of noun incorporation in Eastern Cushitic languages. In Plank (ed.), pp. 243–68.

1986. A southwest Ethiopian language area and its cultural background. In Fishman et al. (eds.), pp. 327–42.

1987. The thetic/categorical distinction revisited. *Linguistics* 25: 511–80.

Sauzet, Patrick & Anne Zribi-Hertz (eds.) 2003. *Typologie des langues d'Afrique et universaux de la grammaire*. Paris: L'Harmattan.

Schachter, Paul and Victoria Fromkin 1968. *A Phonology of Akan: Akuapem, Asante and Fante*. UCLA Working Papers in Phonetics, 9. Los Angeles: University of California, Department of Linguistics.

Schadeberg, Thilo C. 1981. *A Survey of Kordofanian*, 2 volumes. Sprache und Geschichte in Afrika, Beiheft 1/2. Hamburg: Buske.

1986. Tone cases in Umbundu. *Africana Linguistica* 10: 423–47.

1987. Zwei areale Sprachmerkmale im Ostsudan. In Mukarovsky (ed.), pp. 213–29.

1990. *A Sketch of Umbundu*. Cologne: Rüdiger Köppe.

1999. Tone and case in Umbundu. *Studies in African Linguistics*, supplement 9.

2003. Historical linguistics. In Nurse & Philippson (eds.), pp. 143–63.

Schadeberg, Thilo C. & M. Lionel Bender (eds.) 1981. *Nilo-Saharan: Proceedings of the First Nilo-Saharan Linguistics Colloquium, Leiden, September 8–10, 1980*. Dordrecht: Foris.

Schadeberg, Thilo C. & Philip Elias 1979. *A Description of the Orig Language*. Tervuren: Musée Royal de l'Afrique Centrale.

Schladt, Mathias (ed.) 1998. *Language, Identity, and Conceptualization among the Khoisan*. Cologne: Rüdiger Köppe.

Schuh, Russell G. 2003. Chadic Overview. In Bender et al. (eds.), pp. 55–60.

Sebeok, Thomas A. (ed.) 1971. *Linguistics in Oceania*. Current Trends in Linguistics, 8. The Hague, Paris: Mouton.

(ed.) 1973. *Current Trends in Linguistics*, vol. 10. The Hague: Mouton.

Serzisko, Fritz 1989. The Kuliak languages: a structural comparison. In Bender (ed.), pp. 385–404.

Shay, Erin 1999. A Grammar of East Dangla. Ph.D. dissertation, University of Colorado at Boulder.

Shay, Erin & Uwe Seibert (eds.) 2003. *Motion, Direction and Location in Languages*. Amsterdam and Philadelphia: John Benjamins.

Sherzer, J. 1973. Areal linguistics in North America. In Sebeok (ed.), pp. 749–95.

Shibatani, Masayoshi 1985. Passives and related constructions: a prototype analysis. *Language* 61: 821–48.

Singer, Ruth 1999. The inclusory construction in Australian languages. *Melbourne Papers in Linguistics and Applied Linguistics* 18: 81–96.

Singler, John V. 1979. The segmental phonology of verb suffixes in Talo Klao (Kru). M.A. thesis, University of California, Los Angeles.

Smieja, Birgit & Meike Tasch (eds.) 1997. *Human Contact through Language and Linguistics*. Frankfurt, Paris, New York and Bern: Peter Lang.

Solé, María Josep, Daniel Recasens & Joaquín Romero (eds.) 2003. *Proceedings of the 15th International Congress of Phonetic Sciences*. Barcelona: Futurgraphic.

Sommer, Gabriele 1995. *Ethnographie des Sprachwandels: sozialer Wandel und Sprachverhalten bei den Yeyi (Botswana)*. Sprachkontakt in Afrika, 2. Cologne: Rüdiger Köppe.

Spagnolo, L. M. 1933. *Bari Grammar*. Verona: Missioni Africane.

Staden, Paul M. von (ed.) 1993. *Linguistica – Festschrift E. B. van Wyk*. Pretoria: J. L. van Schaik.

Stanley, Carol 1991. *Description morpho-syntaxique de la langue tikar (parlée au Cameroun)*. Epinay-sur-Seine: Société Internationale de Linguistique.

Stassen, Leon 1985. *Comparison and Universal Grammar*. Oxford: Blackwell.

2000. AND-languages and WITH-languages. *Linguistic Typology* 4.1: 1–54.

Steeman, Sander 2003. Some issues in Sandawe sentence structure. Paper presented at the 33rd Colloquium on African Languages and Linguistics, University of Leiden.

Stegen, Oliver 2002. Derivational processes in Rangi. *Studies in African Linguistics* 31: 129–53.

Stéphane, Robert (ed.) 2003. *Perspectives synchroniques sur la grammaticalisation*. Louvain and Paris: Peeters.

Stevens, Kenneth N. 1983. Design features of speech sound systems. In MacNeilage (ed.), pp. 247–61.

Stewart, John M. 1967. Tongue root position in Akan vowel harmony. *Phonetica* 16: 185–204.

1976. *Towards Volta-Congo Reconstruction*. Inaugural lecture. Leiden: Leiden University Press.

1989. Kwa. In Bendor-Samuel (ed.), pp. 217–45.

1993. The second Tano consonant shift and its likeness to Grimm's Law. *Journal of West African Languages* 23: 3–39.

1995. Implosives, homorganic nasals and nasalized vowels in Volta-Congo. In Emenanjo & Ndimele (eds.), pp. 162–69.

2000–1. Symmetric vs. asymmetric vowel height harmony and *e, o* vs. *i, u* in Proto-Bantu and Proto-savannah Bantu. *Journal of West African Languages* 28.2: 45–58.

2002. The potential of Proto-Potou-Akanic-Bantu as a pilot Proto-Niger-Congo, and the reconstructions updated. *Journal of African Languages and Linguistics* 23.2: 197–224.

Stolz, Thomas 2002. Crosscurrents – the Mediterranean region as a potential linguistic area. In Masala (ed.), pp. 52–73.

Storch, Anne 2003. Dynamics of interacting populations: language contact in the Lwoo languages of Bahr el-Ghazal. *Studies in African Linguistics* 32.1: 65–93.

forthcoming. Hone (Jukun). In Dimmendaal (ed.) forthcoming.

Takács, Gábor 2003. South Cushitic sibilant affricates in a comparative-historical perspective. In Bender et al. (eds.), pp. 143–62.

Taljaard, Petrus C. & Sonja E. Bosch 1988. *Handbook of Isizulu*. Pretoria: J. L. van Schaik.

Tchagbale, Zakaré 1977. Le statut phonologique de (p) en tem. *Afrique et langage* 8: 45–51.

Thomas, Jacqueline M. C. 1972. Aires de phonèmes et aires de tons dans les langues d'Afrique centrale. In Thomas & Bernot (eds.), pp. 111–19.

1991. *Encyclopédie des pygmées aka 1, fascicule 4*: la langue. (LACITO No. 50). Paris: SELAF.

Thomas, Jaqueline M. C. & Lucien Bernot (eds.) 1972. *Langues et techniques, nature et société I, approche linguistique*. Paris: Klincksieck.

Thomason, Sarah Grey 1994. Hypothesis Generation vs. Hypothesis Testing: A Comparison between Greenberg's Classifications in Africa and in the Americas. Manuscript, University of Pittsburgh.

2001a. Contact-induced typological change. In Haspelmath et al. (eds.), pp. 1640–8.

2001b. *Language Contact: An Introduction*. Edinburgh: Edinburgh University Press.

2003. Contact as a source of language change. In Joseph & Janda (eds.), pp. 686–712.

Thomason, Sarah Grey & Terrence Kaufman 1988. *Language Contact, Creolization, and Genetic Linguistics*. Berkeley: University of California Press.

Tosco, Mauro 1992. Dahalo: an endangered language. In Brenzinger (ed.), pp. 137–55.

1994a. The historical syntax of East Cushitic: a first sketch. In Bearth et al. (eds.), pp. 415–40.

1994b. On case marking in the Ethiopian language area (with special reference to subject marking in East Cushitic). In Brugnatelli (ed.), pp. 225–44.

1996. The Northern Highland East Cushitic verb in an areal perspective. In Griefenow-Mewis and Voigt (eds.) 1996, pp. 71–100.

1997. *Af Tunni. Grammar, Texts and Vocabulary of a Southern Somali Dialect*. Cushitic Language Studies, 13. Cologne: Rüdiger Köppe.

2000a. Cushitic overview. *Journal of Ethiopian Studies* 33.2: 87–121.

2000b. Is there an "Ethiopian language area"? *Anthropological Linguistics* 42.3: 329–65.

2001. *The Dhaasanac Language: Grammar, Texts, Vocabulary of a Cushitic Language of Ethiopia*. Cushitic Language Studies, 17. Cologne: Rüdiger Köppe.

2003. A whole lotta focusin' goin' on: information packaging in Somali texts. *Studies in African Linguistics* 31.1–2: 27–53.

Traill, Anthony 1985. *Phonetic and Phonological Studies of !Xóõ Bushman*. Quellen zur Khoisan-Forschung, 1. Hamburg: Helmut Buske Verlag.

1993. The feature geometry of clicks. In von Staden (ed.), pp. 134–40.

1994. *A !Xóõ Dictionary*. Quellen zur Khoisan-Forschung, 9. Cologne: Rüdiger Köppe.

Traill, Anthony & Douglas N. Young (eds.) 1987. Sounds, Structures, and Varieties. Special issue of *African Studies*, 46.2.

Treis, Yvonne 2000. Komplexe Sätze im Kxoe (Namibia). M.A. thesis, Institut für Afrikanistik, University of Cologne.

Tryon, Darrell & Michael Walsh (eds.) 1997. *Boundary Ride: Essays in Honour of Geoffrey O'Grady*. Pacific Linguistics Series C-136. Canberra: Australian National University.

Tucker, Archibald N. 1967a. Erythraic elements and patternings: some East African findings. *African Language Review* 6: 17–25.

1967b. Fringe Cushitic: an experiment in typological comparison. *Bulletin of the School of Oriental and African Studies* 30.3: 655–680.

1994. *A Grammar of Luo*, ed. Chet A. Creider. Cologne: Rüdiger Köppe.

Tucker, Archibald N. & M. A. Bryan 1966. *Linguistic Analyses: the Non-Bantu Languages of Northeastern Africa*. London: Oxford University Press for the International African Institute.

Tucker, Archibald N. & Peter E. Hackett 1959. *Le groupe linguistique zande*. Annales du Musée Royal du Congo Belge, série 8, Sciences de l'homme: linguistique, 22. Musée Royale de l'Afrique Centrale, Tervuren.

Tucker, Archibald N. & J. Tompo Ole Mpaayei 1955. *A Maasai Grammar, with Vocabulary*. London: Longmans, Green.

Tyllesskär, Thorkild 1986–7. Phonologie de la langue sakata (BC34): langue bantoue du Zaïre, parler de Lemvien Nord. Mémoire de maîtrise, Université de Paris 3.

Ullendorff, E. 1955. *The Semitic Languages of Ethiopia: A Comparative Phonology*. London: Taylor's.

Ultan, Russell 1969. Some general characteristics of interrogative systems. *Working Papers on Language Universals* 3: 1–31.

Vekens, A. 1928. *La langue des Makere, des Medje et des Mangbetu*. Bibliothèque – Congo, 25. Ghent: Editions Dominicaines "Veritas."

Voeltz, F. K. Erhard (ed.) 2005. *Studies in African Linguistic Typology*. Typological Studies in Language, 64. Amsterdam and Philadelphia: John Benjamins.

(ed.) forthcoming. *The Dative and its Counterparts in African Languages*. Amsterdam and Philadelphia: John Benjamins.

Voeltz F. K. Erhard & Christa Kilian-Hatz (eds.) 2001. *Ideophones*. Typological Studies in Language, 44. Amsterdam and Philadelphia: Benjamins.

Vogler, Pierre 1987. *Le parler Vata*. Travaux de l'Institut d'Ethnologie 3, Université des Sciences Humaines de Strasbourg.

Voßen, Rainer 1985. Encoding the object in the finite verb: the case of ‖Ani (Central Khoisan). *AAP* (Afrikanistische Arbeitspapiere) 4: 75–84.

1997a. *Die Khoe-Sprachen*. Cologne: Rüdiger Köppe.

1997b. What click sounds got to do in Bantu: reconstructing the history of language contacts in southern Africa. In Smieja & Tasch (eds.), pp. 353–66.

(ed.) forthcoming a. *Handbook of Khoisan Languages*. London: Curzon.

(ed.) forthcoming b. *Problems of Linguistic-historical Reconstruction in Africa*. Sprache und Geschichte in Afrika, 19. Cologne: Rüdiger Köppe.

Voßen, Rainer, Angelika Mietzner & Antje Meißner (eds.) 2000. *"Mehr als nur Worte . . .": afrikanistische Beiträge zum 65. Geburtstag von Franz Rottland*. Cologne: Rüdiger Köppe.

Vydrine, Valentin 2004. Areal and genetic features in West Mande and South Mande phonology: in what sense did Mande languages evolve? *Journal of West African Languages* 30: 113–25.

Wagner, Joachim 1988. Untersuchungen zur Grammatik des Hadza. M.A. thesis, Hamburg.

Wald, Benji 1994. Sub-Saharan Africa. In Moseley & Asher (eds.), pp. 289–309.

Watkins, Calvert 2001. An Indo-European linguistic area and its characteristics: ancient Anatolia – areal diffusion as a challenge to the comparative method? In Aikhenvald & Dixon (eds.), pp. 44–63.

Wedekind, Klaus 1985. Thoughts when drawing a tone map of Africa. *Afrikanistische Arbeitspapiere* 1: 105–24.

1994. Ethiopian Semitic languages. In Asher (ed.), pp. 1148–9.

Weinreich, Uriel [1953] 1964. *Languages in Contact*. London, The Hague, and Paris: Mouton.

Welmers, William E. 1974. *African Language Structures*. Berkeley: University of California Press.

Werther, C. Waldemar (ed.) 1898. *Die mittleren Hochländer des nördlichen Deutsch-Ost-Afrika*. Berlin: Hermann Paetel.

Westermann, Diedrich 1911. *Die Sudansprachen: eine sprachvergleichende Studie*. Abhandlungen des Hamburgischen Kolonialinstituts, 3. Hamburg: L. Friederichsen.

1927. *Die westlichen Sudansprachen und ihre Beziehungen zum Bantu.* Mitteilungen des Seminars für Orientalische Sprachen, 30. Berlin: Walter de Gruyter.

1935. Charakter und Einteilung der Sudansprachen. *Africa* 8.2: 129–48.

1940. Die Sprachen. In Baumann et al. (eds.) pp. 375–433.

1949. *Sprachbeziehungen und Sprachverwandtschaft in Afrika.* Sitzungsberichte der Deutschen Akademie der Wissenschaften zu Berlin, Philosophisch-historische Klasse, Jahrgang 1948, 1. Berlin.

1952. African linguistic classification. *Africa* 22: 250–6.

Westermann, Diedrich & Margaret A. Bryan 1952. *Languages of West Africa.* Handbook of African Languages, 2. London: Oxford University Press.

Williamson, Kay 1983-4. Vowel merger in harmony languages. *Journal of the Linguistic Association of Nigeria* 2: 61–82.

1989. Niger-Congo overview. In Bendor-Samuel (ed.), pp. 3–47.

2004. Typical vowel systems and processes in West African Niger-Congo languages. *Journal of West African Languages* 30.2: 127–42.

Williamson, Kay & Roger Blench 2000. Niger-Congo. In Heine & Nurse (eds.), pp. 11–42.

Williamson, Kay & Timitimi, A. O. 1983. *Short Izon–English Dictionary.* Port Harcourt: University of Port Harcourt Press.

Wilson, W. A. A. 1989. Atlantic. In Bendor-Samuel (ed.), pp. 81–104.

2007. *Guinea Languages of the Atlantic Group.* Edited by Anne Storch, with a contribution by John Stewart and a foreword by Herrmann Jungraithmayr. London: Curzon and Routledge.

Witkowski, Stanley R. & Cecil H. Brown 1985. Climate, clothing, and body-part nomenclature. *Ethnology* 24: 197–214.

Woldemariam, Hirut 2004. A Grammar of Haro with Comparative Notes on the Ometo Linguistic Group. Ph.D. dissertation, School of Graduate Studies, Addis Ababa University.

Woldu, Kiros Fre 1985. *The Production and Perception of Tigrinya Stops.* Reports from Uppsala University Linguistics, 13. Uppsala University: Department of Linguistics.

Wolff, H. Ekkehard 1991. On the morphology of the verb-initial consonant in Maba (Nilo-Saharan). In Rottland & Omondi (eds.), pp. 277–85.

Wolff, H. Ekkehard & Orin Gensler (eds.) 2000. *Proceedings of the Second World Congress of African Linguistics, Leipzig.* Cologne: Köppe.

Wolff, H. Ekkehard & Ludwig Gerhardt 1977. Interferenzen zwischen Benue-Kongo- und Tschad-Sprachen. *Zeitschrift der Deutschen Morgenländischen Gesellschaft,* supplement 3: 1518–43.

Wolff, Hans 1959. Subsystem typologies and area linguistics. *Anthropological Linguistics* 1.7: 1–88.

Wrigley, Christopher 2001. Frontier linguistics in Uganda. In Nurse (ed.), pp. 575–93.

Yigezu, Moges 2001. A comparative study of the phonetics and phonology of Surmic languages. Ph.D. dissertation, Université Libre de Bruxelles.

Yimam, Baye, Richard Pankhurst, David Chapple, Yonas Admasu, Alula Pankhurst & Birhanu Teferra (eds.) 2002. *Ethiopian Studies at the End of the Second Millennium. Proceedings of the 14th International Conference of Ethiopian*

Studies, Nov. 6–11, 2000, Addis Ababa. Addis Ababa: Institute of Ethiopian Studies.

Yip, Moira 2002. *Tone.* Cambridge Textbooks in Linguistics. Cambridge: Cambridge University Press.

Zaborski, Andrzej 1991. Ethiopian language subareas. In Pilaszewicz & Rzewuski (eds.), pp. 123–34.

(ed.) 2001. *New Data and New Methods in Afroasiatic Linguistics: Robert Hetzron in Memoriam.* Wiesbaden: Harrassowitz.

2003. Ethiopian language macroarea. *Sprawozdania z posiedzem komisji naukowych. Tom XLV/2 Lipiec–grudzien 2001 r*, pp. 60–4. Polska Akademia Nauk. Cracow: Wydawnictwo i Drukarnia "Secesja."

Zima, Petr (ed.) 1995. *Time in Languages.* Prague: Institute for Advanced Studies at Charles University and the Academy of Sciences of the Czech Republic.

Index

28277860R00215

Printed in Great Britain
by Amazon